Growing Dumb:
An Autobiography of An English Education

Growing Dumb:
An Autobiography of An English Education

Peter Quartermain

Zat-So Productions
Montréal — Vancouver
2021

Growing Dumb © 2021 Peter Quartermain

All rights reserved. No part of this publication may be reproduced or transmitted in any form or by any means, electronic or mechanical, including photocopying, recording, or any information storage and retrieval system, without permission in writing from the publisher and author.

ISBN: 978-0-9867595-5-0
Revised First Edition: with very minor corrections 10 April 2021

Text design: Elisa Sampedrín
Cover and inside photos: Peter Quartermain

Published by Zat-So Productions, Montréal
zatso.productions@gmail.com
available for purchase at Lulu.com or order through your independent bookseller

for Pete Griffiths

Growing Dumb

Preface	9
1: Upheaval	13
2: The Village	25
3: Adapting	39
4: The Farm	53
5: Dad	65
6: Woodroughs	81
7: Rushbury	91
8: Spalding	105
9: Little Marlow	121
10: Boarding School	135
11: Chocolate	147
12: Keeping Mum	161
13: Marathons	173
14: Small Pleasures	189
15: Mrs Bailey	199
16: Dolly and Angus	217
17: Letters Home	229
18: Bike Riding	245
19: Sundays	257
20: Self-Help	273
21: Wartime City	289
22: Air Raid Shelter	307
23: Wartime Farm	323
24: Farm Girls	339
25: Milk and Apples	353
26: Punishments	369

27: New Headmaster	383
28: Broggie's World	399
29: Nosey and Godfray	413
30: After the War	429
31: Robin and Jim	445
32: Pete	465
Afterword	487

Appendices	489
Appendix 1: *People and Places*	490
Appendix 2: *Sketch Maps of Brewood Village and of the School Grounds*	494
Glossary	496
Acknowledgements	497
Author biography and other publications	499

Preface

Growing Dumb is the story of an English boy whose education occurred during the last gasp of the British Empire in the Second World War. He was expected to join the managerial class or take up a post in something like the diplomatic corps or the Colonial Service. He would be, above all, a salaried worker, responsible for people working under him and totally reliable to his employers. He would have social standing in the community and achieve middle-class prosperity. For his parents and grandparents, it was important that he go to the right kind of school, not a state-funded council school, but rather a private preparatory and grammar school, a school which would lead to matriculation at one of the best universities in England. That was the road to success.

That boy was me, and these expectations led me and my brother to end up as boarders in a small country grammar school, which catered to farmers, country shopkeepers, and managers of local industries. So many teachers were away in the War that the school could no longer meet the expectation to provide normal preparation for university, a task which was supposed to include French, German, Latin and Greek. The school was stuck with the better dregs of the teaching profession not at the Front, but nevertheless persistently modeled itself on English public schools, such as Rugby and Wellington. As in *Tom Brown's School Days*, life in boarding school mimicked that in the adult world, with the same rivalries, distresses, and pleasures of belonging and excluding.

Such schools operated on quasi-military lines of authority, chains of command from Headmaster to Senior Masters to Prefects and Monitors. Rank was key, a question of who could order you about and who you could order about. Who naturally had authority because they were good at sports or a star in Math or Chemistry, and who didn't. Like my peers, I desperately wanted approval in that system for I was not a star in anything, just a bookish kid who continually tried to do better than his friends.

Boarding school made all relationships institutional. It left no room for the intensely personal. We never got away from watchful adult eyes. We felt we were always being inspected or assessed. As a rule, boarders did not have close friends, did not confide in one another, except when they could get away from the very public life of the institution.

On the one hand, education gives the child an institutional identity, but on the other, it denies the private. How does the growing child reconcile this apparent conflict, torn as he is by loyalty to his friends and family and obedience to social authority? His vocabulary, the terms of his visibility, works against any viable resolution. And in fact we don't really know why we do what we do, we can't really account for our behaviour.

The narratives in this book involve travelling to places of bewilderment and non-understanding that lurked within and on the edges of the regime of my formal education and family guidance, which, on the surface, uniformly upheld social distinctions and judgements of who was respectable and who was not. I enter zones of bafflement and perplexity where speech is inadequate. This is partly a matter of vocabulary, no words for the situation, and partly a matter of too much to say, floods of images, memories, possibilities, a dumbfounding.

Dumbness has acquired a pejorative connotation which I do not in any way intend. For me to be dumb is to be bereft of speech and if it also includes a sense of stupidity it is a stupidity that contains intelligence and wisdom that preserve sense in the face of social oppression. Dumbfounded means founding my being in speechlessness, where I struggle to articulate the disconnected without limiting possibilities of meaning.

To 'utter,' a word I love, comes from deep in the throat. It comes from a void. We don't know what we are doing when we come to utterance. Closer to stutter than to mutter, both of which contain it. To utter is to bring language to the edge of the sayable.

As it moves toward utterance, language takes us to a threshold, a cusp of the potential, hovering between articulate and inarticulate, between certainty and silence, where feeling resides. It resides too in the irrationality of speech patterns and the pulse of the breath. Hence rhythm is crucial, language occurring as music rather than as explanation of the world. Its insistent rhythm transported me aurally in the headlong rush of childhood perceptions before thought. Writing this enabled me to restore my bewilderment to its rightful place in life.

1
Upheaval

There's *Before The War*, and there's *During The War*, and of course *The Day War Broke Out*. After the War got going, Robb Wilton turned that watershed into the catch-phrase for his once-a-week comic routine on the wireless, his soft Lancashire voice'd set us all laughing, always starting the same. "The day war broke out, my missus said to me she said, What are *YOU* going to do... ?" his preposterous and perpetual helplessness in the face of her well-worn scepticism, her "What good *ARE* you" leaving him trapped in nonsensical dilemmas, and we'd settle back just like everyone else to relish his haplessness and her nagging voice. We didn't know anyone who spoke like that, so unrespectable and so insistent, and we loved it, that catch-phrase popping into your head at all sorts of times and places. You couldn't help but chuckle even *thinking* it. Robb Wilton eased the reality lurking behind *The Day War Broke Out*, to say nothing of *During*, he calmed people's worries about a German invasion and about Hitler, and even us kids'd repeat what he said and laugh.

But September the third, 1939, the actual day war broke out, wasn't a bit like what he said, not for my brother Phil and me anyway. It was the dust hanging in the air from the coconut matting all rolled up one side of the kitchen and catching in your nose, it was the slow drip of the kitchen tap I could hardly reach, nobody bothering to turn it off, everything topsy-turvy, and Mum and Dad hurriedly filling the last suitcases and boxes *Watch where you put your feet! Don't trip over anything! And stay out of the way!* Nothing for Phil and me to do, toys and games all packed away, no *Beano* or *Radio Fun* to look at, not even any pictures on the walls, they'd all been taken down *No you can't go outside!* Nobody else outdoors anyway, and nowhere else to go. Mum and Dad wrapping last bits of china and kitchen cutlery, checking shelves and cupboards over and over, *just to be sure* Mum said, the car waiting in the driveway with its boot wide open *Good job it's not raining!* haste and anxiety you could smell, breathe it in breathe it out, dustsheets on the furniture ready to go into storage, Phil and me prowling back and forth knowing it was serious but not understanding what was up, *It might be War* didn't mean a thing, me five and Phil not yet eight.

Dad looked at his watch. "It's eleven," he said, "we've *got* to listen" and we all clustered round the wireless in the dining room, I didn't even shuffle my feet, everyone so serious, and we heard Alvar Liddell say "Please stand by" and we waited, and the Prime Minister said *This country is now at war with Germany*. "That's that, then," Dad said, "You're going." Going to leave Birmingham, get away from the Air Raids, Mum and me and Phil and Alice the maid, off to some place called Wheaton Aston miles out in the Staffordshire countryside, we're going to live with Mr and Mrs Davis, people us kids and Alice'd never met and I'd never even heard of, her a distant relative of Mum's, "They run the village shop" Mum told us, and after he's dropped us off Dad'll come back to Birmingham but not to the house in Solihull Road, he has to be at work tomorrow "and clean up," he said, "make sure everything's put away."

"It'll be very different," Mum said in the car, "not what you're used to, not like Shirley at all" – that's where our house was – "there won't be any indoor plumbing." Dad chuckled a bit. "This is all very serious, but it'll be like an adventure, living in such a small place, it's just a village. It's not like the city at all, I don't expect there'll even be any buses, not often anyway." Mum turned her head to look at Phil and me, stuck on the back seat with Alice, crammed with what wouldn't go in the boot. "But you'd better be warned, except for a couple of taps over the kitchen sink and perhaps one in the scullery, there's not a proper bathroom, and there's no electricity. No hot water except when the boiler's lit." Dad shook his head. "It'll be just like our farm that way, you'll soon get used to it, perhaps wash at the pump in the yard. But they *have* got an Elsan."

I didn't know what an Elsan was, so I had to find out, and we hadn't been there five minutes before Mr Davis led me past the pump in the cobbled yard, pushed open the green plank door and gestured me through. Cold whitewashed room, clean cement floor and a small window at the side, in the corner a metal barrel with a lavatory seat on top and a pipe running up the wall behind it to let the smell out, a gush of outside air where it went through the wall up above my head, toilet roll in a holder, a bit damp-looking. "You can wash in the scullery when you're done." He pointed back the way we came.

Pungency clamped the back of my nose, cold and chemical, not a bit like the privy at Dad's farm at Alcester, with its two holes cut side by side in the wooden seat and pages from *The Farmer and Stockbreeder* strung on a nail. My skin tightened on my face a bit damp and sticky and I still had my hand over my nose when I came out and Mum said "it's just disinfectant, to get rid of the germs," but it was so chilly, not the least little bit like home. A tall square tin on a shelf by the window with a screw top, dried blue stuff all round it where it'd spilled, *that must be where that smell comes from* I touched it with my finger but it wasn't even sticky, and I lifted the scrap of curtain over the window. No vague dark patch of outbuildings and blurry green lumps of trees softened by pebbled glass the way it'd been at Shirley, no mottled glow of the sky stretching up, not even the gleaming cream paint of the windowsill. Just a couple of dead flies, legs in the air, and through the dusty smeared glass nothing but the yard I'd just come from, a low brick wall, a bit of a tree. *Oh!* A fleeting touch of disappointment, *Well, what did I expect?* I let the curtain drop, and wondered how I'd been daft enough to think the window'd open up to something new like in the Rupert story in the children's corner of Dad's *Daily Express*, somewhere different and exciting, with someone like Billy Badger or Pong Ping to keep me company. But *they* were just drawings, weren't they.

It must've been a bit of a shock for the Davises, us five almost complete strangers turning up just like that for the duration, they must've felt we'd simply dumped ourselves on them without so much as a by-your-leave, even if Mum and Dad *had* arranged it ahead. "A lot better than having a bunch of scruffy evacuees shoved down our necks," Mrs Davis said a few weeks later, "We've seen more'n enough of them thank you very much. Glad we got *you* instead. Most of those townies are just dreadful, slum kids, don't know how to behave. Never wanted to see them, not in *this* village, not enough room if you ask me, not for the likes of *them*." Wheaton Aston felt a long long way from Solihull Road, what with just two buses a day from Wolverhampton ten miles or more away, a good hour on the bus, hardly any shops, not even a Market Day once a week. Looking back now I realise the Davises must've been glad of the extra ration books as well as whatever money it meant. They ran the village shop slap bang in the middle of the village kitty-corner from the church, Leabank Store, outbuildings across the cobbled yard at the back and side, houses all around and not a lot of room in the yard with that pump sticking up where it was. Three rooms wide and two deep but most of the front and part of the back given over to the shop or to storage, a bit crowded sharing it with the Davises. Phil and me had a room up a dark staircase, blackout curtains on the window, two beds side by side with a chair between them, a candlestick on a chest of drawers, crinkly red cellophane in the grate just like at home or at Grannie's in Spalding, but no fire screen, a few bits of soot that'd fallen down the chimney, a bit cold.

Peggy and Timmy Davis were both older than me, Peggy the biggest and Phil just a bit older than Timmy. "You two show them around," Mrs Davis said the morning after we got there. "Not that you're likely to get lost." And she laughed. The village school was just down the road from the shop, and Phil and me started there the very next morning, Peggy and Timmy, they're the ones who taught us to call each other *Our Kid*, walked along with us till they pointed where to go. "Over there!" Timmy said as he ran off to play with some other kids, lots of jeering and shouting and running about, girls with skipping ropes, boys kicking stones, grabbing each other, playing catch, swinging conkers. I didn't stop to watch but went straight up the stone steps, *find out where to go*, big double doors above my head, shiny brass handles, small windowpanes, and a Teacher's loud scornful shout *"You!* Don't you know you're a *boy?"*

and I froze as she pointed, *was she shouting at ME?* "GIRLS" the deep carving said on the sandstone lintel miles above my head *How could I've possibly seen that?* "Boys over *there*!" She tossed her head and spoke to somebody else, another grown-up, and both of them laughed. Back down the steps. "*You!*" another shouted, this time a man, and pointed. "You'd better run!" Cross the front of the building, climb the steps *there*, they looked just the same. Another laugh. "Run, boy! or you'll be late!" My hot flush sweated my face, eyes blurred up in front of all these strangers, other kids and all the grown-ups looking, Peggy and Timmy out of sight *Where's Phil gone? Nobody ever told you anything*, and I'd never even noticed that the girls'd been skipping in a playground behind the building and the boys in the front and at the side. Through the tall door, clatter of kids' boots on the lino, echoes from the high ceiling. A grown-up pointed and I scuttled, scrape of seats and bang of desk lids, a gap in the front row. "Sit *there*. We'll sort you out later." He looked towards the door. "Now," he said, and he sounded angry, "Settle down, *all* of you. *Now.*"

Mrs Roe'd never talked like that to us in Birmingham, her school in the house next door to ours where she and Sammy lived, but that evening when Mum asked, "How did you get on, then?" I said "I didn't like it much," and before I could tell her what'd happened Mrs Davis leaned forward in her chair and said "Well, you used to be in kindergarten, didn't you, and now you're going to a *real* school. Bound to be different. More grown up now." *Oh!* Peggy flashed her eyes at me, "Went up the wrong steps, didn't you" she grinned, and Tim smirked a bit. I felt myself going red. *How did they know? I didn't even tell Phil.* I didn't understand why I'd been shouted at for going up the wrong steps, the GIRLS'd had to use *their* steps and *their* big double doors, and then *all* of us, boys and girls together'd ended up in the same classrooms. *How daft!* But I didn't know how to explain how I must've got it all wrong. *They know something I don't.* It was all too tangled, and I couldn't even say anything to Phil, like all the others he wasn't bothered by it at all, and I didn't know how to ask anybody else, not even Mum or Mrs Davis, I didn't have the words.

And I thought of the Teacher's desk, a lot taller than what Mrs Roe'd had *but why should I tell Mum that?* and the map on the wall behind it just like the one in Shirley only a lot bigger, all the seas in blue and a Union Jack at the top, it had coats of arms round the edge and the British lion, and a lot of the land in bright pink especially Canada so big on one side and India and Australia big on the other, and dotted lines leading to tiny Great Britain up there near the middle. We all knew without being told that we lived in the centre of the universe, we'd seen maps of the world with all that pink or sometimes brilliant red all over the place, in post offices and shop windows, but only a week or two after Phil and me got to Wheaton Aston they started to take all the public maps down and put them somewhere out of sight along with the fingerposts which told you the way to the next village and how far it was so that the Germans wouldn't know where they were if they got shot down and got loose in the countryside or even invaded. I liked the fingerpost at the Watling Street corner, it said "Brewood 1½ Codsall 4," but when they took down even that we still had all the maps in school, one in every classroom, a lot of them with "The Empire on which the Sun Never Sets" or "Highways of Empire" written across the top, and you'd see the same map but smaller and without the label at the very front of your school atlas, and in a home atlas too if you had one.

At the end of every day, Mr and Mrs Davis'd count the money in the till and write it down, sometimes fussing till they agreed they'd got it right, and every so often Mrs Davis'd call us over, "Here's George the Second" or whoever, "come and see" and we'd peer at a thin copper disk worn almost smooth, a date like 1748 dimly traceable, faint strange-looking head, "It's a ha'penny, looks like a Roman emperor, doesn't he? Won't spend *that*," and she'd put it to one side. Nobody bothered about all the ha'pennies and pennies with Queen Victoria's or King George V's head on them, they were just money, coppers really, nothing to bother about except of course people *did*, money mattered in a shop, but lots of people not just kids, had a few old coins tucked away somewhere, didn't spend them, curiosities to hang on to, I've still got an 1806 farthing with George III's head looking off to the right. You couldn't help seeing the King's head on all the money and we all had our stamp collections, we all wanted Sammy Roe's 2¢ Canadian stamp dated XMAS 1898, a map of the world with the British possessions in red and "We hold a vaster empire than has been" printed across the bottom, we breathed all that in through our pores, we never had to think about it. The idea of Great Britain was just *there*, we knew it'd been there for ever.

When I started writing this Our Kid sent me a battered copy of a book he'd had at school, he paid Gavin Frost sixpence for it, *The Little Oxford Dictionary of Current English*, the same size and colour as the old *World's Classics* series, his big red-crayon handwriting cramped into the small inside front cover, "14/6/42," we'd long left Wheaton Aston by then, and I was surprised to see its last three pages list "Some Foreign And Colonial Moneys" at their rate of exchange. Lots of dictionaries and guidebooks had lists like that, they always pegged everything to the British pound, and we learned from them what we learned every day at school. Nobody questioned the rightness of all those pink bits, and whenever General Smuts or Mahatma Gandhi came up in the news or in conversation most people changed the subject, they all read the *Daily Express* or the *Daily Mail* and loved Lord Beaverbrook. So far as Mum and Dad were concerned if you mentioned the *Daily Herald* you had to wash your mouth out, and I never even heard of the *Daily Worker* until the War was over, it was a terrible rag just like the *News Chronicle,* not fit even for navvies and labourers.

Our Kid'd put his name above the date as well as his two addresses on that inside front cover, one at School in Brewood and one in Rugby, they filled the page and reminded me how almost all the kids including me'd make their address as long as they could, they'd add "England, Britain, Great Britain, the British Isles, Europe, Western Hemisphere" before adding whatever else they could think of, "Earth, The Solar System, The Milky Way, the Universe," we copied from each other and we competed. One kid crossed out "Europe" with a thick black line when his dad told him to, "England is *not* a part of Europe" he said indignantly, "we got *nothing* to do with them!" and we all thought he was very clever when he wrote "The British Empire" instead.

When they'd darned all the socks and gloves and turned the cuffs and collars on the shirts, then Mum and Mrs Davis and Alice might sit in the evenings unravelling old socks and pullovers and us kids'd roll up all that crinkly wool into balls. "I can't knit anything with this," one of them would say, "it's too far gone," and she'd pass it on to one of us kids. Some evenings, when we'd done our homework the three of us'd sit at one end of the table especially in that cold winter of 1939 working away at our knitting spools, what we called corkers, producing long knitted strings we could spiral into mats, pot holders, tablemats, things like that. I vaguely remember somebody, probably Peggy, trying to cobble together a scarf that way, what a mess that was it was so thick it wouldn't bend, and Our Kid still has a little spiral doily he made, it sits under a china pot he's got on his windowsill in Worcester, the colours of all those different scraps of re-used wool neutralised into a salt-and-peppery browny grey, it's almost felt now. "You never know," Mum would say, "it might come in useful." It wasn't anything like sewing socks for soldiers, and what you made was pretty useless really, but "Waste Not Want Not" got so deeply engrained that we saved everything, even old torn parcel-wrapping if it wasn't too tattered, and then we'd put it in the wastepaper bin for Salvage collection, and we certainly wouldn't throw it away any more than we'd throw away food. We'd carefully undo all the knots when we opened a parcel, sometimes a package even from a shop'd be held together by all sorts of scraps of different string tied together, we never had enough in the shop even to sell, for some reason it was always in short supply, and we all became dab hands at salvaging and re-using stuff, always had packets of Economy Labels to sell, they let you reuse old envelopes lots of times.

"Don't be a Squander Bug!" the posters said.

And there'd be posters and adverts everywhere you looked, and slogan after slogan, in the school and even in the church. "A clear plate means a clear conscience" was one, probably from the Ministry of Information, "Mystery of Propaganda" one of the kids at school called it, he shocked me when he said that, how could he be so disrespectful. Somebody told us that Inspectors from the Ministry of Food were looking into people's dustbins and cupboards *How dare they!* Mrs Davis said, and checking restaurants and canteens *Can't let it get to the black market* Mr Davis said. Alice wondered "But that's better than throwing it away, isn't it?" and all the grown-ups started arguing, but I didn't know what *black market* meant, I knew it must be something bad whatever it was, and Mrs Davis told everyone about the woman in Barnet, she'd heard it on the BBC News, got a pretty hefty fine for feeding bread crumbs to the birds, and everybody tutted she should've used them for rissoles or she could've made an apple charlotte with them, but chucking stuff just for the birds was wrong, unless it was to chickens. Later on, in the blitz, food clubs kept pigs and chickens and rabbits on bombed-out plots and even in their gardens or on the roof if it was flat, sheep grazed on what used to be famous lawns in stately homes as well as municipal parks, and in the towns everybody saved their kitchen scraps, put them in the pig bin for collection, the pig bin out where everyone could get at it, it wasn't half messy on the pavement all round it.

 A lot of this came vividly to mind when Phil took me back to Wheaton Aston a few years ago, and on *that* visit I looked at those school steps and turned round and saw the small red-brick bungalow across the street. "Why, that's the Headmaster's house," I said, "Mr Button's. We *never* went *there*!" and he grinned, "We all dreaded him, didn't we. I think even Mum did." We both marvelled a little, Mr Button such a fierce little man, his plump tight flesh filling his pin-striped three-piece blue suit, always chucking his weight about, always stern and impatient with us when we played in the street. "You children clear off!" he'd shout, sometimes he'd wave his fist, "take your noise elsewhere! You've no business near here!" and that was just daft really, where in the village would we play if not by the school? I was a bit shocked when as we ran away one of the kids shouted, "It's our village too!" That was so rude. If Mr Button's daughter was there, he'd grab her and her tricycle and hoick them back into the house, "*Stay away!*" Not that we saw her very often, nor her mum, hiding away from village life. Mrs Davis and Alice said that with his schoolmasterly ways he thought we were all beneath him, "We're just shopkeepers to him," Mrs Davis said, and "Really!" Mum said, "he's such a *vulgar* little man." We all had nothing but scorn for the sore thumb of that little red bungalow so new-looking and out of keeping with the other buildings on the street. "Too big for 'is boots," Mr Davis said once when he came in from the shop. "Look at 'im, wearing 'is *suit* when 'e's got 'is *boots* on."

The Davises would never've said anything like that about Mrs Roe back in Shirley, they wouldn't even have thought it. We liked her. Her house was much nicer than ours, bigger, and Phil and me went to the kindergarten down the road she ran as part of Woodroughs School, and back before the War, in June 1939, Phil and me'd glimpsed Mrs Roe through the fence with some people we didn't know setting something up in the garden, the noisy motor-mower trundling back and forth over the grass and heavy furniture being shifted about inside the house, people telling people where things belonged and where to put them, windows being washed and doors held open, chairs being carried out into the garden, and when we went next door for Sammy's fifth-birthday party Mum stayed with Mrs Roe in the house, Phil and me put our presents on the table where we were told and went straight through to the back garden, it didn't nearly look like where Sammy and I played it was so different, everything so clean and tidy, the sandbox hidden under a table that stretched as far as the shade under the tree, benches alongside, plates on the cloth, a leaf fluttering down to the table, one'd already drifted down into one of the glasses. I went over to see, and the tablecloth wasn't cloth it was paper, pinned down at the corners with drawing-pins, a bright pattern of green and red lines, I could just rest my chin on it the table was so high so I sat on the bench to find out and a woman's voice said "No, don't sit there yet! We've got games to play," Mum's voice said *I think we'll have to sit some of the small ones on pillows so they can reach*, and some other kids arrived. I watched a small green spider crawl across a plate, and wondered if I should try and move it, I didn't want to touch it.

We started with Blind Man's Buff, "That'll get you all loosened up" Mrs Roe said, she'd worked out a lot of games we could all play before we sat down for Birthday Tea, but once the blind man had nearly fallen into the rockery and hurt herself and someone else had blundered into a flowerbed Mrs Roe said "Let's set the chairs up" so we could play musical chairs and somebody else opened the French windows and played the piano so we could hear, the pianist couldn't see us children galumphing around the chairs on the lawn, rockery on one side, flowerbeds on the other, and as the music went on and on you'd get more and more giggly and breathless and linger round the chairs in the middle of the row, an extra chair set away from each end and facing away *That's not for you to sit on, you have to go round it!* you'd keep a hand on the last chair and slow down and then rush in a great leap across the gap to the extra chair, scramble round it and leap again to the first chair on the other side, bumping into whatever child was hanging on to it to be safe when the music stopped, and there'd be a sudden mad scramble you could never be quite ready when the music stopped and you'd plump bang down into a chair, some other kid on top of you pushing and shoving and out *she*'d go, another chair would be taken away and the music would start up again you'd get up and move on, one time the pianist stopped right after she'd played just one note, a loud start-up sort of chord, and there was this huge rush, one kid at the end running all the way down to the middle of one side to grab an empty chair, one kid so caught by surprise that he was still getting up when another kid slipped underneath him when the music so suddenly stopped and out *he* went, breathless children laughing and whooping so hard people could hear them through the trees and across the field at the back, too caught up in the delicious energy of the event to be sorry they didn't win. And the grown-ups made sure that everybody won at something, Blind Man's Buff or Pin the Tail on the Donkey.

After we'd played musical chairs we all sat down at a long table, I ended up sitting next to Our Kid, and we had fishpaste sandwiches and cucumber sandwiches and Heinz sandwich spread, how we all loved that it was so sweet, with lots of lemonade to drink, and then the grown-ups came round with bowls of raspberry jelly and chocolate blancmange. I didn't like the blancmange very much, the faintly bitter aftertaste, there was always a bit of thick skin, so I ate it first tried to eat it without tasting it, saving the jelly till last to take the taste away, jelly was my favourite treat, and just as I'd started on it a grown-up came round giving everybody seconds and like all the other kids I hurried up, you couldn't have seconds till you'd finished your firsts, and when she saw I didn't have any of the chocolate in my bowl and I was wolfing down my jelly she smiled and said "Oh, *you* like blancmange!" and gave me a great big dollop. "Well, you silly thing," said Mum, "that'll teach you what to eat first, won't it."

Looking back, I now suspect – though nobody said a word to me or Phil about it and I never did ask – that Sammy's birthday party was really a farewell party for him and his mum, all the grown-ups knowing they'd soon be off on a boat to Canada just in case there really was a war, part of the great exodus of children along with some of their parents fleeing threatened air raids and invasion, emptying the cities. I read much later that thousands and thousands of kids were moved whether their parents wanted them to or not, but Mum and Dad'd had a choice, we'd not been forced where we weren't wanted.

2
The Village

In Wheaton Aston we smaller kids didn't see much of Mr Button at all, in school or out, he was much too important to be bothered with the likes of us, and he told Mr Davis that he had to run *every*thing, "'E tells us that all the time," and along with most of the other teachers he looked after the older kids in their classes, they had to learn *real* stuff, but I can't remember who they were at all; us smallest kids were mostly in the hands of a young woman who I only knew as "Miss," she had us do a lot of reading aloud, just the same as I'd done with Mrs Roe at Woodroughs and I liked it, I liked the sound of words, "Don't read ahead," she told us, "listen to the others when it's their turn, they had to listen to you" but I couldn't help myself and did it anyway. All of us liked long words, and the sentence I got described a church and the high-up windows in the clerestory, cler*é*story I said without a pause I liked the rhythm of it and I didn't even stumble, it sounded right and I loved how posh it sounded, but she smiled and shook her head and said "clear story." Years later Mum said her name was Miss Chapman, she can't have been more than about nineteen years old and she taught us reading, writing, and simple arithmetic. It was a bit like being in a one-room school with the older kids helping the younger ones, and I didn't find out she'd got it wrong until I was ten, I'd just got into the Third Form at Brewood, Nosey Parker was talking about churches in Scripture class and he asked what those windows were called and after nobody answered he said "cler*é*story." I wasn't half glad I'd kept my mouth shut and not said "clear story," he was always scornful if you got something wrong, and I was really quite astonished years later, when I was browsing in Banister Fletcher's *History of Architecture* I found that it was called both, sometimes with a hyphen and sometimes without. I wasn't at all pleased to find out that for all those years all of us had been wrong, at Brewood you just weren't *allowed* to be, there couldn't be two proper ways to say things, both of them correct, and we all loved it when a know-it-all got it wrong. We all knew how to be withering.

But Miss Chapman wasn't like that at all, she never made you feel daft or resentful, she was so friendly we all behaved ourselves, and she taught us everything. When we started Arithmetic the kids in the class who already knew'd help the younger ones do simple sums. We did a bit of French, geography and history, not much Scripture except for a few bible stories, and a lot of reading. Hengist and Horsa were supposed to be heroes, but I couldn't sort them out from Ethelred the Unready and the Alfred who burnt the cakes, they none of them had anything to do with anything, and the silly empty pictures didn't help. But it didn't seem to matter, Miss Chapman didn't insist the way other grown-ups did, and with the news of evacuees and people moving from one place to another perhaps we all knew we wouldn't be there very long, it wasn't Private like Woodroughs it was only a Council School, and as it turned out we only went there till Easter 1940, that's not even a year. Miss Chapman didn't last long either, what with a critical shortage of labour she might've got called up, anyway she moved to somewhere else perhaps the way Alice did before we left Wheaton Aston, when she got married. Dad stayed on in digs he'd found, some place in Moseley Phil says, and we didn't see much of him except at weekends, and a couple of times not even then.

Dad had some petrol coupons because farming was an Essential Activity and now and again he'd drive, but to save petrol he usually took the bus, never an easy trip with the bus wandering all over the place to get about inside Birmingham and then to Wolverhampton and if he missed the one to Wheaton Aston he'd have a long empty journey back to his digs, him not getting off work on Saturday until six, closing up for the weekend, and he must've got a bit anxious especially if they were held up by an Air Raid, the bus picking its way through rubble-strewn streets. Most times even if he had the car he'd get in when we were in the middle of bathtime, and he'd leave again next day. The car looked ever so funny with a cowl hooding its headlights so that only a little shaft of light could get out, it was easy to drive off the road at night and one weekend he was late because the car got caught in an Air Raid and couldn't get through for hours, and another he didn't get in at all because another car ran into him. There wasn't any way he could telephone, there were only two in the village that we knew of, and phone-calls were like telegrams, you only got one if it was bad news, but he got a message through somehow, and when we came downstairs to breakfast we asked "Where's Dad?" Mum must still have been worried sick, but I don't think we paid attention except to notice he wasn't there. Grown-ups worried all the time.

On bath night Mum and Mrs Davis or Alice would haul the great big galvanised tub in front of the fire, put a screen round it while us four kids – me and Our Kid, and Timmy and Peggy Davis – sat around the oilcloth table with its pooled light from the oil lamp, carefully not looking at the screen and its glow, blackness because we had drawn curtains, quick little glimpse of bare skin through the screen when someone shifted a towel, sudden rush of cold air as Dad came through the door careful of the blackout, one of us in the bath the others hunched over a comic or a book or a game, dark shadows round the room, pools of yellow light from the fire and at the kitchen table, a glimpse through the screen *Don't you dare look!* Eyes half-closed, face pointing the other way, we looked. Sidelong. *You should be ashamed of yourself! Want a good hiding?* Peggy often went first she was the eldest so if the weather was nice the rest of us would be sent out to play so we *couldn't* see, and it didn't matter if you got a bit dirtier, towels hanging on a clothes horse near the fire not in front of it so you might feel its heat when you were in the tub or getting dry after. Subdued splashes, laughter, scolding from a hot and tousled grown-up, voices from behind the screen nattering away at whoever was in the bath. You'd get out of the bath and shiver away before the fire while a grown-up fiercely rubbed you down, and someone else poured another hot kettle of water in for the next child, but the water got colder and colder and the towels got damper and damper soggier and colder no matter how hard the grown-ups tried. They'd hold the towels real close to the fire while you shivered away in the lukewarm water, skin prickly from the cold, goosebumps on one side and fireglow on the other, every little move you made making a new bit of cold, eyeing the others all wrapped up in their dressing gowns looking warm and pink and sparkly-eyed.

Because I was the littlest I should've gone first, but I was always the muddiest, not just my knees, the dirt engrained no matter how I struggled to clean myself off in cold water at the kitchen sink, I went last, especially when Timmy and Phil'd let me tag along to play Pooh Sticks where the stream ran under the road at Lloyd's Farm. *You'll have to wear those clothes until they dry, you know* Peggy'd smirk at my discomfort and maybe a bit envious as I came back muddy and wet, *Serves you right, you'll be the last again!* The bath by the time I got in a thick scummy mess round the rim, grey mucky suds floating on lukewarm water, *had anyone peed in it?* everything soapy and slick, and you got your hair washed, scrub of carbolic Lifebuoy soap, a big enamel jug of water to rinse it off. That was usually warmer than the bath, but it wasn't much relief, by the time it had trickled through your hair it was stone cold and ran down your back and chest and under your arms and you'd climb out pink and shivery and still feeling a bit mucky, only now the muck was all over instead of just here and there, some of it wiped off on the towel, and you'd get into your pyjamas and dressing gown, almost fall over from the hard scrub Alice or Mum'd give your head with yet another towel damp from drying someone else's hair, and be given a bit of something to eat and drink before being sent up to bed, at the table the others whiled away their uncomfortable time talking or reading or playing a game.

The first Saturday we were at Wheaton Aston Mrs Davis said, "I've got a treat for you lot before you go to bed," and I perked up I felt so sticky and a bit cold after the bath. "Bread-and-milk!" cried Timmy and Peggy, "can we have a dab of butter? Please, please?" and Mrs Davis plonked a bowl down in front of me full of chunks of white bread soaked through in a bath of hot milk. But it smelled horrible, cloying the back of my mouth, my tongue felt thick, and I shook my head. "Go on, try it," she said, and I dipped my spoon through the oily scum of butter greying as it spread and took a bit, the bread all hot and slimy in my mouth. I put the spoon down again. "Don't you like it? Here," and she took a precious spoonful of sugar and dumped it in *Fancy that! Never heard of anyone not liking bread-and-milk!* and Timmy looked a bit scornful as Peggy laughed. I stirred it up, and it just smelled worse, the sweetness hanging on even more stubbornly in the back of my mouth and I knew, I simply *knew* that I'd never be able to get it down, my stomach rebelling in a lurch. I couldn't swallow, and I sat there shaking my head and I looked down at the bowl. The others lapped theirs up in record time, *Can we have his, then?* "I think you'd better have cold milk," Mrs Davis said, "I know you drink that, but it won't warm you up the way hot milk will, we've got plenty." "Can I have a piece of bread with it?" I asked, I loved bread, I still do, and everybody laughed. "You won't get any jam!" Mum said and chuckled as Mrs Davis gave it me.

Me with my milk and a piece of bread and them with their hot bread-and-milk got to be a Saturday ritual, the others thought it was a treat but for me it was just a thick slice of white bread with a bit of jam on it. Bread didn't get rationed until after the War, so there always was some for us kids *But not between meals!*

Even with treats now and again Wheaton Aston never felt like home, home was in Shirley, lots of houses, lots of shops, lots of buses and cars and the baker's boy and the milkman delivering stuff every morning and a set of traffic lights and a public park with lots of flower beds and a playground with lots of swings and a sandbox. Wheaton Aston had nothing like that, and there we were, four kids along with four adults, and Dad not there except weekends if he could make it, all of us crowded together, the furniture all wrong and not even ours, the shop right off the kitchen and not even a separate dining room and no carpets anywhere. We kept getting in each other's way and the grown-ups tried to find things for us to do, an old set of Ludo and a much worn pack of Happy Families lying on their shelf and all of us irritably hanging about the place in wet weather, unravelling old socks and pullovers, carefully undoing seams on shirts. Peggy tried to teach Phil and me to knit, "Sewing socks for soldiers!" she said, but when I picked up the knitting needles after she'd done a couple of rows and she took my hands in hers, sitting behind me, I couldn't see what she was doing her fingers got in the way she threaded the needle through a loop and then hooked the wool over it, we did it over and over "Hold it like this" she'd say, and "This goes over this, here" and if I did it right what we got was a bedraggled mess of loose loops sticking out and hanging down. "You've got to get the tension right!" Mrs Davis poked, "Pull on that bit. *Gently!*" and the whole mess'd simply unravel until there was only one row of stitches left on the needle. "This is hopeless," Peggy said, "I don't think you'll ever learn" and Mrs Davis said that even if we learned to knit a nice clean row and move from one needle to another we'd never learn how to cast on, let alone turn a heel or finish up a toe. "You can't teach *boys* how to knit. And anyway," she said, "us women have too much to do. You'd better take up corking." And that's how *that* got started. After a while Peggy or Timmy would sigh, "Can we go now?" and Our Kid and Timmy'd hare for the door to get into the village maybe grabbing a rubber ball and Peggy'd be off to play with her pals, dolls or something like that, but chattering away and I'd sit there with the corking or perhaps with a drawing-book.

"You can't always be going off with Timmy or those girls," Mrs Davis said one morning before the others all went out, "you need someone your own age to play with," but I didn't know anyone and wanted to be with Our Kid, the grown-ups didn't want me aching about and underfoot all the time. "Here's a book for you," she said, "Timmy and Peggy both loved it, I did when I was young. It's got lots of pictures, it's a good story," and she put it on the table, *The Water Babies*, on the cover a greenish-brown picture, two big fish, red speckles on their back, peering at a small child looking out at them from a cleft under the water, "You'll like it a lot, it's about being the youngest," she said, and Peggy said "Tom the chimney sweep, what a wonderful time he had living under water, wouldn't you like to do that?" but it was such a lot of words and there really weren't many pictures, I couldn't understand the white room that Tom fell into from the chimney, it just didn't make much sense, and I didn't believe anybody could be as namby-pamby as Ellie was. Mum said she'd read it when she was little, "It gets much better after Tom falls into the river and becomes a water baby" so I kept at it when there was nothing else for me to do, but what with words like Naboth and Cinquecento, when I asked nobody really knew what they were, it was too hard to enjoy. Who'd ever have a name like Mrs Doasyouwouldbedoneby and Mrs Bedonebyasyoudid? What could I do with a word like *anastomosing*, none of the grown-ups had ever heard of it and Miss Chapman didn't know when I asked, she couldn't even find it in the dictionary. Dad thought the book was too old for me and called it "a bit preachy," and I thought it was a bit bossy, things like "Sir John was a very sound-headed, sound-hearted squire," saying he was "just the man to keep the countryside in order," like listening to Mr Button, or strict Grandmother at Marlow, everyone so very proper and polite. Why would anyone telling a story call its hero "Naughty Tom"? *You never did like to be* <u>told</u>, Mum wagged her finger at me long after.

Mr Davis arranged a barge-ride for Our Kid and me, "fixed it up at the pub," Mrs Davis told us. "It'll be a half-day off school," she said, "let's hope it's a nice day." None of us four kids was allowed to play down by the canal, but we knew it well enough, the canal narrowed under the bridges and the towpath curved out under the arch so horses could get through. Fastened to the corners of the sandstone or brick arch and reaching from the ground to somewhere nearly level with my head, big tapered pieces of smooth black iron full of deep grooves at different angles. None of them the same, the grooves quite shallow at the top and the bottom, some bridges you'd see faint grooves in the sandstone or brick corner above the iron, some of the grooves in the middle were so deep I could only just reach the bottom when I poked my fingers in, on hot days the iron at the bottom of the groove cool in its own shade, sometimes there'd be

a bit of grit, sometimes it'd be a bit wet. One Sunday walk I asked Dad "What are they for?" and Dad just said "Wait and see," and in a little while we met a horse pulling a barge along the canal, a nosebag over its face, brasses on its harness winking in the sun, the long rope dipping now and again into the water, the bargee at the back of the boat leaning on the rudder so the horse didn't pull the barge into the bank and we all stood still out of the way until the horse got past us. "Watch," said Dad, and we all turned round and moved slowly along behind the barge. When it got to the bridge the horse moved out towards the middle of the canal as the path curved out so that it was almost right in front of the barge and then it was through the bridge and it disappeared as the path curved back, and as the rope lifted out of the water the groove caught it, you could hear a faint singing as it rubbed water off the rope. "It took a long time to carve those grooves," Dad said, "a lot of barges." Like feet on stone steps, I thought. "It's a bridge guard," Dad said. "Sometimes the rope slips off and wears a groove in the brickwork. Not here, though."

It was Alice who walked us up the towpath towards Church Eaton, to Dirty Lane bridge, everyone else had too much to do, "That way," Mr Davis told her, "they'll get to ride right through the village, they'll get a longer ride and won't have so far to walk back. The weather's good." The barge really slowed as it went under the bridge it almost stopped and we hopped on, Alice said who we were, it wasn't horse-drawn but had a motor and the bargee wasn't a man but a big comfortable-looking woman with a bandanna round her head. She had a couple of kids but they were off playing in the fields somewhere. I asked her if they ever got lost and she smiled and said, "they can always find the canal." Then she said "Once we get through the village you can 'elp us get through the locks. Then you can steer us a bit." We chugged through the village at a walking pace, a sudden chill from the abrupt shadow under the bridge next to the Hartley Arms, the engine boomed as the sound bounced back under the arch, the sign for "Banks's Ale" so much higher over the canal than over the road it almost looked as if it was falling on you, and the pub garden came down nearly to the water. The village seemed smaller, a bit distant, but some of it closer and higher, a bit over your head, one or two houses and half-timbered cottages, you could see into the back gardens, quiet and peaceful, grass and trees and flowers and old brick. The water level was just below my waist where I was sitting in the cockpit, the wall between me and the water cold, the wood at the top of the side painted and warm from the sun, *the gunwale!* I thought, proud of the word, but *no it couldn't be that, not on a barge*. The bargee's big round arm on the rudder handle, lots of wrinkles, pink and freckly skin, she looked a lot stronger than Mum or Mrs Davis, lots of lines on her face but comfortable and relaxed, enjoying herself, smiling a bit, looking along the side of the barge so she could see around the cabin, a great flat expanse of wood and canvas beyond it covering the cargo. If we stood up on the benches we were sitting on we'd be able to see over it, but I wasn't sure we should.

Our Kid stood on the seat to see better and she didn't say anything, I remembered we'd trodden on the seat when we climbed down getting on, but I just sat still and looked, everything so different, like nothing I'd ever done before, and then we were through the bridge and we could see the locks coming up. "There's a rise of seven feet here," she told us, and moved the barge towards the towpath, here made of brick laid in ribs so the horses could get a good grip. "You can work the gates." We ran down to find the gates at our end pointing away from us, already open, the gates at the far end held closed by the weight of the water on the other side, they sprayed fat streams where they met, muddy brown-green, weed hanging down. Our Kid hung carefully onto the rail with one hand as he walked over the gates to the other side of the canal, came back to the open gate across from me, and when the barge was safely in the lock we heaved away, each of us pushing the heavy balance beam to close the wooden gate through the water behind the barge and she threw a rope up as the lock-keeper came out, he tied the barge up and opened the upstream valve, cranking the big windlass handle she'd given him to let the water come spouting in the side wall of the lock. I stepped over to the rusty iron ladder going straight down the lock wall so you could get onto the barge while it was all the way down there at the bottom, its narrow round rungs, but the bargee shook her head and we stayed up top. As the water rose in the lock and the loop in the mooring line got bigger and bigger strands of weed stretched out away from the ladder and then disappeared in surging brown water, the waving green tips the last bit you could see.

Once the lock was full my gate was so heavy the lock-keeper had to help me start it off, Our Kid could just move his, but once it got started it wasn't too hard, straining against the great thick square baulks of weathered rough timber rubbed shiny by years of hands pushing, smooth enough not to give you splinters, bits of grass and weeds in the cracks and crevices in the top. As soon as the gates were open we stepped across the narrow strip of swirling brown water between the edge of the lock and the barge, flecks of greyish foam and bits of twigs and leaves, eddies and little whirlpools, it was already moving as we got on. "What stops the canal from getting empty?" I asked. "I mean, it always goes down from the high bits when you use the locks," and the bargee said "Well it would, ducks, but they keep it topped up. I'll show where if we go that far," and Our Kid asked when we'd get to steer. "Once we get past the next bridge," she said, "the Wheaton Aston bridge" and she gestured, it was only about fifty yards away, and then we were through it, that boomy echo again, there was a long straight stretch through the Lapley Wood bridge a couple of hundred yards away and she gave Our Kid the rudder, he had to stand on the seat to see. "Keep it in the middle," she said, "we don't want to run aground. There's no tide to lift us off!" and she laughed at her own joke. She explained that most canals just had a narrow channel down the middle sometimes not as wide as two barges "What would happen if we met one?" and Our Kid said "Come on, Pete, you've seen. One of them ties up to the bank," and he gave me a look. "You can do that without any trouble most places," she said. "You can always push it off, but you don't want to travel that close." She took me down below to make a cup of tea, "Call out if you get any trouble," she told Our Kid.

The cabin had an oil stove for cooking, and a wash basin; it was lovely and warm with bright colours and curtains over the windows, a bit of a rug on the floor, a door at the end. "There's bunks for the boys," she said, they let down over the table opposite the stove. It was all very tiny, with a special place for everything, buckets and mops and brooms. A small pole stuck out of the top of the cabin, and another one at the front of the barge, they hung the washing on a line strung between the two, "'aven't you seen that?" she asked, but I hadn't, and I thought of the three grown-ups in the back scullery on a rainy washday, hands and arms shiny and red from hot water, big wet patches on aprons and pinnies, steam from the copper in the corner smothering everything with damp, smell of carbolic soap, Alice turning the mangle while Mum fed the sheets through, Mrs Davis rubbing away at something in the sink, pools of water on the tile floor, basket of wet laundry waiting to go on the big airing rack to dry clothes on that let down from the ceiling in the kitchen behind the shop at Wheaton Aston and at Grannie's in Spalding and what a nuisance it was, the rack always too small for all the wash, two bedsheets took up a whole rack and you had to keep lowering the rack and refolding the sheets and hanging them again with the damp side on top and keeping the fire going so everything could get dry and getting the sheets off before they were too dry so they could be ironed properly, we had to dry a lot of sheets at Wheaton Aston with four kids and three grown-ups, four with Alice, and then once all the sheets were done, the rack would go up and down twice as often, the rope forever getting in everybody's way, hanging up everybody's underwear and pyjamas and towels and shirts, socks and hankies, the rack going up and down all day long, and what with rationing there was never enough coal to keep the fire going and you wanted the clothes *hurry up! hurry up!* to get dry.

"Don't pull it up too fast!" Mrs Davis would scold, "You'll hit the ceiling" or "You'll break it!" but when it was full of wet stuff it was too heavy for me to pull up to the top. I loved lowering it though, I liked running the rope through my hands, "Don't let it come down too fast! You'll break the pulley" and "Mind you don't get rope burn!" the table always cluttered with clothes being folded or sorted and chairs cluttered up with baskets of clothes, everything smelling of damp, the whole room clammy and hot and steamy, nowhere to sit, everybody in each other's way, we all hated washday when it was raining, the whole day got cluttered and all the grown-ups got short-tempered, somehow you had to eat dinner or tea among all the clothes, somehow somebody had to cook the food, the kids aching about the place, or running about playing some game or other, or squabbling. And there'd be the ironing too, going on with the wet clothes still all over the place, hanging over people's heads and draped over chair backs, piles of ironed clothes on the table, hot dry ironing-smell mingling with the damp, rumpled and wrinkled clothes in the basket, two irons on the hob, a swing trivet on the cast iron range each side of the grate, the irons big and heavy, you didn't want to drop one it'd smash up the big red tiles of the floor, so hot Mrs Davis or Mum or Alice had to wrap a bit of cloth round the handle before they picked it up. She'd reach over from the ironing board and pick the iron off the hob right next the coals, lick her finger and dab it on the iron real fast, or with a bit of spit, always a bowl of water on the table where she could get at it, test the iron. Mum'd dip her finger in the bowl and flick the water hitting the iron, a little hiss of steam, to make sure it wasn't too hot, and then she'd run the iron fast over the cloth, "If you stop it'll scorch!" she'd say, "you can't go slow!" the room a thick fug with all that steam from the damp clothes and the water to sprinkle on the clothes if they'd got too dry, all the women with shiny red faces from standing so close to the fire when they were ironing, one of them perhaps doing the cooking, hair in damp strands down the sides of their faces, all us kids hanging about and fretting because it was raining too hard to go out, grumpily folding clothes or putting them away because there was nothing else to do, too crowded and cluttered for any play, not even word games there was so much noise and bustle, everybody busy.

Our Kid shouted "There's a bridge coming up!" and we both scurried back to the cockpit, "Would you like to steer it through?" she said, and she slowed us down a bit so he could steer this long narrow boat through a hole not much wider than the barge, you could easily touch the bridge on one side and it was only a few inches to the towpath on the other, the edge of the towpath lined with stone and with black iron at the rounded corners to fend you off if you hit it. We sat in the cockpit drinking our tea, milky with lots of sugar, and I looked at the wonderful bright paintwork, flowers and vines and leaves on a red background just like a gypsy caravan, yellow and blue and green and white, the name of the barge in a panel with a fancy border, "Meadowsweet." After the War, when the barges were nationalised, they all got painted dull grey and given numbers instead of names, and we hated the Labour government for doing that.

All around us were fields and woods, copses on hillsides, farms, cows in pastures, bits of villages across the grass, a church spire in the distance. After we got through the bridge the cut we'd been going through ended and then the ground gradually dropped away and we were up above the fields going along an embankment, we chugged sedately on, the only sound the motor, now and then a splash against the bank or against the barge, moorhens and rabbits, or some villager's dog rooting about the bank, and birdsong and the odd cow lowing and an erratic bit of breeze that made you half-close your eyes. We could have stayed there for ever. We asked her where she was going, and she said she was carrying a load of chocolate from up near Liverpool down to Birmingham, "I bet you're going to Cadbury's" I said, but she didn't answer, she pointed off to the right to a big lake behind a dam on the other side of the aqueduct that carried the canal over the Watling Street, we could hear the traffic now, probably an Army convoy, "That's the Belvide Reservoir," she pronounced it *Belvidee*, "there's a stream that comes from there, just on the other side of the aqueduct, that's where the water comes from to top up the canal." *How does the water get from down there all the way up here?* Before I could ask, she said she'd better let us off at the start of the aqueduct, her children would likely be waiting there. I wondered where they went to school, but she slowed the barge down told me to steer and disappeared inside the cabin for a moment, the canal just a bit wider than the barge as it went over the bridge. "You've got a bit of a walk back to Wheaton Aston," she said as we got off, and she handed each of us a brown paper bag, the traffic rumbling and roaring by underneath us on the Watling Street. "It's a bit of chocolate," she said. I looked inside at crumbly grey-brown lumps full of little holes, just like lumps of coke we burned in the stove, "It's ever so good," she said, "it just 'asn't been made into bars yet. This is 'ow it arrives at the factory." By the time we got back to Wheaton Aston hot and tired we'd got none left.

3
Adapting

Once or twice after we'd had our supper the sky full of stars and the moon, "a bomber's moon" Mr Davis called it, we heard planes in the distance, lots of them and we'd go outside to look. Even if you couldn't see, you could tell they were some of ours, Timmy always said he heard a Defiant, that'd've been made in Wolverhampton, but Mr Davis simply said "You can't always tell, not if you can't see it. A Nazi plane sounds different, no matter how big it is. Listen to the engine, if it throbs like that it's German. Our planes sound nice and smooth" and we'd cluster outside listening and looking out towards Wolverhampton ten miles off, searchlights criss-crossing, sometimes smoke rising from distant lights on the ground "that's bombs" somebody would say quietly but they were very faint, the air raid was too far off, nothing much to see. "Oh," said Peggy, "Look at the moon!, it's ever so clear" and after a bit Timmy said, "I can see the man-in-the-moon, look, he's right there," and I wanted to see it too. But no matter how hard I tried I couldn't. "Here, let me show you" Peggy said as she crouched and pointed her arm over my shoulder, "Look along my finger! There's his eye, see it?" But from where I was her finger hardly pointed at the moon at all, and as everyone chimed in with different suggestions Mum said "cover one of your eyes, try it that way," and after a few minutes me looking and them telling me what to do Mrs Davis and Alice shook their heads and the others began to sound a bit annoyed, and I began to wonder *perhaps he isn't really there!* and on the heels of that *but he must be, I've seen those pictures!* and I began to be a bit cross with myself. I felt a flash of annoyance and I didn't say anything when we went to bed that night and Our Kid said "It's funny you can't see it when everyone else can, isn't it?" but it was a long time after Wheaton Aston before I actually did, and that happened when I just glanced up and *lo-and-behold!* there it was. I suppose I'd been looking for what I'd seen in all those pictures in fairytale books and on calendars with phases of the moon, a huge grin on a face as clear as in those drawings, and I could only see the fuzzy grey shapeless patches that everybody else sees on the moon's yellow. You have to *learn* to see things the way other people do.

Most days weren't that way, they were all the same except the once when we got home from school, a wizened man in a worn and grubby grey suit turned up outside the shop, he leant his bike against the wall with a couple of bags in the handlebar-basket, he didn't look quite clean, he simply started talking to us as we came up, he nodded and smiled and talked to us as though he knew who we were and'd come to the shop specially to talk to us. He winked at us, and shrugged, and listened when any of us said something. Peggy knew who he was, he worked on one of the farms nearby, he'd been there for years, and he'd got a ferret in a bag, he took it out and stroked its neck. Mum saw him through the window and came out shaking her head. "Don't you all have chores to do? Timmy, have you swept the outhouse yet? Peggy you're needed in the kitchen, Philip and Peter, you come with me" and the four of us scattered. He stayed where he was and it wasn't long before we all clustered round him again, the ferret still there. "Don't touch!" he said as he leaned over it, "'E ain't 'alf got teeth, sharp 'uns too! Gobble y'up!" and he laughed. As we examined this lean fierce creature with its small red eyes and off-white fur he told us he used it to go rabbiting, "Got two last night" he said, "You'll be 'avin' one of 'em for your dinner I expect," and he showed us a string contraption he'd put round its head and snout before shoving it into the warren, he called it a cope, and he told us the ferret chased the rabbits out of their burrow and he could catch them with his dog, or he'd sometimes set a snare or two. "You got to put the cope on," he said, "or it'll kill the rabbit down the 'ole and eat it and then it'll go to sleep it'll be so full, and you've lost your ferret" and he laughed. We wondered at that tiny ferret eating a whole rabbit all by itself, and Peggy asked him if he'd ever lost his, he said yes he had a couple of times, sometimes they got rid of the cope down the hole, though he'd got one of them back. "But they're quite tame," he said, "and you don't really 'ave to train them, no, just get to know them a bit and get them to know you, keep 'em 'appy" and he laughed again. "They know you but they don't like you, no, they don't 'ave any love in 'em, not like a dog. No loyalty" and he laughed again, "but they don't 'alf breed, worse'n rabbits. Two litters a year." He loved talking to us and we liked it too, remembered what he said, he just explained things to us because we wanted to know, he wasn't like a lot of the grown-ups we met. "He's a poacher, isn't he?" said Timmy, and Peggy said, "Of course not!" and "I bet he is," said Timmy, "he's bound to be. He swopped that rabbit for something from the shop." "*Rabbits* aren't poaching," Peggy said. "Other animals are!" said Timmy, and I wondered, *do the rabbits belong to somebody?* "Like pheasants and grouse," Timmy said. "The farmer's not the landowner," and Peggy didn't say anything.

One of the things the ferret-man had said became a catch-phrase of ours for a while, and we'd chant the last part of it whenever we could and chortle, we must have been pretty tiresome with it, it sounded like he'd got it from a book, an encyclopaedia I expect, "When irritated, it is apt to give painful evidence of its ferocity," said in a posh voice, warning us about the ferret's bite. And he laughed at his own joke. He was so friendly to us kids.

But his snooty joke accent reminded Mum of Mr Button the schoolmaster. She let us overhear this a day or two later as she told Mrs Davis she thought he was too irascible to be a teacher, "Always whacking the kids," Mrs Davis said, "That's what I've heard." "At home, too, I shouldn't wonder," Alice chimed in, "honestly, you'd think someone with a name like that could think up a better name for his daughter than Pearl," and they all three began to laugh. "But Pearl's a pretty name for a girl," Mrs Davis chuckled, shaking her head. *Why was it all so funny?* Shy little three-year-old Pearl who looked a bit like her dad and always wore pretty little dresses and never said anything very much, she'd sometimes catch my eye as she stopped riding her trike for a bit or look up from playing with a doll and just stand there and watch us till her dad hauled her indoors or chased us away.

It wasn't long before evacuees arrived, mostly from Black Country places like Dudley and Walsall, they billetted I think no choice with villagers who had room, townies whose very presence reminded us constantly and forcefully that the War wasn't far off. We could feel *its* effects alright as rationing began to bite, shivering outside and getting chilblains in the cold raw weather, not much of a fire indoors if there was one, a spoonful of cod-liver oil every morning after breakfast to keep the colds off and burping oily fishy taste all day up into the back of your nose, you might smell it on someone's breath, it'd even penetrate the boiled potatoes at dinner no matter how much gravy you managed to drown it in. The only thing that helped really was a great doorstep of bread to gnaw on, with a bit of dripping if there was any, Mr Davis called it mucky-fat, the melted beef or pork fat strong enough to overcome the fish oil. But there was not much of that, the butcher never had any to spare nowadays with meat in short supply, and we didn't get much fruit except for a few wizened winter apples, cox's orange pippins if you were lucky, good storers they were, we *loved* them, we only knew about bananas because of a faded notice for Fyffes near the store, and we hadn't even seen an orange since the War started. It was a real treat when Mrs Davis managed to get hold of a jar of Radio Malt, "just as good for you as cod-liver oil," she said, "you can even spread it on bread," but a jar didn't last very long with us four kids getting a spoonful every day. Timmy and Peggy began talking about the summer when we could have fresh fruit, cherries and strawberries and plums.

We got colds. Timmy and Peggy told us that some village kids "but not us!" 'd had their chests slathered with goose fat in October and sewn into their underwear for the winter, we didn't really believe them until Our Kid ended up sitting next to one of them in school, "I changed desks as quickly as I could," he told Mum years later, I'd forgotten all about it till he said that. "By the time December rolled round they were pretty ripe I can tell you." But Phil got away from all that in January, we hadn't been in Wheaton Aston as much as six months when he started as a weekly boarder at Brewood Grammar School in the next village over, when he was eight. That was a Private School, and we all sneered at the rough townies billetted with village kids, "They all think milk comes from bottles!" Mum laughed. "Bunch of ignorant little B's," Mrs Davis called them, they all got slathered with Vick's VapoRub every night or had great wodges of some patent cotton wool like Thermogene, bright orange and smelly, sewn inside their vests, we bet that'd be itchy, but it might be warm too, and we didn't know what we felt about that, had such terrible colds all the time, and it wasn't long before we wore Thermogene too, only ours was held with safety pins front and back. Phil remembers asking one of the townies where he came from and he said "Wa'sa'," we'd heard about Warsaw on the BBC and Phil was amazed that he spoke English at all and asked Mum "Did he come from Poland?" She made a face and laughed and said "No, no, Walsall's in the Black Country, it's all factories, working-class." And then she said "They don't speak properly, I can't really understand a word they say either, their accents are so thick. They're just urchins really, they don't have much to do with us, don't like the countryside." Us four kids began to feel a bit ashamed of the Thermogene, its mix of capsicum and wintergreen oil *it doesn't half stink!* even if it did soon wear off, the VapoRub made your chest all sticky and the Thermogene even itchier, worse than wool. It said we were just like *them*, and if the thick cotton wadding kept our chests warm it didn't stop our noses running or keep the colds off like Mum and Mrs Davis said it would.

Phil really had a hard time of it, he got a terrible pain in his ear, most of us got an earache now and again of course, kids do, but his simply wouldn't go away, it kept him awake half the night and more in that pitch-dark room with ice on the inside of the windowpane and its unused fireplace, the hot-water bottle slowly getting colder and colder, and in the morning his pillow would be all stained with what had come out of it, yellow pus sometimes with a bit of blood, his earhole all crusty and red-looking deep inside. He had an awful temperature, the doctor had come more than once, and sometimes on that side he couldn't hear what you said. After a bit of a search Mrs Davis found a roll of pre-war cotton wool in the shop snug in its roll of blue paper and every morning Mum would warm a bit of it up in front of the fire and put it in his ear to keep it warm, but it didn't help much, just sopped up the mess coming out of it. But while she was looking for the cotton wool Mrs Davis found some fireworks from before the War, and Dad found a few more in the stockroom at Woolworth's in Birmingham. She even laid hands on a pre-War Christmas pudding all wrapped up, though it might've been in a tin, everybody was pleased about that, you couldn't get all the ingredients to make one not even at that stage of the War.

Guy Fawkes was on a Sunday in 1939, so Dad stayed late and set them off in the garden outside the window so Our Kid could watch them. He nailed a Catherine Wheel to the fence just outside the window but like all the others I ever saw it didn't go round the way it was supposed to; the Roman Candle and the Burning Schoolhouse were amazing, and I wanted him to set off some rockets but nobody had any, and all the grown-ups said "You can't do that in the War; you're not even supposed to have any fireworks, certainly not in the blackout." One or two kids from the village came to watch, Dad made them stand back, and Our Kid sat up in the window in his pyjamas and dressing gown with a hot-water bottle and all the lights off in the room, a bandage round his head to keep his ear warm.

Everybody was terrified that he had mastoiditis, whatever that was, and a few days later Mum and Mrs Davis shooed Timmy and Peggy and me out of the house and told us to *stay out!* With Alice they spent the whole day washing and scrubbing floors and brushing all the cobwebs down and cleaning the curtains and the carpets and the furniture and the stairs and our bedroom and lighting a fire to get that bedroom warm, and at the end of the day when it was getting dark we at last came in, everywhere filled with a strong carbolic smell *Take your boots off before you come in!* and *Keep quiet!* One of the grown-ups kept a close watch on us as we got a thorough wash at the pump outside and then let us near the fire to warm up a bit before bed. Next day after school we were all sent out of the house again, but it was so cold and wet we came back into the kitchen and stayed there *No noise, mind! Read a book or play a game!* but before we settled into that two men wearing dark raincoats each with a small suitcase and scarves and trilby hats drove up to the shop, so shiny and tidy in the rain they looked as though they'd just been cleaned in a laundry, and spoke for a bit very quietly at the bottom of the stairs to Mum and then went up to where Our Kid was. We were all bursting with curiosity, so to keep us quiet Mrs Davis told us they were two doctors come from Birmingham to operate on Our Kid's ear. A few years later a new kid about my age who came to Brewood had a monstrous hole behind his right ear, looked big enough to put a baby's fist in, where they'd chipped and ground away the mastoid bone because of the infection, you couldn't do anything else about it, not then. That night, when they'd gone back to Birmingham, Our Kid had the bedroom to himself and I slept in Mum and Dad's bed with them.

Next day at breakfast Mum and Dad told us Our Kid didn't have mastoiditis after all, *What good news that is!* they smiled a bit, but they still looked tired and worried, "He's going to need a bit of attention, and you'll have to help too, you know, all three of you. We can't manage everything when Philip needs looking after," and Peggy nodded. "He's going to be alright but it'll be a few weeks." He'd had an abscess in his middle ear and the doctors'd cured it up there in the bedroom by puncturing his eardrum to let the infection out, and he'd need a warm poultice over his ear to draw all the poison out *That's why we need your help, all of you, We really can't do everything.* And it took Phil two or three weeks to get better enough to get back to school and even play outside, and after that he'd still sometimes have terrible earaches. He never complained, he just sat still, near the fire if he could, draw in on himself. His eardrum never really grew back properly and if there was any chance of getting water in his ear he'd have to put his earplugs in, hard rubber things, they must've been really uncomfortable, and they didn't work very well, he once tried them out swimming and one fell out and water got in, the terrible pain took more than two days to go away. He was mad about joining the Navy, loved sea stories and pictures of ships, but he knew that abscess'd likely put paid to his ever being in the Navy. It didn't make any difference to his dreams though, his drawings were always of ships, never of anything else, and his favourite book became E.C. Talbot-Booth's *Ships And The Sea*, lots of maps and fold-out pages of silhouettes and drawings of ships and parts of ships and flags and funnel insignia, as well as all sorts of stuff about their length, tonnage, and displacement, he just lapped that up, but it didn't mean anything to me *You've got to be older before you can understand it!* I couldn't get interested in all that detail, I just liked the idea of ships. Dad'd found the book in Birmingham and gave it Our Kid as an early Christmas present, and Phil just couldn't let go of it it was so magical, he'd make a beeline for it as soon as he got back from school, and spend hours and hours going through it, and he's still got it, it sits close to hand on the windowsill in what he calls his den. Once the War was over he spent a lot of his pocket money on books like *Jane's Merchant Ships* and *All the World's Fighting Ships*, hundreds of pages of silhouettes along with technical details about each ship.

In the War of course we were all mad about joining up. At first I wanted to be in the RAF just to be different from Our Kid, and I'd draw camouflaged planes shooting at other planes or dropping bombs on them, curly loop-the-loop lines to show how the planes flew, the RAF roundel carefully coloured in, the swastikas in black, crooked rows of dashes making sure that the British guns didn't miss their German targets. When the Battle of Britain was going on we'd sometimes see dogfights high up, a distant intermittent buzzing they were so far away, all of us looking and pointing, cheers if a plume of smoke a plane span out and down, a long slow plunge to the ground faster and faster a long way off out towards Wolverhampton way or even far-off Birmingham, you could hardly see the planes at all just small dots and the blurs of the trails, we'd begin to argue and then fall quiet trying to see if it was one of ours or a Nazi, wait for a parachute. We'd argue quietly about that, always somebody absolutely positive it was a Messerschmitt, or a Hurricane or a Spitfire, but too far off to tell.

But when Our Kid found he couldn't be in the Navy I decided I wanted to be. We both cut pictures of ships out of *Picture Post* and *Illustrated* and the newspaper and glued them in scrapbooks and the drawings in my drawing books began to be of ships, page after page of them, harder to draw but more exciting because they had more on them, pompoms, torpedo tubes, huge guns, HMS *Nelson*, we had a dinky toy with its sixteen-inch guns sticking out of three big turrets, you could draw smoke coming out of funnels, men walking on the deck, shells flying through the air, explosions and flags flying. And you could draw German ships sinking, men crying "*Achtung!*" and "*Kamerad!*" words we'd picked up from comics and cartoons in the paper, and parachutists being shot at. At Christmas and birthdays all through the War not just in Wheaton Aston we'd get picture books of *Our Fighting Forces* and *Our Glorious Navy* full of photographs of tanks and ships and planes and soldiers in full battledress and we just devoured them, copied the pictures. Impossible heroics. I began to fill my drawing books with pictures of tanks knocking down buildings and crossing ditches and crushing German soldiers and shooting down planes while getting blown up. Someone in the village said that the only news we heard was what the Ministry of Information let us hear, and Mum and Mrs Davis were shocked by that and Alice said "Why, the BBC and the papers even tell us the bad news, we're not like the Germans. We don't lie."

And then Alice left us, went back to Birmingham to live. "She's gone to get married," Mum told us, and then, to Mrs Davis, "we'll miss her. We gave her a good wedding present though, a whole month's wages. With the shops so empty that's the best we could do." Phil was inconsolable, sixty years later he told me on the phone, "I couldn't get over it. I cried myself to sleep every night," and if he dwelt on it even now, he said, he could feel bereft the way he did then, "I thought she'd deserted me"; she was such a fixture in the family that neither of us understood, nobody'd said anything to us about it, not even her, she just said her goodbyes the day before she left. "Well," Peggy said, and she laughed, "she did go away every weekend didn't she, back to Birmingham. Not surprising she had a boyfriend" and Mrs Davis chuckled, "Of course she did, attractive young woman like her. Lots of people are getting married nowadays, there's a war on. That's what people do."

At almost the same time Dad told Mum that he'd managed to get Phil into the school about five miles away in Brewood. "He's old enough now," he said, "to live away from home. He'll be starting in the new year. It'll do him good to get away, make a fresh start, especially now Alice's leaving," and it's true that going away as a boarder to a new school helped him push away the loss of Alice, what with having to make new friends among kids his own age, new routines and tasks to learn and get used to, interesting and some of it quite exciting. "There's even a woodwork shop," he said one week-end visit, "smashing tools we can use, chisels, saws, set-squares, clamps, proper work-benches with really strong vices, we can't go there by ourselves, there has to be Prefect or a Teacher, but there's proper cupboards to store what you're doing in. I don't know what some things are for, but someone'll tell us."

No matter how much he liked it, though, he still found the change, the sheer newness of it all, a bit bewildering, and when he went to Mr Bailey the Headmaster and asked for permission to go home for that weekend, every boarder could do that once every half-term, Mr Bailey gave him the bus fare and wrote it down in a little book, "There's a bus at 1220, you can catch that if you hurry!" he said, "You're to be back before lights out tomorrow!" But when he got to the Square it was the bus to Wheaton Aston, he didn't want *that*, what he wanted was the bus to Wolverhampton so he could go home to Birmingham two hours or more away, "*That's* where home was," he said, "so I didn't get on. Why would I want to go to Wheaton Aston?" and he had to falter his way back to School. "That was terrible," he said. "I had to tell everyone I'd missed the bus and so wouldn't be going, I couldn't let on to the other kids that it was the wrong bus, I'd never live that sort of mistake down. If one of them asked I just said there'd been a change of plans." And he paused. "I went off to be by myself for a while."

Perhaps the Davises heaved a sigh of relief when Our Kid went to Brewood and there was only Mum and me to take care of during the week, but Peggy and Timmy didn't want me tagging along with them all the time, they were much too busy with their own friends to bother with looking after me, and it must've been a real nuisance for the Davises with just Mum and me there, only two extra ration books instead of four, not so much rent coming in now Phil and Alice'd gone, Dad still struggling to come every weekend, and I think Mum and Dad got more and more tired of it, what the Davises had to offer really wasn't a solution. How could it be, when Mum only saw Dad at weekends and then not always, Phil away in the next village all week and not always in Wheaton Aston for the weekend, and no matter how friendly and welcoming the Davises were she was still living in a *shop* really not a *proper* house, and all day she had to be at other people's beck and call, no private or personal time at all, not even in the evening and never with just us kids, never just sitting at home with a quiet cup of tea and a book, and no piano to practise on and we didn't even have a cat.

Phil and I had it better. Compared to the evacuees, we were *habitués*, old inhabitants almost, and like most of the village kids and nearly all the grown-ups we looked down our noses at them, *they'd* been evacuated on trains and in buses, luggage labels tied to their collars or round their necks, dumped among complete strangers, some of them stuck with unwilling hosts, and most of them scorned because they hadn't even known what a cow was before they came. Some of them'd never even *seen* a cow before. And Phil and me had, lots of times. *We* knew about the countryside, *we* knew about country life; *we* had the advantage of Uncle Tom and Aunt Dot and cousin Brenda who lived on the farm, and who we visited. And the farm was how Dad could keep running a car when lots of people'd had to disable theirs or give them up completely.

But the Davises tried hard enough. One clear Saturday morning as he came in from the yard right after breakfast Mr Davis looked at me and said, "You're coming with me to deliver the bread." Mum smiled as he put a big basket of bread on the rack on the front of his bike and another over his arm and gave me a smaller one and door to door we went round the village, houses I'd never paid attention to or even noticed. Two big loaves for the Joneses *Oh! That's where Trev lives, is it!* a Hovis and a malted for old Mrs Crooks, four white and a brown for the Purdy family. We got back to the shop after about an hour, everything carefully counted and remembered, and he wrote it all down in a little book. We don't 'ave to deliver everyone's bread," he said, "a lot of 'em pick it up at the shop." He looked at me. "Are you tired?" he asked, "we're going out again, I'd like your 'elp, there's a long way to go." And he slung a great sack of bread over his shoulder, and gave me a bag with a shoulder strap, four two-pound loaves in it, crisp fresh baked crust warm against my coat. And in answer to my question, "We can't take the bike. Come on, then." And we set out across the fields, the long wet grass swishing against my socks, the odd thistle or burr scraping my legs. Watch out for the cowpats. Climb the stile. Open the gate. Close the gate. My bag of bread kept sliding down my shoulder and I kept hitching it up, holding it with my hand. "'Ere, let me move it to the other side," he said. "It's a lot further by the road," he said, "and it's 'arder on me feet." "It's Mrs Philps," he said. "A big family. 'Er 'usband's in the Army. 'E's a Sergeant. In the South Staffs regiment. Somewhere in the War. Overseas I think" – the short sentences punctuated by the grassy sound of walking. It was hot. I wanted something to drink. "There's a stream coming up, under that 'edge." My pace quickened a bit. I cupped my hand, licked up some water, splashed it in my face. It didn't taste very much. "In the winter," he said, "when it snows, they sometimes get cut off, and they 'ave to pinch to make do. It's a bit remote." We stopped for a bit of a rest. "Don't want to rest too much," he told me; "it gets 'arder to start each time. Come on." My bag of bread was a bit damp from the grass, and my crisp loaves of sandwich bread were beginning to lose their sharp four-square edges. "Don't worry about that," he said; "not much farther." My bag kept getting closer to the ground, dragging on the odd tussock. They usually fetch the bread themselves, he told me, every Wednesday. But this week they're poorly. I stopped. "Doesn't the bread get stale?" I asked. And he told me they wrap it in damp cloth. "You're just wrapping it a bit early," he said, looking at the sodden bottom of my bag. I thought of horrible soggy bread and bread-and-milk and made a face, and he laughed. "It gets a bit mouldy by the end of the week," he said, "especially in the summer. Scrape the mould off." I was glad we lived in the village. "And you can toast stale bread," he added; "makes good toast." He looked at me and winked. "Or fresh it up a bit in the oven." He took my bag as we climbed over a stile, the tread a bit mucky, and "'Ere we are" he said. A red brick cottage, patch of garden, a gate, some chickens out the back, empty pigsty. Mrs Philps gave me a drink from the pump, and chuckled as she looked at my battered loaves of bread. "You're a bit of a small one for that long hike," she said. Friendly. Glad. "Couldn't 'ave managed without 'im" Mr Davis said, and he ruffled my hair. My socks were covered with burrs. I could smell my own sweat and I said, "I liked that" and felt proud. We turned round and walked the mile-and-a-half back to a big cup of tea with sugar. It almost felt like home.

Eight or nine years later, me fifteen-and-a-half, on my first Sunday morning as Senior Prefect to all the boarders at Brewood, I marched the regulation two-by-two crocodile, all the boarders under my care, to morning service. I felt quite proud. And a stoop-shouldered man, with missing teeth and ragged whiskers, a bit grubby in a battered grey suit and down at heel in his scuffed dusty shoes, reached out, his fingers brushed my sleeve; me in my School blazer and cap and best black shoes. "Excuse me, Sir," he said, "Are you Peter Quartermain?" I stopped, gestured to the crocodile to keep going. "I'm Charlie Davis. Do you remember me?" And I was astonished. *How could I possibly forget?*

The kids trooped by. He told me: the shop was long gone, his wife had died; Timmy and Peggy in separate foster homes, and he had no job; living in a Salvation Army shelter in Wolverhampton somewhere near St Peter's Square. Red-rimmed eyes and desperate breath. Could I spare five bob. And I didn't know what to do, the Headmaster in his reserved pew, me with my School cap in my hand its silver badge warm from the mild sun, standing there in the churchyard while the rest of the boarders trooped past me into compulsory worship. The sheep's bell stopped its hurry-up, the church door began to close, a blackbird's abrupt song in the suspended silence and the double-decker bus changed gear as it went down Dean Street on the way back to town. "I've got to be in there," I said. "But after I come out. Wait" my voice making a question. I *had* to be in there, I was the Prefect that day, the only one there, I was in charge, and I had to take the collection plate round and take it to the altar, and I didn't want to be seen talking to someone who looked like this, the two of us in the churchyard. And all I had was sixpence, my week's pocket-money, I didn't give it to him, it wouldn't even begin to pay his bus fare back to town; the gravestones around us, the path where we stood, the whitewashed cottage across from the Admiral Rodney bright over the churchyard wall. He turned away. And after I'd planted myself in my proper place in the boarders' pew at the back I began to think I should have taken him straight to the new Headmaster Mr Finney, or better yet gone to trusty old Henry Houston, said who Mr Davis was, and asked for help. Perhaps they could phone if they had one, phone Mum and Dad, I didn't know the number but surely they must have it at School even if the office was closed for the weekend, no School Secretary there till Monday.

I kept shifting about in my pew, couldn't just sit there in my pew, in charge of all these kids, and do nothing. *But what can I do? I can't just get over to School* now, *there'll be nobody there! Mr Finney down the aisle up towards the front in the Headmaster's pew, he has to be there, no choice, the two Church Wardens hovering round the nave to take the Collection and see that we all behave, Henry Houston as usual probably down at the Admiral Rodney, Matron taking her Sunday off who knows where she might be, and* nobody *in the kitchen except maybe one of the maids* I simply couldn't settle, the hard seat of the pew continually distracting the urgency of my heart and breath. *I simply don't know what to do.*

It took ages for the service to end. But as soon as Church was over I just looked at the next-most senior kid and in the quiet hubbub of everybody chatting and gossiping with their neighbours and getting ready to leave I tore out of the Church as quickly as I could not talking to anybody. And Mr Davis was *gone.* I never saw him again.

What demons of shame and irresolution possessed me, where had I learned such hesitation and indecision?

4
The Farm

Uncle Tom was the bailiff Dad had put in to manage a farm south of Birmingham, sometime after the First World War, they might have gone shares, but I don't think it was a Partnership in any formal legal sense, I don't know that Tom put up any money and I've no idea how they met. Our Kid knows a lot more about that than I do, I haven't asked him, but there must have been some sort of written agreement. Dad really wanted to be a farmer Mum more than once said, and it was pretty obvious his heart was set on it anyway, he looked so different on the farm, relaxed, free of the constriction of a three-piece suit, not that he ever said anything about *that*, his face a bit fuller. He smiled more, he talked more, and he listened, paid attention to the sounds of things. He loved the countryside and the fresh air, the animals, the feel of crops growing round you that you'd planted and could harvest, loved the work and the steady pace of it and of country life. He was a dead keen gardener no matter the weather, I can still see him when we lived in Lichfield long after the War at the end of the day after he'd parked the car out the back it'd take him more than an hour to get across the sixty feet or so to the house, he'd get waylaid by the plants, he'd really get caught up by the weeds, he'd disappear into the shed and come out with a spade or the secateurs, or a bit of green twine, even in the snow he'd stop and carefully disentangle a struggling coreopsis or pentstemon, he even knew their Latin names, and when at last he got to the back door *Oh Leo look at your suit!* Mum'd cry, *and your shoes!* and he'd look a bit crestfallen and smile, "I was a bit worried that geum wasn't going to make it" or "I must do something about the greenhouse, get some heat in there," pleased and relaxed, hands all covered in rust and spider-webbed muck from the old stove that hadn't been lit for years, and the two of them would set to cleaning up his clothes for the next day, he wouldn't let anybody else press his trousers, he did it himself the damp tea-towel laid carefully over the legs, the iron firmly running down the crease, that was *his* job, like cleaning shoes, he'd learned that in the Army, "You'll have to learn that too," he told us, "so you don't get tram-lines running down your leg," and every night he'd put his suit-trousers in the trouser press, tenderly pulling and tucking and adjusting, a big sheet of brown cardboard under the trousers, another sheet laid gently on top before he closed the press down like a door and tightened up the screws, I think it was the cardboard that'd come with the press when he first got it, a bit scruffy round the edges, a bit brittle, but perfectly usable, he liked things to last, took care of his tools, wiped them with a rag after he'd used them, loved reading seed catalogues.

But it didn't matter how often Mum'd ask him to change into his gardening clothes as soon as he got home, he still took ages to get through the garden though sometimes he'd remember, I suppose it got to be a bit of a ritual for them, a shared domestic task. I don't know what Mum thought about it what with clothes rationed even after the War, it always meant extra work for her after she'd been at it all day, but she never said anything that I heard, not even a sigh, and I was really surprised soon after Dad died when she told me, I'd said something about Uncle Tom, that she was never really very happy about the farm, yes of course she'd enjoyed the summers there especially in the War but she didn't trust Tom much. She thought he always managed things to his own advantage, what nowadays we might call good at manipulating. Of course by the time Dad died we didn't have anything to do with the farm any more, he'd been so ill for such a long time. "I'm glad we stopped going there," she said with a slight grimace, "when I think about it." It wasn't long after that, it can't've been more than two or three days, she asked me if I'd go up to the bedroom and sort through Dad's clothes, both of us in that sort of shock you get with someone dying, Phil away at his job in Birmingham, me home from University. "I couldn't bear to do that," she said, and sniffed, her eyes all wet, "Just the wardrobe," her bleak face. "Do you think his sports jacket would fit you?" I shrugged, didn't think any of us'd be able to stand me wandering round, the slightest glimpse of me out of the corner of your eye, me in that beautiful green lamb's-wool jacket, grim punctuation. She looked relieved when I said I don't want it. "Somebody's coming tomorrow to pick them up, you'd better go through the pockets" she said; "I expect they'll end up at the Salvation Army, somewhere like that, unless he's a jobber," and I realised I'd never thought about it at all, all the things to be looked after after somebody died.

Faint trace of mothballs as I opened the wardrobe door, the camphor overlaying the *Muguet des Bois* from Mum's clothes on the right, Dad's clothes tucked away in the dimness on the left. Laying them on the bed one by one I went through his suits, the scent of stale cigarette smoke getting more and more noticeable as I reached further into the wardrobe, at the very back a baggy double-breasted suit, old stains here and there. As I reached it out a faint puff of dust from the shoulders and lapels, my finger-marks as I took it from the hanger, he must've worn it for gardening but goodness only knows when, and there in the inside jacket pocket, the only thing I found in all those clothes except for a clean hankie, a cheque. The best part of thirteen years old, fountain-pen in slightly fading washable-blue ink, Barclay's Bank in Alcester, made out in December 1941 by Uncle Tom, paying Dad four hundred pounds. He'd never cashed it. A huge sum of money, more than twice as much as I had to live on in 1954 as an undergraduate at Nottingham when my two-hundred-and-fifteen quid had to pay for everything, food, clothing, lodging, bus fares, all those books, the lot. In 1941 it must've been worth the devil of a lot more, and I just looked at that cheque for a moment or two, and I wondered what Uncle Tom had thought about that, whether he'd said anything to Dad. I tore it up and stuffed it into my pocket. I didn't tell Mum, I didn't dare, she'd've been so upset, I never told her, there was no point, and I never told anyone till now, not even Our Kid, yet there's a small corner in me somewhere that wishes I'd hung on to it, a memento of difficulties. But I didn't want Mum to *know* what she'd suspected, how much Dad must've put into the farm and into Uncle Tom's pocket over the years. If that cheque is anything to go by, he must have spent quite a bit on the farm every year. I'm pretty sure it never actually brought any money in, precious little anyway at the best of times, I suppose it was a more-or-less unacknowledged bone of contention between them, though of course they never breathed a word of their disagreements, if they had any, not to us. Dad's near-obsession with the farm and farming was, they must have agreed without ever much discussing it, a necessary vice, needed because the farm kept him sane.

Not that Phil and I thought *that*, we never really gave any thought to Dad's job, managing a Woolworth's store was simply what he did, leaving the house at half-past seven six days a week, during the War going off on his bike, coming home for dinner at twelve-thirty on the dot except at Rugby when the store was too far away, getting back to the store within the hour, coming home again at night after dark, nearly always too late for the six-o'clock news. *Mustn't set a bad example for the girls!* meaning the girls behind the counters, about twenty-five of them altogether, *if I'm not punctual I can hardly expect them to be on time.* It wouldn't be fair to dock their pay for doing what he did, and they could even get the sack. On Mondays especially what with it being wash-day Mum really had to scamper to make sure that dinner was on the table when he came through the door, the potatoes and greens nice and hot to go with the cold meat leftover from yesterday, the custard keeping warm on the cooker along with the pudding for afters, dinner invariably a proper sit-down meal, a brief domestic break in the middle of the working day, sacrosanct. "Martha Spriggs," he'd tell Mum, "the girl at the confectionery counter," and Mum would say "Oh yes, the pretty one with curls, she looks so very young." "She told me she's getting married," he said, "when I was doing my rounds. Sweet young thing, shy and proud all at the same time when she told me. Excited. He wants to be a baker when he gets out of the Forces," and they'd quietly worry together about people not getting back from the War, how young they were, "They'd better get married while they can," Mum said, and Dad "They're going to live with her parents." They'd think about the difficult times young people had nowadays what with the housing shortage and Air Raids, impermanence and change. Nothing said about what Dad would have to do to make sure Martha got a bit of time off for her honeymoon. Mum would detail her news and gossip to accompany his, how sudden rain ruined copies of *Picture Post* at the newsagent's when the wind tore the old canvas awning or how Mr Jones's bike has been stolen, how terrible that is when he needs it to get to work. Difficult times we live in, how people need to help each other. The only time he ever talked shop in front of us at the dinner table was the day he said to Mum as soon as he got through the door "I had to give Gladys Potter a week's notice this morning," really down in the mouth, Mum saying "Oh Leo, what will she do, her mother sick the way she is and the other children still at school?" Dad saying how he'd had to talk to her over and over about not doing her job properly and how much theft there'd been from her counter, her giggling away and gossiping instead of looking after her till. "She's just not responsible," he said, worrying about his job as much as about Gladys; "I can't carry that dead weight, we can't afford it."

That deep-seated midday routine would be severely disrupted by Mr Porteus on his Annual Inspection of the store. It was a big event not only because he was Dad's Superintendent but because he always expected to be brought to the house for dinner and given a good home-cooked meal, even in the War, and Mum'd spend the weekend cleaning all the windows and vacuuming, Dad'd polish the cutlery and dining-room furniture, the whole house spick-and-span for the Visit, no difficulty getting Phil and me to be on our best behaviour as we sat at dinner in awe of this important and powerful man, immaculate in his scrubbed face and fine suit, everyone ill at ease. Mr Porteus's Inspection would last two or even three days, thank goodness he only came for dinner just the first day, and with Mr Porteus ensconced in the small office at the back of the store going over every scrap of paper in the accounts, examining all the stock records and movement, checking the payroll and quizzing the staff, Dad always got home late having to catch up on all the ordinary business of managing the store after Mr Porteus'd gone back to his hotel. Mum'd always ask how it'd gone, and Dad'd always say "I think it was alright" but he really couldn't tell, Mr Porteus never opening his mouth except to ask a question, never even hinting how satisfactory or how disappointing anything was.

When he'd finished Porteus might say he'd be sending his report to Head Office at the end of the week, and he might say there's nothing to worry about, but that didn't mean much, Mum and Dad worried anyway. Phil and me had no idea at all, except once, on the run-up to Christmas at Lichfield, Dad came home all grumpy, he'd been rebuked because he'd put together a paper cut-out toy fort, he'd taken it out of stock, spent a whole Sunday afternoon enjoying himself carefully trimming and pasting, and put it on display in the window. He'd been pleased with himself, and he sold all one hundred of them in no time. "I wasn't supposed to do that," he told Mum, "It wasn't what they wanted, I was supposed just to display some boxes in the window. Too many people would be disappointed." Long after Dad was dead Mum told me that he would talk at such times about the rumours circulating among store managers, how some Superintendents lied, telling managers one thing and Head Office something else, that the manager of such-and-such store didn't discover he'd got a bad report until he got moved at the end of the year or even lost his job.

The hardest time of the year, Mr Porteus or not, was right after the Christmas holidays, four hard days of stock-taking, going to work early and coming home after midnight, finding out how much the total shrinkage for the year was on projected sales and profits, and getting from that a pretty good idea of how much he'd actually earned that year. Once we reached our early teens they'd talk a bit about it in front of us, perhaps over dinner before Dad went back to work, him relieved that it looks as though the shrinkage might be within the permitted range, and sales for the year probably enough to cover what he'd been drawing every month against his salary. If there was anything left over, and there always was, he'd get it in January, which was when he'd give Mum her allowance for the year. I don't know how much that was, but she had to carry all the household expenses out of that, pay for her clothes and stuff as well as ours, and every now and again when we were home for the holidays we'd hear Dad ask her how she was doing, did she need more. Not that she could necessarily have any, since Dad didn't know what his salary would be until next January. Naturally, he had a pretty good idea he was so careful, and it's not as though there wasn't enough to live on, but they both watched their pennies. If sales were low and shrinkage was too high then he'd be posted to another store, the dread of that wasn't just the expense of the move, sell the house, have to buy another, in a strange town, settle in, but that he might get moved to one of the notorious stores like the one in the Bull Ring in Birmingham, Dad said no manager lasted more than two years there, there was so much theft, if you got moved there it was because they wanted to get rid of you. He'd heard that in some stores the manager'd ended up owing the company money because he'd drawn more than sales justified. So Mum and Dad both had to be careful, and I know she sometimes had a bit of a hard time making ends meet. I don't think Dad ever told her how much he'd actually earned, he looked after the money, that's what the head of the household was *supposed* to do, Mum carefully totting up the bill every week in the grocery book, Dad writing the cheques for coal and electricity and gas, and of course the car, and the mortgage, and Phil's and my school fees. Certainly he wouldn't have told Mum about that cheque I found. I'm a bit surprised he hid it instead of destroying it, but he'd think all that was none of her business, it was an aide-memoire I suppose, and it's not surprising that she was uneasy about the farm, money that went into the farm didn't go into the household, but she understood Dad's psychic need for it.

She didn't like Uncle Tom very much, him too much of a know-it-all, nor Aunt Dot and Brenda. They weren't really relatives, we just called them that. They looked down their noses a bit at us, *we* weren't really farmers, coming from the city as we did, and of course it was Dad's money that had got the farm started, not theirs. Mum told me that Dad bought the big old black-oak bureau because of Uncle Tom, it's a drop-leaf desk with three big drawers, it's sitting across the room from me here in Vancouver, lots of pigeon-holes, a couple of draw-supports for the drop-leaf so you don't break the hinges when you open it, bits of plank really with a knob on the end, set in slots each side of the top drawer, you just slide them out. She didn't know how much he paid for it, she said it was quite a lot, Tom found it in an antique shop in Redditch or somewhere round there and took Mum and Dad to see it all excited in his quiet way, a sort of gleeful look of someone who's got a secret, and he pulled out the one on the right and said *Look at this!*, some child it looks like had written on it with a broad steel nib a long time ago practicing his copperplate, careful lettering, the nib scratching a bit into the wood the black ink soaking in. "William Wesla . . ll" it says, bits so faded you can't read them, and a couple of dozen goes at a script letter *a* in the same ink, on the other side of this bit of plank some pale faded illegible scratches made with a pen, and a few pencil marks. And then he walked round and pulled the left-hand support out, "Look at this! Who'd have thought it?" he'd said, a bit like the way Dad showed us Lichfield cathedral when we moved there in 1949 by leading us round the worst end first, saving the best till last, all that statuary covering the west front such an extravagant shock, to please us with the town where we were going to live and make us proud. *Isn't that something!* Tom said, and pointed, and there, burned with a poker on the left plank as you pulled it out, etched in the wood, PQUARTERMAN all in capitals the lettering cramped and awkward pale browny grey. But it wasn't long after Dad bought it, four or five years, that the letters began to fade completely, you can hardly read them at all now just faint unevenness in the wood, ash-grey. Mum was convinced Tom had burned them there himself. "He was in league with that shopkeeper," she said, and I think she was probably right. That black-oak looks a lot like pine or fir to me, deal anyhow.

But Dad when he came back from the War in 1919 grew to love antiques and bought what he could, a painting or two and some etchings, that bureau, a pair of solid silver carving-rests one a bull the other a monkey. He had a couple of books on old furniture and one on old porcelain, a lovely black-oak grandfather clock which Our Kid's got, it really is oak, "vse time well" it says on a frieze, palm-tree pattern carved on each side of the motto, and "1716" arranged in a diamond the "17" vertical the "16" horizontal. A friend of Our Kid's who knows quite a bit about antiques says the clock's a fake made some time in the 1870s, the palm-tree pattern's a dead giveaway, "an antique fake-antique," Our Kid laughed on the phone, the carved relief on the case door actually mouldings. He found that out when some of them fell off, he glued them back on. "It looks alright," he said, "still keeps time," and we both love that clock with its slightly tinny Westminster chimes. It's not anything Dad's parents would have cared about at all so far as I can see, any more than they cared for a collection of assegais and moth-eaten buffalo-hide shields from the Boer War that Dad picked up, "in some junk shop" Mum said, "Rubbish," but I think he wanted things that had lasted or had a bit of history, there was some sort of stability about them perhaps, a continuity. I wasn't half pleased when I read *King Solomon's Mines* to know that I knew what an assegai looked like, I'd even held one in my hand, its beaten iron tip a bit stained and battered.

I think all that stuff, along with the clock and the bureau, are all of a piece with Dad's utter determination to keep the farm, they're a part of what the War gave him after it took so much away, retrieval of a kind of lost civility. Part of growing up too, I suppose, of becoming more than a simple extension of your parents, moving into a sense of your own self. When I was staying with Our Kid a couple of years back he said he still had Dad's walking stick, and he pulled it out of Dad's umbrella stand, a heavy oval barrel varnished in dark-oak stain, hardwood, six iron hoops clasping the staves, ornamental studs spaced all round, three hefty dividers splitting the open top into six compartments, pretty useless nowadays. Solid as a rock. I looked for an ebony stick with a scarlet knob above a silver band for the hand and a steel or hard black-iron ferrule for the tip, its hexagonal knob mildly domed, possibly stone but if so, I don't know what, its original gloss dimmed a bit with use. But it wasn't there, and we both wished it was. Phil didn't really remember it till I asked, hadn't thought about it, and we both decided that Dad must've been a bit of a dandy when he struck out on his own when he got clear of the Army, I remembered reading somewhere that the London Rifle Brigade, that's where Dad was, used to be called *The Dandies*. Phil dug out a snapshot taken in the 1920s of Dad in his motorbike gear, taken one holiday by his younger brother Gilbert, Mum remembered that bike well with its up-to-date belt-drive – Dad said the belt kept slipping – but she never got a ride on it, and I thought of his hats, his gaiters and spats, his suspenders to keep his socks up and his armbands, his neat moustache and meticulous haircut, he got it trimmed once a week, manliness and gentility drawn mainly, as I  look back on it, from books by Rider Haggard, or *Sherlock Holmes* or *Raffles* and stories in *Strand* and *Argosy* or, when he was a child, the *Boy's Own Annual*. And, of course, from his mother and father and from life generally in middle-class Edwardian London, the King a notable dandy himself. I think, too, of the rarely-if-ever-used pipes and pipe-rack hanging on the wall above the bureau, the heavily carved wooden dining chairs with their worn leather seats, a set of eight with an armchair for the head-of-the-table. And of the red velvet chair Our Kid still has. We weren't allowed to sit in that when we were kids, but it was uncomfortable anyway, the velvet much too prickly for anyone wearing shorts or even a frock, this was a *man*'s chair, the seat too deep for anyone undersized. Phil's son Matthew, showing the chair to his new wife Sue when I was there said *he* wasn't supposed to sit in it when he was a kid either, nor his sister Liz, and I don't recall that anyone actually did. So I sat in it, and oh my, it's really quite comfortable, though a bit saggy and rickety after all these years. And I wondered just how much of all this stuff Dad had brought to the marriage, much of it rarely if ever used, but iconic, perhaps affording identity. The pipe rack carved the way the chair was, the Bavarian tankard with a lid that Mum used to keep rose petals in, the fake Swiss cowbells hanging from a bracket in the hall.

Dad'd been wounded in the War, a chunk of shrapnel had ploughed into the back of his neck, it must have been terribly painful even after they cut it out, a big Y-shaped scar you could have sunk a ha'penny in, soft flesh all folded in, the scar all dark where it folded in on itself, a bit blurry from the short hair where the barber trimmed growing round it. I was fascinated by it. Once, when we were walking along the towpath at Brewood or more likely Wheaton Aston, Our Kid was going to Brewood but I hadn't gone yet so it must've been around 1940, Mum and Dad in front, and Phil and me tagging along side-by-side, I was marching along I was holding a stick out in front of me a bit like a flag like on a parade almost strutting, marching between crowds, it was a bit droopy and had a few leaves on the end I kept looking at Dad's scar I couldn't keep my eyes off it I was feeling all cocky and full of myself, humming away, I wanted to see how close I could get it to Dad without touching him I must have been really daft to think he didn't sense this thing hovering round the back of his neck, Mum and Dad enjoying each other's company talking quietly together but I still remember how chirpy I felt marching along, Our Kid by my side behaving himself just walking along the canal, me being all clever, smiling away to myself, eying distances and angles, the droopy stick all wibbly-wobbly as we walked over the uneven stony towpath. And it suddenly dipped forward just a little bit I flailed it back, a leaf just brushed Dad's neck at the edge of the scar it must've tickled, and Dad wheeled round on me really annoyed, really cross at me, and told me to get rid of that stick and leave him alone, "And don't throw it in the canal!" he really scowled at me, I was shocked, I hadn't done anything really, all I'd done was just touch him a little bit with a little bit of stick with a leaf on it. But he was right, it was that scar I was after. It was a mysterious object, we knew it was in the War but we didn't dare ask how he'd got it, he never talked about it or even mentioned it, I think now that he was a bit self-conscious about it, a disfigurement, though to me it was just a fascination. Every now and again he'd lift his hand, usually his left, and stroke it a little, gently, cupping the back of his neck in a little brushing motion, a comforting little gesture. It must have bothered him sometimes, ached, it was so deep, but that sort of thing never occurred to me then, that scar was just part of Dad, like his nose or his moustache, it *was* him really, and its enigmatic quality made him different from other dads, special.

5
Dad

He never talked about that scar, we knew he'd got it somewhere in Flanders, but we never knew where or when, except it was in 1917, Dad'd change the subject if we asked, or ignore it altogether, so it was Mum told us *that*, just as she once told us, Dad out in the garden somewhere, that he'd been hit by British shrapnel. I didn't understand that at all *Why would you shell your own troops?* A book of war memoirs I read long after the second War was over described a creeping shrapnel barrage bursting on top of the mist, the flash going in front of you as you advanced, it had to be really accurate, you could advance nice and quick, the flash telling you where you were, and it was easy to go too fast, right into the barrage and through it, clammy and hasty in your fear wanting to get it over with, getting wounded and even killed by your own side, and perhaps something like that'd happened to Dad, everybody in a panicky hurry-up urging each other on to get the enemy, things looming through the mist as you stumbled over broken ground, or slogging through the mud, treading on god knows what.

Phil and I didn't have the remotest idea what it was like, the terrible thick mud, the rats and flies, the stink, the endless noise, I'm not sure we even tried. A grainy photo or two of shell craters and leafless fractured trees was all we'd seen, and if I thought about that scar on Dad's neck at all it called forth a vague picture of him all bandaged up in a nice clean hospital bed somewhere, being looked after. Certainly we hadn't the least glimmering of what he'd been through in a landscape so ruinous that one night in October 1917 it took four strong men working hard for six hours in the dark to move a wounded Rifleman only to find, when day broke and enemy sniping forced them to take cover, that in all that time they'd only moved him fifty yards. That'd happened in Dad's regiment, but nobody ever talked about it that'd be boasting or making a fuss, drawing attention to yourself. Other people had done much more difficult things, had much more terrible wounds.

So Dad's life in the Army was a closed subject. Like everybody else who was there he kept it to himself, never said a word even to Mum so far as we could tell, not much anyway. Women had to be protected from that side of life, though of course he must have told her something, couldn't not. Perhaps he felt the way Clifford Halliday did, an Old Soldier from the First World War, 104 years old, interviewed in Toronto's *Globe and Mail*: "When I came back," he said, "I just blanked it out of my mind. I didn't want to relive it." The world of the trenches must have been so remote from the world we lived in now, Dad managing a store, us away at School, that even in the Blitz it didn't bear thinking of. In any case you wouldn't impose your private thoughts and feelings on others. "The personal is *personal*," he'd say, "*private*. Nobody else's business." Talking in bed at night in the school dormitory none of us ever talked about his mum and dad, if somebody lay awake worrying about his dad getting wounded or taken prisoner or something he wouldn't say anything, everybody had a relative somewhere in the War even if it was only somebody like Uncle Edward, off in a safe place like South Africa in the Air Force, and if a kid suddenly disappeared from School for a day or two or even a week or more nobody ever said anything more than "He had to go home," and you didn't dare ask. You might find out later from one of his friends that his house had been destroyed, with his Mum in it, in an Air Raid or that his brother in the Navy had been killed, or his dad, but you couldn't go up to him and talk about *that* after he came back, what on earth could you say? You didn't really want to know anyway, you couldn't get too close, and after all everybody'd been somewhere in the War, the last war as well as this one, done something, you couldn't possibly claim you were somehow special. It wasn't anything special, that sort of thing just happened in the pages of *The Wizard* or *The Hotspur*, we devoured those but we knew they weren't real. If you did ask, people just said something vague and changed the subject. How could anything anyone actually said tell you what anything was really like anyway, in North Africa or at Dunkirk? There weren't any details in the *Picture Post* or the newsreels, so you didn't really think about the clumsy bewilderment and disorder, even if you'd gone through an air raid or two yourself. Maps in the paper with black and white arrows and lots of dotted lines showing where the Army advanced or retreated were as close as we got to any real battle, names of places you'd never heard of till now. And if it wasn't your business why would you want to know anyway? *Careless talk costs lives*, we saw that slogan everywhere.

Dad was quietly proud of having been in the London Rifle Brigade, he didn't boast about it, but every November he'd carefully press his green-and-black LRB tie, dig out his medals and clean them up to wear in the Armistice Day Parade, big expensive poppy on his lapel, he insisted that Phil and me get one, *lest we forget*, he said. Not like his of course, we had to pay for it ourselves, but we didn't need to be told. You couldn't not buy a poppy for Poppy Day any more than you couldn't not buy a lifeboat flag on Lifeboat Day, for a while Mum got to run the Lifeboat Day collections when we lived in Lichfield, scrambling to find people to put in an hour or two in the market place or near the bus station, she'd stand outside Boots the chemists on High Street smiling away at people she didn't know, tray round her neck and rattling her money tin, the girls at Boots or even the manager now and again coming out to chat a bit. Every Armistice Day Dad'd go down to the Legion for a drink or two after, talk to other Old Soldiers, spend the afternoon in his armchair by the fire if he didn't have to go back to work, he wouldn't do any gardening Armistice Day and he didn't read anything he just sat there after he'd put his medals away till next year. *We will remember them*. Sometimes he'd fall asleep.

After he died I never saw those medals again nor did Our Kid, I think when Mum moved to Worthing at the end of the fifties they went to some jobber along with a lot of the stuff in that big Lichfield house, simplifying her life, but she still kept his big elaborate discharge certificate, Phil's got it now, a drawing in the bottom right-hand corner of a stone tablet like the ones you see on the wall in Church, a mix of careful handwriting and calligraphic type, saying

"No: 302308 Rfn Clifford Philip Quartermain of the 5th London Regiment" – Mum called him *Leo* he hated the name Clifford which is what Grandmother and Grandfather always called him – "served with honour and was disabled in the Great War. Honourably discharged on 22.5.18." The first time I ever laid eyes on that piece of paper was when I went through Mum's papers after she died in 1994, I didn't even know it existed. She had it carefully tucked away in an old chest that used to belong to her great grandmother, she once told me it dated from the seventeenth century but it doesn't. It's where she kept all her private stuff, spiritualist bits and pieces from White Eagle Lodge, bits of writing she did for a course she took in her eighties, things to do with Dad. Our Kid and I had always thought he'd at least been a Lance-Corporal or a Corporal because that's what he was when he joined the Home Guard in 1940, but the London Rifle Brigade was different from everyone else in the Army, they didn't have Lance-Corporals they called them Acting Corporals, just as they didn't call the men Privates but Riflemen. With their special vocabulary and their great reputation as sharpshooters and skill at rapid rifle fire the LRB distinguished itself from other regiments, gave Dad a special knowledge which let him hold his head up among other men without ever saying anything, inwardly proud that he belonged to a special regiment.

  Even so we got the odd clues to his Army life if we stopped to think about it. Like the way he hated flies, especially bluebottles, he'd get really disturbed, genuinely cross if one was in the room, chase it down, try to kill it, it was years before I read about the bloated and torpid flies in the dugouts, sometimes asleep on beams or in bits of sacking, flopping down your neck as you brushed by or banged your head, that world of glutted rats. No wonder he was so fastidious. Even on the farm he couldn't stand to see dirt tracked into the house, *Clean yourself up before you come in!* he'd rebuke, if you didn't you'd better watch out. And he always followed the Bisley sharpshooting contest in the news, he always commented on who'd won what, expected us to pay attention, follow the details. The Rifle Brigade walked off year after year with trophy after trophy as best shots in the Army. Knowing how to handle guns was an essential part of growing up, just like the art of self-defence, he'd given the two of us boxing gloves that Christmas but we neither of us used them, we didn't want to learn how to box properly. No matter how often he told us *Keep your guard up!* Or *Use your left!* And that if you knew even the least little bit how to box you'd easily beat someone just flailing away no matter how big they were, *All you need is a good right hook.* It made no odds to us. Why would you want to get hurt, why would you fight somebody just for something to do? We didn't understand that, we didn't have Boxing at School the way the stories said in the *Boys' Own Paper*, not many schools did, it just wasn't part of a gentleman's education any more. He must've thought we were a bit sissy, but he never said he was disappointed, didn't tell us how to run our lives so long as we were truthful, just quietly let it drop.

Likewise, his attempts to teach us to shoot had limited success. One weekend just before Christmas, Phil and me home for the holidays, he came home all pleased with himself. He'd just got an air rifle from someone he knew, he broke it at the breech and held it up to the light so we could look down through the barrel towards the muzzle, "Look at it" he said, a smile in his voice, an intense silvery shine the mirrored brightness almost stinging the eye nothing to focus on such straight bright intensity much harder than anything I'd ever seen, dazzling, "not a speck of rust, and the spring is really tight." He snapped it back shut and then he opened the breech as wide as he could, the butt in his left hand, and folded the whole gun nearly in half before it gave a small *clack*. He really pulled at it. "That compresses the air. If you don't do that nothing happens when you pull the trigger" and he walked over to the open window pointed it at the sky and pulled the trigger a loud hard *snap!* almost a *bang!* followed by a short puff of rushing air. "It's pretty powerful," he said, and I wondered why he'd gone over to the window *Why not just point it at the floor?*

"You never point a gun at other people," he said. "*Never.* And you've *got* to watch for ricochet. Even if you *know* it's not loaded." We already knew that really from watching him and Uncle Tom at the farm, they always carried their shotguns broken at the breech, but "You can't be told too often," he said. "It's the first thing you learn in the Army." He told us what luck it was one of the Masons'd found a couple of boxes of pellets in Halford's stockroom warehouse along with the gun, he was really pleased and excited in a quiet sort of way, a glow on his face and a suppressed sort of grin at the corners of his mouth, his eyes shining. Mum compressed her lips, a funny sort of reserved look on her face, but Dad said we had to learn how to handle guns properly, better learn from someone who knows than from someone in School who probably doesn't know anything, and he took us down to the tennis courts. "Can we shoot it? Can we fire it? Please?" and he told us no, not until he got some proper targets, perhaps the Home Guard can spare one or two. "I wonder if you can manage to prime it," he said and when we got down to the grass he gave the gun to me "Can you open it?" he asked. I put it across my knee and pushed it open a bit, soft click, smell of oil, and "Can you open it all the way?" I pushed and pulled heaved away but I couldn't compress the barrel down till it nearly reached the stock. I wasn't strong enough and anyway I couldn't reach far enough along the barrel to do it. "I didn't think you would" he said, "That's a good thing" and he gave it to Our Kid who really got his shoulders into it and got it all the way down, *clack*, red in the face. He closed it. *Watch where you point it!* Dad took the gun and fired it at the sky, and then he had us lie down on the grass and hold the gun the way soldiers do, nestling the butt into your shoulder, sighting along the barrel. "Squeeze the trigger don't pull it" he told us, "Hold it steady," but he had to prime the gun first for us to do that, the trigger was all slack if he didn't, nothing to squeeze, but then we got a satisfactory *bang* out of it. After he got some targets he pinned them on a bit of beaverboard he'd hung on the garage door and we practised, Dad deciding we should take the gun to the farm next time we went. I don't think we ever did, though. Shooting never really took hold.

When I was getting ready to leave School around 1951 or 52 and began worrying a bit about doing my two years' conscription, I wanted to do it in the Navy but knew I'd probably have to settle for the Army, he really surprised me when he said if I ever thought I was going to get into a serious fight *And you will get into one, you know*, I should put a roll of coins in my fist, "Get them from the bank," he said, "ahead of time; keep them in your pocket. Ha'pennies're best, they're good and heavy, fit nicely in your fist, get a bob's worth." When I asked he said, "Of course they hurt your hand, but it's better than getting beaten up." He learned that in the Army, he said, just as he learned that if you get drunk on brandy "Don't drink any water as soon as you wake up or you'll feel drunk all over again, terrible." Those two bits of advice were the only things he ever deliberately let slip about his Army life, all Phil and I really knew was that he'd been wounded and that he'd been in hospital, but we didn't know where or when, but the scar looked so terrible that we knew he must've been in hospital for a very long time, he had a War Disability Pension that kicked in, 23 May 1920, two years almost to the day after he was discharged, he had to wait longer than that, nearly three years, for it to be officially confirmed on May Day, 1923. So we both had the idea he'd been in hospital for ages, why else would he've had to wait so long for his pension? For a while I wondered if he'd been wounded at Vimy in 1917. People still talked about what a great victory that was, but when they said how terrific the Canadians had been, it was them that won that battle, I knew Dad couldn't've been there. I wanted him to have been wounded somewhere heroic, and once, when he was sorting through some old envelopes and stuff for our stamp collections, he gave me a picture postcard of the Avenue de la Victoire, the Verdun War Memorial, Marlow Grandfather had sent to him in 1937 from France, he was there on business, he'd been to see it, and I wondered *Was he wounded at Verdun?* I've still got that card, I came across it again when I started writing this, I remembered *ils ne passeront pas* that great French victory holding the line in 1916, Dad could've been there I suppose, he was old enough, but the Memorial at Verdun is a French National Shrine, nothing to do with the English, so it's not likely. Grandfather's card doesn't really tell me anything at all, and when I wrote to the Public Record Office at Kew I found out that most of the war records for Non-Commissioned Officers and Other Ranks, including Dad's, had been destroyed in a German Air Raid in 1940.

The gap in Dad's life, his silence, remained a mystery. What did the War do to him? Where was he wounded? How much was he in the trenches? What did he do? Masses of grunt work, that's obvious, and a lot of hurry up and wait, half freezing in half-filled icy trenches. Phil said Dad once told him, almost the only time he ever

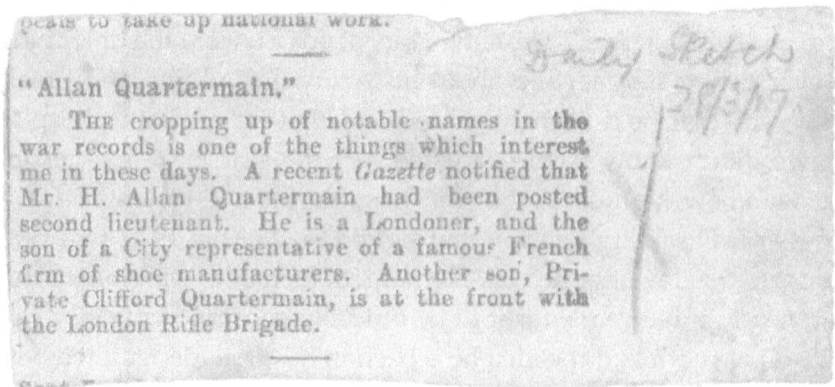

said anything to him about the War, that he'd lied about his age so he could get in. "So he must have been in the Army pretty well from the very beginning. He must have joined up in 1914," and that seemed quite possible, he'd've been almost 17 that October. I've got a studio portrait photograph of Uncle Allan, Dad's older brother, it was in the bottom of a battered old portable desk along with a scrap of newspaper, once-lovely Victorian walnut veneer bound in brass, it used to be Dad's, one of his antiques, Uncle Allan in his brand new uniform, officer's peaked cap but no insignia, with a note on the back in Grandmother's handwriting, "H. Allan Quartermain (19 yrs 4 mths) joined 2nd City of London Royal Fusiliers, August 1914." It struck Our Kid and me that with his elder brother's example before him Dad simply joined up as soon as he could, but he never overcame his reticence. If he'd lived until I was a grown man I suppose I might have been able to ask him straight out, man to man, over a drink perhaps, what he did in the War and where and when he got wounded, ask if his old wound bothered him, things like that.

Then Our Kid found a bit of paper in Mum's old bureau, *Army Form B. 2067*, "Character Certification," dated 22nd May 1918, on the back it says he joined up on 13 December 1915 so he was 18 after all when he joined up, and he didn't get to the Ypres salient on the Western Front till 24 January 1917 in the build-up to Passchendaele, and he spent over a year in England, probably training new recruits, and got sent home on the 28th of September. With a lot of help from retired Colonel J. H. McCausland at the Royal Green Jackets Museum in Winchester I realised Dad was most likely wounded about 1500 yards from St. Julien in an attack on a farm the British called Von Tirpitz, zero hour was twenty-to-six in the morning on the 20th of September, heavy mud, and three or four hours later when the battle was to all intents and purposes over, fifty percent casualties, all officers killed, it turned out that Von Tirpitz Farm was not only a German stronghold but a medical post. It's funny that Dad never even hinted he'd been treated by captured German doctors before being carried through the mud to a casualty clearing station, he must've known it was Germans who'd saved his life, and he had to wait eight days before he got back to England. You didn't get discharged from the Army till you got out of hospital, so it turns out he was in hospital for only about eight months instead of the years we thought, though goodness knows that's long enough. Phil and I both knew, it was a sort of family legend, that the week before he got out of hospital, the Doctor asked Dad what he was going to do now he was getting back into the world outside, and he said "I'm going to buy a farm." He'd saved all his pay through the War or at least – and that's more likely – since he'd been wounded. "I'm going to be a farmer," and the Doctor said "No you're not. It'll be the death of you within a month. You probably shouldn't have a job at all, but you certainly can't do anything as strenuous as that. You'll probably be alright in an office or somewhere quiet, but you've got to be very careful for the rest of your life." The mind boggles that nobody said anything until he was almost out of hospital, but Mum or whoever it was told me this said Yes, that's what they did in those days; he went back to live with his mother and father at 52 Lowlands Road, Harrow, a nice suburban house named "Rycot."

And what sort of life was it for him, coming home at last, living with his mum and dad and his two younger brothers Geoffrey and Gilbert, how could he settle down, that painful aftermath of war on the back of his neck, what was it like, walking down the road in Harrow the War still going on, him invalided out, no other young men anywhere that he might see. Did he feel lucky, I wonder, or did he, like Siegfried Sassoon after the War, see corpses wherever he went in London, lying about on the pavement, dimming the sunlight and muffling the traffic. *What shall we be,* the soldiers sang, *when we aren't what we are?* How could he tell Grandfather and Grandmother that, or anything like it? Dad was 21 in October 1918, five months out of hospital the War not yet over, and he'd probably never been alone, all by himself, never had any privacy at all from when he'd joined up three years ago, and after convalescence he wouldn't've had much choice but to take up his old life where it left off, a clerk, Our Kid says, in the Admiralty earning five bob a week. In the Army he got a shilling a day. Did he just accept it all as something you can't help, or did he think it was all wrong, the waste, the blood, the quiet surface of the London streets. How could he take up his French lessons again, or music or drawing, the polite accomplishments of conventional middle-class suburban life, posh Harrow School just down the road, his mind trying to get over all that death and loss, split masonry and flame-lap, ruined walls, broken bodies, friends and comrades he could never see again? What did he dream, no doubt fighting terrible headaches? What could he talk about at home?

"Steady the Buffs!" Grandfather used to say to settle things down whenever anything ruffled the smoothness of the day, like somebody nearly dropping something as they picked it up or stumbling on the edge of the carpet, anything like that. Our Kid and I'd pay no attention or maybe grin a bit to each other, the old man's empty reflex, but without fail Dad's face would instantly freeze for a moment, expressionless, his whole body immobile, his breath suddenly quiet, his gestures stalled. Phil and I simply didn't know what to make of that catchphrase until I came across it in a story by Rudyard Kipling, but even then I didn't understand that The Buffs was the Royal East Kent Regiment, Dad would've known soldiers there, The Buffs had been alongside the LRB in all sorts of battles in the run-up to Passchendaele, Grandfather unconsciously stirring up the grim realities of Flanders every time he said it. After the War one soldier from the Rifle Brigade said that in a way he'd lived his whole life between the ages of 19 and 23, "everything that happened after that was almost anti-climax."

In September 1919, sixteen months after he got out of hospital, Dad bought a Stanley Gibbons Simplex Blank Album for his stamp collection, taking up a constant from his life before the War, that album quite expensive with its little metal clasp inside the back cover to support the heavy pages. He'd already got one, he'd got it in January 1913 when he was fifteen, perhaps when he'd started work if it wasn't a Christmas present, it would've cost twelve-and-sixpence in 1914, more than a fortnight's wages, and it strikes me now, writing this, that his stamp collection must have afforded an island of cohesion and coherence, him poring over his Stanley Gibbons catalogue identifying and sorting the stamps, getting them into some sort of order, a page of Australian stamps, light notes done with a hard pencil, "Wmk Type 2" in the left margin. If you gently lift the bottom of the stamp a little you can see where he's written the perforation (11½ - 12), and the date of issue (1914-15) on the flap of the hinge holding it to the page, and below that the catalogue value, anything from a ha'penny to a shilling; he worked it so that all you saw, if you looked at the main body of the page, was just the stamps themselves, the important information tucked away out of sight. Sometimes he'd write down the catalogue number as well, mostly when it was hard to figure out, *how shiny is that shiny paper? How slaty is that grey?* I see him sitting at a table reaching for the black watermark-tray and benzene-dropper, tweezers and perforation gauge and magnifying glass close by, picking up his pencil, leafing slowly through the long illustrated lists of the stamp catalogue, looking at other stamps from the same issue, rubbing his face, perhaps sitting a long time without moving, or asking his father or his younger brothers Geoffrey and Gilbert what they thought, quiet moments of intense concentration affording some relief from that Other you have in the last three years and more become, a stranger to your family and to yourself, working away at the uncertain provenance of that small scrap of paper until its unstable identity settles, the decision no doubt a small step back towards who you are or think you used to be. But what would he have thought as he neatly pencilled "Pf 14 wmk lozenge" at the edge of the page, alongside that 1905 re-issue of a German stamp, 2-marks, blue, with its mythological tableau? Did he know it was a much-reprinted propaganda stamp celebrating Bismarck's unification of North and  South Germany in 1871, its caption *Be One, One, One!* A rallying cry for unity, an allegorical call to arms? Neatly arranging row after row of carefully identified German stamps, picture after picture of Germania, symbol of Imperial Germany. Dulling the memory perhaps, removing its bite, restoring an older perspective to his view of his ex-enemy as well as of himself.

Some time in the 1920s Dad put up what money he'd saved plus what must've been nigh on £125, almost three years' back-pay at sixteen bob a week, the pension he'd at last been awarded on Mayday 1923, to put Uncle Tom in a farm, somewhere in Worcestershire, not far from Redditch, south of Birmingham, and when I was about three moved to a farm a bit further off from Birmingham, just outside Alcester, eight miles from Stratford-on-Avon, a lovely big square Georgian farmhouse you could see from the Stratford Road at the top of a rise, a hundred acres, arable mainly but good land, enough pasture for a couple of dozen cows, a few pigs, poultry, and an orchard, a river along the bottom edge that you could swim in. Great big housing estate now, the farmhouse turned into flats. Some time in the late 1940s, after the War, Uncle Tom began to specialise in poultry, incubators everywhere, tiny little yellow chicks running about and cheeping underfoot, but not in the War, not any incubators anyway, always a smell of paraffin, and sometimes we'd get to the farm and be told a lot of chicks had died it'd been so cold. We spent a lot of wartime summers bringing in the cows or bringing in the harvest, wheat, oats, and barley, what we all thought of as corn, always some beans stuck in there with the barley, black and brittle when we brought it in. We wouldn't be there for haymaking, but now and again in the spring we'd spend the weekend hoeing beets or turnips or tending some sort of fodder.

Dad couldn't wait to get to the farm, with its ducks in the duck pond, and geese. Great big cart-horses to do the ploughing and harvesting in the War; farm cats to keep down the rats and mice in the barns where the feed was. *Leave 'em alone! They're not pets!* They didn't even have names, most of them. Disaster when an epidemic of cat flu killed most of them off, later on you'd occasionally come across a raggedy scrappy mess of fur and bones in some corner where it'd crawled off to die, then you'd have to take it away and bury it somewhere. Hayricks and cornstacks dotted about the farmyard, thatched, wheat and oats waiting for the threshing machine to come round and the big traction engine to run it. Paraffin lamps and candles flickering your way to bed up the stairs, open the door to another flight of stairs, perishing cold once you left the kitchen area, blow the candle out when you got there. You didn't have any matches so if it went out on the way you'd have to grope and grope in the dark, easy to lose your way with the blackout over all the windows, quiet voices in conversation perhaps a muffled laugh or two drifting up behind you fainter and fainter as you got higher, or a door closing. Pour cold water into the basin on the wash stand but leave half of it in the china jug so big I could hardly lift it, in the winter have a shivery wash, clean your teeth, empty the lot into the slop bucket. Some mornings that would have a thin crust of ice, you'd have to empty it downstairs along with the chamber pot if you'd used it, taking it outside. Me and Our Kid huddled under the blankets till Aunt Dot or sometimes cousin Brenda she was a month or two older than Phil clattered in, seven-thirty in the morning, and pulled the covers off. "Come on, look alive! You'll warm up once you get moving! And don't forget to empty everything now you're up. Breakfast's getting cold!" Everybody else would've been up for hours, the cows milked, the horses fed, and it was still dark, but no Woolworth's to get to, no shop-girls or shrinkage to worry about, no Superintendent Porteus. And no School.

If you opened the gate to the farmyard at the right time of day the cows would walk in without being told, but there was a dog to remind them, and now and again I'd be sent out to fetch them in, Our Kid busy with something else, everybody older than me and with jobs to do. As it got towards milking time the cows were coming in on their own anyway, but they didn't always. If it was raining I'd put my mac and wellygogs on, stick an old sou'wester that was kept in the mud-porch on my head, and the dog'd find me, it knew what to do and it didn't need me at all except to open the gate for it and for the cows, now and again I'd have to chase down a cow that'd strayed off from the rest, but most times they all just mooched along, I'd tell myself they'd be glad to get to the nice dry cowsheds but it was obvious really that they didn't look ahead like that at all, they were just doing what cows do, which was nothing much. Marching off through the fields by myself was fun, just the dog for company, sometimes I'd have a stick to behead a thistle or swish at the grass or the cows, but I soon learned that when you hit a thistle or anything else tall with a stick in the rain the water'd shoot up and scatter all over the place, hit you in the face and make you jump. The shock of cold made me turn it into a game, pirates or prisoners fighting back *Don't let him land a blow!* But what I liked about it was that it was always so quiet, nobody else there, just your boots swishing in the grass, and your mac rubbing on your bare knees, the scrape of the brim of the sou'wester catching on the back of your collar when you turned your head, but you were in charge of those sounds even if a trickle of cold water did now and again somehow get down the back of your neck when you shrugged or moved your arm too fast, water always got in your boots, your hands cold and wet, it was what *you* did that made it happen, you could hear yourself think, the cows jostling and mumbling perhaps a bit of cud in the background the soft brushing clap of an udder against a leg as you all walked along. When you got back with the cows scrambling round the open gate as you let them in the barnyard you felt you'd done something, they were so much bigger than you were, and they did what you told them to. Well, of course, they didn't really, they just went there because that was what they did that time of day. If you started out late they'd all be clustered round the gate anyway but it was you that helped it happen, the deep familiarity of routine, lovely smell of field and grass flavoured with mild acridity from cowpats, sweet and sharp pungency and fresh breeze.

6

Woodroughs

With Alice gone, Our Kid five miles off in Brewood and Dad still in Birmingham all week, Mum's life must've felt a bit empty stuck out there in Wheaton Aston the way she was with just me and the Davises for company and the shop nothing like busy enough to give Mrs Davis let alone the two of them very much to do. "I heard this week from Mr Belben," Dad told Mum early in the new year. "He's going to re-open Woodroughs, and if he does then Peter can go back there, it's a good school, and he'd be much better off there than stuck here in a Council School, no matter how good everyone says it is." I wasn't so sure about that, I enjoyed Miss Chapman's classes, I enjoyed sossing with the other kids in the stream down by Lloyd's farm, and I loved reading, I was good at that, perhaps that made me feel as if I might belong, and I didn't know who Mr Belben was. Besides Mrs Roe and Sammy,  all I remember is Mr Hawkes, all of The Woodroughs School along with the kindergarten belonged to him, tall and thin, close-trimmed grey beard, always wore a grey herringbone suit with a subdued waistcoat and a silver watch-chain, always signed his name "W.J. Hawkes M.A." I thought he was the oldest man I'd ever seen, older even than Grandfather, and Mum said that like Grandfather he frowned as if he thought everybody was doing something wrong, perhaps that's why people said he was very learned and whenever they got the chance talked to somebody else. What could they talk about with somebody who knew Latin and Greek *and* had been to Oxford? We didn't know anybody else like that.

My mind boggles a bit when I look at my School Reports, the one for Christmas 1938 says I was one of fourteen boys taking nine different subjects, and I really can't remember any of them at all. What could Mr Hawkes possibly say about a four-year-old's understanding of "Geography" when he could barely pronounce the word? What might the child learn from "Science or Nature Study" that might warrant a more detailed assessment than "Has made a good start"? The closest my School Report came to critical judgement was the comment "Is inclined to be inattentive." Most of these "subjects" were simply convenient fictions designed to keep the parents happy, what on earth could a four-year-old actually do in school except play a few games and learn the basic three Rs, and I vaguely remember picking my way through the words on a cereal box at breakfast and being surprised to learn that not all the other kids could do that, untouched by its magic. Dad said Mr Belben'd found a really terrific place out in the countryside, miles away from any possible air raids, a big old house called Stanway Manor Farm, at Rushbury, at the top of Roman Bank half a mile or so outside Wall under Heywood, a small village near Church Stretton in Shropshire, close to the Welsh border. "Not the same as Woodroughs was before the War, of course, but you'll be safe there, and it'll still be Woodroughs. And I know Mr Belben'll need help, everyone's short-staffed nowadays. I'll arrange something."

So Dad stayed on in his Birmingham lodgings, twenty-five miles away from Our Kid who'd just started at Brewood, and a good forty miles from me and Mum, who moved with me to Rushbury. Nowadays, of course, with Motorways and easy transportation, those distances don't sound like very much at all, but back then, even with the roads clear and no delays from Air Raids or Army convoys, it'd easily take a good two-and-a-half to three hours on the bus to cross those twenty-five miles from Birmingham to Brewood, and a lot longer for a cross-country trip to that tiny Shropshire village. When I think about that wretched place, my mind skitters off some place else, that huge barn of a late Victorian house with its more-or-less derelict outbuildings, gaunt and inhospitable, even in the summer months, some stockbroker's notion of a leisured country home and model farm. And the school itself a far cry from what it'd been before the War, ten kids rather than the close to twenty in what was now called "Form 1" and not even that many in the remaining four Forms, all of them meeting in the same room. Mr Belben's was the only name listed on my School Report, but I wasn't in his class, he just looked after the older kids, and other than the initials "H.S" I have no idea at all who taught us. But Mum was there, perhaps because she couldn't bear to think of me out in the wilds of Salop by myself, no matter how safe it was. And she could hardly stay on in Birmingham to all intents and purposes by herself, her and Dad having to find a place to live, move all the furniture out of storage, and what would she do with her time anyway when there was a War on. Mum and Dad would've been mortified to have her go out and get a job, a lot of people did that, but in his position that'd mean he couldn't afford to run a proper household, and that was a matter of pride. Both of them, anyway, were glad to get her as well as me out of the War zone now that Dunkirk and the fall of France had turned the Phoney War into a Real one.

"My name is Stephen J. Belben" he told us, that first day, "but you will address me as *Sir.*" Mum never called him anything but Mr Belben, even years later, long after the War, long after he and the school had gone bankrupt. Mrs Belben looked a bit like a gypsy in a book about Spain, dark black hair and red lips, really red, a very definite sort of person, you knew it when she came into the room, taller than Mum and the other women, big hooped earrings, red or patterned blouse and swirling black skirt, vividly different, she always looked at you as though you ought to be doing something, *Little children should be seen but not heard*, or sometimes as though she couldn't be bothered, *Why are you here at all?* not interested in kids or caring about them, she never spoke to us kids except to tell us what to do. They had two boys, Jeremy and Graham, both much older than me and a lot bigger, around twelve and fourteen; "lummoxes" Mum called them but not while we were at Rushbury where she might be overheard.

Stanway Manor Farm hadn't ever been a proper working farm, what fields it'd once had long sold off, it'd been built some time in the 1860s at the top of a long sloping drive, old farm-sheds and stables off where the drive branched to the left and behind, big stone balls on top of two gate-posts with no gate, a dense and wonderfully unkempt shrubbery higher than my head next to the house as you came round the curve and up the slope toward the building *that'd be a great place to play!* three Victorian Gothic storeys, a paved and cracked forecourt on your left just after the driveway branched, a derelict shooting brake in it, rusty patches in weather-dulled buff paint, no top at all, steering wheel all cracked and peely, glassless frame windshield. A rear side-window poked up a bit on the left, rubbery threads hung from the flat tires, the doors so rusted you couldn't open them, and dried up feathers and droppings all over the place, chickens'd been there a long time ago, perhaps laid eggs in the clutter on the floor. A great big open car like that *What a super thing to have in a playground!* we swarmed all over it as soon as we got there, didn't even go indoors, couldn't wait to drive it or sit in the back like a Nazi Staff Officer and bully the prisoners about or wave at the cheering crowds like the King on parade, fire wooden guns over the sides, or simply just jump about. *Terrific! Smashing!* But we hadn't been there five minutes before Mr Belben called us all in to The Big Room, big bay windows and a screened fireplace, desks and tables in a cold and mostly empty room, with a couple of blackboards on easels and a teacher's desk at the front, and he told us "The forecourt is out-of-bounds! When you come into this building you use the back or the side door," and he gestured, "never the front! The front door is not for you children to use!" and then *Stay away from that old car!* "It's not a toy and it doesn't belong to any of you. It's a car! If I see or hear of any of you in or anywhere near that car you'll be caned. And it will hurt, I'll make sure of that!" Nobody had ever spoken to me like that before, he was the most terrifying man I'd ever met, I didn't meet his eyes but looked at his chin when he was speaking so he wouldn't notice me, and he uttered not a single word about how tempting a car like that might be to play in, or how dangerous or unhealthy it might be or that it should be taken away. He simply told us what we should and shouldn't do, and said that if ever we came up the drive, *Not that there is any call for any of you to be in the road for any reason that I can think of, so there is no reason for you to be in the drive or that forecourt,* we were to go round the back along by the stables and never go near there at all.

On a Sunday morning soon after, everything a bit damp and almost on the edge of rain but the sun still warm, Mrs Belben shooed us all outside to play "Go and play in the paddock" she said, "Choose two teams and have a game of rounders" but the ground was so tussocky and uneven I kept tripping, and so did the others *Don't you dare get dirty! Those are your clean clothes!* and there weren't enough of us to play something like Fishes in the Net.

We couldn't settle on anything except tag, hide-and-seek was no good when we weren't allowed to hide in the shrubbery or go off round the back of the building, but Jeremy and Graham went off anyway, they just ran off and made for the car, it made a wonderful fort, them defending and us attacking, all of us shoving and climbing and shouting, and all at once there was Mr Belben running out his face bright red and we scattered, Jeremy and Graham stuck in the car, *Get away from there! All of you go into the Conservatory and wait there!* he meant The Big Room where it was always cold. When he came in he didn't say anything except "Sit down and be quiet!" he just stood there and looked at us with his lips all tight and compressed and then wrote a whole series of sums on both blackboards, "No one can leave this room until he's finished all these," he said, "even if you're here all day. You won't get anything to eat until you've finished." A smothered blue kind of breathless quiet, air just before a thunderstorm, and I looked at the first board

$$\begin{array}{r} 40689 \\ 95377 \\ 14883 \\ \underline{24604} + \\ = \end{array}$$

and underneath,

$$\begin{array}{r} x \\ = \end{array}$$

"Add them first, then multiply them!" he said. "No rough work! Just one sheet of paper, neatly done. I want to see the answers, not a lot of untidy scribbles!" So I had to do it in my head, and I didn't know what to do, I didn't know how to do it, I'd only ever added up short columns of double figures and that not very often, mostly single figures, and at the age of six I didn't really know about tens and units. I held my chewed red-painted pencil over my sheet of paper, wanted to cry, but didn't dare. Mr Belben walked up and down across the room whacking his cane softly against his trouser leg and I looked at the next sum. Two sets of numbers, one six-long, the other three, with a sign I didn't know alongside the bottom one though I must've seen it before, it looked like a plus that'd got a bit scuffed. I looked at what the kid at the next desk was doing, he'd copied all the sums out onto his paper and left a lot of room under the second so I did too and he was looking at the other blackboard and started writing, whatever he was doing it didn't look like adding. I waited till Mr Belben turned his back it was cold in there I shook my hands about a bit to get them warm and stuck them in my pockets and then reached over *What if Mr Belben sees me?* to that other kid and he mouthed at me we didn't make a sound *It's long division* and I didn't understand, and he whispered "Divide!" and coughed to hide it as Mr Belben whipped his head around. Afterwards somebody said it was all "long addition" and "long division" and "long multiplication" but I'd never seen any of that before, I didn't know what long division was.

"Make sure nobody cheats!" Mr Belben said to one of the older boys at the front, "No noise!" and he left the room. The sun went in, the monkey puzzle tree on the south side of the building got black, and the room got colder. *What was eighty-nine and seventy-seven?* I thought, and in my head slowly worked out 56 at the end, carry one, so *what was sixhundred-andeightynine and threehundredandseventysix* made *seven-hundred-andsixtysix* and somebody scraped his chair and *what was that number I began with was it fortysix and sixhundredandseventythree?* and there was this sharp catch just above my stomach *hadn't there been a five somewhere?* and I had to start all over again and over and over this happened everybody else in the room writing things down and I hadn't written *any*thing yet I had this huge number in my head 134255 I didn't dare write it down I only had the one piece of paper and I had to add 14883 and the door opened and Mr Belben came in and said "Jeremy. Graham. Come with me" and a senior boy said "Please Sir I've finished." I felt all slow and stupid and all three left together and none of them came back and I'd lost it all, all those numbers, and had to start again. It wasn't like Brewood would be, later, where they taught you to do sums in your head, but when I got into the Third Form there four years later I got into trouble in French and annoyed the Teacher because the first time we had homework I didn't think you were allowed to look at the Vocabulary in the back of the book and so didn't. *That's* what I learned from Mr Belben. I got a lot of it wrong, I thought everybody else had cheated and Jim called me daft when I said so after. When Mr Belben came back and told us all we could go to lunch I was shuddering with the cold and sweating, Jeremy and Graham already there before us pushing and shoving to get lots of potatoes, looking pleased with themselves.

There were no more than about twenty of us living in at Rushbury. I don't have a School Report for Easter Term when there were a few more, all older than me, but the one for Summer Term 1940 says there were "ten Boys" in Form I. At Easter 1941 there were only five of us, no girls, perhaps a couple of children from the village came every day, and Mr and Mrs Belben, and Mum, and Bert Critchley's mother who acted as School Matron – we all Bert included had to call her Matron or Mrs Critchley, he couldn't possibly call her Mum, not there – and Hannah, and a cook. A young woman from the village helped in the kitchen, and an odd-job man turned up about once a week.

Somebody came up every day from Wall under Heywood to help with the teaching but I never saw who it was. Our Kid came from Brewood for the Christmas holidays in 1940 they were much longer than ours, and Mrs Belben had to find somewhere for him to sleep, he wasn't due back at Brewood until the middle of January so at Rushbury he had to go to classes with the older boys, nobody knew else what to do with him. It was horrible, he told me much later, they did all sorts of lessons he didn't have at Brewood and he was supposed to take part, he was expected to catch up in Latin when everyone'd taken it for at least a term or even longer and he'd never had any at all, they didn't do it in Prep school at Brewood. And he didn't have any books. Mr Belben was the Teacher, and he couldn't understand why Our Kid couldn't conjugate irregular verbs, and scorned him in front of the other kids and they laughed. Mr Belben always looked a bit angry, he never played games with us or told us any stories or even read them and there weren't many books, not for kids anyway, though the *Beano* and the *Dandy* came in the post for somebody and soon got tattered as they got passed around. When it rained, some of us'd sneak off to the old farm buildings round the back, there was a heap of old straw stacked up in one corner under a big gap in the ceiling, trimmed ends of broken lath jutting beyond broken plaster, and you could climb up through the trapdoor above the manger where they used to pitch hay straight down to feed the horses and ponies, clamber along the rickety flooring to the end of the building, light chinking between the roof tiles, and jump down through the hole onto the straw. In one of the side-stables there was an old two-passenger pony-trap with a wheel missing, the door to that stable padlocked to keep us out. But the loft ran the full length of the building and one of the kids'd pulled up a couple of boards, we could scramble through, climb down and play there, the trap threatening to seesaw a bit, the shafts lifting and stirring in the old straw, dust arousing in the patched light, wonderful smell.

Until Mr Belben found out. Then we had to play in the Big Room on rainy days, but late one winter afternoon on a damp day three or four of us got sent out and went down to the edge of the old garden, a long broad hummock at the edge of the trees, cold and gloomy and dank, water dripping from the branches. We were shivering a bit, we'd none of us been down there before, didn't know if we were allowed, at the end of the hummock the ground fell away towards a sunken lane, all scraggly grass and twigs and stunted bushes and one of us wandered off a bit we couldn't see him and *Crikey, there's a door down here! It's all falling off!* came from below all muffled and echoey, so the rest of us rushed round to where he was pushing through wet branches and shrubs like a cave all clammy musty mouldy smell an old wooden door hanging by one hinge against the bank crumbly bricks and stone, wood walls orangey big fungus sticking out, dark green stuff almost black stains, you could hardly see inside, a blurry dark pile of murk at the back, white shreds and lumpy strings hanging over our heads everything cold I hung back near the door shifting from foot to foot breath steaming a bit and then *What's this?* whoever it was said, *Ugh!* and dropped it, we crowded round, a wizened droopy glistening black nastiness but it didn't move *Ugh It's a carrot! Was! Wouldn't eat that!* I poked at it with my foot something stuck to it, wrapped itself on, white glistening mould and black wet, it wouldn't come off no matter how much I scraped I bent to pick it off and it tore, slimy sacking on my shoe and on my hand, foul smell, I cried out and all of us ran out the door as fast as we could, *what was it?* We looked at each other, panting a bit, *There's something in there,* one of us said *Something moved!* and we strained to hear, one of us had thick black cobweb in his hair, our faces pale and smudged, our knees all red, socks down at our ankles, mud and muck, and shivery in the cold we got back to the house as quick as we could, we had to get cleaned off, we all smelled, a thick horrid skin, I didn't want to touch even the tap handle, stink pinching right up between my eyes hard to breathe, scrubbing away at the outdoor tap, cold. Then at tea our hands clamped around warm cups and carefully picked up slices of bread, but once we'd started we simply packed it down we were so hungry, Mrs Belben stood up and said in a stern voice "Some of you have been playing down in that old root cellar at the bottom of the garden by the lane. It's dirty, and what's more it's very unsafe. It's dangerous, it might fall in, and you could get seriously hurt. It will be sealed off. None of you is to go anywhere near it, or Mr Belben will hear about it." The touch of that horrible sacking with its stinky rotting potato slime on it is still with me, the old damp rotten brick and stonework and cement and mouldy wood, sour earth in the dark. We looked at each other, we thrilled at it, glowed a bit at the fright of our adventure, we'd done something the others hadn't, that they couldn't. Our secret.

7
Rushbury

So long as it wasn't raining the one great pleasure at Rushbury was getting out of the school to fetch the milk. You'd get up earlier than the others, you and somebody else, sometimes there might be three of you, and with a large billy-can between you, it'd easily hold two gallons and wouldn't spill with the lid on, you'd walk through the dark across the fields about half a mile to Mr Blacker's farm. Sometimes it was misty and you had to hope you were still going the right way, as the month wore on the path got clearer and clearer as our feet trampled it down; on a frosty dark morning the pale grass picked up the clear sky and the hedgerows stood out, the buildings slowly got bigger your breath puffing out all white and settling clammy round your ears and neck, your scarf 'd be damp when you got into the dairy. You had to be sure to shut all the gates behind you, especially as you went into the barnyard and across to the cowshed and dairy, a huge pile of straw and manure from the cowsheds in the middle of the yard, a great stinking pool of cess on the cobbled yard around it, brown-green and yellow, rainbow patches here and there catching what light there was, even in the gloom of early morning when it looked jet black, odd bits of straw floating, sometimes the heap still steaming from when they'd cleaned out the sheds the night before. You'd open the cowshed door, pushing through bits of heavy sacking to keep the light from shining out, they smelled of jute and grain and seed, and you'd suddenly be in a different world, the smell of cows, the steady rhythm of milk hissing tinnily into pails, the note shifting as the milk rose higher, straw on the floor and a cow pissing into the gutter behind it, black ropy spiderwebs up in the rafters, rich heavy smells, sharp clear and milky, cats now and again underfoot, chains and halters and bits of rope muttering and scumbling against wood, cows chewing hay or cud as they breathed heavily back at the murmuring grumble of the cowmen as they talked to Buttercup or Daisy or Burdock or Cowslip, all the cows named with flowers or plants, quiet clatter and unhurried bustle in ammonia-laden warmth. You'd dawdle, the cold metal sharp on your legs as the hairs rose against the warmth, and a voice'd say "Oh ah, you're here then. Come on, don't waste time, bring 'em through," and you'd go through to the clean-smelling dairy, someone would come in with a pail of warm milk climb a couple of wooden steps and pour it into a hopper as high up as their head and you'd watch the milk spread out as it flowed over a cold metal washboard cooled with tap water running through it, down a trough and into a churn. "Don't need to cool yours," Mr Blacker would say on a cold morning, "it'll be cool by the time you get back" and he'd fill the billycan with warm milk, using a big enamelled quart measure, white with a blue rim, dark metal flecks on the outside from where it'd got bashed. It took a lot longer to carry the milk back, and heaven help you if you spilled any. You'd stop and rest as the milk got heavier, and sometimes one or two of the bigger boys would come over the fields to help you get it back, everyone impatient for breakfast. "I loved fetching the milk at Rushbury" Our Kid told me when I read him this paragraph over the phone, "I can still feel exactly what it was like. An adventure, that, and a relief." We jealously guarded our privilege to fetch the milk, sometimes the farmer or one of the hands'd give you a drink of milk straight from the cow to get you through the journey back, I loved the warm animal taste of it. Sometimes we'd fetch a few eggs.

Deeper into the winter it became almost too adventurous, and for a while we managed with no fresh milk at all, hoarding what we had. January 1940 was bitterly cold, and when the snow got really deep the milk ran out. There were terrific blizzards and one morning it'd been snowing all night and in the dark the kitchen help went down to light the fire in the cold cold kitchen; she opened the back door to get some firewood and there was a great wall of snow, a round dent where the doorknob had been and the square pressed mark of the door panels, a tiny bit of green paint that'd come off the door, she couldn't get out, and the snow just sat there, it didn't spill into the room at all except off the knob but it didn't melt when it hit the floor. "It was ever so funny and quiet," she said, "all muffled," she couldn't stop talking about it, and when it got light it was still dark in the kitchen, a white glow seeping in through the windows, "it's just like the glass in the bathroom," she said. But it wasn't like frosted glass really, when you looked at the window you could see it was snow, there were ripples and creases in it and little holes reaching away from the window where the light looked different, a bit bluish, grains of snow pressed up against the glass. The snow was piled as high as your knees against the front door and got deeper and deeper so steeply up to the front porch roof you couldn't see the sky when you looked up. Somebody scrambled through and round to the stables for a spade and it wasn't long before there was a path out from the front door to the forecourt, you couldn't see the shooting brake under all the snow, and by lunch time there was a tunnel dug down from the top of the snow to the kitchen door so you could get out that way. The utter strangeness of opening a door and finding myself in a tunnel of snow that reached over my head was exhilarating in its mystery, I couldn't tell where the corners were, where the floor ended and the walls began, just surrounded by cold light, all round and under, everything silent, the sky up there in front mixed up with the edge of the snow, like something I'd only read about, magical, every step a soft crunch, small squeaks as I walked surrounded by the branches of the monkey puzzle tree, close as close, they weren't way over my head any more, I ran my hand along their knobbled prickliness, it smelled cut green, faint sweetrot edge, cold wet ferns, faint pine.

Upstairs we saw a great expanse of snow stretching out with black bare trees sticking up, perhaps a few twigs poking above the snow where the hedges were, the snow right up to the upstairs windowsills on the south side of the house. Mr and Mrs Belben told us we couldn't go on the snow that side, looking in through the bedroom windows. It was ever so strange with the big boys able to reach up to the gutter at the edge of the roof, the bricks of the wall outlandish so close as though you'd never seen them before, the eaves jutting above my head smelling of wet dusty wood, flaked paint, muddy dirt. Everything quiet outdoors, just the crunch of footsteps, the soft plop of a falling clump as I brushed against a branch, no wind, and no birds, a bit of smoke from a chimney over by Mr Blacker's farm, perhaps a horse whickering or somebody's voice coming muffled from across the fields, under a hard pale sky, tough light everywhere, in great dazzling drifts covering the hedgerows and filling the lanes, landmarks changed or simply gone, I had to turn round and look back at the house to sort it out, slightly surprised and reassured to see it was still there. Up by the road there was this swollen bulge just level with the snow, it was hard as hard and intensely cold, it just sucked heat through my mittens, the wet wool, and I couldn't think what it was until somebody said "we've reached the gates," the top of the gate post at our feet. In some spots, mostly under trees or around the shrubbery next the forecourt, near some of the hedges, we plunged up to our waist, boots filling up with cold cold snow, mac flung up round my face as I went through, my cap came off, snow in my eyes in my hair in my ears, laughter ringing out in the frosty afternoon and suddenly soaked to the skin and frozen cold my hands and knees red and raw, sodden, blue from it. When we got back we put our wet clothes in the Big Room but the radiators weren't working and there was only a small fire in the kitchen and another in a half-furnished room we could sit in and we'd all stay there, our teeth chattering, trying to get warm again, shivering and shaking in great spasms, the funny numbness of your nose and ears awful cramps and aches as the blood started circulating again, hands and feet.

When one of us plunged up to his neck and it took one of the grown-ups to pull him out, and that was a struggle, we had to stay away from the deep snow, but by then we all knew that we couldn't get through to the village or to Blacker's farm, we were completely cut off. That must have been a nightmare time for the adults, what with firewood almost impossible to find because of the snow, all of us getting cold, and coal nearly non-existent. I've a vague recollection of being sent down into the coal cellar, or just going down on my own to see what I could find, black festoons round the single bulb up between the dusty joists *where'd the spiders go? were they watching?*

scrappy day-light outlining the top of the coal chute, I had to strain to see, dark lowering shadow, cold dry as a bone, my own shadow looming huge in the dingy light, gritty underfoot, patchy whitewash glimmering through black coal-dusted walls, echoey half-presences lurking, the building sighing behind me creaks and murmurs through the doorway, not even the odd scrap of anthracite caught in a corner or wedged between the bricks of the floor, strong smell of coal, broom and dustpan tracks on the floor, edgy perceptions in that edgy memory and I scurried out, steamy ballooned breath cold on my face.

There was still gas in the cylinder for cooking and the electricity still worked but it was only a couple of days before we ran out of milk. There was still plenty of water, the pipes didn't freeze, and we were all encouraged to scavenge where we could for fuel *but only take dead stuff, don't break ANYthing off a tree!* Somehow the grown-ups got things so organised that there were always two rooms with a bit of a fire for us to dry off in, we didn't get much schoolwork done, I can't remember us having any classes but I suppose we must've done, and there were half-a-dozen hot-water bottles to share among the kids when we went to bed we'd shiver and shiver away wrapped up in our pullovers, two pairs of socks on, even a scarf, our breath pluming in the night air, pillow bitterly cold, your nose red and stuffy in the morning, ice every day growing thicker and thicker inside the windowpane, so thick and hard you couldn't even scratch your initials in it if you didn't have a nail or some other bit of metal, your breath freezing on the window as you scraped away, and all you'd see was just the brick of the wall and snow. Snow, and the dark vague trees.

It was three days before anybody got through from the village, and that was the postman. Not that many of us kids saw him, and not that any of the grown-ups said anything about it until one of the kids asked who'd made the tracks from all the way through the gate, it wasn't anything we were supposed to be bothered with. But he'd struggled through one day to see if we were alright, people in the village'd been worrying, he said, bringing a handful of letters with him. Looking back it feels a lot longer than that, memory is so forgetful and inventive, but it was a hard time, and it soon stopped being an adventure, we got sick of snowball fights and snow forts and struggling into wet raincoats and boots before going out, trying to run about in the snow to get warm.

There weren't many toys at Rushbury, and we got so expert at the few scrappy jigsaw puzzles that we could do them in nothing flat, children's tempers got short and adult tempers got shorter. It wasn't just the milk ran out, so did pretty well everything else. Bread and cheese and meat and all the supplies came up from the village at the bottom of Roman Bank, and rationing meant that the school couldn't lay in big supplies for when the bad weather came. Bread wasn't rationed, of course, but that went mouldy if we didn't eat it, there wasn't that much anyway and when it ran out it ran out, but the cellar held two or three sacks of potatoes and the pantry two big bags, large tapioca in one, sago in the other. They'd been put to one side because there was no call for them when the school moved into the building, nobody knew how old they were. One morning when we came shivering down to breakfast the cook said "I've made you potato pancakes for breakfast, you can have two each"; we put salt and pepper on them and swallowed them down with cups of weak milkless tea – *You can't have much sugar! we've nearly run out!* – and then for dinner at mid-day we got boiled potatoes with some dried parsley on them, followed by a bowl of large tapioca boiled in water, the main meal of the day, with a bit of jam. Mum said years later that the cook had been at her wits' end having to feed something like twenty people on so little food. "How many ways can you cook potatoes?" she said, "when you've no milk and no butter, you've run out of bacon fat and you've hardly any dripping for the frying pan and you've got to make it last. Not even any onions! That cook was heroic."

It can't've been more than two or at most three days, but they felt like forever. Cook managed to vary the potatoes for each of those sorry meals, miserable children snuffling away with self-pity and runny noses for the cold as they picked away, hungry but loath, at baked potatoes, roast potatoes, mashed potatoes, potato pancakes blacked on one side in an attempt to give them some flavour. And at dinner. And in the evening. Followed by boiled tapioca or sago. Large tapioca, boiled in water, big glutinous balls perhaps half an inch across – almost completely inedible once we'd run out of jam and sugar, barely edible with them, utterly unappetizing to look at, semi-transparent opaque starchy balls sitting in a faintly slimy gelid mass in the middle of your plate, sticking together so hard you had to work at detaching them from each other with your spoon, you'd put one in your mouth, scraping it off the spoon with your teeth and lips, and bite into it, scrape it off your teeth with the spoon or a finger, gradually work it into lumps so you could bite again so it could stick some more, and flush this lumpy mess down with a drink of cold water so you could take another. Some kids put salt and pepper on so they'd taste of something not tapioca, but nothing could make them palatable, and the adults would sit at the end of the table, bravely smiling with revulsed enthusiasm as they chewed their own helpings, making sure that everyone ate what was before him. "No, you *can't* give it to Jimmy, it doesn't matter if he *does* want it." Years and years later, in the seventies when we first met, Meredith made me a treat, a wonderful and strongly flavoured peach and apricot pie, her wonderful pastry, I could smell the hot fruit as I came through the door, delicious, but when she cut me a piece the scent of the tapioca came through, a teaspoon of instant was all she'd used, to thicken the juices, "How *can* you smell it?" she asked; all that fruit, and I tried but simply could not eat, my gorge would not let me.

But eventually the snow melted and mud got tracked in and food got on the table, the weather still bitterly cold, everyone with a runny nose, crusts of ice on the puddles and not much heat in the house, Mrs Belben stood up at the end of tea, rapped with a spoon so we'd listen, and said "We've all got lice. Head lice. We've got to get rid of them." Mum remembered that before the First World War, when she was a child, old people said lice just simply grew from the dirt, that's where they came from, spontaneously, so they had nothing to do with respectable people, all you had to do was stay away from the dirt and keep clean. *Cleanliness is next to Godliness*, Grandmother would say. What a shock of dismay, then, what a shock to the system, to have that stigma, to have head lice yourself!

Like when I got home to Lichfield for Easter about a dozen years later, itching from head to foot, Dr Saunsbury carefully reassured me that scabies, another parasitic infection we all associated with ignorance and dirt, was nothing to be ashamed of. "You can get it anywhere, you probably picked it up from somebody's blanket at school," he said, "did you sit on somebody's bed?" and Mum and Dad both firmly warned me "Don't tell anyone you've got it!"

Those lice, of course, had to come from somebody in the village, it couldn't possibly've been one of *us*, and their riddance was not easy, all of us in a couple of attic rooms specially set up to treat us, no heat, after dark. I hunched over a chipped enamelled basin with a thin blue rim, a towel over my shoulders, feet like ice, other kids the same or just waiting, three or perhaps even four women in the room all in splashed white or yellow pinafores, damp cold children by the doorway *You'll get in the way in the kitchen!* Mum in the next room vigorously rubbing away at a child's head with a white bath towel, the towel getting wetter and heavier with each child scrubbed, Mr Belben nowhere to be seen, Mrs Belben scraping scraping and scraping left to right across my scalp, working from the front to the back then right to left then starting again from forehead gradually back to the crown, and again and then again, pressing a fine-toothed black Bakelite nit-comb over and over through my hair, hard, over the scalp, crying it hurt so much, *Keep your hands down! we MUST get all the eggs!* the stink of kerosene soap, a room full of bawling children trying not to cry, soap getting their eyes *Don't make such a fuss!* weepily going over to the next room to be towelled off by somebody else, those who were finished taking hopelessly wet towels down to the scullery to the copper for Hannah to boil and wash and dry, at least it was warm down there and in the kitchen, a watery cup of precious cocoa, bright red scalps under wet hair, off to bed, to be told the next morning by exhausted gaunt-looking adults who'd been up half the night combing each other, that "we'll be doing it again in eight days." Everybody bad-tempered, Mr Belben blaming the lice on people from the village, the school poisonous with hostility and resentment, looking for scapegoats as all the bedding got cleaned with kerosene soap on that freezing day, damp and condensation everywhere, no one allowed out, Hannah gaunter and gaunter. Extra doses of cod-liver oil, punishment for the dangers of ill health, and increasingly hard to find.

Mr Belben announced that "We all need a break. I've arranged for a school outing. A week from Saturday," and like everyone else I wondered where we'd go and what we'd do when we got there, Jeremy and Graham smirking away "We can go bird's nesting!" and like everyone else I looked round and smiled. "The weather is getting warmer," he said. "We shall explore the countryside, and discover what grows here, not what the farmers grow but what grows here naturally. We'll examine the hedgerows and go into the woods, see if we can find a fox or a badger, look for rabbits and birds. See where they all live, and how. We'll learn to be Naturalists." And then he explained that it'd be a long hike, as much as eight or ten miles, we'd be gone all day and have to carry our own food and water. He looked at Mrs Belben and told us "Not all of you can come, just the older and bigger boys." He looked at me, *You're too small*, he said, *and so are you, and you. You'll have to stay behind*. The day they'd all left, Mrs Belben clapped her hands and said "Well. What shall we do?" and then answered her own question: "We'll go for a walk too. Get your coats, put your boots on. And when we get back we can play a game in the paddock." But more often than not Mr Blacker kept cows in the paddock, we weren't supposed to go there at all on our own *There's no need for you to*. It was out of bounds really, all yellow and bright green tussocks, we'd all been in it of course, uneven ground with lots of cowpats most of them all dried up, but it was getting muddy now the weather was warming up, watch where you put your feet *You'd better not let Mr Belben catch you*, and now all at once here we were, trying to play a bat and ball game in the long wet grass, the ball wouldn't bounce, it just lay where it landed, wet and lifeless, sometimes you couldn't see it at all and we had to stop till one of us found it. We all kept tripping on that broken bumpy field and it wasn't long before Mrs Belben said we should all go indoors to play, or we could read, and Mrs Critchley said "I'll see if I can make us a nice cup of tea to warm us up. There's not much sugar though."

It was dark by the time Mr Belben got back with the big kids and I was in bed with an extra blanket in one of the attic rooms where we'd done the lice, the other stay-behinds in the room next door, and I edged off to sleep with the fainter and fainter outline of the doorway to the landing and stairs blurring into dark, the clatter of the older kids finishing up their late meal, the distant sound of their boots scrambled with their arguments and laughs as they went over the day's adventures, the sounds slowly waning into a drifting faraway murmur broken by occasional bursts and waves of indistinct shouts or laughs, Mr Belben's orders and Mrs Belben's questions and it got colder I could feel my breath condensing and I shivered my head under the blankets, not a sound from the other room a grown-up woman's voice answering a man's, small creaks and groans as the building settled and I burrowed further into the warm bed, heavy steps on the stairs, boots coming up, somebody called out, silence and then a scrape on wood, a rasp like a match on a matchbox but no flare of light, slow heavy tread, and then loud splintering wood *was that right outside the door?* and then a cry somewhere downstairs, hard laughter, a low scream cut off, a murmured urgent voice, a scrunch of wood splintering and breaking, groaning and then a sharp loud screech *that was in the next room!* and then another louder crunch of breaking wood, my blood thumping in my ears I suddenly *knew* that all the people the Belbens had invited to the house in their grey suits and party frocks had moved through the house, they knew what they were doing and they knew where they were going and they knew where we all were and their heads leapt from their shoulders on tight coiled springs crunched through the plaster-and-lath ceiling and through the floor above, the coils wrapped in bright red tissue-paper looping down, squeezed my eyes closed tight, the loudest crunch of all *right next my bed* wide grimaced Jack-in-the-Box-Head fat clown lips its grin all teeth, unblinking eyes flat and wide, hair thick under its pointed hat, it blocked the hole it had just made in the floor where my shoes should be, but I didn't dare look, I could not get my eyes open I didn't dare try, the heads all over the house I could hear them as they scrunched away at the building all around me, thick steps slowly coming up the stairs crunching plaster. I lay there the covers tight around my head, they grinned the house to wreckage, my room the only one still left, *Were they in the doorway?* nobody but me, the bare wooden floor, the Gog-and-Magog head. And I awoke to thin sunlight red through my eyelids I couldn't open my eyes, didn't dare, did not believe the distant racket of the other kids jurbling down to breakfast and the distant rattly *chunk* of dishes at the table until at last Mum came into the room to see if I was alright and I slowly pulled my head out into the cold air and peered over the edge.

Over and over that dream came back to me, it took a long time for it to lose its power, I couldn't tell anyone about it not even Mum or Our Kid. *It's only a dream!* they'd say, *it's not Real!* and once I'd moved back into a dorm with the other kids all of us chattering quietly away in the dark I knew that put in words it'd just sound daft even if I told it as a story, we were all too busy wondering if there'd be any extras to eat or feeling the hard pinch of too-tight shoes, grown-ups thankful we had fuel for the kitchen and hot water *Don't be daft, think about something that matters!*

The food didn't get any better or any more plentiful and if we grew out of our clothes, we still had to wear them. By that time I was wearing black leather boots like most of the other kids, noisy clodhoppers up to my ankles, labourers' boots, that's all they'd had in the shop at Church Stretton, steel tips on the heels and on the toes "They make you look like a navvy" Mum said but she smiled, "but thank goodness we got *them*, they should last." *Fat chance of that,* said one of the kids, *I'll grow out of mine in no time!* Our Kid still wore shoes though, black ones, you had to if you were at Brewood, brown shoes were vulgar and of course *no*body had suede, useless stuff in the rain and mud, only travelling salesmen wore *them*. Phil was supposed to keep his shoes polished, there was a shoe-cleaning kit which the kids were supposed to use all the time, brushes and polish and cloths scattered all over a bench or around it under the stairs near the gym, still there when I left the place ten years later, but hardly any kids bothered except on Sundays going to Church, it was too much of an effort traipsing across from one building to another just to clean your shoes, especially when nobody except Matron or the Housemaster noticed you'd done so. We all had crooked and sometimes overlapping toes, that was simply what wearing shoes did and there was nothing anybody could do about that.

Much earlier in the War, before the big storm and before troop movements and German Air Raids made it almost impossible to get about on the train, Mum took me to Shifnal, not much bigger than a large village but grubby from the ironworks, a slow cross-country journey, it took nearly all the day to get the thirty-odd miles from Rushbury. Did we go on the train or did we take a bus? Mum thought it was a mucky place, pinched and mean, sooty brick railway bridge narrowing the road as the bus went into it. When we got there, we took a taxi, just Mum and me, I can remember being in a car and Mum having to pay, and we got out at the hospital where I was to have my tonsils out, a grimy red and yellow brick building. I can't remember it very clearly at all, it can't have been much more than a cottage hospital really, but it was two or three storeys, it looked a lot like Stanway Manor Farm only bigger, it loomed more. Once we got in I don't remember Mum being there at all but of course she must've been until they'd got me ready they wouldn't've just sent her away, what I do remember is lying down in a starchy white gown that tied up at the back, on a stretcher, it was on a trolley in the hallway outside the lifts it must have been a lot bigger than a cottage hospital after all, and a dark-haired man in a white coat sitting in a chair leaned over and said "Can you count backwards from ten?" it was all very strange, big cylinders against the wall, and I kept looking about me, the man smiled and I chirped "yes" and he said "I'm going to put this mask over your nose and mouth and I want you count backwards when I've done so. I'm going to be giving you gas." This big mask with a tube going up into its nose settled over my face, it felt powdery and smelled of rubber, and I could hear the gas hissing, it didn't smell of anything, and I wondered if it was going to work, I didn't feel anything, and he said "why don't you start counting?' and he said "ten" and I said "nine," and then "eight," my voice booming at me a bit, and I started to feel a bit funny, my lips all blubbery and loose the gas hissing away and I said "seven," it sounded as though my ears were plugged up but I don't think I got as far as "six" and when I woke up I was in a ward with some other people, blackout, and pale yellow electric light, my bed screened off.

Everything was woozy. Mum was standing at the bottom of the bed a plump woman in white lifted me upright leaned me over a white bowl and I was sick, great heaves into the bowl, and it was all red with blood, bright red, and my throat hurt terribly and I fell back, she must have lowered me back, Mum's voice saying I was going to be alright, the nurse saying I'd probably be sick again but I wouldn't know much of what was going on for a while so why didn't she get something to eat and I nodded off feeling terrible, sore throat, dry mouth, couldn't swallow "could I have a drink" a sip of some cold water from a funny white china bottle a bit like a teapot you drank out of the spout I wished it had a taste and I went to sleep and then I was half awake and sitting up and leaning over the bowl and I was sick again, more blood, bright red, and I rinsed my mouth to take the taste away, blood tasted like a penny, coppery and sharp, and had a sip of water and slept only to wake up with blood all wet down my front where I'd been sick again, Mum was nowhere around it was the middle of the night but the nurse she was a new one came in and lifted me up and cleaned me off and gave me a fresh nightgown and as she was putting it on I threw up again, a mass of bloody liquid all over the sheets and the nightgown and her and the floor and I couldn't stop. Every time I lay down and went to sleep I'd wake up and be sick, there were dim lights in the room the taste of blood and it was dark outside wanting a drink and it was late, you couldn't hear any traffic, I couldn't keep the water down, everyone else in the ward was asleep there was a screen around my bed the light dim and I couldn't see them or the other beds everything a sort of noisy busy blur, someone snoring, someone turning over, lights and darks, no focus, nothing clear, and I'd sit up and miss the white bowl and as the night wore on what I threw up was black in the dim light and another nurse would come in turn on a light and wipe me off and I'd lie there wondering what was happening would it stop, the blood a bit paler now you could see it, but plenty of it, the nurses wearied, drained and irritated, too many patients, I think they got tired of it all, or they ran out of sheets, but they just wiped me off and let me lie there, bloody mess all round and over me, clammy wet clothes and bedding, smell of the rubber mattress-cover, and at a bewildered loss *Where was Mum?* I told myself I'd tell her in the morning how many times I'd been sick too many to remember but I counted anyway and at last I went to sleep, I woke up when it was light and everyone was awake, they gave me a blanket bath and cleaned me up, a nurse held me, her warm arms soft voice, soft cardigan, her breath and hair on my face, smiling "now you feel better" while they changed the bed, they gave me a bit of ice cream for my throat and a little bit of jelly, I could hardly talk and she said "have you ever had ice cream and raspberry jelly for breakfast before? Won't your friends be jealous!" and as my mum came in I croaked proudly "I was sick seven times!" still feeling poorly but preening my own heroism, a soldier wounded in the War.

8
Spalding

Poor Mum. Lice and snivelling children wasn't at all what she'd been brought up to expect in Grannie and Grandpa Wilson's house in Spalding. It stood in a row of tall red-brick Georgian houses near the middle of town, facing the River Welland just across the road. That house with its dark front door looked huge even if it was only two rooms wide, layer after layer of windows stretching up four storeys. The ground floor of the house included a gloomy-looking sweet shop that belonged to old Mrs Spencer. A worn stone step led from the pavement to the front door, with its wire cage on the back so the post wouldn't get dirty when it came, two deliveries a day. The maid'd put it on a brass tray in the front hall. Bang, the front door closed behind you as you walked down the hall to go upstairs or to the back part of the house, past the side door to the sweet shop. I'd hear the letter cage rattle all the way to the back of the house, where the kitchen was, and the Breakfast Room, and a hot and steamy Conservatory with pipes all over the place above your head, and a stove in the corner against the brick house-wall, white-painted cast-iron furniture, tables and chairs, and big dark green plants, looking out over the garden.

Grannie sometimes had Tea in that hot glassed-in room full of plants, or sat and read, but the sweetish mouldy earthy smell of all the plants and the damp soil and fertiliser always stuck at the back of my nose, it didn't make the food taste too good, I didn't much like being in there, it was so steamy I had to breathe with my mouth open and my head felt stuffed up, my clothes stuck to me in the heat and I just knew that beetles and woodlice, bugs and bits of bark and leaves were all the time falling onto my head or into the bread and butter and jam, even the cake tasted wrong.

Cook and Mary lived in and a maid came in every day to do the cleaning, the back part of the house was theirs, they had rooms at the top of the back stairs, the stairs dark as dark, but they spent most of their time around the kitchen with its cotton curtains and no carpet on the floor except a scrap of coconut matting over by the sink, light and open, cheerful, a door with a glass pane in it straight into the garden. We *liked* the servants' quarters.

I'd forgotten till Our Kid reminded me that there was a well in the corner of the Conservatory with a manhole cover over it, round and nubbly black iron with lettering on it, once a year Grandpa opened it up and dropped a bucket down to test the water, the first time I saw him do it I couldn't understand why he dropped the bucket in upside down so he let me try and I found out.

With the Welland just across the street it must have been river water in the well, filtered by the sandy soil the house stood on, and Grandpa tested the water by tasting it. The river flowed under the house and every now and again it flooded. How exciting to have water lapping at the front door just like in *Swallows and Amazons*. People travelling in sailboats instead of by bicycle or car. Holiday country. "Did you go to work in a row boat?" we asked Grandpa, and with a quizzical look on his face Grandpa playfully puffed out his cheeks and said "Of course not! I've got *boots*."

"Terrible mess, real damage too," he said, "water soaking into the walls, all the mud to be cleared away, new wallpaper, painting to be done once it all dried out, everything moved back downstairs. Good job we have no heavy furniture down here. Nor carpets." Not like at Berril's Department store where he managed the furniture department. In the middle of the night he'd got up and mucked in with all the other staff to move brand new merchandise upstairs. Didn't think anything was beneath him.

It was a Victorian household with all the formal rooms and all the family-living upstairs on the first floor, bedrooms higher, velvet and heavy mahogany where you could look down on the street, just the Breakfast Room downstairs, next to the kitchen, a couple of steps up from the entrance hall, and the conservatory. "Sometimes the water even got as far as the kitchen!" Grannie told us and Cook nodded. "Couldn't get a fire going, could we mum, but we managed somehow, had to boil a kettle on the drawing room fire upstairs," and everybody smiled. "Oh yes," Grannie said, "That was a funny time wasn't it, you eating your meals up here with us," and she chuckled. Cook had been there for years, ever since Mum was a small child, and Grannie and Grandpa had taken eighteen-year-old Mary under their wing when she had a baby, "a by-blow" Our Kid called it, sotto voce. "I'm traipsing up and down those stairs all day long," Mary'd say when she felt grumpy, but "We get a nice long sitdown here all afternoon," Cook always reminded her, a small ritual, "till tea." And in the summer they sat on the garden steps in the sun doing chores they'd saved up, chatter and laugh together, gossip.

Grannie liked her peace and quiet and I think Phil and I were the only disturbance tolerated in that calm house with its closed doors, heavy velvet curtains everywhere, furry brown mohair or tapestry hangings behind the doors to keep the draft out, we even had one in the living room at Lichfield long after the War, lots of houses did. As you opened a door it'd lift the heavy curtain hanging on its rail, a soft whooshing sound, and as it closed the curtain billowed behind it, the curtain-rings scuffling. I had to cram under the draught-excluder and stretch like mad to get at the doorknob it was so high, except in schools and places that's how doorknobs were, that long-haired-curtain-smell of dust and of Grannie's house, long thick heavy itchy, it made a wonderful place to hide, if somebody opened the door I'd have to lumber quickly a clumsy crab in a sideways clambered stoop try not to kick the door or make any noise. Especially in the dining room I loved that hidey-hole, the stuffy air as the curtain closed round me, the mohair making my neck and my legs all scratchy, the price of that small discomfort well worth its reward, a secret vantage to hear the muffled goings-on as people went about their business, *That's Grandpa's voice, he's not supposed to be home right now! Where's Mum?* the delicious thrill of anxiety not to sneeze *Mustn't give myself away!*, Mary's footsteps along the flagstones of the hall downstairs, rattle of the wire cage on the front door as she collected this morning's post. Sooner or later the household noises would fade and stop, off in the distance perhaps the back door into the garden would bang closed and I'd creep forth, *Where's Our Kid? What's he doing?* I wasn't even supposed to be in that room without any grown-ups, a laugh downstairs, Mum's faint voice. I'd worry *What's going on? Where's everybody gone?* and strain to listen, I'd hear a footstep, turn away toward my hidey-hole my heart pounding like mad and Grannie's voice, "What are you doing up there? You're supposed to be outdoors. Be off with you!" Or Mum and Dad, cross, "Have you been behind that door again? You'd better not kick it, scratch the paintwork!" or Our Kid, "You must be daft! Find something better to do!"

Voices got muffled to a murmur in the still air, someone quietly putting coal on the fire the only disturbance in the drawing room, all red velvet and deep plush chairs and sofas, or ringing for Mary, and the quiet chink of cutlery and cups at Tea, best-behaviour territory, sit on the edge of the sofa, reach for a slice of bread and butter, balance your plate on your knee, spread some jam, you'd better not drop anything, drink some tea, Granny asking you if you'd like a piece of cake, and at last be released, go downstairs, get away from that mahogany velvet gloom, get back to the kitchen, sit with Mary and Cook at the big square worktable, help yourself to more bread-and-butter without having to ask, light and open, warm and cheerful, my favourite place in the house, the kettle forever muttering softly to itself on the hob, everything scrubbed clean, faint trace of carbolic underlying all the kitchen smells. It felt like something was always going on there even if all they were doing was having a quiet sit, there was always a bit of work waiting to be done, greens to be washed, something to be put on the airer, the light from the garden flooding through the window, the door straight into the garden, a couple of fruit trees, a small greenhouse.

Every morning Mary or sometimes the maid who came in for the day woke us up and we went straight to the kitchen, usually Cook gave us breakfast there, a small wooden table against the wall opposite the range, the stone floor warm from the fire which had been banked all night, cornflakes and lashings of toast and marmalade, perhaps hot buttered toast for a treat, *Don't eat it too fast* Mary always echoed Mum or Grannie, *it'll give you indigestion just like new bread that's warm from the oven!* We always grinned, and always wanted more, the cheery clatter of dishes and hot water running, Cook and Mary bustling about looking severe but pleased to watch us eat and the jangle of the bell made us all jump, Grannie wanting her breakfast in her room, or Grandpa wanting more hot water for his tea in the Breakfast Room before he went off to work. I loved to watch the bell-board, rows of numbers in a glass-fronted box in a small room just off the kitchen, high on the wall near a row of bells up near the ceiling, wires disappearing into holes. When a bell rang a red disk dropped down to cover one of the numbers on the board, and Mary would get up from the table with a sigh and fill the teapot, smoothe her apron, fuss a bit with her hair, pick up a tray and go off to the Breakfast Room, or over to the dumb-waiter in the corner of the kitchen. "Don't you go pulling of them bells," she'd tell us, "we've got enough to do without you two up to your tricks," and "No, Mary," we'd say; and "I can't go charging all over the house just because you two want to play with the bellpulls," and "Yes, Mary," we'd say, and we'd finish our breakfast and go off somewhere to find something to do. The dumb-waiter was magical, it was all very well to see this funny little cupboard with its two unpainted shelves, nothing in it, but to see Mary close the door before she went upstairs and a minute later hear the rumble behind the wall and after that hear another rumble and have the door then open to show the empty cupboard behind it fascinated me, sometimes I'd try to open the door and Mary'd say "Leave it alone. It's not there," but I didn't understand how she knew.

Then on one visit when we were sleeping in the room above the dining room Our Kid climbed on the chest of drawers to look at a wooden panel in the corner, "Hey!" he said, "It's the dumb-waiter" and he poked and fiddled about a bit I don't know what he did or how he did it but a faint rumble started behind the wall and got a bit louder and louder and then the panel jerkily slid up, Our Kid had to help it, and there it was, the same little cupboard with its shelves. "You can get to the kitchen from here!" he said, "have a ride. Just like a lift." But he was too big. *What if it broke?* I thought, *What if we got caught?* "It'd be fun getting to the kitchen like that," he said, "take the shelves out, better than sliding down the banisters. Go on, Pete, try it! You could easily do it. Get in." But that was such a small place I'd have to scrunch up terribly, me in my pyjamas, nothing to hold on to, closed space over an endless drop, strange noises, all of it in the dark, there'd be cobwebs, spiders and things *they'd crawl all over me. What would happen if it got stuck in the middle of the wall? what if my finger got caught going down?* We wouldn't half get into trouble if we broke it *What if it fell?* And *how'd I get out at the bottom, could I open the door from the inside?* Our Kid was a bit narked that I wouldn't get in and every now and again he'd give it a long look, fiddle with the door, he couldn't leave it alone, and I couldn't stop wondering what was lurking on the other side when the cupboard wasn't there, waiting to get out.

That dumb-waiter in the bedroom was much scarier than the great big bathroom with its high ceiling, paint peeling everywhere, and cracked lino floor, it drew me the way the dumb-waiter drew Our Kid, the first thing you noticed when you went in was the smell, just like the Conservatory but cold, sweetish and clinging. A washbasin facing you as you went in, a big cast-iron enamelled bathtub on the right, and a big upright tank a lot taller than me on stubby little legs against the side wall on the left behind the door, "Acme Water Softener" on it in metal letters, next to it an Ascot hot-water tank just as big, hard white stuff hanging down in great gobs where pipes came out from the top and went in at the bottom, they looked like crumbly plaster, soft at the foot of the tank, it came off on my hands or fell in bits and marked the floor, at the top rock-hard and almost too hot to touch. I thought it was this that smelled until Our Kid said *It's dry-rot under the floor,* I didn't know what that was, its sweet putridity once smelled never forgotten. Both tanks gurgled at you or made a little hissing noise, listening and watching, breathing, they knew you were there, they muttered and murmured to each other, you'd turn the hot tap on because the bath was getting cold and the Ascot would whoosh in a great roar as the gas lit and then a barrage as water rushed through the pipes around the flames in the firebox and the heat went up the chimney and the water came out of the tap too hot to touch, the enamelled jacket creaking and crackling as it added *its* smell to the room. I never sat in the bath for very long, the air so cold and the room so full of strange echoing noises, everything alive. Cobwebs and dust in the dark cave made by the water-softener's legs, big spiders under there living in the dry warmth. Every time I had a bath one would sooner or later come out and stop for a moment for a look around then scuttle to the Ascot or to the corner under the bath, I'd heave out of the water as quick as quick, feet on the cork mat, dry in a hurry with one of the big rough white towels, the steam from the bath clammily settling, cram my feet into my slippers shivering away clean my teeth and get out of there toothpaste rim round my lips pyjamaed and dressing-gowned and slightly damp, scramble off to bed slippers flip-flopping. I couldn't get past that room during the day without stopping to look, the room was so full of noises and smells, and I'd seek reasons for coming back to it, wondering at those monstrous strange devices that growled and grumbled away their creaks and groans doing things to the water, I'd hover in the doorway, shifting from one foot to the other. I wondered if they would notice me, and I'd cautiously run away, the mutterings and whistlings softly calling behind me.

But our life at Spalding was never adventurous, it wouldn't dare it was so tidy, and we kept in our proper place. If we had breakfast in the Breakfast Room, so did the grown-ups, except Grannie. Mum, Dad, and Grandpa read the paper and talked quietly together. When Grandpa left a jigsaw puzzle out for us to do after he'd gone to work Mary would put it on the breakfast table after she'd cleared away his breakfast things, we were supposed to finish it before the next morning so he could eat his breakfast, and one or two evenings each time we visited he'd say "Let's play skittles" and set up its square wooden board all shiny brown varnish on the Breakfast Room table, "Mahogany" he'd say every time, we weren't allowed to play unless he was there, and he wouldn't let us set it up, that was *his* job, the nine varnished skittles set in their shallow sockets to make a square in the middle of the board, in the corner of the board a pole with a wooden ball fastened by a green string hanging from the top, the string so short the ball could only just reach the skittles on the far side and you only got three goes to knock all the skittles down. "Peter goes first," Grandpa said, and I stood next to the pole where he told me and swung the ball out, "Not too fast!" he said, "watch what it does!" and he chuckled as the ball swung out so high it didn't touch the skittles at all as it went round the pole, "You've got to catch it," he said, "You can't let it go round twice!" But if it did go round twice it simply climbed higher and higher as the string wrapped its way round the pole, it didn't hit anything at all. When it was Grandpa's go he looked sideways-on to the board across his right hand, his breath fluffing his moustache as he grinned and just let the ball go, it swung out in a lazy slow arc grazed the front-corner pin and got a bit of a wobble as it hung on the string and with a neat *click* hit the pin in the middle of the back row and bounced off to hit the pin next to it and all the pins went down in turn, rattling away together as the ball ended up in his left hand or just hung there on its string, nestled at the foot of the pole. But I was too impatient, I kept thinking that if I flung the ball out in a wide swing it'd swoop down and bash all the neatly arranged pins to smithereens, all of them crashing down in noisy mayhem, no matter how often he'd tell me *No, easy-does-it wins the game*. So I was hopeless at it, I wanted it to be like an explosion, skittles flying everywhere, enemy soldiers getting blown up by heroic artillery, I didn't want to let gravity do the work the way Grandpa said, I wanted it to be *me* that made it happen. Grandpa would chuckle and write down his score while Phil and I set the skittles up for our turn, a bright sparkle in his eye. I'd keep telling myself to do it Grandpa's way, but as soon as I got the ball in my hand I just *knew* that if I could only swing the ball hard enough it'd go in a straight line and I'd win with a spectacular victory. But of course it didn't, and I'd get so cross with myself but even more with the string and the pole as the ball zoomed round and round the pole climbing higher and higher, I'd write down my miserable score on the paper with all those twos and threes next my name and see Grandpa's nines and Our Kid's sevens and eights marching across the page. I never did win, but I enjoyed it, that funny mix of laughter and crossness, the three of us doing something together, that skittle set one of Grandpa's precious things, Mum said she'd played with it when she was a girl, so he must've had it for a long time.

Grannie never played with us or really found anything for us to do, I suppose if we'd been girls she might've found something for us to do, given us dolls or let us play dress-up, stuff like that, get a doll's house, but we didn't have any of our own toys at Spalding, *What if we left them behind?* Mum'd ask, *you'd have to do without them for a long time!* and Dad told us not to be silly, *We're not going to be here very long*, he said, *There's lots of things to do.* But I missed our lead soldiers and Dinky Toys, *H.M.S. Nelson* with its rotating gun-turrets, the tiny Spitfire with its propeller that went round, the Wellington bomber, and we didn't have wooden bricks and boards to make roads and towns and airfields, we didn't even have our marbles. More than once Grannie told us to go for a walk or play in the too-small garden, and sometimes we went with Mum over to Berril's, the big Department Store, walked about and looked at things, always ending up in the furniture department, where Grandpa was in charge. In the afternoons we'd walk down to Ayscoughfee Gardens. "Look at those lawns," Mum would say, she never got tired of them, "they've been there for two hundred years, they're wonderful. I've never seen anything as good as them."

On Sundays if the weather was nice Grannie and Grandpa would come with us, Grannie all dressed up, Grandpa in his Sunday suit, and we'd sit in a row on the deck-chairs in front of the bandstand, the chairs set out in rows and rows, there must have been hundreds of them, people in their Sunday best walking about saying hello to each other perhaps chatting a bit and moving on, and then coming to sit down, some little clumps of people come just for the concert, some of them sitting where there was nobody else, some of them like Grannie and Grandpa where they always sat and they could meet people they wanted to be with, Grannie smelling of powder in her flowered dress and sunhat and white gloves, a parasol at her side a quiet nod to somebody walking by. Half of the chairs were in the shade, the brass of the musical instruments winking under the bandstand canopy as the players shifted in their seats. You could see the sun on the trees on the other side of the bandstand, they looked darker, more intense than the others in the park, the light changed by the shade of the canopy, the dark blue of the band uniforms, more like a picture because of the frame you saw them through. The park attendant always came round in his uniform and Grandpa always paid the thruppence for grown-ups, a penny each for us kids, and got in exchange a blue or white ticket off a roll, holes punched in them, while we sat there, legs cool in the shade from the seat in front, face and arms hot from the unshaded sun. I couldn't get comfortable anyway, the seat so stretched and saggy that the wooden bar holding the front of the canvas hurt as it pressed against the back of my legs, I couldn't really swing my feet, there wasn't room. Mum quietly nodded her head in time to the music, Our Kid slumped back in a sprawl with his eyes closed, one leg tucked under him, Grandpa just sat there in the sun his eyes half-closed. I wondered how long it'd be before Mum or Grannie told Phil to sit up properly but nobody did, it'd disturb the music, and all at once I recognised the tune and began to hum it and when it got back to the beginning I sat up straight and beat the time with my hand and grinned to myself "a duck may be somebody's mother." Grannie looked askance and wagged her finger at me, Mum said *Ssssh!* and whispered *I like that tune too, Peter, but people didn't come here to listen to you, did they?* the shouts of children playing somewhere over across the grass, the crunch of footsteps on the gravel walks, the bark of a dog, a car on the street outside, the sun bleaching the smell of canvas up to our faces, the grown-ups nodding and falling asleep as the band played. Sunday the same wherever we were, nothing to do but sit there. I asked, "can we go?" in a quiet voice and Grannie wondered why but Mum simply said "Don't go far! Don't be long!" and Grandpa winked as he told us "Don't get lost!" As if we could. Most times we went over to the duck pond and watched other boys sailing their toy boats, but we didn't talk to them, there'd always be one boat stuck out in the middle of the pond, someone vainly throwing stones to make waves to wash it back to shore, but we couldn't help, it wasn't our boat. But oh, how we longed for a fancy wooden yacht.

The War changed all that. The iron railings round Ayscoughfee Gardens were torn down like all the other iron railings in the country to be melted down into guns, you couldn't rattle a stick along them to make a wonderful noise and annoy everyone, and there was no one to cut the lawns and they grew all hummocky and coarse. Mum mourned their passing. The plants in Grannie's conservatory had gone there was no fuel, sweets were rationed and Mrs Spencer couldn't give us the occasional chocolate dragee or liquorice allsort as we went past her door on the way to the kitchen or upstairs to Grannie's drawing room, with rationing she had to keep strict control of her stock. Before the War Grannie always had a tin of humbugs sitting there on the mantelpiece, Callard and Bowser probably, "the best" anyway, or at least the tin was, Callard and Bowser made wonderful treacle toffee, but in the War even with the resources of Mrs Spencer she couldn't always get them and instead there'd be Pontefract Cakes or my favourite, Coconut Teacakes, I can still taste them when I think about it their lovely toffeed paste, their gritty sugar coating, I loved them much more than I liked the big and knobbly humbugs all that peppermint a bit too strong though I wouldn't say no. Sometimes they stuck to your teeth and you'd stand or sit there frantically trying to pry them off with your tongue and you'd suck away at your teeth without letting anybody spot you, that sticky mess clinging there, sooner or later you'd give up and bend your head down and poke your finger in your mouth and nudge it off, what a relief that was, and then your finger out of your mouth all wet and sticky, a bit of peppermint or liquorice p'r'aps caught under the nail and you had to hang your hand between your knees where nobody'd notice and feel it get cold as it dried off a bit sticky, perhaps you'd furtively lick at it a bit to get it off so nobody'd notice, *What if you had to shake hands with somebody or pass them a plate or something* but nobody ever let on, if they did see you you were at least trying to be polite and well-mannered. Grannie'd bring down the tin, it was always the same one and I'd reach for the wrinkled white paper beckoning from the tin and rustling round my hand as I carefully pushed it apart, I'd peer into the gloomy insides, *what sort was in there this time,* there'd be a sudden little shock as the tip of my finger met the soft and yielding or hard and sticky surface of the sweets. I'd draw back just a little, Grannie holding the tin *Don't touch any of the others in there,* she always said, *You can only have one!* The humbug or the liquorice you'd got hold of would cling to its fellows resisting its little adventure and you'd wiggle your hand about to get it free, sometimes two or even three would come out especially if it was a Pontefract Cake *No you can't have all those!* her soft voice firm, *break one of them off!* the tin bobbing about as you tried, but now and again you could get away with two, when that happened you'd give your brother a little grin and try to look shamefaced and of course *he* had to get two as well, or another if he'd already had *one.*

    She was a bit forbidding I suppose, looking back from now, when I'm writing, but we really liked it at Spalding and we loved her, Mum and Dad always seemed at ease there, nobody really on their best behaviour the way we all had to be when we stayed with Dad's parents, we had to call *them* Grandmother and Grandfather and the formality of that is still how I think of them. Grannie had her formal side, she wanted everything to run smooth and unruffled, and set great store on observing the proprieties, she liked life tidy and stable, but she enjoyed conundrums and tongue-twisters, laughed over them, and one afternoon she and Mum had a high old time as she challenged us kids with "She sells sea shells by the sea shore" and the long one about how "Peter Piper picked a peck of pickled peppers" that kids used to chant at Wheaton Aston, that one had rhymes and went on for ages. It's funny the traps you set for yourself when you're a kid. I could never get it right never mind remember it, and I never dared let on that I couldn't when everyone else could, so I couldn't ask what the words were really so I could learn them. The others always gabbled through it so fast I couldn't learn it just by listening, and I couldn't pretend the gabble, that'd be a dead giveaway. I daresn't. The one I remembered for ages after, I loved it because it let you make noises like being sick, a bit like that wonderful sound poem François Dufrêne did by swallowing a microphone but not really, Grandpa liked it too, recited it now and again, was "The sixth sick Sheikh's sixth sheep's sick," it was so wonderfully silly. But the most difficult one was Grannie's favourite of them all, "The Leith police dismisseth us!" That one even had Mum stumped, she'd had it pulled on her when she was a little girl, and I know I got crosser and crosser as I couldn't do it, I expect Our Kid did too, but it stood us in terrific stead in the dorms after we got back to School, nobody else could do it either, two rows of kids lying in the dark trying it out one after another round and round the room till somebody said "I've had enough" and went to sleep.

Grannie relieved the mild tension of looming boredom by letting us play with her kaleidoscope, a heavy brass cylinder a bit like a telescope with three mirrors inside, set up to make a triangular tunnel you looked through, "Be careful with it!" she always said, "It's very precious. It came from Germany a *long* time ago. It has real mirror glass in it, that's why it's so clear." She'd look through it, give a little hum of approval, and pass it to Mum. And as Mum passed it to one of us she'd remind us *It's not a toy, so don't drop it! Be careful when you put it down*. It was clearly a special treat for us to see the wonderful patterns made as you slowly turned it, the tiny coloured glass rods and discs tumbling round each other, coloured diamonds squares and triangles, tiny prisms catching and scattering the light. "They're never the same," she said, "so you've got to share it when you get a really good one." She'd carefully hold it while we took turns peering over her shoulder to see, and without fail it would get jiggled and the patterns change, you'd look into the kaleidoscope and you'd tell her how nice it was when it really wasn't because all the coloured bits'd slumped down in a corner, and you'd fidget about waiting for your turn *C'mon, Our Kid, hurry up! Pass it over*, wanting to see the patterns fall into and out of place as *you* held it. When I was about fourteen I realised that it was originally a grown-up entertainment and imagined Grannie's parents gravely seated round the table or before the fireplace entertaining their dinner guests, pointing the kaleidoscope towards a source of light and passing its patterned glitters from hand to hand. Edwardian if not Victorian, about the same vintage as an old magic-lantern somebody dug out from their attic and played in the school hall at Wheaton Aston, carefully setting it up in front of a screen us kids fidgeting *When would it start?* the older kids saying how wonderful it was when all it was really was boring, the poorly coloured minarets or alpine landscapes so faded and gloomy you really did have to be told what they were. The old-fashioned curiosity of magic lanterns and kaleidoscopes is thoroughly redolent of Grannie and her ways.

Grannie always wore a choker, mostly pearls but perhaps just as often dark velvet, with a cameo. In her living room Bess used to have a studio portrait of Grannie I think Our Kid's got it now, single-strand pearl choker and dark dress probably velvet, yet mauve is how I remember her, *frocks* not dresses in the summer, lilac and mauve, a child of the 1880s with their wonderful rapidly-fading Victorian postage stamps produced when the craze for the new colour, it was called mauveine, was so widespread even if it did fade quickly in sunlight. All of us in school at Brewood really coveted those stamps, Marlow Grandfather passed some pretty faded ones on to Phil and me for our collections, and there's something quintessentially Victorian about that colour, I think it was Grannie's favourite, and the house in Spalding especially the drawing room with its heavy velvets and plush and its mahogany and its balloon-back chairs has the flavour, there's no other word for it, that I associate with her and with the 1880s when she was growing up, whether they were like that or not. Grannie in her formal elegance ruled the household and us with a firm hand, but she and Grandpa laughed a lot, were kindly folk, chapel but not serious about it, her father had been a master baker with his own shop, "Worked hard old Mr Williamson did," Mum said, "up all night baking and then delivering bread for half the day when he started, kept at it even when he had two or three working for him." There wasn't much pretence about Grannie.

Every single time we went to visit, we knew without fail that Grannie'd tell us, the evening before we left Spalding, *Come with me,* and she'd beckon us both upstairs and towards the back of the house to her bedroom, her private place, where she'd open the wardrobe, reach down a slim box, open it. We'd lift the edge of the paper, a drift of white sugary powder in a small cloud settling on our lips and in our noses, and she'd say, "Have a piece of Turkish Delight." It was always the same, densely sugared soft pink and white cubes, always the top layer in the box with three or four pieces gone, but Phil and I knew enough to look surprised as well as pleased, and if we said "Thank you Grannie" in the right way she'd sometimes invite us to take a second piece. That went on exactly the same even after the War, in formal and upright contrast to Grandpa's twinkled vulgarity. "Silent like the *p* in bathing," he'd say, and "Albert!" she'd say back, "Really! And in front of the children!" and he'd laugh and stick his chin out a bit, he loved lavatory humour more even than he loved riddles and puns. More than once, separate times we were there, he belched softly after eating his pudding at dinner, "Aaah," and turned it into "Aaahples" Grannie looking severe shaking her head over "*Al*bert!" and he'd look at us and wink. A lot of his jokes became old friends. "Why can't a deaf and dumb man tickle nine people?" he'd ask, and before you had time to reply, "Because he can only gesticulate," his eyes twinkling and him chuffing away to himself, delighted at its sheer inconsequentiality. He'd nod and smile at Grannie and she'd look back at him, her mouth softening a little as she drew herself up. We usually had soup for the first course at dinner, oxtail or mock-turtle, and he'd break his bread into small bits toss them in the air one at a time and catch them in his mouth, "There!" he'd say, and twinkle at us, and we'd try too only we'd get into trouble, Mum sounding shocked, "Where's your table manners?" Grannie sounding cross, "*Al*bert!" she'd say with a severe look, "You *are awf*ul. How *of*ten must I tell you!" He'd grin, and out on walks or sitting at a table Phil and I secretly practised throwing all kinds of things up to catch them in our mouths, berries, bits of apple, even paper pellets or bits of twig, so we could show off when we got back to School or went to the farm, and next time we went to Spalding, and if there was soup at dinner we both tossed our bread in the air and caught it in our mouths and grinned proudly. "Where did you learn to do that?" Grandpa said sounding cross, "young savages!" and Grannie and Mum said to him "Now see what you've done? You ought to be ashamed of yourself!" and they both tried to look cross and forbidding, reluctant quirks at the corners of their mouths. But next time we did it they *did* look cross. "All right, enough's enough. We know you know how to do it. Don't be tiresome."

9
Little Marlow

We never tried anything like that on Dad's parents, they were a different breed altogether, never showed affection for each other, not that we saw anyway. They asserted their identity in their name, insisted that we call them *Grandmother* and *Grandfather*, and upheld their respectability through their house, a cottage really, a ten-minute walk over the fields from the River Thames in Little Marlow. Grandmother's back was ramrod straight, unbending, she terrified us kids, and even Mum was a bit afraid of her, her disdainful governance, her unyielding air of superiority. Phil and I ate our meals at a small table across the room from the grown-ups, had to keep quiet, the dining table only large enough for four. *Little children should be seen and not heard.* Even Mum and Dad said that when we were at Little Marlow.

Once, when I was nearly twelve and she was in a friendly mood, pleasant chatter round the grown-up table, Mum and Dad making sure we were alright, saying things to us here and there, it was when teachers from before the War were coming back to their old jobs and we'd just got Mr Embleton back from the Army, he'd been an Officer in the War and had even been to America, he had a leather support strap round his right wrist because of a bullet wound, he was an exciting figure, and practicing with his golf clubs on the School playing fields made him really exotic, I'd never even seen anyone who played golf before, "Grandmother," I piped up from the kids' table, "we've got a new Teacher at School, he wears his wristwatch ever so funny, he has it on the front of his wrist so he can see it like this" and I gestured, the inside of my wrist before my face. She drew herself up with a loud sniff. "What's the matter with that, child?" she said, and I watched her right hand twist her own watch round on her left arm, she didn't even try to hide what she was doing. "I wear mine like that, and always have." She held her arm up. "Look!" and she turned away to Mum, disdainful of children and their ways.

In Grandmother's book children existed to be disturbed and uncomfortable, she only ever spoke to us to order us about *Fetch me this* or *Find something to read* or *Go and see what your Grandfather's doing* and in all the times we stayed there, Phil reminded me when I was writing this, we never once got to go upstairs, neither of us. It took us quite a few phone calls to reconstruct the layout of the cottage with its kitchen at the back, the scullery behind it alongside a pantry, two rooms upstairs where the adults slept, and two more down, the living room at the front and the dining room opening up into the kitchen behind, and Phil and me always felt cramped. If we'd managed to bring any toys or games we had nowhere to spread them out and play, and only ever-so-old books like *Chums* or *Boys' Own Annual* to read, Grandfather telling us after he'd dug them out from some cupboard or other with a pleased air *You boys be careful with that, it belonged to your father*, or *It was your Uncle Geoffrey's when he was a boy, look after it properly*, Uncle Allan and Uncle Gilbert both long dead, Allan of cancer before I was born, Gilbert some time early in the War, but we never got to see any of their stuff, I don't know whether any of it still existed. I expect Grandfather might've held on to it, I know he hung on to their stamp collections, but I think Grandmother with her practical and managing habits might've said "Stuff and nonsense!" as she threw them out. Though you never know, she'd hung all sorts of family photos on the walls, including all four sons on the wall by the fireplace in the living room, and it was her that made sure Dad got that studio photograph of Allan in his brand new uniform in 1914. But she kept her personal feelings *quiet*, nobody's business but hers.

Phil reminded me that she used to keep bees, she had a couple of hives in the garden, she did all the looking after them, the old man had nothing to do with them though he enjoyed the honey right enough, and she wouldn't let Phil and me anywhere near them. I think the honey was the only indulgence she gave anybody in that house, she never indulged herself that I saw, everything kept under strict control. Her fierce tongue was scornful if any of us including Mum shied from a bee that'd strayed into the house *Don't be ridiculous!* she'd say, *Why would it be interested in* you? *Just leave it alone and it will leave* you *alone. The world isn't here just for you children.* More than once she told us how often she'd been stung, *hundreds of times, don't be such a baby!* and once when she got stung in the house she called us in, that in itself was a marvel, and we all watched as the bee delicately walked clockwise, anchored by its sting till it'd unscrewed itself and could fly away. "That doesn't kill the bee," she said, "If you slap it you squeeze all the poison into *you*, and then it really can hurt. So just leave the bees alone!"

Not long after the War, I must've been about twelve or so, the grown-ups at Marlow busy together in the kitchen and Phil off somewhere and me reading, Mum and Grandmother's impatient voices burst out louder and clearer, they never did get on. Mum came out of the kitchen and closed the door quietly behind her, looked about her and beckoned, "Peter," she kept her voice down, almost a whisper, frowned a bit as she hurriedly looked round. "Here." She handed me a Yale key tied with a bit of brown string to a scrap of paper. "It's to the Taylors' front door, the white bungalow just across the street, the one with the hedge in front." But there were two like that and I didn't know which one she meant me to go to, and as she started to explain, still whispering, Grandmother's irritated voice called "I really think you might hurry, we don't want to be cooking all day," and Mum sounded a bit irked as she said "Never mind! I'll go myself. You can help carry." So we both went to the Taylor's house to retrieve Grandmother's lamb roast from their refrigerator. Grandmother never had one. Mum grumbled "I've got a pudding on and I don't want it to get all stodgy the way Grandmother's always do. There's too much to look after." And then, "I don't want *her* to tell *me* what –" but she bit off the rest of the sentence.

In the same low voice she told me Grandmother'd bought a small roast of lamb on Wednesday and couldn't put it in the Taylors' small fridge till Friday after the Taylors'd gone away, the lamb'd been in Grandmother's meat safe till then. "I hope it'll be alright," she said. We heaved the door open where it stuck a bit, *Oh!* Mum said as a warm rush of air, a bit musty, flurried over us. *We should open a window in here.* The floor creaked a bit and sagged as I trod on it and Mum sniffed, a couple of dead flies on the floor, and as we crossed the room a mouldy mushroomy smell got stronger and stronger, its pungent sweetness settling behind my nose, a bit like the bathroom at Spalding only much more clogging. I opened the fridge, Mum took the cold package, white butcher's paper, and sniffed at it, said "Here, you sniff it" but all I could smell was the air in the kitchen *How could anyone tell if it was any good with all that smell?* "Never mind," she said, "Let's get out of here, I'm sure it's alright." But on the way back across the road, even in the bright sun of the garden we could still smell it and I said "Mum, it's that package" and she sniffed it, "No I don't think so, I think it's alright. Yes, I'm sure it must be alright." She sniffed at the package again and asked *Was the refrigerator door closed properly before you opened it?* which it had been, and then, "Of course it's perfectly good. Don't you say a word to your Grandmother. If she finds out I don't know what we could possibly do. It'll be lovely once we've cooked it." And I wondered. I'd never seen her in such a dither, and Grandmother greeted us with the words "Well! You certainly took your time, didn't you!"

But when we sat down to eat it, roast lamb with mint sauce and gravy, redcurrant jelly if you wanted, lots of spuds and peas, even a slice of bread to mop up the gravy I didn't want, I wasn't hungry, I kept thinking of the house across the road, the smell of it hiding between my teeth, I looked at Mum at the table where the grown-ups were, they were all chattering and eating away, Mum caught my eye and smiled but didn't say anything, I looked at Our Kid and he was wolfing it down, he wanted more but didn't dare ask. Grandmother looked at me pushing my food around the plate and said "What's the matter child?" and I took some potatoes and peas on my fork and tried not to get gravy on them I didn't want to touch the fork with my lips tried to swamp everything with mint sauce I didn't want to close my mouth I scraped the food off my fork with my teeth mashed it against the roof of my mouth with my tongue, the mashed potatoes were easy, and swallowed as best I could without tasting, the vinegary sharpness of the mint sauce a real blessing. "Can I have a drink of water?" I said, and "Nonsense!" said Grandmother, "it ruins your digestion to drink while you're eating," Grandfather and Dad each with a glass of beer in front of them. "You won't get any dessert," she said. "Apple pie," she said, and I struggled along. Mum looked at me and said "Everything's perfectly alright, Peter, there's nothing to worry about" and smiled, but she didn't say anything more and looked all nervous, Grandmother looking, and I picked away at what was on my plate, little tiny bits of meat smashed in among the potatoes and peas to hide the taste and at last everyone had finished, they were tired of waiting for me, and Mum took my plate away, Grandmother frowned and scowled and said in a vex something about waste and shook her head, it was such a long meal I hated it my stomach heavy each time I smelled the food. There was nothing wrong with the apple pie, but I didn't have any enthusiasm even for it, and later, when Mum and I had a moment alone Mum said there'd been nothing the matter at all with the meat, it was just my imagination. That night in bed I kept expecting to be ill and I wasn't, and when I thought hard about it I realised I actually could have enjoyed it the way everyone else did, it really had tasted fine. At tea time Mum told me there was dry rot under the floor at the Taylors, that's what made the smell, "that and the damp, and probably a few mice under the fridge or under the floor" and I thought *Dead ones, yes,* but tea was a grumpy meal, I'd missed out on the lamb.

Every afternoon once dinner was over, Grandfather got in his favourite armchair where nobody else was allowed to sit, his tetchy voice telling Dad some story or other about the racket from the pub next door, Dad wanting to read the paper, Phil and me in the scullery helping do the dishes *Watch what you're doing!* or *Mind you don't drop it!* or *It doesn't go there, child!* Once the dishes were at last safely in their cupboard, us two kids all grumpy, damp sleeves clinging to wrists a bit chill from handling those wet dishtowels, Mum pursing her lips in subdued aggravation, Grandmother sent Grandfather out of the house, "Take them for a walk!" she'd instruct him, "You can't lie about all day" and we'd get out, our sense of relief tempered by the absolute need to behave ourselves with polite restraint in Grandfather's uninviting company, no running about, no noise. He always wore a three-piece suit, grey herringbone with a touch of red in it, a small man with a round belly his beard like King Edward VII's, a gold watch-chain and fob across his waistcoat, every now and again he'd reach down and pull out his half-hunter, peer at it, open it up to make sure he'd read it right, shake it gently and put it back, most times he'd take us down by the Thames and he'd cast about for something to talk about, ask us about School and what we were reading or tell us about his stamp collection, drop the odd comment about life in the village, who'd died and who'd moved, complain a little about the vulgar people coming down from London for the weekend or to drink in The King's Head pub. He took Our Kid without me for a walk when Phil was about sixteen or seventeen, "He was checking up on me," Phil said years later, "making sure that I'd got everything straight, wanted to know if I smoked or drank *Don't do it my boy!*" he took him for a walk along the river and they came across a bare-chested bloke, he'd taken his shirt off it was such a sweltering day, *Look at him,* said Grandfather making sure the bloke heard, *Bloody Barbarian, should be horse-whipped!* and muttered into his beard about "the sort of people you get nowadays," glaring. It was the only time, Phil told me, that he ever heard *any* vulgarity pass Grandfather's lips. "I was quite shocked," he said, "he never said things like that. Never."

On visits he'd as a rule take me and Our Kid aside one at a time on a walk round and round the garden or into the village or along the river or even perhaps into the pub garden next door and he'd harrumph and harrarh a bit "Well my boy, it's very important that you do well in school, you've got to work, very hard, really hard, at your lessons. You owe it your family, to all of us, to be at the top of your class. Yours is not an ordinary name, you know, there's a book about it, you're from the Nobility, your ancestors came over with William the Conqueror, your great great great great grandfather was William the Conqueror's right-hand man, there's a castle in Oxfordshire that belongs to the family" – he never mentioned that the castle was in ruins and had been for five hundred years or more and probably didn't belong to anybody really, and when we asked he never said where – "and you must live up to your name, you have to be worthy of the tradition that your name carries, you have a coat of arms you know, your name is a responsibility" and he'd go on and on about how we had to live up to our name, we had no business being Ordinary we should Set Our Sights High, go into the Diplomatic Corps, we deserved The Best because of How Ancient Our Name Is but we had to Do the best and Be the best, we had to Work for the sake of our Ancestors "You must never disgrace the family name, my boy, it's something you should be proud of" and eventually we'd get back to the cottage and Our Kid would say in bed that night "Did you get the usual lecture?" and we'd shrug it off, we never paid any attention to him, he was so pompous and self-important, "Yes Grandfather" was all you could say *Yes, Grandfather. No Grandfather, I won't forget. Of course, Grandfather.* The other side of that coin, not that anybody held it up to view, told us that Mum's family was nobody. Wilson! Bessie! What kind of a name is that?

I remember all that more vividly than I remember his kindnesses, his telling me in no uncertain terms at Rugby once just after the War when such things became available again, that Whitfield King's was a much better stamp catalogue than Stanley Gibbons's *Simplified*, "Buy one, my boy, if they're publishing it again. It only has the British Empire." I think it cost me five bob when at last I got it, that was five weeks' pocket-money, and he was right even though the illustrations were much reduced and a bit muddy. More than once he showed me how to soak stamps off envelopes with a bit of clean blotting paper in a saucer, *Don't let the water get on the surface! The ink might wash off*. I can still conjure his rotund little figure, his herring-bone tweed trousers and waistcoat, arm-bands on his shirt sleeves, carefully carrying a saucer of water to the table and just as carefully laying a clean piece of white or pink blotting paper in it, slow and ponderous, laying down the law with his *Don't do this* and *You must do that*, his belly resting against the table. "You have to be patient," he said, "Wait for it to rise clear from the paper it's on," and I'd have to stand there and watch, waiting and waiting, I'd fidget from one foot to the other, wanting to pick it up and lift the stamp off, and he'd just stand there looking down at it, he wouldn't say *any*thing, and at last he'd slide the stamp off the paper and say "Now we must let it dry," and we'd stand and watch *that*, and it took ages too, he'd stand there in his carpet-slippers a faint persistent odour of tobacco and dusty wool, he didn't seem much taller than me but I know he must've been.

The other day Phil reflected that *he never had anything very much to say to us kids, did he?* and then suddenly remembered that sometimes on a walk talking to himself more than to anybody else you'd hear him say

>A collie dog a melon saw,
>And thought it would be jolly,
>The collie dog a melon ate,
>Was filled with melancholy.
>The collie dog is in his grave,
>Dog roses grow upon it.
>Oh watermelon cauliflower.

Neither of us ever knew what to say to that, it was so exactly the sort of terrible pun we'd hear from Spalding Grandpa not from him, that glimpse of fun in the old man, surfacing briefly only almost immediately to subside. Always a small shock of surprise. Like my surprise years later when Dad told me that the hauntingly persistent song he used to sing dandling me on his knee came from *his* father in turn, Horsey, horsey, don't you stop / Just let your feet go clippety-clop. But he didn't excite my wonder at all, it was so hard to get away from his grave pomposity, and hard in his presence to conjure any pleasure.

He'd retired long before the War, when he was about fifty or so Mum said, which would've been in about 1938, and nothing in Little Marlow seemed to engage his energy or his imagination. I was completely astonished to discover, when I was an undergraduate at Nottingham, that Cookham was only about two miles along the Thames from Little Marlow, but we never walked in that direction, where Stanley Spencer'd done his amazing painting of "Swan Upping," but Grandfather never mentioned any of that. I doubt if he even knew of Spencer's existence, he'd certainly've got hot under the collar at the thought of immoral artists and their scandalous ways.

But then he never mentioned Swan Upping, the age-old annual count of the Queen's swans, either, no doubt because it brought charabancs full of outsiders into the neighbourhood to disturb his peace. Mum was surely in the right of it when she said, "I don't think he knows what to do with himself," and the constant need to manage him as well as the household and no doubt the budget must have driven Grandmother nuts. No wonder she sent him out for a walk every day.

Mum said he'd trained as a cobbler and shoemaker and worked his way up to some sort of managerial job with Favre & Picard which that old clipping about Uncle Allan in the *Daily Sketch* called "a famous French firm of shoe manufacturers." Except for that clipping the only thing I know about them at all comes from old postcards and envelopes he gave us for our stamp collections, "Duplicates" he called them, sent to the shop where he worked near Regent Street, and over the years he gave us quite a few. "Covers. You really should save those, boys, if you want to be a serious collector. Don't take the stamps off the envelopes. Make sure they have a clear postmark."

When we stayed at Little Marlow, Grandmother mostly talked to Mum, and Grandfather mostly to Dad. Except at table, I don't think he really had anything very much to say to Mum at all, and she simply had no patience with him. "The old fraud!" she'd say later, but never to him, I wonder if she did to Dad, "He was just a *shoe salesman*! He hasn't done a stroke of work since I don't know when, before you boys were born anyway, and his grandfather was just a farm labourer, I'm not sure *he* was even literate! He doesn't tell us to live up to *that*." But when I was working on my Honours Essay in 1954 at Nottingham, to get a Reader's Card at the Bodleian Library I had to put my hand on the Bible, I'd laugh later and joke it was the works of Sir Thomas Bodley though I don't know if he ever had any really, and at the main desk just inside the entrance, everybody round me all po-faced, "recite in a clear audible voice" and then sign the stilted oath printed on the back of the Card, not to write in the books not to steal anything nor smoke in the library, and to obey all the rules. No sooner had I finished than a wizened old man came up to me and said "Quartermain? Did I hear Quartermain? Very old name, that! Came over with William the Conqueror." We argy-bargyed a bit about that and the history of surnames, "Significant name," he said, and for the next week whenever I went into the library the people behind the counter were all friendly with a cheery "good morning!" They greeted me by name. A book Grandfather got so puffed up about, Dad had a copy, was called *The Quatremains of Oxfordshire*, with a coat of arms as frontispiece, four right hands and a blue stripe on a red shield. I don't remember Dad ever even opening it, but Uncle Geoffrey, his younger brother, kept trying to put us straight. "The Old Man means well," he'd tell us whenever he visited us, "but he's got the wrong end of the stick. You've got an unusual name, that's why it's important, people don't let you forget it if you do something stupid, or wrong. They remember, and they hold it against you." And like his father he'd tell us endlessly, "Keep your nose clean."

But of course it worked both ways. I had all sorts of advantages when I needed something in the University library or the bookshops at Nottingham, they all knew my name, recognised me, made feeble jokes about Rider Haggard; all my pals had to stop and ask before anyone paid attention but I'd walk in and whoever was behind the counter would look up and say "That book you wanted is here" and give it to me without checking to see if I'd got too many books out already. But they also knew if I had a book overdue or hadn't paid my bill "Mr Q you owe us fourpence" they'd say and my pals all grinned as they snuck on by, them owing huge library fines, a lot bigger than mine at any rate, but the librarians didn't know who they were. Uncle Geoffrey was a prosperous businessman at Covent Garden in London, he was just as pompous as Grandfather, lectured us just as interminably "It's not what your Grandfather says, you don't have to live up to the family name, nothing like that, no, your ancestry doesn't matter. But people always remember your name, it's distinctive" – he liked words like that – "so you'd better watch out." Like Grandfather and like Grandmother he never paid any attention to what Phil and I might want or think, but I did once overhear him ask Dad what Phil and I would do for a living after we left school.

"They've got to be *some*thing," he said, and was a bit puzzled when Dad said he expected we'd each find our own way. "Can't decide for them," Dad said, "can't make plans of that sort. So long as they like what they're doing, that's what matters."

Even so, names mattered. Mum was only a Wilson, after all, or had been before she married Dad, and the Wilsons were nobody. And her own name, well! What sort of a name was Bessie for a grown woman, that's the sort of name you give a serving girl or a cow, not respectable at all, really! And that sort of assumption persisted a very long time. When I went to collect the death certificate when Mum died in 1994 her regular doctor wasn't there and the locum got her name wrong, writing *Elizabeth* instead of Bessie, and he was surprised when I put him straight, "I didn't think *anyone* was christened *Bessie*," he said as he apologised. Grandmother always pronounced *Girl Geh-el*, a little break in the middle of the long-drawn vowel, and it would be a long time before I realised that it too was a clear class-marker, her habits as well as her pronunciation, polite middle-class late-Victorian and Edwardian London, an unshakeable formal reflection of social protocol.

When Dad was just two years old, Grandfather gave him a silver serviette ring, with the following note to his wife Ada: "Please accept this ring on behalf of your Boy my Godson teach him to fear God and honour the King whilst loving us all as a Son should – as I did my Mother." He signed it "faithfully yours, HG Quartermain." It's hard to believe that he was saying this to his wife. But that was the kind of formality their relationship had. In Dad's family, certainly, like in Mum's, serviette rings almost had the status of sacred objects. Everyone we knew used them, silver usually, and they treasured them, a bit like heirlooms. Clear signs of respectability, they said we belonged.

But Mum too had her class prejudices, claiming Dad's family were pretentious and really just farm labourers, and it turned out she was completely wrong. The letterhead on Grandfather's note with the serviette ring was The ORIELS, Kingston Rd, Merton, an elegant new garden suburb of London. Dad's grandfather, far from being a farm labourer, was a well-to-do architect who'd designed the suburb of Merton. He was named Henry Goodall Quartermain, and it was *his* address on that letterhead.

Dad as well had some pretty strong beliefs, some of them inherited from his parents, some from his time in the Army, about things like when you should get married and what a husband should do and what his social position demanded. He'd learned from his time in the Rifle Brigade never to swear. Swearing was really frowned on and quite severely punished, all ranks. And he'd learned from his parents and their generation that you shouldn't get married till you could afford to – that was supposed to include buying a house. If everyone'd followed that injunction then of course nobody would've ever got married, but Dad certainly fretted over living in rental property, like Grandfather he knew that gentlemen had to be property owners, "That's why it's called *Real* Estate," he'd say.

And like other families, of course we set up our own rituals, some of them hung on for years. It's more than half a century since Dad died, long before I met Meredith, but we both ask, just as Bess did when somebody poured a cup of tea that's not full to the top, "When do the trams start?" *The Wars of the Roses are still going on*, Dad told Mum not long after they first met, *Yorkshire against Lancashire*. Nobody needed telling about those, in every school they were central in the telling of English history, and Dad told Bess that when he got his first real job at Woolworth's, as an Assistant Manager, up in Sheffield, the standing joke amongst local Yorkshire people had to do with the tram service in Manchester, the other side of the Pennines, they said there was no such thing as a timetable, trams didn't leave the terminus until they were full, they'd sit for ages before they had enough passengers to start. We none of us believed that, of course, it's so daft, but we all enjoyed it, *how could anybody down the line possibly catch a tram if it was always full when it arrived?* We'd think of all that rain Manchester was famous for, no roof upstairs on the tram you'd get soaked if you sat up there, and you'd never get anywhere on time. That's obviously the point of the joke, but "When do the trams start?" became a family ritual, shared affection that it holds us together even as we explained it to Meredith the first time she heard it said.

Mum was a shorthand typist when she met Dad, Grannie and Grandpa insistent that the girls earn their keep, but for Dad, coming as he did from Grandmother's and Grandfather's upper-middle-class respectability, what enabled you to get married was that your wife would never have to work, she'd be looking after the children and running the household, it wouldn't be a *job* it would be a *responsibility*. What mattered was that Dad worked for a *salary*, and that meant that Mum's marriage rescued her from wage-labour, and she could hire a maid to help with the children and the house, lead a proper life the way both Grannie and Grandmother did. The War changed all that, and once it got well and truly under way, like most women her age Mum had to get a job, the Direction of Labour Act made sure of that, and Dad was absolutely furious, "You can't end up on a factory floor making munitions or running a lathe like all those women, scarves wrapped round their heads or their hair all in curlers, not *my* wife!" But what really rankled was that she'd be a *wage*-earner. "That's not right, he said, "We're *respectable* people, not working class" and he called on all his Freemason friends, senior management people, landowners, doctors, and even a magistrate he knew, for help, he pulled every string he'd got. But the War had frayed a lot of those strings, and the best he could manage at the beginning of 1942 was part-time work in the telephone exchange at British Thomson-Houston, a big factory in Rugby. He soon managed to get her moved, though, to the Post Office telephone exchange. It was late in 1941 that he'd moved to Rugby, to replace the manager who'd got called up as a major in the Army, but this was a step down, to find himself living in a flat instead of a house.

10
Boarding School

Brewood. Our Kid loves browsing around rag-and-bone shops looking for books, he's quite a dab hand at it, gets back home gleeful with his loot, especially if it's bound volumes of *Punch*, they're too heavy to read comfortably on your knee, at least they are for me, but he'll spend hours with one, listening with half an ear to a record or to music on the wireless in front of the fire in his worn saggy armchair, and he sounded quite chuffed, pleased with himself when he recited on the phone a really terrible limerick he came across in the February 16 1935 issue:

>An old-fashioned spinster from Brewood
>Was such an impossible prewood
>That she got in a state-o-
>Ver peeling potato
>And serving it up in the newood.

"Well," he said, after I commented on its attitude towards women, "yes. It *is* pretty awful. It's prissy, and it's lazy. That last line doesn't really rhyme, does it. But it's still a good way to tell strangers how to pronounce the village name." Of course all us kids took a certain pleasure in knowing that ordinary people wouldn't know how to spell it if they heard it, or how it *should* sound if they read it. Once we got settled, *Brewood* was such an everyday word, how to say it second nature, but like everybody else a tiny corner of me was secretly proud of that knowing, it set us apart and said we belonged. A few years later, at everyone's insistence especially Marlow Grandfather's, I read a version of *Tom Brown's School Days* which began with an epigraph from the 1835 *Rugby School Magazine* saying that School is "a complete social body, a society, in which by the nature of the case, we must not only learn, but act and live; and act and live not only as boys, but as boys who will be men." That idea, without me noticing it until I read it, was drummed into me pretty much without pause, until I left eleven years later.

Our Kid'd been there for over a year when I started at Brewood. I was seven and a bit, and Mum came upstairs with me and Phil to see the dormitory I'd be in. We met a grey-haired woman in white, her clothes crackled and shooshed whenever she stirred, she had a sitting room just round the corner where she kept bandages and medicines as well as a warm fire and a kettle, a table and comfy-looking chairs, even when she breathed there was this faint creaking her clothes were so stiff, and Mum said "Matron will look after you, Peter, you'll be alright, won't he Mrs Grant," Our Kid restlessly shifting his weight from one foot to another, me holding onto Mum's hand, and Mrs Grant took my other hand she smelled a bit like TCP antiseptic mixed with face powder and Mum bent down and kissed me goodbye and turned away to go downstairs, Our Kid already halfway down the hall on his way to Dormitory Two to see his pals "Where did you go for the summer?" "What did you do?" "Look at what I've got!" and I was still watching after Mum when Matron said "This is Dormitory One, you'll be here with the other new boys, they're not all here yet" and she ushered me in, four other kids already there. A long room, up two steps to go in, big white wooden beam running across the room and through the plank wall into the corridor, sloping ceiling above the beam at the end and then it levelled out above the middle, five iron beds along the side with two windows, four along the wall with the door, one bed blocking another door further down. "That door's kept locked," Matron told me, "we don't use it at all."

Polished lino on the floor, a battered chest of drawers with a mirror just in front of you on the left, three washbasins at the end on the right in an alcove just past the window, made by a chimney jutting out at the end of the room, sponge-bags hanging under a narrow shelf above the basins, a couple of wooden towel rails on the wall alongside, and another chest of drawers up against a blocked-up fireplace. Radiators under the windows, lockers next to each bed, black painted coat-hook on the yellow wall above each locker, somebody's flannel dressing gown hanging on one of them, nothing else on the walls anywhere, no pictures, nothing. Everything bare, four kids already in the room, all of them older than me. And one older boy, about ten or eleven years old, in charge but not back till tomorrow. One empty bed, not made up. "Another new boy is coming on Wednesday." He'd have to start from scratch, then, when everybody else knew each other.

"This is your bed" – the third one down, blocking the other door, under one of the two ventilators opening out into the corridor – "and this is your trunk" at the foot of the bed. The tartan blanket you bought at Beattie's with Mum in Wolverhampton a few weeks ago is on the bed. That's how you know it's yours. It's got your name (on a Cash's nametape) sewn on one corner. All your clothes have your nametape on them, even your socks and handkerchiefs (white). "Every morning you make your own bed. Clean sheets once a week" (the sheets have your nametag, too). Our Kid in Dormitory Two along the hall on the left, mirroring the same layout, and the House-prefect's bedroom opposite, between the two bathrooms (one has one tub, the other two) and the w.c., you soon learned to call it the Bog, but not to grown-ups. There's another bathroom just off the top of the stairs, but we can't use that or even go in, it's Matron's. Third Dormitory runs across the end of the corridor, there are more dormitories upstairs, where the senior boys are. Everything strange, even though I'd seen it the year before when Our Kid came.

All of us in Dormitory One except an older kid, he'd be looking after us, were in Prep School, getting ready for entry into the Grammar school. We were all new, three of the four kids already here watching another who was sitting on a bed steering a toy car. It had a black cord stretching from a small steering wheel sticking out of a box in his hand down to a shiny red car on the floor and as he turned the wheel the car turned, I'd seen one before, one of the kids I'd known in Shirley before the War had had one, it said *Distler* underneath and a lot of funny words I couldn't read, it looked just like a real sedan car, it wasn't a Dinky Toy much too heavy, it had windows you could see through, with a couple of batteries tucked away inside where you couldn't see them. "Too expensive for us," Dad'd said. "This is Gravette," said Matron, pointing to the boy with the car, "This is Quartermain Minor." She told us each other's names, Smithe, Jones, Hart, "you're all in Prep class," and we stood around in silence, looking at each other when the other wasn't looking, shuffling our feet, gazing round the room, awkward faces. "Malpas is here too, he's in that bed" and she pointed to the bed under the window across from the door, "he's the senior boy in the dormitory, he was here last year. He'll show you round."

I could see where Dad had painted "P A Q" on my trunk the letters all shiny black at the end under the handle, and I liked where the bed was, I could lean on the plank wall behind the pillow and see outside and not just look at the other beds across the room. Hart followed my gaze and said "what's that tree? I've never seen anything like that" and I told him it was a monkey puzzle, proud to know something he didn't, but he didn't know whether to believe me or not, he was older than me, they all were. "There's only six of you here tonight," Matron said, "the others will be coming tomorrow, except for one," and I still recall trying to sleep that night, lying awake in that big half-empty room, the three empty beds, two patches of dim light stretched across the ceiling from the ventilators high in the white plank wall, right over my bed, two glimmering huge truss beams their white bulk reaching across the room and through the ceiling, black iron stanchions a faint line sensed more than seen, one end of the beam disappearing out through the wall over my head and across the corridor outside, doubled shadows of beams stretching out and across and down the other side of the room in the gleam from the ventilators, a kind of roomy oppressiveness nothing at all like home, sounds of footsteps in the corridor outside, the Housemaster or more likely the House-prefect patrolling, Malpas and Hart whispering to each other in the corner of the room, Gravette snuffling to himself, me missing Mum, wanting to be in my own bed with my battered yellow Teddy-bear, under my blue quilted eiderdown, the sound of the grandfather clock in the hall ticking away, Mum and Dad talking quietly. The room was so big, so cold and strange, no pictures on the walls, no carpet on the floor not even a rug, echoes and noises from outside, the sheets so cold blankets so light, bedsprings creaking as somebody turned over, footsteps as someone in shoes climbed the cement stairs, the dim outlines of the two rows of beds, the chests of drawers at each end, an owl in the garden somewhere, the row of washbasins gleaming grey, the weight of my dressing gown across the foot of the bed, the pad of someone in slippers going down the hall to the bathroom, the sag of the mattress, the tap dripping in the corner, sudden light when someone opened the door and then closed it again, and the sound of somebody frankly crying, all of us sniffling, "I want to go home," blubbering for Mum. Oh Mum.

Once the War was over and bells could ring again, Nunc or more often Young Nunc would go round the halls in the morning *clang clangety clang clang clang!* ringing the handbell to jerk us all awake, a terrible racket we all learned to ignore, but it hadn't taken as long as a week after I first arrived at Brewood to stuff my head under my pillow and snuggle down to grab another five minutes in bed and then rush into my clothes at the last minute. When I first got to Brewood, Matron or a Prefect'd come round and chivvy us out of bed, breakfast was at half-past eight, but within that week we were competing to see who could stay in bed longest and still get down to the Dining Hall in time. You devised ingenious ways of undressing and arranging your clothes the night before so you could get your vest and shirt and pullover on all at once the tie still looped round the neck with a knot in it all it needed was pulling tight, and you'd pull your underpants and trousers on all at once, tug your socks on, slip your shoes on, you'd kept the laces loose, at least I had, but the first time Birdie tried that his shoe came off and he tripped, somebody grabbed him on the stairs so he didn't fall and after that even tying his laces didn't seem to slow him down, we'd all of us learned to be quick, you'd grab your blazer and shovel your arms in the sleeves as you fled downstairs. You couldn't be late for breakfast, you'd get punished, older kids'd told us you might even have to do without, but I never saw that happen. You had to be there for saying grace *For what we are about to receive may the Lord make us truly thankful Amen* sometimes a quick gabble, but we all thought it was cheating to sleep in your socks and underwear, we scorned that, that was what ignorant townies or even the kids at the Nash School did, evacuees or worse, dirty, not that there were many of them around any more and not that we knew anything about them anyway, they weren't anywhere near us. We'd all be in a mad scramble to get our clothes on, all of us leaping out of bed at twenty-five-past when the Prefect on duty or Matron crossly told us we'd got five minutes to get downstairs and out through the Quad to the Dining Hall, some kids not even bothering to wash if they could get away with it. You'd comb your hair with your fingers as you clattered down the cement stairs, I could never find my comb anyway, the first kid leaping down the first eight steps all at once hands on the metal banisters, getting to breakfast all puffed and red in the face and feeling terrific, we'd wolf our breakfast no matter what it was. In the winter there'd be thick patterns of frost on the inside of the window the lino on the floor freezing cold some of us would pull our clothes into the bed under the covers to get them warmed up especially if you slept under a window, it slowed you down getting dressed but you stayed warm wriggling into your trousers under the blankets and hauling your socks on, that got to be a different kind of game it didn't really make things much better, instead of being a bit cold for a few minutes you ended up a bit warmer with your clothes all twisted round and rucked up, you'd see kids going down stairs wriggling about trying to get everything comfortable, poking and tugging at their underwear red in the face trying to run down the Quad at the same time as they tucked their shirt in or tightened their tie.

But when I first got to Brewood, and until the War was over, Matron went round the dorms first thing *Come on! No lazy bones here!* ringing in our ears *Time to get up!* she might pull the covers off the bed closest to the door jumping us awake, ten minutes later she poked her head round the door to make sure we were all getting dressed properly "*Don't forget to wash behind your ears! Use your flannel! and lots of soap!*" towels all higgledy-piggledy near the washbasins. On that first day she escorted us down to breakfast in the big echoey half-empty Dining Hall, other kids tearing down the stairs to get past us, shouting to each other or stumbling along behind us, clatter of boots shuffle of feet, long empty tables big enough so everyone in the School could sit and eat all at once, all 140 of them, right now room enough for all of us kids ranged along both sides of one table, with a small table for the Masters at the end of the room where the kitchen was, and when the other new kids arrived that afternoon we all felt better, they were the ones feeling lost and shy while we all knew each other and had got lockers already even if we did have to share them, we got one shelf each, in the Billiard Room downstairs, a big room with a fireplace at one end, a couple of sofas and a battered armchair, the lockers all along one wall wooden cupboards really stacked on top of each other all the way to the ceiling, and a few chairs and benches round the walls, in the middle an enormous billiard table with a big green lampshade hanging over a huge expanse of fading dark green cloth cues in a couple of racks on the wall by the window and a wooden scoreboard with sliding brass pointers above the fireplace, and we knew that the Billiard Room was what the Headmaster meant when he talked about the Boys' Common Room. And we already had our names on hooks in the entryway and knew where to go to clean our shoes and where the classrooms were and what times meals were, we all knew you couldn't sit down at the table until grace'd been said, and we all waited to see if one of the new kids'd sit down before grace and get scolded, it'd serve 'em right, yesterday we'd been warned not to sit down until grace'd been said, they should've been here yesterday shouldn't they.

And Matron knew our names and we knew each other's names, Matron at the head of what'd be the Junior table, we'd seen the Headmaster at his table at breakfast, sitting with his wife and the Housemaster; they had toast and it was in a proper toast-rack, and marmalade from a proper marmalade-pot, they had a tablecloth and serviettes, a little dish of butter for their toast, and a china teapot with a teacosy and a jug of hot water, and after a bit a uniformed kitchen maid popped quietly in through the door behind High Table with a rack of toast and another jug of hot water to give them seconds. We knew how to find the Croft and where the football fields were and the Changing Rooms. But this was the day nearly all of the boarders came back, and now there'd be close on forty boys, some of them as old as sixteen, where yesterday there had been about ten, and tomorrow would be the first day of Term and all the dayboys would be there. That's when lessons would start. On weekdays, all the boys would eat the midday meal in the school dining room, the Teachers and the Headmaster called it *dinner*, the way we did at home, not *lunch* the way some of the dayboys did.

The kid who arrived on Wednesday was a weekly boarder, newer even than us, he didn't know what we knew, so we had the advantage. He didn't last long, but he was a Weekly Boarder and he didn't care, he went home every Friday night on the bus, right after school, missed Saturday morning's classes in Prep School and didn't come back till Sunday night or even Monday morning. The first Wednesday he arrived all full of himself, a cocky little bloke from Wolverhampton darker than us like a street kid, sharp brown eyes, curly black hair, like one of those urchins at Wheaton Aston, his dad was a jeweller, Ezra Pound might have called him one of the sturdy unkillable children of the very poor he was so knowing and rambunctious, and he absolutely refused to cry, instead he crowed it over us all. How we all hated him, he was so indomitable in his talk and his refusal to buckle under, so undisturbed by anything we said or did. He told us the facts of life "Your dad sticks it into your mum," he said while we were still crying in bed for our Mums, "That's what it's for." That was shocking, yes, and we incredulously laughed, he must've made that up. A couple of nights later he announced he was Jewish, he sounded angry and impatient about it – or about us. I hadn't the faintest idea what that meant, I'd never heard of Jewish before. I couldn't see why he sounded so defiant, that he didn't come to School Prayers every morning, but I was startled. Other kids weren't so baffled, and some were scornful and hostile right back, noisy about it too, even after Lights Out when we were supposed to shut up. "Oh yeah, your dad's a jeweller, isn't he?" "He's got a shop in the Arcade." "Bet he's got a lot of money!" " Where's all your toys then?" and the voices jeered on, in the dark, and after the Houseprefect came and shut us up there were still furtive whispers from one bed to another, "there's a lot of them in Hull," "keep themselves to themselves," "wear funny clothes for the weekend." Chuckles and scornful mirth, "money is all they care about."

What was going on? Life as a boarder was so unlike life at home, there was no one to ask, but you learned very fast not to show ignorance if you didn't want to be laughed at. You never talked about personal or private things, your family or how you felt about anything, and it all gave us a secret sort of knowledge, strangely secret even from ourselves, that removed us from the secure rule of grown-ups, made us less dependent on the cosy world of family, kept us clear of intimacy, separated us from dayboys and weekly boarders. You'd look into their eyes and see nothing you could recognise, no affinity, no response. Nothing, that is, that was anything like you. They looked self-contained. They all had abilities and interests from which you were completely excluded, they were strangers, lives of their own, i.e. not yours. Aliens. What with three holidays, four weeks, four weeks, and seven weeks, and a long weekend at Whitsun on top, most of a boarder's life had nothing to do with home except when Mum or Dad wrote a letter, they couldn't come on a visit, take far too long in the War without a car. When you went home you were a stranger to other kids your own age, they thought it was funny you went to a place called Brood if they remembered, and you got tired of explaining. Phil would ride the Outer Circle bus round Brum, took all day, Mum'd pack a lunch for him, a sandwich, and an apple. If I could I'd go stay with friends from School, the odd weekend, like Norman Laycock in West Bromwich, or Robin Salmon at Agardesley Park Farm near Sudbury. You had to make new friends, break into settled circles or make friends anew.

At home in Brum or Rugby I was afraid of being laughed at or looked down on, had to wear School Uniform because that was all I'd got for clothes – flannel shorts, grey; long-sleeved shirt, grey; School tie, grey, with green stripes; green School blazer, green and grey badge on the pocket; School cap, green, with a solid silver badge sewn on above the visor; School socks, grey wool with a double green stripe where you turned the top down to hide your black garters; black leather shoes – and boarders weren't allowed to wear anything else, at School or in the village. But village kids, like Gerald Wakelam or like Ivor Williams from Codsall four miles down the road, they had sports-jackets, and they wore them at weekends or even in the evening! I remember the shock the first time I saw Gerald in a grey herringbone jacket, in Term time. His dad ran the cycle shop in the village square, and he'd help out some Saturdays. Boarders had to wear School Uniform during the Term, even when I was sixteen, wearing long trousers, still had to wear my School cap whenever I left the School grounds, you'd get Gated if you didn't. "Prefects have to set an Example!" But the daykids went home every day, had tea, ate supper, could go for bike rides in the evening. They came to School after their Mum had cooked breakfast (even if it was only cornflakes, and what horrible grey cardboard they were in the War – but you didn't know what they'd had), they brought exotic sandwiches for Break or for mid-day – cold toast and bacon! the pungent smell of cold toast wafting out of somebody's satchel filling the room, we boarders never got toast – had games to play (indoors and out), friends to visit, other people's houses to go to at weekends, family, grown-ups they could actually talk to, listen to and even take part in adult conversations, go to soccer games, trips to the pictures. They could talk to girls, in the village and at home. They were mostly country folk, quite a few of them farm labourer's or local shopkeeper's sons or – more of them – farmer's sons (like some of the boarders), and they had relatives all over the place, went visiting, high tea on Sundays, perhaps; a game of ha'penny nap after with all the relatives and friends, celery sticks in a jamjar of water on the tea table next to the salt. "Would you like another piece of cake, Bill?" They knew each other's mothers! They had dogs, and cats. Jeff Hayward would know Jake Bickerton's pet canary. They could go to town on the bus, watch the Wolves at Molineux Football Ground, do a jigsaw puzzle on a Sunday morning. They'd all grown up together, gone to the same village school before coming here, roamed the fields and woods summer and winter, fought and played, knew each other, knew each other's sisters (and later, perhaps, married them). And what you saw, when you looked into their eyes, was that knowledge, that world they shared with all manner of mysterious folk and animals and each other. Dayboys. Living with mum and dad and family, not to be trusted – and in School they belonged to a different House, Kempson or Parke.

After we'd all got back to school at the end of my first Half-Term holiday, a new kid turned up in the dorm after supper, all of us as usual in a hurry to get up to bed after clattering up the concrete stairs but we bottlenecked at the door *There's somebody new in here, never seen him before* sitting on that bed by the washbasins, it hadn't been anybody's bed pretty well since I'd come to Brewood, it'd been a great place to put things or to sit and wait to clean your teeth and now this kid I'd never seen before, sitting in his pyjamas, wide blue-striped flannel so neat and tidy they were obviously brand new, his toothbrush in his hand next to a sponge-bag on the bed. I didn't notice him at first, a cluster of kids round his bed they weren't even getting undressed *What are they doing over there?* that wasn't anybody's bed it was empty, Alan Franks had escaped it when Morris West left, so many people sat on it drying themselves or cleaning their teeth it always got into a damp mess towels and wet flannels left on it or on its locker West'd had to keep defending it, fighting people off, none of us'd liked him very much, and somebody said "What's your name then?" and that's when I noticed him, just a slight little bloke small delicate bones and neat black hair, big brown eyes, real tidy-looking kid, neat.

"Prince?" somebody said as I came closer, "What sort of a name is *that*?" and just as he said "That's my name" in a strangulated sort of surprised voice somebody else said "We can't call you *that*! Everybody'd think you're Royalty!" and laughed, "too big for your boots!" and another voice, somebody close to the kid's bed, asked "What'll we call him then?" chiming with someone else's "We've got to give him a name, we've got to call him *some*thing!" And the next moment we were all talking at once loud and scornful as if he wasn't there. "He doesn't look like any Prince I ever saw," "I dunno, look at those posh pyjamas, they're not like mine!" and we all laughed, after a few weeks of dormitory life ours were all rumpled and worn they'd been through the School Laundry so many times, not that the School had a laundry really it just sent them out to be done, once somebody's pyjamas had come back all starched and stiff and uncomfortable, we'd all laughed. This kid's pyjamas looked like that. He shifted a bit and looked up at us and then away "He looks *winsome*" somebody said, "Yeh, 'e does doesn't 'e, just like a bloomin' *girl*!" and somebody laughed. "Look at 'is eyelashes and those lovely lips, ooh-er, a Princess! 'e ought to be in the films" and the kid shrank a little into himself, sat without moving. "Not like Princess Margaret though!" We all liked her, "Lovely rosy cheeks" another laughed, and the kid went a bit pink. Somebody nudged me and whispered "He looks like a bird really, doesn't he." He pulled himself upright and turned, at a loss, to put his toothbrush in his sponge-bag, his eyes blinking, eyelashes dark with wet, "Just a little bird" came a voice and then "That's what he is, he's a bird! We'll call him birdie!" goodness knows who said that, we all took up the general cry we chanted "Birdie! Birdie! Birdie! Birdie! Birdie!" over and over and he turned back towards us his back absolutely straight an uncertain trembly smile he looked at all of us his eyes moist he hadn't said a word since that once and started to climb into bed "Yeh, that's what we'll call you" and "Now you've got a name" and "That's who you are, you're Birdie." We began to drift to our beds all pleased with ourselves as the Prefect came in and said "Come on you lot! it's way past Lights Out! You should have been in bed ages ago and you're not even undressed! Get on with it." And after we'd all settled down in the dark, faint light through the ventilators up on the wall, somebody said "Good night, Birdie" in a relaxed sort of tone and then somebody else "Good night Birdie," and I lay there wondering how he'd managed to get through all that, he'd been so dignified, it was fantastic he'd hardly even twitched, all of us shouting at him. "You're all right, Birdie" somebody said. He hadn't even cried, we couldn't make him cry. "Yeah," we all said, "G'night." One of us.

11
Chocolate

One night no more than two or three weeks later, the usual quiet chatter after Lights out and most of us only half-awake, Ron Malpas said "Keep the noise down you guys, it's after Lights Out. But listen, I've heard the Second Dorm might raid us tonight, we'll have to be ready for 'em if we can!" and Henry or somebody like him, under the window anyway, said "Who is? What d'you mean?" I was wide awake, thinking of Mum and Dad at home talking quietly or listening to the nine-o'clock news with Phil and me tucked up in bed *What on earth are they talking about?* And right behind my pillow it sounded like, the other side of that blocked door, a soft scraping sound, a slight bump against the plank wall, a suppressed giggle, and a *ssssh!!* the sound carrying the way whispers do, *everyone must've heard that!* but I nudged Brian in the next bed anyway and whispered "someone's out there!" and we strained to hear. A door softly closed down the corridor, the pad of a foot, a quick stumble, more feet, and then *BLAM!* the door flung back against Alan's bedside locker the muffled *thud* of the locker against the bed shook him up he'd almost been asleep, some kid from the Second Dorm slammed his pillow into Alan's face, tried to anyway but couldn't do much the door was in the way, a silent bunch of kids from the Second Dorm boiling their striped pyjamas into the room pillows flailing, down the room between the rows of beds, soft thumps as they jumped from bed to bed flailing away, some of us scrambled from under the covers whirling our pillows, Morris West leapt out of bed and shouted "Get 'em!" and charged at a bunch of them, scrambling his pillow in a fierce arc *He'd been ready for them!* and some of the kids on the window side of the dorm ganged up together and charged, drove the invaders out, "Chase 'em! Come on, get after them!" but as you got out of the door there was a whole clump of them ominously staring back down the corridor at us, red-faced and derisive, big-looking.

We hesitated, Martin Franks said "Don't be daft! It's just pillows!" and he charged at them, the rest of us crowding behind him narked and laughing, all of us breathless, feet sclabbering away on the floor you didn't want to get trodden on bare feet or no, and *Slam!* went the Second-Dorm door, one of us trapped behind it, Tom Fearnley, in there with them, a prisoner, bangs and thumps and shouts and laughing, we couldn't open the door a bed pushed against it too many kids jammed up against it, you'd push and it'd open an inch or two and then slam shut *Don't get your fingers caught!* shouting and thumps, bangs and crashes *Ouch! Gerroff!* the door suddenly opened but only a bit Tom scrambling as they pushed him out his face bright red he didn't have his pillow any more he'd lost his pyjama jacket and we all piled up against the door but we couldn't budge it, we didn't know what to do it was no good hanging about here and anyway it was too cold for that, we stood helplessly about all speechless shifting from foot to foot, quiet peeling sounds of slightly tacky feet shifting on the cold lino, waiting and someone said "I dunno about you lot but I'm going back to bed" and we all trooped back puffing and panting, full of palsied beans, it was no good there was no way we'd just go back to sleep, heart and breath pounding away, and then there was Fearnley and Franks and West going out the door to see if they could raid the Second Dorm back and get his pillow and we all watched and wondered, sitting up in bed all on edge except Gravette, he'd rolled his blankets round him pulled his pillow over his head "Quit it!" he said, "No! I want to go to sleep!" We couldn't hear anything at all from the corridor, not a sound, then the soft scrape of a pillow or a pyjama jacket dragging along the wooden corridor wall, a light footfall and then a shout and a bang, Fearnley and Franks and West going at it like mad and Hart shouted "Come on! Up the First Dorm! Get their mattresses! Grab their clothes!" and we were off, even Gravette's lanky soft body galumphing along behind us and suddenly there's Alan flailing back towards us, Morris and Tom scrambling along, all of us in full retreat

Watch out! they've put shoes in their pillowcases! to the safety of the dorm.

I thought of a pillowcase swung round the head and then *WHAM!* a shoe in it, that'd knock you flying, the noise was terrific, and what about your teeth, *oh no!* so I scrambled under the bed Alan somehow closed the door I clung to my mattress nobody was going to steal *that*, other kids flailing around me in their pyjamas so close together they couldn't really get a hefty whack in and I just hid all out of breath thinking about shoes and the door swung open, the sound of shoeleather on lino the light clicked on. Along under the beds a pair of pressed grey flannel trousers just above ankle level polished black shoes just inside the door. "What's going on here? You! Stop that!" as Fearnley swung a pillow he'd somehow stolen from the Second Dorm, he couldn't stop the swing his face blank as sudden silence, complete and motionless, breathless, a consternation, one quick loud panting breath a gasp a muffled furtive clump as was it Malpas lowered his pillowcase *had he put a shoe in his?* behind him, sheets stripped off beds tangled and messed, dressing-gowns jumbled topsy-turvy, shoes all over the place, clothes scattered everywhere, one pair of bare feet scampering down to the Second Dorm. I peered out, I slowly stood up hoping not to be seen, my bed a shambles. An appalled silence.

Mr Bailey.

There were only supposed to be eight of us, and all in bed, all fast asleep, but there were over a dozen, tousle-haired and sweaty-red, panting and shocked, some of us in only half of our pyjamas, everyone crestfallen looking guilty, not daring even to lift their feet, pillowcases clumping to the floor, but there was nothing you could say. A panic-stricken "Nicks!" from down the corridor, "It's Mr Bailey!" the sound of climbing into bed in Second Dorm, creaks, cautious whispers, light clicking out. You couldn't say "Nothing Sir" you couldn't say you'd come to find something or to ask about your Prep, that would be daftly idiotic even if you could think of it. There was no possible excuse, how could you say you were going to the lavatory, that was the only reason to be out of bed; no one had an excuse, and into that awful silence he said "Gravette! Go to my

Study. Hanging on the wall behind the door you'll find my cane. Bring it!" "Oh no uncle," Gravette said, and we all looked at him. *Uncle?* "Please," said Gravette. "Please, uncle." "Fetch it! At Once!" Gravette didn't even put his slippers on, didn't dare. "You other boys go back to your own dormitory. I'll see to you when I'm finished here." And there we all were.

"Line up," he said, "Smaller ones first." And then, "No. Malpas. You first:" – pointing to Ron – "In your position you should know better, you're supposed to be in charge. Put your hands on this chest of drawers," he said, *"flat.* And bend over." I was littlest but somehow I came third, and Ron walked up as we shuffled into position, a whole line of kids in front of the chest of drawers "Stand back to give room, boy!" Mr Bailey said. "Mind my back-swing!" and Ron bent over as Mr Bailey flexed his cane with its tip in his left hand. It looked just like the ones in the comics, thin and whippy and pale yellow the colour of straw with a curved hook of a handle nestling firmly round his hand, and he said "Straighten your legs child, don't slouch!" and Ron straightened an abrupt tight little upward hump and a sharp thin *Whack!* you could hear the cane singing in the air and *Whack!* and Ron flinched a little jerk I grimaced and as he recovered the cane came down again and then again. We watched Ron as he straightened up his face as red as red could be, blinking like mad his hands at his sides. "Get into bed, boy. Next!" Waiting was a sickish trembling sweat, standing there in line in your pyjamas knowing you were for it, but Ron had stood up straight, like in the Army, and hadn't made a sound, so did the next, so I did too, you had to be brave, *Bend over!* and the evenly-paced *Whack! Whack! Whack! Whack!* left ridges across the bum, great welts, one just at the top of my right leg, the tip of the cane whipped round you, flicked like a bite, *unnngh,* hard into the skin, sharp needle's slap and you waited for the next, that really hurt, *slap!, slap!,* much fiercer than the whacking on your buttocks and you bit back tears and blinked and didn't rub your bum until you got into bed you didn't dare, what would the others think, your rear end wide awake, tingling, you were proud you didn't cry, choking it back. But when it got to his turn Gravette started to cry and said "No, uncle, no!" before he'd even got there and cried aloud, bawled and snivelled his way back to bed rubbing his bum and crying out again his snotty face and we all turned our backs on him, such a baby. What had being his uncle got to do with anything.

"Gravette *cried!*" we said next day to everyone as they stood around wanting to hear all about it, and we sneered at him. But Shag Callahan or one of the other Prefects said, when he heard, that he wasn't surprised Gravette'd cried. "Pussy hit him harder than the rest of you, didn't he? Bound to've done, he can't show favouritism, and Pussy *is* his uncle." And that rankled too, what a twerp for not telling us that! But Shag hadn't known that either, till we told him. "No," Shag said, "don't be so silly. What would you think of some kid if he came up and said to you Pussy was his uncle? Putting on side like that?" But what a sissy for crying. "Oh stop it," he said, "you kids are hopeless! Think what it'd be like if you were in his shoes! You'd do the same. Leave it be."

But we didn't, of course, and as I look back now, thinking of him as I write this, his perhaps astonished fearful cry *No, Uncle!*, I wonder that I never felt ashamed of the way we treated him, paying him no attention, refusing to be friends. We never learned anything about him, where he lived or what his dad did, he might have been in the Army or something, not that we ever shared that kind of information; he might even have been killed in the War, and after that Term we never saw him again, he went to some other school and none of us asked where he'd gone. But of course next day he must have hurt just as much as the rest of us, and most of us spent a lot of the next day standing up. I know I did, rubbing myself tenderly, on a radiator if I could for its warm comfort, the wooden chairs and desks so hard, and one of the dayboys smirked a bit and said the best thing to do if you're going to get whacked is stuff a few sheets of blotting paper down your trousers, "You can hear ordinary paper," he said, "it echoes, and he makes you take it out and then he whacks you again, only harder. And a book's no good you can see it." I only ever got caned again once, it must have been five years later, Mr Bailey long gone, it was with Broggie, the next Headmaster, and I didn't have the chance to pad my behind then, either.

I can still conjure that terrible panicky helpless feeling when I knew it was coming up, not so much my stomach plunging down to my boots as a great wave flooding up through me from the floor, my stomach tottering, my legs not doing what I wanted shaky no longer mine, my lips blurry I didn't dare even try to speak open my mouth, a detached numbness almost taking over, not really me, not there, mouth dry, sweaty palms, sphincter edgy, eyes unfocussed can't look at anything as they wander, but the floor steady through it all, and the wall, the firmness all outside. Allen Fisher in 2003 told me that he got caned sometime around 1960, at Battersea Grammar School because he got caught reading Jack Kerouac's *The Subterraneans*, he'd borrowed it from the public library, and I think that's a pretty monstrous thing to do to a kid, whack him for reading a book, especially a book like that, about on par with Basil Bunting in 1916 or so almost getting expelled from school when one of the Teachers came across him one Sunday crossing out all the unnecessary words in Shakespeare's sonnets, he confiscated the book, but I can't think that Ken and Taffy and me were anything like that enterprising and imaginative. Broggie hardly ever caned anybody, you had to do something really really wrong like when Jeremy Ascough it must've been a couple of years after the War climbed out of the Third Dorm window way after we'd all gone to bed and scampered across the roof and rang the School bell *clang! clang! clang!* in the middle of the night, he must've rung it for a good minute and then scarpered back across the roof and back into bed, he'd hardly got there when the dorm door opened and Broggie walked in flicked the lights on made all of us quake and simply said "Ascough! See me in my study in the morning. After breakfast" and walked out again, didn't say another word *How did he know?*

With Ken Hatton and Taffy Evans and me, we'd probably been caught out-of-bounds or taunting Nunc or something as ordinary as that but persistent. Broggie announced after Prayers that we had to come to his Study immediately, we knew we were in for it. When we got there he told us he would have to cane us and told Ken to come in and shut the door, the sound of Broggie's voice with me and Taffy stood outside listening to the *Whack! Whack! Whack!* as Broggie administered six of the best. A brief silence, the murmur of voices. Then the door opening, Ken, blond hair falling over the side of his red face. We didn't look at each other, and it was my turn. Broggie standing there with his cane in his hand, it wasn't like Pussy Bailey's it was heavier, dark brown, but just as whippy, and he said "Bend over that chair. Lift the tail of your jacket clear," and after he'd given me six, all evenly spaced, well aimed as well as timed, I didn't make a sound and nor had Ken, he said "Stand up" in an indifferent sort of neutral voice and reached across his desk, picked up a box of chocolates and said "Well taken!" and he smiled. "You deserve a chocolate," me blinking the welling moisture, catching my breath, wanting to get out of there fast. Cadbury's *Dairy Box* brand new, one chocolate gone, I didn't notice which I chose I just took one I was so astonished, anxious to get through the door said *thank you* in a strangled sort of voice, and "Yes, Sir," he opened the door and I left. I didn't look at Taffy but just left, my awkward walk. Ken was nowhere around I didn't want to see him anyway, not yet, went and washed my face could feel the welts through my trousers. None of us talked about it together, not then nor ever, just shoved it to the back of the mind. It was nothing to talk about, really, except somebody said, nod of fellow-feeling, one of those kids who was always getting whacked or so it looked to us, "Did 'e give you a chocolate?"

There really wasn't very much caning and with Mr Bailey it was hard to tell what you would get caned for, it had to be a terrible misdemeanour. With only the Headmaster or if necessary the Assistant Headmaster allowed to do it it existed more as deterrence than as punishment, and at the same time it invested Mr Bailey with great Authority, he never spent any time with the boys, mostly left us to our own devices, we had no idea what sort of bloke he was, he was remote especially to us young ones but nobody wanted to be drawn to his attention, and you certainly didn't want to invite his disapproval. But getting whacked for that dormitory raid in the first Term didn't stop us from having a Midnight Feast in the third, though we were terribly careful about it, we didn't want to get whacked again. I've no idea how it came up, but we all knew about Midnight Feasts, we'd read descriptions of them in places like Billy Bunter books and comics like *Hotspur*, now and again some uncle or family friend who hadn't seen you for a while on being told you were going to Boarding School would smile jovially and ask "Had many Midnight Feasts yet?" or tell us "That's what you do in dormitories," and follow it up with a "Don't get caught or you won't half get into trouble!" but they made it sound like an adventure, and one night in the third Term, it can't have been a weekend night unless it was a Sunday because Willy Pratt was there, he went home every weekend, and he brought the potato crisps, a whole tin full of packets of crisps, his dad owned a factory in Wolverhampton, and he sent along a whole case of orange pop as well, twelve bottles of it in a wooden case, smuggled it upstairs somehow, p'raps his dad helped when he brought him back to School in the delivery van and carried it up himself, Willy put all of it under his bed shoved up against the wall, being a weekly boarder he didn't have a trunk at the foot of his bed. We'd all of us saved our pocket money, every Wednesday after lunch we'd go to Mr Bailey's Study and he'd give us thruppence for the week, older boys got sixpence, and enter it in a book, I thought it was so he'd know he'd given it us but Our Kid said it was so he could send Mum and Dad the bill, just like there was a one and a penny item on the Term bill, that was a penny a week for the Church collection but I never knew about that till Mike Blackman wrote me about it when he lent me an old School Magazine in 2001, "One-and-a-penny gravely recorded in the accounts at the end of every Term," he laughed, "church collection." Jimmy Osborne'd told him I was writing this, it never occurred to me that Mum and Dad had to pay for everything and Dad never showed us any of the bills, or talked about them or about money, none of our business, and I never thought about it till now, didn't even take it for granted. I knew about the pocket money of course, because some kids got a shilling, their parents had arranged that with the Headmaster, that was a huge amount of money.

We saved up our pocket money for weeks, along with our sweet coupons, and we kept coming back again and again to what we should get and how much it would cost, and every now and then somebody would remember something we'd all forgotten, like *do we need plates*, or *what'll we drink out of*? Harry's mum told him we should keep it simple, *You don't need plates, how're you going to wash them up? Use a page out of your notebook! or just use your notebook. Smuggle stuff out of the Dining Hall. You can't have jelly or tinned fruit – if you're lucky enough to find some! – nothing like that* but somebody said he could try and get some sausage rolls from the butcher shop in the village, that'd be Fatty Gwilt's dad, and when it came time for the Feast it turned out we'd all got a terrific lot of stuff, piles of it. Ron and Tom and I had stood outside the baker's window for ages that day after school eying the cakes in the window worrying over how much they cost and what kind to get, Tom wanted a chocolate Swiss Roll and I wanted one with cream and jam in it, it wasn't real cream of course not in the War, but I liked it anyway, and Ron had his eye on what he called a French sponge, and while we were mucking about trying to make our minds up somebody from the village went in and bought the chocolate one, it was the last there was. "Here," Tom said, "we'd better get cracking or we won't get anything!" so we tossed for it, I said *heads* and it came up tails so we went in and asked for the French Sponge, the woman gave us a smile as we took off our School caps and asked about the cake, she said "Somebody's birthday, is it?" and I said "No" just as Tom said "Yes" and he gave me a look and I went red, and she smiled again, real amused, and said only it was almost a whisper as she leaned forward "Are you planning a midnight feast then?" We didn't know what to say to that, but Ron pulled himself up a bit and looked out the door, gave a bit of a nod without really giving it away and she said "I wonder if I can find a box for it" and went into the back.

    Of course after Lights Out it was impossible to go to sleep, we were all obviously excited when Matron came to turn off the light she must have known something was up, all the toothbrushes nice and tidy by the washbasins, and all the spongebags hanging up where they were supposed to be, not the way they usually were. "Have you washed behind your ears?" she asked and looked round at all of us, she was much more particular than usual, me, and I expect everyone else, praying like mad she wouldn't get it into her head to have a look under Pratt's bed where all those bottles of pop were, he'd moved the potato crisps to his locker they hardly fit in there were so many packets terrible crumpling noise as he pushed them in *I hope they didn't break to smithereens* and she went over to Blondie's bed and then turned away and tugged at Harry's ears in the next bed over to have a look and he just squirmed a bit and said "Ow" and "Yes, Miss, I really scrubbed them" and she asked "Whose flannel is this on the floor? Hang it up. Be quick about it!" and somebody or other got out of bed and did what she said. The rest of us all just lay there in bed shifting about a bit all restless and impatient, nobody saying anything unless he was talked to, all the usual chatter just gone, everyone quiet, and she gave us a look as she went to the door and said "You make sure you go to sleep now!" and smiled round the room, "No mischief!" and turned the light out. "Good night, boys!"

After we chorused our reply none of us said anything, not like other nights when we'd usually gossip and chatter a bit or play some sort of word game for a while before settling down. We just lay there staring at the patches of light shining on the ceiling through the ventilator, and after a while somebody said, "What time is it?" and somebody else said "The Third Dorm hasn't come up yet." They didn't have to go to bed till half-past eight, you could hear them talking away in the Billiard Room which was right underneath us, and we just lay there waiting and waiting, how long were they going to be? A hoarse whisper, "Hey Pratt, chuck us a packet of crisps," and we had a furtive whispered argument about how we couldn't start yet, somebody said "Did anybody bring a knife" and a small chorus of voices said to a lot of *ssssh*ing that they'd pinched one from the Dining Hall. Blondie Hart said in an almost ordinary tone of voice "Hey, you lot, keep it quiet! My Dad says whispering carries for miles! Just speak in a low voice" and Birdie said "Yeh, it'll sound like Ron snoring!" and we all giggled, "they won't notice that!" We just lay there and lay there and Harry said "I don't know how she missed it, but I left my knife on my locker, she must've seen it, I bet she knows what we're doing" but Blondie said "your locker's always such a mess nobody'd ever see anything on it. Your snot rag's still there, I can see it!" and somebody giggled, "Going to cut the cake with a snotty knife?" and we all chortled a bit, even Harry. And then we just lay there and lay there, we lay there forever, and at last a door opened downstairs voices suddenly louder, a laugh or two, "Come on, hurry up! It's bedtime," a door closed, clatter of shoes, feet and talk coming up the cement stairs, the patch of light on the ceiling suddenly sharp and bright as a light turned on, chatters and mutterings and the sound of running water and the bright patch on the ceiling turned pale, the Third Dorm slow settling into the night, quiet, the Fourth and Fifth Dorms coming up ten minutes later, quieter, and a tiny whisper from the corner *Red leather yellow leather red leather yellow leather* "Who's that?" A hissed *shurrup you fool!* "I'm just trying to pass the time, do you know any tongue-twisters?" A bed creaking as someone turns over and a quiet voice said "Hey, that's not a bad idea. D'you know this one? Shut up the shutters and sit in the shop?" a quiet gurgle, *w-h-a-a-t?* and what popped into my head was *Polish it behind the door,* I giggled, a faint susurrus of whispering round me and a voice from the corridor, "You boys go to sleep! It's ten o'clock!" *It's Matron!* and Willy Pratt said in a sleepy-sounding voice, bless his heart, "Yes Miss" with a loud yawn. And we just lay there tossing about, Martin said, "I bet it's not ten o'clock, nothing like!" and we lay there and lay there and lay there all this bubbling up going on inside, how could you sleep with all that glee.

Wait.

Wait.

And wait some more. Lie on your stomach, listen to the wind in the monkey puzzle tree, lie on your back, roll over, hang your arm over the edge of the bed, wonder why the window's rattling, pummel your pillow, back on your stomach again, swing your arm back and forth trying to reach the floor, yawn, turn over. Somebody walking down the corridor, a light at last clicking off outside, just a dim glow through the ventilator, drifting off, nice snuggled up *mustn't go to sleep,* warm blanket tucked round my ears, quiet, dark. And *Ouch! Gerroff!* big rustle of paper *What d'you think you're doing?* and there was Harry clambering about on Alan's bed, frantic whispers, *Hold me up, Alan!* standing on the bedstead reaching up, crackle of stiff paper, Blondie flashing a torch in their direction *Point it at the floor you doofus!* and I could see Harry pinning a big sheet of paper over the ventilator, he'd brought it from art class, "Watch out!" he said, "I dropped a drawing pin" and "Hope it's not in my bed" Alan said, somebody giggled, and there were Ron and Tom covering the other ventilator. *Alright, it's OK now!* that was Willy, *We can start now*, a flurry of activity and giggles and murmurs as we pulled our tartan rugs off our beds and spread them on the floor, three or four torches going, mine so feeble there was just a faint glow, the bike shop in the Square hadn't had any batteries they were always in short supply and even if you could find one they cost a lot, rustling sounds, bumps *Here, give us a knife!* crinkle of crisp packets suddenly loud as somebody undid the twist of salt and shook the packet to spread it about, *hey! not so loud!* all of us fidgeting away half-on half-off our rugs trying to keep clear of the cold lino, dressing gowns dragging and drooping as you hunted your socks out, draggy scraping noise as Willy hauled the pop from under his bed, clink of pop bottles, *Blimey! 'Oo's got an opener* scuffling sound of Alan coming up with his fancy knife it'd got everything on it, scissors, nailfile, screwdriver, corkscrew, pig-sticker, three blades, it was a smashing knife, even a bottle-opener, "Made in Switzerland," he'd told us proudly, "My Dad got it when he went there before the War," gurgle of pop being drunk. All of us just munching away, all of us on edge, listening for noises from outside, and Harry as usual stirring about and restless. He suddenly said "Hey did you hear this joke? It was in the *Beano*" and as he said it we heard a door close, *Nicks!* we all froze, off went the torches, you didn't dare breathe, a bit of cake halfway to my mouth, my hand poised in midair, what good that'd've done if anybody'd come in I didn't know, the bog flushed, a door opened, footsteps down the corridor towards the Third Dorm, bare feet not slippers, mutter of a deep voice, a door closing again, and we all breathed a bit. A soft clatter followed by a quiet *glug* and then another, and Birdie said *Oh no!* quite loud, he'd knocked his pop over, he was a really fastidious kid, always looked neat, it'd spilled all across his rug, and Harry got up he was closest to the washbasins and threw him a towel "That'd better not be mine" Tom said as Birdie tried to mop it up. "I'll rinse it out," he told him "you can use mine tomorrow," but whose was it? I felt a bit disgruntled about that, we none of us used each other's towels, that was like using each other's toothbrushes or wearing somebody else's dirty underwear, and in the middle of a chuckle Willy yawned *I wonder what time it is.* Martin peered at his watch in the gloom, he was the only one of us had one, and then "'Alf a mo'," he said. "No, give us a bit of light" and as he looked he leaned back, a small crunch behind him as he sat on a bunch of ladyfingers, crumbly dry powder all over the rug next his bum, and then "I dunno, I think it must've stopped," and he held it to his ear, "No, it's still ticking. It's just after twelve" and we couldn't believe it, it was hardly even midnight, some kids' parents wouldn't've gone to bed yet. My bum was getting a bit numb from sitting on the floor and I looked round at the others, there were crisp packets and bottle caps and empty bottles and bits of paper and cutlery, crumbs and broken ladyfingers and stuff all over the place, there was a sausage roll over by Birdie's foot, someone'd contrived to get some, and us without ration books, who managed that I wonder *Crikey! We'll have to clean all this up before we go to bed* and suddenly I gave a great big yawn and stretched my arms out, Birdie looked at Willy and Blondie said "I think I'm going to sleep" and as we gathered up our rugs to put them back on our beds munching at bits and pieces of stuff as we cleared up there was a loud clatter as a couple of knives and a full bottle of pop fell to the floor and we froze, all the torches off, listening, proud sort of giggle bubbling up barely held down, my heart pounding away my mouth chock full of sausage roll and my feet getting colder and colder. *Okay,* somebody whispered, I took a quick swig to get it down, and Ron turned his torch back on, rushed sleepy exhilaration, we stuffed all the rubbish any old how into our lockers, frantic that we'd been heard yet wanting to chirp. The floor was cold, and so was I.

In the morning Matron just banged on the door and opened it a bit to get us up, she didn't even stick her head round the door, *Come on! Rise and shine! We're a bit late this morning! You'll have to hurry even if you* are *tired!* and there was a big sticky patch in the middle of the floor where Birdie had spilled his pop. There were still bits of crisp packets and stuff all over the place, mostly under the beds. "Hey!" Willy said, "look!" and he held up three twists of blue paper, one of them open, "I've got salt all over my bottom sheet!" and we laughed, but the floor when I got out of bed was all gritty too, salt and crisp crumbs sticking to my feet. "That's it!" Alan said, "That's enough adventure for me!" but he grinned as he flinched his feet across the room to the washbasins, his slippers in his hands. "I'm going to wash my feet before I put anything on them! I don't want to walk about on salt and crisps all day, get it in my socks and shoes" and while some of us washed, the rest of us scurried about trying to tidy everything up *We should do it again* we said, it was a terrible mess really even after we'd finished, we didn't have a dustpan or a broom or anything like that, and Birdie picked up his tartan rug and grimaced it was all soggy and sticky at one end, "I'll wash it after breakfast" he said, and we shrugged. We were all a bit droopy after too little sleep, and everything felt strange, the room was different now, it was really ours. And at Breakfast Mrs Grant looked us over, and said "Smithe, you look as though you've been dragged through a hedge backwards" and Martin came over all innocent, "I know you boys have been up to something, I don't want to know what, but you'd better not get caught, and you'd better pull your socks up or you'll get in trouble," and up at High Table the Housemaster gave us a sidelong glance and Mr and Mrs Bailey studiously ignored us. We all grinned and felt a bit sheepish, pure little lambs, and she laughed. "It's a good thing it's me," she said as a murmur drifted over from High Table, "and not a Prefect, who gets you up in the morning. But don't take advantage!"

There are rules, and there are rules. "Play up!" we read that morning, in class, Sir Henry Newbolt. "Play up! and play the game!"

12

Keeping Mum

When I'd first arrived in September, ages ago, that first morning with all us boarders there together for the Term, a loud voice at the seniors' table'd said at breakfast that New Kids had to fag for the Seniors and especially for the Prefects, "Didn't you know?" and laughed, "You'd better not get Russell, he does terrible things to his fags" but he wouldn't say what, "You don't want to get caught in the Prefects' Sitting Room, not with a fire lit and they can close the door!" You couldn't get into the building or out of it without passing that small room just inside the boarders' entrance, and I had visions of Flashman bullying his way through *Tom Brown's School Days, Would they burn me? Torture me just for fun?* but somebody at our table said "Don't be daft" in a low voice, "he's pulling your leg. You're too small anyway," and next day Brian Holland, a New Boy in the Third Form, he'd be about ten or even perhaps eleven, older than me by quite a bit, was sent by a Prefect to buy him a bottle of pop at Mrs Roberts's tuck shop just down the road from the Gates and the Housemaster was really cross, "You don't deserve to be a Prefect at all if you behave like that, it's a complete abuse of your authority!" And that was all that happened, nobody did any fagging for anyone after that, nobody forced kids to run errands or give something up the way they did in *Tom Brown's School Days*, at least not openly, and fagging just disappeared if it'd ever gone on in the first place.

But I wasn't the only smaller kid whose vague sense of dread made him sneak past that door, those Prefects were so much bigger. I never dared glimpse inside if it was even half open, we'd all read too much about Prefects and bullies in stories about Greyfriars or Dotheboys Hall, and knew it went on in other schools. I felt a lot easier when Matron told us at bed time early in the Term, "Don't worry about it. Fagging doesn't happen here at all, it's not allowed, and don't you let *anybody* try it on, they'll get punished if they do. We've put a stop to that," and it was a bit of a shock at Break about a week later to see a new boy scurry back through the Gates from Mrs Roberts's and hand over a penny bag of sherbet to a bigger kid and I didn't know what to do. I told Our Kid and he shrugged. "I dunno, Pete" he said, and after that I kept my eyes peeled.

"Gibson's one of the worst" I heard one fourth former say, "'e can be a real terror if 'e gets you alone, especially if you've got any sweet ration left." But you didn't talk about it, if anything happened you just had to take it, you couldn't report it to a Master or any grown-up, it'd just make a kid like Gibson lie in wait for you once he found out, you knew he *would* find out, some other kid'd be bound to tell him to save his own skin, so you kept your mouth shut and put up with it. But we all knew who the bullies were, there were so few of them, we just kept clear. On more than one Saturday a bunch of us'd wait in Dirty Lane for the Second Eleven before the game started and you'd see a kid walking round the edge of the field over by the Spinney avoiding everybody, or going along the border of the drive. I'd been at Brewood for a couple of years or even more before I really began to notice something was going on and we none of us thought the Masters knew at all. Our Kid told me on the phone when we were talking about bullies and life at Brewood that when Brian Harley died in 1991 – he had become Professor of Geography at the University of Wisconsin and was the same age as Our Kid, quite a small lad, according to my brother, they were in the same Form – his friend Paul Laxton in the *Independent* talked about the "miserable treatment" Harley'd had at Brewood, and I wrote away and got a copy of Harley's obituary. What an "easy target" he must've been, Laxton wrote, "a country boy in hand-me-down clothes but with a sharp intellect." His parents didn't have much money, "impecunious" Laxton called them, and they weren't even his mum and dad really, they were just foster parents, the other kids certainly would've held that against him especially if he had any brains, he wasn't like the rest of us. Another obituary, in the *Times,* said a bit pompously that Harley had been "predisposed to champion the cause of those deprived and dispossessed by the establishment, whether of state, church, or social class." It suggested that his work on maps was as important as it was because he spoke "not only from what was in his fertile mind but also from the heart." When I was in my forties one of my colleagues in the English department talked in a meeting about the necessity for what he called "blooding" graduate students, I expect he had something in mind like what we did to Birdie Prince, giving them a hard time with impossible exams and hostile orals, *you've got to test them under fire*, he said, *make them think under pressure*, and there he was, the schoolboy bully all over again, but smugly self-satisfied, shoving something or other down people's throats, terrorizing. Small wonder, that jolt of recognition when I read *Great Expectations* later on, Pip screwed down so hard by Mrs Joe and that ass Pumblechook and then Estella.

But Our Kid and me were probably lucky; I know I was. A couple of days after School first started I walked into the Billiard Room, I had steel tips on the heels of my shoes so they wouldn't wear out so fast, *clink-clunk clink-clunk clink-clunk* really loud on the tile floor outside the door, one of them a bit loose, and this really big kid in a brown jacket, much older than me, he could have been one of the Teachers almost, stuck out his arm as I went in and said "You've got a heavy tread for somebody so small! What's your name?" and my voice got all wavery I couldn't tell if he was friendly or not, and I told him, and he said "How old are you?" and the other boys at that end of the room stopped talking and I told him and he said "You must be the Youngest Boy, then" and I said "Yes," I was about a year younger than the next youngest in the whole School, proud of the distinction but bothered too, there were other people listening, the whole room had gone quiet, everyone was looking, and he said, "Your brother's Phil isn't he?" and I said "Yes" and he said "Then you're Little Phil, aren't you!" and turned away dismissing me, but I didn't know it, to talk to somebody next to him, another big kid carving away at a piece of wood with a big clasp knife. I just stood there wondering what to do and a voice from the other side of the room said "Hey Little Phil come over here!" and somebody laughed. I slowly worried my way all round the billiard table *What've I done wrong?* keeping well away from someone leaning over the table to take a shot, he'd waited while Fatty called me over and quizzed me, and the name stuck, it would be a while before I got called Scat instead, and this kid said "Do you know who that was?" and I said "No" worrying I'd done something wrong, everybody around listening, and he said "That's Fatty Bullimore, he can beat anybody in the School in a fight except Bud Flanagan, that's who he's talking to" and I worried some more, and this kid said "You'll be alright, then," meaning that Fatty had taken me under his wing, and he was right, Fatty was a gentle bloke, but I didn't see that then, and for a couple of years I felt protected. There wasn't much bullying anyway, but most of us'd got the idea, mostly from school stories like *Tom Brown's School Days* and what we read in the Biggles books – we *devoured* them – that in an unruly world we all needed protecting from the villainous.

I'd get into fights, of course, kids always do, and I couldn't go twitting off to Fatty for anything like that, I couldn't go twitting off to Fatty at all anyway, wrong or right, but there was no need to, everybody knew Fatty had called me Little Phil, I'd got my nickname as easily as that. But I couldn't put on any side, you couldn't go twitting anyway, kids didn't tell on other kids, not to the Masters nor to older kids, you always shouted *Nicks!* if there was a Master coming, whether anybody was doing something wrong or not we all stuck together, you had to warn the other kids, let them know there was a grown-up around, or even a Prefect, and it was always funny to read that in other schools like ours, schools like Greyfriars or Dotheboys, kids called *Cavey!* as though that was the proper word for *Nicks!* We knew better and thought they were a bit sissy. We never queried such things, any more than we wondered why the Quad was called the Quad, we knew it stood for Quadrangle, but it was nothing like one really, it was just a sort-of oblong shape with two or three arms sticking out if you made a map of it, not a bit like the Quad you read about or at an Oxford college, square and tidy; it was years before I thought about it enough to realise that *Nicks* was really *Nix* and was Latin, like *Cave*, some sort of holdover from the time when everybody learned Latin and smaller boys were ruled by older boys and subject to their every whim. You just knew that if the Masters saw you enjoying what you were doing they might stop it.

Even that very first night in the dorm, Gravette snivelling away me wanting my Teddy-bear, I just knew everybody'd mock if you had a Teddy-bear at School, they'd taunt you relentlessly and play piggy-in-the-middle with it. None of the other kids'd brought theirs, you didn't dare even ask if they'd got one, you knew you'd probably pretend you didn't have one yourself if anyone asked, *what're they asking for?* Gravette was the only one who'd brought any fancy toys that you knew about, of course we'd all got a couple of Dinky Toys but only the little ones you could put in your pocket, cars or perhaps a model destroyer or spitfire, none of the big fancy things like lorries or Wimpeys, they were far too precious. When everybody got back to School you found out some of the older kids had brought things like Meccano sets and Totopoly, things with lots of pieces, they kept them in their lockers, games and toys like that were sacred, they really did belong to someone, you might've wished you'd got one yourself the way much later on we all wished we had Robin Rawlings's game of *Dennis Wheatley's Invasion!* that was obsessive, we'd play it for hours and hours, no one fooled about stealing them, or hiding them; like jigsaw puzzles, lose a piece of them and you were all losers. But Teddy-bears were fair game, they wouldn't last long at School. Nobody'd protect you if somebody snitched a Teddy-bear and tormented it, Fatty couldn't protect you from that, nor could anybody else, you just knew that without being told.

Or you found out soon enough. Poor Graham Harvey, one morning at Break a pair of kids came up while he was playing with a couple of Dinky Toys on the tarmac in a corner of the Quad and helped themselves, took them off him, we all knew he'd get them back when Break was over save he might have to scramble for them a bit, they weren't *thieves*. They started jeering at him for playing by himself they'd got his toys, he started shouting, lost his temper, flew at one of them and then there was a fight, Graham and one of the kids, and we all gathered round and started shouting the way kids do, a Master came up *What's going on? Stop this fight!* and we all fell silent. *What's this all about?* and Graham said "Please Sir they took my

Dinky Toys when I was playing with them," and after the Master broke it up and had gone away we all stood in a circle round Graham and chanted at him "Twit! twit! twit! twit! twit!" I was shouting with the rest "Twit! twit! twit! twit! twit! twit! twit!" louder and louder insistent heavy beat "Twit! twit! twit! twit! twit! twit! twit! twit! twit!" until he cried and the Master came back and sent us all away. It was really very frightening, and next day I said "hello" a lot of us did but didn't know what else to say to him we couldn't meet each other's eyes. He never did get a nickname.

Bud Flanagan was Black Irish, black black hair and blue blue eyes, compact build, he and Fatty were inseparable, he didn't speak to anyone hardly except Fatty that I remember, they'd sit and talk quietly together in what we all knew as their corner of the Billiard Room, Fatty's watchful bulky presence keeping a clear space around them, if you wanted to speak to Fatty you'd stand in front of him and Bud and wait till he noticed you. He always did, even if you had to wait for what felt like ages while he finished what he was saying to Bud, sometimes he'd simply look up and start talking to anybody near, ask you what you were doing or wanted, we liked him, but you didn't waste his time. Bud was mad about ships and the sea, "the open sea and the sky" is how Fatty put it, "a poem by John Masefield." Bud shook his head, "Not like being in a classroom" he said, "who'd want to be *there?*" and laughed a little. He couldn't wait to leave school so he could join the Merchant Navy, always reading about it, had pictures of ships in his pocket; always carving away at a model. Some evenings, after he'd done his Prep, or in the late afternoon and at weekends, he or one of the Seniors'd get permission to open up the woodworking shop and he'd be lost there, couldn't tear himself away from the big workbenches with their vices and clamps, racks for woodworking tools, glues and paint and varnishes and brushes and different kinds of saws and chisels and drills and planes, mallets and hammers and screwdrivers, precious in specially unlocked cupboards one end of the room, you weren't allowed to use any of them until you'd taken Woodwork, nobody in Prep School could work in there without an adult. I was too small to be allowed to go in at all. Bud would get a bit of four-by-four somewhere and other kids'd watch as he rough-cut it with a handsaw into the shape of a boat, following carefully measured pencil lines he'd drawn on the wood, he'd got them from books in the library, silhouettes from Talbot Booth or *Jane's All the World's Merchant Ships*, endlessly comparing the three-dimensional solidity of the wood against the flat two-dimensional plan of the paper. After that he'd carve it by hand, at first with a chisel holding the wood in a vice, but mostly with his clasp knife, he carried it everywhere, he'd sit quietly in his and Fatty's corner of the Billiard Room whittling away, sharpening it on his pocket stone, checking his carving with a pair of dividers from his geometry set, dozens of noisy shouting kids, sometimes all thirty or forty of us in that room arguing and laughing and playing, singing and talking. He'd quietly carve away at the hull and smooth it down with a bit of hard-to-find sandpaper or scrape carefully with a wood file. It was hard to watch him do all this because it didn't look as though *anything* was happening, he was so careful and patient, and we kept coming back to see.

Once the hull was done he'd find more scraps of wood and carve and build hatches and cabins and superstructure, tiny hinges and hasps and doorknobs, lamps and wheels and winches, he'd shave away at bits of dowelling to make masts and derricks, he'd paint all the parts, glue them together, nails and thread for deck rails and rigging, portholes scribed into the hull with minuscule rims put round them, cellophane for glass, absolutely exquisite detailed models of merchant ships, everything scrupulously to correct scale, painted in the proper colours, yacht-buff masts, black hulls painted red below the waterline, white superstructure, lines drawn on the deck for planking, stiff shaped-cardboard propellers, rudders that turned, funnels in the proper insignia for the shipping company. He'd mount it all on a wooden cradle, name on the stern and on the cradle, and stow it carefully somewhere, in his locker, or safe in a Master's keeping.

Our Kid told me a couple of months ago when I was reading this bit to him over the phone that Bud'd cried his eyes out his last day at School when he was sixteen, and that really surprised me, I still puzzle over that, his heart so clearly set on getting into the merchant navy and his *Who'd want to be in a classroom?* but he was such a fixture in Fatty's corner of the Billiard Room, it was so clearly *his* corner too, that I wonder at what he must've felt, ships and the sea pulling him one way and the friendships of school and his close companionship with Fatty pulling him another.

The first morning we came back to school in September 1943 Pussy Bailey told us all at Prayers in Big School that Bud Flanagan had sailed in a North Atlantic convoy in June, his ship had been torpedoed, and he was "missing at sea." Inescapable notice, that, read at Prayers and then posted outside the Masters' Common Room,

>   A.E. Conway, killed in action, North Africa.
>   Michael Flanagan, missing, North Atlantic.

Someone you knew even if only a little bit, however remote he was from us seven- and eight-year olds, was now dead from the War, or missing in action. Or a Prisoner-of-War. What we'd been reading about in the paper was suddenly *here*, where we were, in the Billiard Room and in the Quad and in the classroom. We'd have two minutes of silence at School Prayers, and the formality of it would tell you what you hadn't known. Bud's name was Michael, his nickname from the music-hall team of Flanagan and Allen a curious intimacy, *Michael* the estrangement insulating you from shock, him drowning, and I thought of brasswork and glossy paint, his boat models, where they were, what would happen to them.

That was about as close as the War got, out in the Staffordshire countryside, at least until December 1944, after Pussy Bailey'd got sent to jail and we got a new Headmaster. I went for the weekend to Robin Salmon's, his dad had a farm out near Uttoxeter at the end of a long lane off a secondary road, miles away from anywhere, much too far to walk to the nearest village if you'd got stuff to carry. Cold drizzle on Saturday afternoon we all piled into their sit-up-and-beg pre-War Austin his mum and dad in the front and us two ten-year-olds in the back, *Get your mac on,* his mum said and looked at my boots and nodded, *Yes, they'll do, wrap up warm,* Robin and I wondered where we were off to. *What we were talking about last night,* she said, *the explosion.* I wasn't any the wiser, but Robin said, "A farm blew up, it's gone, it's not there any more" and before I could ask anything else his dad said "It was an arms dump, a big explosion. It's not far away, up at Faulds, we thought we'd have a look," but we kept driving around, the two grown-ups peering through the steamed-up windows trying to find it along unmarked country lanes, some of the landmarks were missing, and at last his Dad said "I know that tree" just as his mum said "There's Whitcombs" so we just parked the car at the gate to a field *It's that way, the old gypsum mine, not far now* and I shivered a bit as we walked in the cold drizzle "You'll soon warm up," his mum said. It all sounded exciting when we started out, but as we got closer I got a bit nervous *Has it all been cleared up? I don't want to see any dead people* and my thoughts shied away from what it'd feel like if I did. *I'll not look,* I decided, but of course I would, you couldn't help looking, the way we all had after an Air Raid in Birmingham after we'd been allowed out of the shelter, a funny mix of hope and dread, hard to think about even if it was someone you'd never heard of *I've never seen a dead body. Except at the pictures, on the news.*

The four of us slowly drifted apart to make a raggedy line across a huge ploughed field, nothing growing, just bare wet dirt, not a sign of any mine or any factory, just mud and small pebbles, grey raggedy scraps that might be concrete, mired stodge, puddles. The furrows went every which way, not really furrows at all, not much in the way of trees or hedges they'd all been flattened, Robin's dad said he'd heard from one of the men that something like three inches of dust had fallen on the whole countryside *a thick blanket* but the rain had settled it, mud built up on my boots, heavy, clinging, when I tried to kick it off it just smeared and clung and spread, got worse and worse, nothing there to scrape it off, not even a stiff twig, utterly useless scraps of wood, my hands getting colder and wetter, my gloves a complete waste of time, rain trickling down my neck, my cap soaked, mud on my mac, puddles and rivulets of water to scramble across, "Not far now," Robin's mum said as I thought *We'll be here forever*, up ahead a handful of people standing at a wire fence where everything had been cordoned off *You can't get any closer*, pointing and talking. Someone said, "It's a hell of a crater, it must be half a mile across, they'll be clearing it up for months" and someone else said "It's a hundred yards deep, water at the bottom" but I couldn't believe that. It turned out later it was more like a hundred *feet*, but the thirty-odd yards those feet made still made a lot of hole, it's called the Hanbury Crater nowadays, more like what you'd see at a quarry but without the lorries and sheds, with that fence keeping us back there really wasn't anything to see, just churned up mud, empty land with a few flattened bits of trees and stuff, no wreckage, and as we turned to go back Robin drifted off a bit to my left or perhaps it was me to the right we got quite a bit apart and in my squelchy leap across some water to a small steep ridge of mud I looked over to see how he was doing and a rank and foul stink smacked across my face right from my feet as I landed, bits of dark muddy red stuff clinging to a long dirty bone wriggly white bits on it *Are those maggots?* a bit of hairy skin, edges pulled back, maggots again, dark red-black spills staining here and there. I couldn't look but couldn't *not*, and I wanted to cry out but didn't dare, I'd have to show it to the others *Hey, come and look at this!* and talk about it but the choking caustic in my mouth and throat paralysed my tongue and breath, my belly heaved as I tried to swallow my flooding spit.

By the time we got back to the car I'd told it anyway, and Robin said he saw it too, "Bet it was a cow leg," he said, "too big to be anything else." And his dad said "Hayes Farm's just *disappeared*," he said, "just *gone*, not a trace. *And* the reservoir." His mum said that's where the water came from that made it so muddy, and I wondered. "The whole thing went up last month," she said, "in the morning. We heard it, all these miles away." Lord Haw-Haw had said on the radio from Hamburg that blowing up the arms dump was a great German victory, but none of us believed that, there'd been no V-2 rockets anywhere near us, it'd just happened the way accidents do, and we sat there, thinking about the devastation we hadn't really seen and I was glad I hadn't really seen it, not out in the countryside. A whole farm obliterated and everyone in it, the farmer and the field he was in vanished without a trace, but it was so huge that it didn't quite seem real, had nothing to do with the War really, just an accident like a natural disaster, but we didn't talk about it, what on earth could you say anyway? After all there was nothing round here that'd make fields and villages just vanish, blown to smithereens, and anything you said'd just be scare-mongering, trouble-making, a bit like twitting only worse.

At the end of morning prayers in Big School a bit over three years later, in May 1948 long after the War was over, School Assembly'd been a bit quieter than usual, we'd finished the hymn and were getting ready to go to class, a Police Inspector, his back ramrod straight and his uniform all sharp creases and his cap square on his head, marched to the middle of the stage, all the Masters still standing without a move, completely erect no smiles or quiet chuckles the way there usually was, Henry Houston as fierce-looking as ever with his ginger hair and red cheeks, the rest unsmiling their gaze levelled straight ahead, and Mr Finney, he'd been Headmaster since April, said "This is Chief Inspector McWilliams from the Staffordshire Police." This was something new. He wasn't even the local bobby. We'd never seen *him* before. And you could cut the silence with a knife, Mr Finney still standing, some kid at the front muttered something and met a hurried *Ssh!* from his neighbour. Nobody relaxed. The Inspector cleared his throat and nodded, and told us in a grave voice that Rex Farran *He's in the class ahead of mine!* had been killed yesterday at home in Codsall when a parcel that he opened exploded *Our Kid knows him*, I thought, and then *No wonder all the kids from Codsall are so quiet*. It was a bomb that'd been sent in the post. "You must all be very careful if you get any parcels or bulky letters that you don't expect, especially if you don't know where they're from or who sent them. Whatever you do you *must not* open them, you shouldn't even touch them if you can avoid it, you should leave them alone and report them to the nearest adult. *Don't* go near them for *any* reason, not even to have a look!" And he told us Rex'd opened it by mistake, it'd been addressed to "R. Farran." "It may have been intended for his older brother who has the same initial," he said, and as we were leaving Big School I heard someone say he'd seen Roy Farran around last week, on leave from the Army, "He's an officer in the Palestine Police" somebody else told me, "He's really tough, he's a hard man."

The two Farrans in the School were a bit frightening they were so much bigger than me as well as older, they threw their weight about on the soccer field and just went their own way, I don't think they ever spoke to me at all, not ever, and nobody talked about Rex very much after, he just wasn't there any more. Gordon Thwaits, he was in the Sixth Form, told one of his pals that the bomb'd been sent by the Stern Gang, he'd read it in the paper, but we never talked about it in class, the Teachers never said anything, and I forgot about Rex pretty soon after. Back when the War was on there wasn't much anyone could say. *Talk won't change it, never will.* Or *Don't make such a fuss! It's just what happens!* In the War we'd all got a bit used to stuff just falling out the sky, especially after V-1s and V-2s came along, a bit like that parcel bomb, but now the War'd been over for something like three years it didn't make any sense, too much of a shock. That summer Uncle Edward said to quite a chorus of tut-tutting that "After all, a bomb-parcel's not as bad as the V-2 was, *that* came right out of the blue, really a terrible explosion straight out of nowhere, with absolutely no warning. A parcel, though, well, that gets delivered by somebody, so there's something to expect, it's been *aimed*. So there's a sort of warning." Some people shrugged, and others nodded in agreement. It was all very odd, how it got swept under the rug. Like Fatty Gwilt's dad saying in his butcher shop in the village, "Palestine's a different war. It's got nothing to do with us."

13

Marathons

Mrs Bailey ran the Prep School in an upstairs room at Rushall House, an old brick building just inside the Gates, two cottages separated by their shared wall. Tall and angular, hard and severe, she looked after us twenty-or-so kids and taught us the three R's with a bit of History and Geography thrown in, stories mostly, and once a week in the Gym somebody else taught us "Music," where we sang songs while the Teacher played the piano. We even got Mrs Bailey for Art, she couldn't draw for toffee, and two afternoons a week she taught us soccer, she called it "Football," twenty-odd mostly bored kids who twice a week chased a ball about for an hour on the damp slope of Second Pitch, a gloomy field a couple of hundred yards across the canal, ridges and troughs undulating across the field, you couldn't run after the ball full tilt and the ball'd hardly bounce at all in the tussocky grass. Years later I discovered the ridges came from mediaeval "ridge-and-furrow" cultivation, but it wasn't a fun place to play, especially if the cows'd been there earlier in the day or even the day before, Mrs Bailey in her brown skirt and jumper running back and forth along the side in the long grass, her little cloche hat on her close-swept hair, somehow she always had her shooting-stick, all out of breath she'd abruptly wave it when she'd blown her whistle, tell us somebody was offside or'd got a free kick. She always carried her shooting-stick to School football matches on Wednesday and Saturday afternoons, she'd open up the butterfly-shaped handle into a wiry leather-covered outline of a seat, lean back to give her tidy buttocks a rest. I used to wonder what sort of print it left on her bum, but I didn't dare say so to anyone, she was so unbending and stern; that wasn't the sort of thing you could talk about anyway, not even to your pals.

She wrote in my report at the end of Christmas Term 1941 "shows quite an interest in football," and gave me 40% for Games. My old School Report Book says the average age of the Prep class was eight years nine months that December; but at seven years and eight months old I was a lot younger, perhaps that's why I hated organised sports so much, bigger people always telling me what to do. I hated soccer and dreaded cricket. Six years later when I was in Form IV A Ticker Ranson would report of me in my 1947 year-end Report that in Games – they didn't give a percentage for that any more – "Plays up to his ability." I liked that, thought it was clever, said I was no good at it without actually saying so.

But I loved playing scratch games of soccer on the Croft, most times someone had a proper soccer ball, one or two boarders had their own and the Gym Master would give the boarders raggedy old ones the school couldn't use any more, but some daykid's mum might be able to sew one up or someone'd snaffle a bike-repair kit, and we'd throw a couple of coats down at each end of a patch of muddy grass on the croft to mark the goals, I loved being the goalie and I'd throw myself all over the place to get at the ball, turn up in class muddy and red-faced and out of breath, 'd had a wonderful time. Our heroes were the Wolves, and when the players came back from the War in about 1946 that'd be when I was twelve they had a terrific team, four England caps including Bert Williams in goal, Tom Galley was the best penalty kicker in the league, Stan Cullis was the captain. If we could get permission and we had the money we'd all get on the bus or ride our bikes to Wolverhampton and cheer ourselves silly at Molineux come back in time for Saturday supper with a copy of the pink 'un with all the soccer scores, other kids crowding round to see the League Tables, we'd all boo Aston Villa like mad, they had Docherty and Gallagher the dirtiest players in the league, Docherty was supposed to have broken somebody's leg in a game and got away with it, they were real villains and we rejoiced when Villa lost though there was one kid I forget his name who lived in Aston and supported them, I suppose now that that must have taken a bit of doing what with the jeers he got because of it. But we cut their pictures out anyway, Docherty and Gallagher and all the other thugs, and stuck them in our scrapbooks alongside all the other players, and squabbled and cajoled over who'd get what, we were soccer mad. But I was hopeless in a proper game with a referee and all, the formality of it, people expected you to do things, they cheered and groaned, you had to play to win and mistakes mattered.

With Mrs Bailey refereeing I never got to play in goal, but then I didn't want to with those hulking great wooden goalposts sticking up out of the ground, you could break bones chucking yourself at one of them, and in any case all the other kids were by a long shot too big. Once or twice she put me at fullback but whenever I went to tackle somebody they'd send me flying or they'd just step round me with the ball and I'd stand there feeling foolish as they shouted at me to get out of the way, so she usually stuck me out on the wing where there wasn't much to do, most of the time on the left even though I was right-footed. "You'll just have to learn to kick with your left," she said, but we never *practised* at anything, and she'd sit at the side leaning on her shooting-stick halfway up the slope to the First Pitch, trot a bit up and down the sideline she couldn't really see what was going on at all there weren't any linesmen, I'm not sure she even knew the Rules properly, and I'd muck about over on the far side of the field waiting for the ball to come my way and hoping it wouldn't, "Quartermain! Chase the ball!" she'd shout, she really hadn't a clue, she'd no more idea how to play than I did and she'd no more seen a professional match with somebody explaining what was going on than Mum had. I'd run over to where the ball was but by the time I got there it was always somewhere else and one of the other kids'd tell me to "Get back into position, you donkey!" so I'd just hang about with nothing to do getting colder and colder I'd jump about or flail my arms around more and more bored trying to keep warm or I'd just look at the grass or the birds in the next field or listen to a horse pulling a cart somewhere or going along the canal. Once there'd been a great big puffball growing on the edge of the Junior Field all dirty brownish white bigger than a soccer ball wrinkly with yellowy streaks, Mrs Hatfield the cook came over to see if she could stuff and cook it *It's too far gone!* she said, I couldn't stop looking at it, and then somebody kicked it apart, great clouds of dry powder coming from its wonder, suddenly the thumping of booted feet on the damp muddy grass and a shout, I looked up at the shock of the ball lurching and bouncing towards me black and heavy-looking against the sky and the trees all these galumphing kids coming at me, faces red and sweaty, some of them in green-and-grey football shirts and black knicks the way we were supposed to be, panting and scuffling scowling "Keep it in!" and I stood there no time even to wonder *Where on earth did they come from?* before the ball got past me I'd hardly started to run when they all smashed past in-the-way me, big kids jostling all arms and legs elbows flying shoving away at each other like billy-oh, all muscly, and the ball went over the line and fudged to a stop in the clumpy grass. Other times it'd end up over by the hedge, but no matter which they always got cross and Mrs Bailey always shouted "Wake up, boy! Stop mooning about!" as I helplessly stood there my face gone all stiff my head as big as that puffball while one of them threw the ball back in, someone would glance at me over his shoulder and say something and they'd all laugh and run on.

    One frosty Sunday in my first Term in Prep School Our Kid'd scarpered with one of his pals right after lunch, and Mason he was a House-prefect stood up in the Dining Hall with a couple of others and said something about the school Marathon, "It won't be until next term, in the Spring, but we must start practicing *now*" and one of the bigger kids chimed in "and Now means *Now. This afternoon!* We can't lose it again, especially not to Parke, and they've got some good long-distance runners again this year." Another one stood up, looked us over, and said "We're *all* going out for a run, we'll have a paper chase, so get yourselves ready, we'll meet in the changing room in five minutes." "Is that the same as Hare and Hounds?" Hart asked, "I've never done that!" and I wondered, it didn't sound like anything I wanted to do, *Do I really have to go?* Gravette he was standing next to me said "I don't want to go" but not loud enough for everybody to hear, and I thought *I don't want to either,* but a lot of the others smiled and looked eager. I wasn't really sure what they were talking about, I'd read about it in *Just William* stories or in *Tom Brown's School Days* or somewhere but I'd never really paid much attention to it, if it was just some sort of running game out across the fields, I supposed it'd be alright.

After we'd all got changed and hung around for twenty minutes or so for Wilcox and Law to run off ahead to lay a paper trail we all piled out across the Croft, they'd told us they were going out Little Hyde Rough way, somebody I think it was Fother Bates said "I'll bet they are! You don't have to believe 'em!" but when we got there a small scattering of paper led us to the canal bridge, they couldn't go along the canal and certainly not down into the village, not scattering all that paper, so we knew where to go, everybody else was running ahead, and by the time we'd got past the First Pitch there was a long string of kids stretched out in front of me. When we were past the tussocky ridge-and-furrow slope of Second Pitch and through the muddy ground between the raggedy bare hedges and we were at the five-barred gate at the top of Dirty Lane, there was just Hay and Phelps and me, a scattering of paper by the stile next the gate so we knew we were in the right place. I had a terrible stitch in my side, Mum told me a long time ago that the best way to get rid of it was to keep running but it was so pointless it was all so daft and anyway I was too puffed, they'd've run for miles by now, so I stopped at the stile just for a little rest looked through at the big field stretching out, it looked miles wide, arms all goose-bumps, woods over to the right and Little Hyde Rough way over across the field on the left, black and white cows standing about, their breath steaming like ours only more of it, a clump or two of kids casting about on the other side of the field looking for paper and running about calling to each other, other kids way off in the distance halfway across the next big field, and as I leaned on the stile I said "We'll never catch them up," we didn't have a hope.

Hay was watching Phelps climb over the gate next the catch that held it shut and "That's not how to climb a gate," he said, he was nine, nearly two years older than me, and he ran back and jumped up at the middle of the gate, got his waist on the top and pitched over forwards his head abruptly down his feet zooming up behind him, he reached his left hand down grabbed the top bar with his right and twisted his legs round as they came over in a swoop and landed on his feet. "See? That's how they do it in the Marathon. It's ever so quick" and he turned round and did it again to get back into Dirty Lane, and "Let's have a go," said Phelps and he took a run and leaped at the gate, his left foot just touched the second bar up, the grey wood all worn into little scoops like the steps at the door of the church, bits of mud clinging to the bar where other kids had put their feet, hit it with his waist and tipped forward and over and down, his hand grabbing the middle bar as the gate rattled, it had mud on it too. "That's fun!" he said, "it's terrific!" so I had a try. But I was too short and couldn't jump up high enough, I had to run and put my left foot on the middle bar and then heave up to get my waist on top, both hands. The wood at the top of the gate was all smooth and worn from people climbing over or cows rubbing it. The three of us kept at it, practicing at climbing the gate, our breath steaming up in front of us us getting sweatier and sweatier in the cold air, and all at once it was ever so quiet the gate had stopped creaking there wasn't a breath of wind even the cows had stopped chewing, clouds moving overhead, Phelps looked up and said "Crikey! Where've they all gone?" There wasn't another kid in sight. "We'll never find 'em now. What are we going to do?" So we got into the field and started running across but it was suddenly cold and damp, big grey clouds coming up, lots of them, a bit of wind, wet long grass. There were sloppy cowpats everywhere, somebody's footprint in one, a great slidey smear where he'd skidded, "Look at that!", and I slowed down to a walk, none of us could be bothered to run after the others and anyhow we didn't know where they'd gone what would we run for anyway, and then we were all trudging across the field towards the copse on the right when Hays said "I'm cold. I'm going back."

  When we got back there were already some kids in the showers flicking wet towels a big snap at each other, hot steam everywhere, Law and Wilcox laughing as they put their clothes on, "Where did you come from? You can't be back yet!" and we didn't say anything but just got in the showers red welts and scrapes across our waists where we'd been at the gate, I stayed well clear of the snapping towels I'd seen them break the target's skin and draw blood, and "Yah! You didn't go round did you? You cheated, didn't you?" they jeered, flicking their towels, *"Don't be such a crumb!"* other kids coming in all hot and cheerful and pleased with themselves. "You'll never get to do well in the Marathon, but you've got to do it anyway, everyone has to. You've *got* to finish, you know, it's alright to come in last, but you'd better finish!" and "We'll never beat Parke if you behave like that? Sissies!" Other kids just kept coming in, "That was a super run. We must have done three miles!" "A bit more than that," Wilcox said, "we led you round the Junior Marathon course," and he grinned. *How could anybody* like *cross-country running?* So I dreaded the Marathon, but by the time it came round in the Spring Mr Pearce said I was too young to take part, he was the PT Master for all the Juniors and he was in charge of the Marathon he said three miles was too far for a boy who wasn't eight yet and I'd have to stay behind and watch, so I didn't have to do it until 1943. I was lucky there, because when Broggie became Headmaster we all got divided into Seniors Juniors and Tiddlers, and even the Tiddlers had to do the Marathon no matter how small they were.

Me and some other kids who had permission not to run, there weren't many of us, had to go out and watch the runners all start off, people milling about by the Pavilion on the First Pitch where they started, some of them jigging about from foot to foot because they wanted to be off, to get on with it, loving it, some of them standing there shivering and listless drooping for the Starter's call, the Juniors going first jamming together through the farm-gate into the Second Pitch and then up Dirty Lane, me and another kid stood in Dirty Lane to watch them coming out through the gate we heard the shout and then the bumbling soft drum of sixty pairs of feet and more all thrabbing on the mud and grass, jostling and heavy breathing, it was a cold blustery day and then they were through and splashing mud up Dirty Lane, already a few stragglers, only I heard a grown-up say "Those are the smart ones, holding back till later in the race," a sudden drift of quiet, just the wind to listen to, and your own clothes as you stirred, hardly any Teachers about, one or two villagers come out to watch all wrapped up in their hats and coats, the Vicar and a shopkeeper or two murmuring together.

We'd seen Mrs Asprey going off on her bike up to the Avenue Bridge to monitor the runners' progress, most of the Teachers dotted about the course making lists to make sure nobody took a shortcut, and after we'd walked through the Croft to the Quad we had nothing to do but wait, we'd watched the Seniors start of course, and we hung about in School Road outside the Gates standing and shuffling about, waiting and waiting, knees a bit blue, you'd stamp your feet to warm them up your bare legs getting colder and colder, I wished I had some pocket money and sweet coupons left so I could go to Mrs Roberts's, there was nothing to do, the morning bus from Wolverhampton came up Dean Street, somebody got off, it turned along Church Road to the Square the rattle of its motor getting smaller and smaller, and a village kid burst out of the alley opposite the Admiral Rodney all out of breath and shouted something, there were all sorts of people wandering over now to watch, and somebody said "They've reached the Avenue Bridge" and "Who's in front? Who's in front?" but nobody knew and then somebody else came along and said "Kempson's in front" *That's a surprise. What's happened to Parke?* I wanted it to be Knightley, the house I was in with all the other boarders, Mr Stowe who ran the stationer's and sweet shop on Church Road said "That's just the Juniors, they don't really count. Mrs Jones when she got off the bus said Parke was in front at the Penk," a cold gust stirring paper and leaves in the gutter. The Seniors had to ford the River Penk three times and I thought how cold it would be slipping and sliding on the stones on the river bed, or the weeds, I'd never even seen that bit of the river where they had to ford, not that *I* knew, over Somerford Way down by the bridge. Of course I'd seen the river itself I'd walked down there more than once on a Sunday, it was about a mile off, about as wide as the canal a little bit wider perhaps, but I didn't know where the ford was, suddenly a picture in my head of the road going through the Windrush in the Cotswolds before the War, cement slope down to the shallow water hardly a ripple Dad carefully driving the car ever so slowly the sound of water gently sussurring under the floorboards me and Our Kid wanting him to speed up to make a great big splashy wake him telling us he didn't know how deep it was and he didn't want to stall "We'd have to be towed" he said but we didn't understand why he couldn't drive fast through the water. The Penk didn't look like that at all, you couldn't drive anything through the ford, it was just for horses and people who didn't mind getting their feet wet.

A shout from the top of Dean Street said the runners had started coming in, Juniors and Seniors all mixed up together somebody had pitched over his head in the Penk soaking wet his feet squelching away socks bedraggled his face all blue round the mouth and chin and he stumbled a bit as he got close to the Gates. One of the watchers laughed and called "Lost your road then did yer Mike?" but people started clapping, cries of "Well done!" and a few more laughs and he grinned a bit but short of breath, he didn't look at all happy and started shivering, huge shivers now the end was in close sight, almost finished, Matron or Angus Beaton the Art Master to hustle him off to the showers. There must have been about fifty or sixty people watching the finish, mostly from the village, bundled up in their coats and scarves and hats, some of them leaning on their bikes or with shopping baskets, peering down the road having a bit of a jaw, and after a bit the runners bunching in clumps there weren't any more coming that you could see but there were still lots of kids who hadn't finished and we had to wait and wait and wait, the road all shiny with wet, all of them getting clapped as they came in, the claps getting fewer and fewer as the afternoon wore on, and after a while just a trickle or two. The first ones in came out to watch, all shiny and scrubbed and pinkly happy and warm-looking after their showers, through with the misery of it, but they'd enjoyed it and were pleased with themselves, 'd come in first, and clapped like mad for the next few runners and then just paid no attention really except when it was a pal of theirs when they'd catcall a bit and clap, mostly they fell silent or joked and talked and scrambled about among themselves.

Mr Pearce came up the hill he'd been watching them ford the Penk for the third crossing and said "That's all the Seniors. I sent Jones Major and Opps home, they were in no condition to finish," Opps'd have a long walk, living out Codsall way as he did. I wanted to go in and get warm, but *You can't. You've got to be here to greet them when they get in. It doesn't matter how long they take* and when at long last the stragglers had dwindled away and we were still waiting, I was freezing cold shivering away like mad goosebumps all over a woman's voice down Dean Street called out "There's a good lad, don't give up, you've nearly finished" and then "Go on, finish it off in a run!" and a single small figure came into view, a couple of village kids wheeling around on their bikes, he picked up his pace a bit *Is that Phelps?* but as he got to the top of the hill he fell back into a trudgy sort of hobbled limp, his face all scrunched up his left shoe flopping it'd lost its laces, his knees red and blue they looked raw and chafed where they met his gym knicks, he looked absolutely miserable spattered with mud and bedraggled, there was a little scatter of faint hand-clapping from a few people as he came up to the finish line outside the Gates. Mr Pearce came forward and said "Well done! You didn't give up!" and then he said "You're the last one in! Well done!" It was Jones Minor, Phelps'd come in long ago, I thought he was going to burst into tears but he gave a wobbly little smile as he winced, *Why did he take so long?* I was a bit cross I was so cold, *Didn't he know we'd have to wait for him?* but everybody said it took a lot of pluck to carry on like that and finish but I was glad I wasn't him, how terrible it was to come in last, the worst runner in the School, nobody clapped him the way they'd clapped the kids who'd come in first, quite a few people'd gone home and Jones Minor got less applause than almost anyone, they were all pleased with him because now they could go home, plucky little kid, they said, made sure he heard. When next year I ran in the Marathon I didn't dare not finish I walked round the last half of the course and had a little bit left to run through the village, faint praise and fake applause, the sheer misery of it, and like Our Kid I learned not to take it at all seriously. Not that we let on but some of us were a bit jealous of the youngest Winston kid, he lived on the Codsall Road about a hundred yards from the Marathon course, and when he got to that part he simply turned aside and went home for tea, so far as we could see he didn't even get into trouble. But *he* was a dayboy.

I wasn't the only one who hated long-distance, but I really enjoyed the sprint, I wasn't very good at it and never won. Sometimes I'd go over to the First Pitch and practise, imagining I was Jesse Owens or somebody like that winning a race in the Olympics. The 440 was about as much as I could ever manage, and even then not often, with about a hundred yards to go I'd mostly fade off completely, so my favourite was the two-twenty, I could just about go flat out all the way and make it, my legs all wobbly and my breath coming in bigger and bigger gasps, another ten yards and I knew I'd fall over all in a heap, but it felt terrific with the wind rushing through my hair whistling past my ears as I tore along as fast as I could, the thump of everyone's feet spurring me on, their breath sometimes so close you knew you could trip each other up if you weren't careful, seeing someone come up from behind out of the corner of your eye and putting on a desperate spurt. I soon learned to pace myself, it was better than the hundred yards because it took me a bit to get up to full speed.

On my first Sports Day at Brewood, in 1942, all the smallest kids had to compete in the eighty-yard dash, there were only about a dozen of us, there were two heats and I came in second in mine so I ran in the Final later that afternoon, I was so full of myself that I'd been in the Final, I strutted about in my gym knicks chattering away to everybody all afternoon. It's odd, I still wince to think about it, even after all these years, and probably will till I go to my grave, I'd hardly moved a muscle, that short-breath fluttering just below my diaphragm all apprehensive, eyes drying out a bit, and when it was all over and everyone had changed, and most of the parents had said their goodbyes and left on the bus, I was still hanging about the Gates a little bit shivery in my singlet and shorts as the sun went behind the clouds, my pullover thrown over my shoulders the way I'd seen Seniors do it it was getting on for Teatime and some older kid said "Don't you think you'd better get changed, Quartermain?" but I wanted everyone who passed by to see me and know I'd been a Competitor, and there was Nubs Derwent coming towards me with his mum and dad they were all dressed up and looked posh and they actually had a car, they'd driven to Brewood from Somewhere-or-other to watch Nubs win his race and goodness knows how they managed that in the War, he was at least twelve years old he was in III A one level above Our Kid in III B I'd hardly ever spoken to him, and I began to shiver a bit more, I knew I ought to go in and get changed but there'd be nobody in the Changing Room and once I'd done that it'd all be over no one'd notice me nothing to do no one to talk to, what friends I had gone off somewhere so I kept hanging about, and I looked and I stood and I looked some more no other kids around except going somewhere on their bikes and Mrs Derwent said "Which race did you run in, then?"

As I stumbled to tell her Mr Derwent said "Why don't you introduce us to your friend, John?" and that was very strange I never knew his name was John, he was just Nubs, someone a bit frightening really, but now he was John the four of us could chatter together and that was a bit exciting I didn't think anybody else knew he was really John, and he had a sister, suddenly I knew a lot about him others didn't know, they were talking about her and his dad had a big posh car, his sister going to a convent somewhere, he called his dad Father and his mum Mother. Nubs went off to fetch something so his mum and dad chatted to me and his dad said "We're going to take John out to Tea, we thought we'd go to Beattie's. Would you like to come too? You'd better go and get changed, hadn't you." "Oh yes," I said, "But please, I've got a brother here, can he come too?" I couldn't go without Our Kid, *What would he think if I didn't bring him along, we had to share a treat like this,* and besides it was him who was Nubs's friend, not me, *what on earth would I have to say to Nubs, we weren't even in the same dormitory!* I didn't really know who he was he always hung around with kids his own age and in the same Form, the way we all did, I was a bit afraid of him him so big and self-contained looking, he was good at cricket and might be in the Junior Eleven next Term, his ears set so close alongside his head and his ginger hair clinging like a cap in dense close waves, not a spiky unruly mess like mine, *What would we talk about?* "Can I go and get him?" He looked at his watch, this tall man neat and tidy in his elegant light brown topcoat, he looked a bit like an Officer in the Army he stood up so straight, and he said, "Yes, of course. You'd better be quick though!" But Our Kid wasn't in the Billiard Room or anywhere around there, *Have you seen Our Kid?*, but nobody had and I ran out across the Croft as fast as I could and got all the way to School Bridge but there was nobody out there at all, there was nobody I could even ask I couldn't even hear anybody, I began to turn back but *What if he's still there?* so I turned around and went over the bridge but First Pitch was big and flat and empty, the Pavilion all closed up all the deck-chairs put away, just a few bits of string and white pegs where the Sports had been, it was completely deserted. I turned back, I was terribly short of breath, *What if he's out in the Spinney or on the Second Pitch?* but I couldn't run all the way over there *That'd be a half a mile easily* and they were waiting for me, I had to hurry and I'd got the beginnings of a stitch but here was the Changing Room nobody in there at all, all of it echoey, the showers all empty and cold one of them dripping the way it always did, damp footprints all over but drying off, big wet patches on the duckboards, the lockers all shut, a pair of pumps chucked under one of the benches among all the fluff, my clothes on one of the hooks behind the door except for my trousers in a heap under the bench, my shoes with my socks in them scattered on the other side of the room, I threw everything on clattered down the corridor and out the door rushed out and there they were the three of them out by the Gates where I'd left them standing about waiting for me Nubs talking to his mum his dad looking at his watch. "Ah, there you are," he said, to my "I can't find him." I wondered if I really ought to go without him, tell them "No I can't come," but they'd been waiting for me *I can't not go, not now.*

In the car the three of them talked about people and places I'd never heard of, and when the waitress came at Beattie's, she was all dressed in black with a little white pinny, she had a scrap of white lace framing the top of her head a bit like a tiara, Mr Derwent looked at Mrs Derwent and nodded and she said "Bread and butter and cakes for four please" and he said "Boys like ginger beer" and looked at us. Nodded. "Two ginger beers." Mrs Derwent said "A pot of tea for two, then." Nubs looked pleased. I'd never had any before, and when I took a sip, it came in a glass with a straw, the strong ginger taste was horrid, it caught in the back of my mouth the fierce fizz of the bubbles went up the back of my nose and I spluttered and choked and spilled a bit of the ginger beer on my plate and table cloth and his dad said "Isn't that wonderful. I always liked it when ginger beer did that to me," and laughed. "It tastes rather strong at first, doesn't it?" and I croaked a damp Yes, I sounded a bit bubbly, worrying about how I could keep a slice of bread on my plate from getting soggy, the others all politely not noticing.

What a treat to have thin bread-and-butter and jam even if it was just margarine, we never got that at school, and only the first piece a little bit soggy with ginger beer. Then we got little cakes, rock cakes mostly, and the ginger beer easier to drink as it went down, and when his dad said "Would you like some ice cream?" I could hardly believe my ears I hadn't had any for so long, didn't think there was any any more, but the waitress came up with a couple of ice creams in two silver ice-cold cups on a stem, a bit battered looking, the name *Beattie's* engraved on it in fancy lettering, beads of condensation, sitting on a paper doily on a bread-and-butter plate, two wafers stuck in the top. The cup wasn't half cold, almost too cold to touch, like the kitchen-door handle in the big freeze at Rushbury a year ago, with the skin almost pulling away just for a moment. The ice cream was so hard it started to roll over when I stuck the spoon in so I grabbed the wafer to hold it steady, and the wafer broke, I poked away at the ice cream with it and it broke again as soon as I dug the spoon in, you had to let it melt a bit or it'd slurp a big rush over the side, I'd already got some on my fingers, my doily was a bit soggy and crumpled looking where the cup was sitting on it, and I looked at Nubs he'd nearly finished his. He'd eaten all his wafers, and his plate was still absolutely tidy, he'd wrapped his hand around the bottom of the cup the stem poking between his fingers warming it up a bit, he knew exactly how to do it. "Wartime ice cream, not very good really, made with turnips probably," said Mr Derwent, "but it's good anyway isn't it" and we chorused our thankyous.

It must have been clear as daylight that Nubs and I hardly knew each other, but we did manage to talk about Meccano sets a little, Nubs had a huge one and'd built a travelling gantry crane with his, I'd only ever seen a picture of one on the Meccano box, we had set 1A he must have had something like set 4 or even set 6. But mostly I fidgetted and wriggled as they asked things I couldn't answer and talked about things I couldn't possibly know about, mostly family stuff and what was going on at home, and it was a relief when we got back to School and got out of the car at the top of Dean Street. Nubs said goodbye to his parents I had just enough sense to go off ahead, the three of them talking in a restrained kind of way and laughing quietly together, his mum and dad shaking my hand and saying goodbye to me ever so politely and me feeling pleased but a bit daft. And there was Our Kid sitting reading in the Billiard Room, "Where were you?" I asked him, I was cross, "I tried to find you!" I told him, "I wanted you to come with us," and he said, "I went to Brian Brown's," he was a day-boy lived on a farm a mile or so away near Somerford, I didn't even know what he looked like. "Why didn't you *tell* me?" I said, I felt really resentful *How could you not invite me too?* and he said, "He's *my* friend not yours." *But you're my brother!* I thought, and I lay awake that night and decided I was secretly glad he'd not been along with me and Nubs even though I hadn't enjoyed it very much and wished I'd gone to somebody's house like he had, with a friend. But I couldn't tell him that, so next day I told him again "We went to Beattie's. We had ginger beer. And ice cream!" and I turned away.

14

Small Pleasures

In Prep School Mrs Bailey taught us everything except French, Music and sometimes Geography, but one day late March or early April 1942, we got young Miss Merrit instead, us kids had no idea until we got into class one morning and there she was. *No Mrs Bailey!* No one'd told us ahead of time, she mostly looked after kids in the Third Form on days she was teaching and she didn't say much except she'd be in charge of us for the rest of the week. After lunch she said it was too nice today to be stuck indoors and took us out onto the Croft to tell us the names of things, showed us plantains and dandelions and buttercups we all knew them, and Cuckoo Pint, she called it Lords-and-Ladies, asked us what kind of cows the school had and did we know why, and about birds' eggs, do any of us collect them. Pussy Bailey'd told us that morning that we must always leave at least one egg in any nest we found, Henry Houston'd told us last week at Prayers that we should always leave three. "That's daft!" a kid behind me muttered, "If you did *that* you'd never get any at all!" but nobody'd say that to Henry's face, he'd fiercely hold you up to public scorn.

Some kids had terrific collections of eggs but all I had was three, a thrush and a robin and a peewit, everybody had those they were so easy to find, and I kept them along with half of a shell I'd got from somebody else nestled in cotton wool in a couple of matchboxes in my locker, and Miss Merrit looked round at us gathered on the Croft and said "Hear that? What's that bird, Jimmy?" a bird's song floating fresh and clear on the air and he said "A thrush, Miss" and someone else said "That's a blackbird, can't you tell?" and we all started arguing, she didn't know what it was any more than I did except I knew a blackbird's lovely song, and we all liked arguing *'Tis!* and *'Tisn't!*, especially when the Teacher didn't seem to know and we could get away with it. Not that we'd've dared try that on Mrs Bailey. Jimmy really did know his birds though he'd given the wrong answer, we admired the cuckoo's egg he had, they're so hard to find, but then Jimmy lived on a farm and knew everything. Miss Merrit firmly said "No!" and in the same breath asked "What's your favourite season, John?" It'd never occurred to me to have one, I'd never thought about seasons that way, they were so much themselves that I couldn't tell, but as soon as she asked I just *knew* what mine was.

I thought of walking across ploughed fields on a crisp morning in November, cold knees warming up as I walked, bits of frost and small patches of ice between the furrows and a couple of conkers in my pocket and a few bits of string, and John said "Spring" and she nodded and said "Yes, that's mine too," and Jimmy said "Spring" and she smiled "It's wonderful when the sun moves round again," and Tom said "Spring" and she said "Isn't it lovely when it gets warm again? You know it's not the sun that moves, don't you? It's us. *We* go round the sun," and she looked at Billy, and he said "It's Spring, Miss. That's when everything grows," and she kept saying how nice Spring is how cheerful the sun is and by the time she got to me at the end everyone'd said "Spring," and I wasn't sure any more. And yes *March comes in like a lion* is what a picture book at home'd said with a picture of a lamb skipping on the grass, it *is* nice in the Spring, *today's a lovely day, soft breeze a bit of sun, everything bright from a few drops of rain when we were indoors, everything beginning to grow, bits of bright green scattered through the trees and hedges, lovely soft air, little spurts of emerald dusting over the mud of the Croft, buds of mayflower just starting.* Perhaps the others'd all thought it a funny sort of question too but they all sounded so sure of themselves, none of them being the least bit cocky, and perhaps you weren't supposed to like anything better than Spring and they all knew that, and when it got to be my turn I heard myself say "Spring, Miss," surprising myself, and she nodded and smiled. I shouldn't have said I like "Spring" when I loved the wonderful *shoosh* you got over and over, lovely rhythm, when I walked through a pile of autumn leaves, the busy scurry of dry leaves swirling in a corner, the fresh sharp scent of a bonfire lingering in my nose. But right then I didn't want to be the only one who liked something better than Spring when Spring was what *they* liked best, and I felt cheated, cross with myself.

I couldn't let on to the other kids that I loved the space of empty working fields and the sounds of distance. How could I tell them that I enjoyed the mild annoyance skirting the edge of tedium as on my Sunday Walk by myself I stumbled over the furrows of a just-ploughed field, wet mud clinging to my boots to make the going heavy, making me teeter now and then as I lifted a foot from the crest of a fresh furrow, or planted it on the next to feel it sink, care in every step. I loved the bits of green in tiny dots hardly there, scattered in a blurry mist of colour against the brown of the field touched with hoar frost, winter wheat, blurs moving into sharp focus at my feet. Cold frosty November day, the brown-ness of it all, the yellows and reds of leaves, black branches outlined against the sky, patches of silvery mist hugging the ground, the air so sharp I'd see my breath, the bite of the air in the gap between my socks and the end of my grey flannel shorts, the harsh rub of cold damp wool, a hard line above my knee at the damp edge of the flannel, the sky a cold cold blue a pale golden glaze over everything the leafless trees sharp against the sun, rooks crying as I walked, they'd land and hunt for worms the cold too much for worms to show themselves. *Caw! caw!* the flurrying of wings, I cried *caw! caw!* my breath a jet of mist, fleeting warmth around my nose as my feet broke through the crust of frozen soil *caw! caw!* I tramped and tramped across everything absolutely right sound carrying over and through the world's energy and my own, all one intense expansive private pleasure, climb a gate and find another field *caw! caw!* the whole world around the trees uprearing, all I can hear is birds, the crows, and me, my breath, the rustle of my clothes, my feet, the hedges bare, quiet scrabble of stones and dirt, perhaps a barge on the canal a field away horse-hooves clipping the towpath or its engine chugging quietly along, the energies of winter and its cold exhilarating quiet more than I could imagine, no other people to be seen except a puff of smoke, faint scent of it a distant bonfire of leaves, some chimney down the village. How could I think of War, or School, or other kids, and lessons and

School food or even Mum and Dad, this so welcomed difference held me, holds me still, its constant other sameness, its slow change, those splendid crows.

The fields constantly beckoned, that first year at Brewood, everything so quiet they conjured strongly the farm at Alcester, there was about twenty-five acres belonging to the school, some pasture, some arable, rotation of crops all the way to the end of Dirty Lane where a gate held back all the School's cattle, about twenty of them. One of my favourite walks on Sunday afternoons once I'd settled down at Brewood but before I felt very much at home with dormitory life, was just to climb over the gate and wander around the fields by myself, they called to me, they reminded me of the farm. In May I found out we weren't really supposed to go into the fields at all, bed-time was a bit later, by then it stayed light for so long, I was walking down Dirty Lane, a lovely warm clear evening, and I heard all these voices and whispering the other side of the hedge. I stopped at the gate to look, tall green wheat as high as my waist, rustling to itself, the leaves and stalks all soft looking, transepts, glimpses of possible architectures, wonderful place to hide, inviting me to curl up and read, and *crikey!* a sudden turmoil in the wheat, and I heard somebody shout *Bang! you're dead!* and then a kid's voice going *a-h a-h a-h a-h a-ha-h-a* a mess of glottal stops sounding the way we thought machine guns sounded, about a foot above the ground a face peered out from between the rows of grain looked both ways *That's Ken Hatton!* another face appeared over the top of the wheat looked round and disappeared as fast as it could *Is that Barry Stokes?* and then another gunfire sound, a stick waving above the wheat, a fake scream, someone's voice saying *You're dead, lie down!* I climbed over the gate "Get a stick!" someone whispered, that was Mike Elrington, "you've got to have a gun!" and then another voice "You're on our side." Oh! I said "Whose?" and he whispered it's us against the Third and Fourth Dorms. I grabbed a scrappy-looking stick by the hedge and scuttled into the field on hands and knees "Quick! Before they see you!" the golden yellow light between the rows, green shade, a garden, started crawling, under and between columns of wheat, huge soft rustling, I wormed along as dry soil wriggled up under my belt, through the leaves I could see Wally Porter facing the other way a hankie round his head he was so much taller than me I could see him against the sky behind him Horace Gwilt his hankie round his arm *Bang! Bang!* I called my mess of glottal stops *a-h a-h a-h a-h a-ha-h-a* starting slowish getting faster as my gun warmed up they turned *Where did YOU come from?* cries of "Not fair! Not fair! Who let Little Phil in here? We didn't know," I'd shot the Commander-in-Chief, and everyone called a truce. We played for hours. As it got dark we sneaked into the dorm way past our bedtime and crept exhilarated and exhausted into bed. At the window early next day Wally saw Mr Hawkins striding into the Headmaster's house, and at breakfast before we said grace, Mr Bailey told us all that "In your thoughtless games you have flattened the crop. It cannot possibly be harvested. That is the food we eat, and you may have ruined it completely. You have damaged the War Effort. It's like an act of sabotage, for which you are all equally responsible, and of which you must all be thoroughly ashamed." And he paused, looked slowly round at us all, "In order for Mr Hawkins to repair what damage he can," Mr Bailey went on, "some of you may find yourselves with extra work to do around the farm and the School, no reward. You have no one but yourselves to blame." Everyone angry at us.

The knowledge that you young rabbits have done serious wrong is punishment enough, Henry Houston told us in class, *but heaven help you if you ever go into those fields again!* And we didn't, except to do farm work like thinning beets. For years and years I wanted to do that again, those arching green tunnels, the magical polished light, the sound, the silence, the concealment.

In late November my Walk led me, no one with me, down Dean Street to the bottom end of Dirty Lane, and I turned up it to get away from the Wolverhampton Road, busy even if there wasn't much traffic at that stage of the War, and hardly anybody was there at all, too far from the playing fields and the school buildings. At the bottom end the lane took me past the tall hedges back of the Headmaster's and other people's gardens on one side, had to keep clear of them alright, and some of the school's farm-fields on the other, a small brick bungalow stuck in the middle of one field it looked like, pasture and crops all round its meagre-looking garden. I soon found out it belonged to the school barber, every Tuesday we'd come into the Billiard Room after supper to find he'd set himself up to cut everyone's hair, each of us had to suffer his blunt hand-clippers once a month, especially us Juniors, but he loved to gossip, liked to talk about what crooners he'd heard on the BBC, chatter about what was going on in the village, all of it pretty remote from us boarders, I liked going past there on my Walk. I liked him and on my Walk I liked going past where he lived. "Nothing to do down there" other kids said. "What are you doing down there, child?" was what I'd hear if a Teacher saw me. If the staff, the cook, or a housemaid or even Mr Hawkins the school farmer saw you along there they'd pay no attention so long as you behaved yourself, and once as I turned the corner into Dirty Lane I almost bumped into Old Nunc, nearly tripped, his red bandanna round his neck, string round his trousers below the knee, his old tweed cap pulled down, sharp blue eyes closely keen on what he was doing, and he didn't say a word he didn't look up he just kept hacking away carefully, laying the hedge on the right. "It takes him three years to get all the way up one side of Dirty Lane and down the other," Henry Houston told us when I asked, in class, "goes at it every winter, mostly when it's coldest," and I realised I already knew that, 'd seen Old Fred doing it at the farm at Alcester. "Got to do it before bud-burst" Nunc said on one of the rare occasions he spoke to me, he never spoke to us kids if he didn't have to, and Henry told us in class that if Nunc started too early then the birds'd have nothing to eat in the winter, all the berries'd be gone. I watched him bend into the foot of the hedge and chop with his mattock, cut at an angle down into an upright stem, close to the ground, it might be as thick as his wrist, or he'd cut into two or three of them, and bend them over and down weave them amongst other uprights, he didn't even pause or take a swig of his cold tea, he always had that by him, knew exactly what he was doing.

I wanted to talk to him but there was nothing I could say he was so like Old Fred, trimming as he went along to keep the hedge the same height, and keep it the same thickness. He'd cut stakes to fill the gaps and then weave the pleachers, that's what he called them, across and around the stake, dig some muck from the barnyard down into the roots for the hawthorn to take, bend the uprights whichever way the gap called for, and sometimes there'd be huge tangles of brambles and dead wood and ferns and grass and other stuff he'd have to clear out before he could even start. It must've been hard hard work what with all the thorns and him not wearing gloves just wool mittens, no room to make mistakes, but I delighted to watch him work the hedge, not a movement wasted; nobody, none of us bothered him then, he was so absorbed, so given over to looking and thinking ahead as he worked without a pause, cut this piece here, bend it there, weave this one round it, cut the next one longer; he just kept at it and made it look as if any of us could do it so long as we had the strength. "You couldn't though," Tom White said, he was a bit older than me, his dad was a farmer, "just try it. You have to keep thinking about what you're doing or the hedge'll die out. Or run wild. It takes a lot of skill. You can't cut all the way through the upright, you've got to leave a good strip of bark and wood connected so it can still grow." I had a small start of recognition when later that year some of us marvelled over a sketch on the cover of *The Rover*, purporting to show the men who took five years to paint the Forth Bridge, only at the end of it to start all over again, one end to the other, over and over, work lasting their lifetime. Just like Nunc, except that Nunc had other things to do as well, a change of pace. If you cut too much it weakens the hedge, but by hook or by crook it has to be stock-proof, you don't want cattle breaking through. "Nor you rambunctious young rabbits!" Henry warned. He'd tell the whole school, assembled as they were every morning at Prayers, to "keep away from those hedgerows! They're not there for you children to clamber about or play in. All sorts of animals and birds live there, and we need *them* a lot more than we need *you* and your imbecilic destructive habits." Mr Page in Biology told us the hedges held the land together, stopped erosion, and kept the ground warm too. "A good windbreak is worth your life in the North," he said, "as good as a wall, and here too, look at the way the cattle shelter under trees or by the hedge, fences are no good." *Good for birds' nesting too*, we all thought, *in the Spring*, but if Nunc waited till then to lay or even trim the hedges it'd drive the birds away.

When Nunc had finished a stretch it looked all bare and squared off. "It's not for your pleasure," Henry Houston said, "it's not supposed to be *pretty*, it's a working hedge, and we have to let it get on with its work. What with the cows coming up and down Dirty Lane twice a day for milking, as well as you kids, there's a lot of work for the hedges to do. Don't ever forget that." And as soon as the leaves started coming out and new growth began to spring up round the edges of all those cuts it was a wonderful living hedge again, thick and green, exhilarating in its welcome. And it did work, you didn't need barbed wire or old hurdles or anything like that to keep the livestock in or to keep the rabbits out, and we none of us clambered about in the hedge, too many thorns even for bird's-nesting.

The cows sometimes went after milking to Bath Field just over School Bridge, a long narrow pasture sloping down to a stream at the far end feeding the old Swimming Pool. The top end of Bath Field, right up by Dirty Lane, was simply terrific, close enough to the Croft for us to get there even during Break, and once we got into its belt of scrub, hawthorn and gorse alongside the canal we'd be pretty well invisible to anyone at school or out on the Croft, we could follow a choppy tussocky path, and where the path ran out look twenty or thirty yards down the bank and through the trees and scrub to see the old sandstone-lined swimming pool, all overgrown, the stream running through the always-open sluice-gate and right under the canal through a brick culvert with a big iron grating over the end to keep the cattle out, and with another always-closed sluice-gate a bit further along the embankment to drain the canal if they had to. Once in a while but you'd have to be watchful and silent, you'd see a kingfisher flashing its bright blue just above the water, its nest further along the canal bank. We couldn't stay away from that band of scrub, lots of hiding places, a lovely pink hawthorn to climb just over the stile as you left Dirty Lane, crooked paths careening round bushes and under small trees, not like the Spinney so much further from the Croft you didn't have time to get there and back at Break, you'd have to cross the Croft, get over School Bridge, and then all the way over the First Pitch along the canal, well on the way to Brewood Bridge.

But once school was over for the day we had time, and the Spinney was another favourite place, not much undergrowth beneath the elms and the slope down to the canal, you had to run like mad to get across one steep bit of hardpacked sand. We weren't really supposed to go there or to the pasture-and-scrub along the canal but once the evenings got light again we ran pretty wild there between Prep and bedtime and at weekends, and I felt a sharp sense of loss when Phil and I went back years later and found the Spinney completely fenced off from the Playing Fields, thin iron posts rearing a tall chain-link barrier. "Can you get into the Spinney? Does anybody go there?" I asked the Head Teacher and was told "No, no, there's no need. We've got a good playground." She meant the tarmac of the Croft, and I thought of the life in the Spinney and Bath Field, the rabbits and the rooks, brambly animal paths, the creaking of the tall elms in the breeze, Ollie Whitworth climbing one, bark dust drifting down from his scrabbling feet as we watched, thirty feet or more above our heads. Not that there's elms left any more, what with Dutch Elm disease. Phil and I tried to get down Bath Field to the old Swimming Pool on that visit, the top half of the field fairly clear, the scrub at the bottom a dense impassable tangle of growth, at least for us in our decent clothes, brambles gorse and broom taking over, rabbit droppings and animal paths, the pink hawthorn still standing guard up by Dirty Lane, we couldn't get through, and I thought of us tearing off the bright green tender shoots of new leaves every spring and eating them, we called them bread-and-butter. "Nobody's been down there for years," somebody in the pub said, "there's nothing down there anyway." But of course there is, even if there's no cows in the field and the School's cattle all long gone, look at Jimmy Osborne at the age of eighty potting a few rabbits in the woods up by his cottage near the rezzer for his dinner. And the Baths're still there, even if they are derelict, the stream still running through.

15

Mrs Bailey

Stuck in Prep School we simply couldn't get away from Mrs Bailey, the Headmaster's wife, who ran it. She locked us down with her watchful eye, she almost never smiled and hardly ever laughed. She just knew we were up to mischief. "You're not in here to enjoy yourselves, you're here to *learn*," and as soon as it was time for Break she shooed us all outside. *You can't be in here when I'm not. Go and play.* We spent a lot of the time doing what I'd done in Rushbury and even in Wheaton Aston, lots of drill in times-tables, lots of addition and multiplication, lots of pounds shillings and pence, and, once she'd found a batch of proper handwriting books, lots of practice at copperplate handwriting. *A A A A A a a a a a* across the page and blank lines underneath so you could copy, then *B B B B B b b b b b* for the rest of the page, stay carefully between the lines and draw the loopy Victorian letters, practise again and again in your Rough Book before doing the neat Copy Book version, *Don't you muddle up the thick strokes and the thin strokes.* When you've finished one page go on to the next, and by the end of the book you're joining the letters into words, real writing. But what with all the muck that stuck to your pen in the inkwells at Brewood, it was a lot harder, no matter how I tried, I couldn't make the up stroke thin enough, none of us could, and it all got smudged anyway "Wipe your nib!" she commanded "*every* time you dip your pen," but all we could wipe it with was a corner torn from our Rough Book, and she'd frown and shake her head, but she didn't show us how to hold the pen at its proper slope or say a word about the nib and at what sort of angle, we all watched each other to see, and woe betide you if you made a mess. "Why can't you be neat and tidy? You *must* try harder."

Mrs Bailey taught Dictation, Composition, and Literature, that's what English was, but mostly we did handwriting and dictation. When we did Literature we read things out loud, simplified stories out of Macaulay, and Lamb's *Tales from Shakespeare*, Horatio at the Bridge or a prosy version of *Twelfth Night*, some of them more than once. Mrs Bailey said Malvolio was very funny in his yellow stockings but she didn't explain, I couldn't understand it at all *Why was it alright for them all to laugh at him like that? He hadn't done anything wrong.* It just didn't make sense, all these people being so cruel *Whoever'd want to be laughed at?* It wasn't fair. Yet when we read about Mucius Scaevola driving Lars Porsena away from the gates of Rome by sticking his hand in the fire without even a quail, he was so heroic, and I thought of me having my tonsils out proud that I'd been sick seven times. I might have read that story in History, sometimes we got Mr Pearce instead of Mrs Bailey, but we certainly weren't taught anything about how the Romans destroyed and obliterated Etruscan language and culture. People talked a lot of the time even in School about how the Germans were trying to obliterate *us*, and like a lot of the songs we had in Music, everything, all the stories, were about Heroes, Hector and Lysander, Drake, Raleigh and Nelson, poems by Sir Henry Newbolt and Alfred Noyes. Learn "Drake's Drum" by heart, and Charles Wolfe's 1817 poem "The Burial of Sir John Moore at Corunna," I've never read that again, not since, but over seventy years later I can still remember bits, even though I didn't quite understand what was going on:

> Not a drum was heard, not a funeral note,
> As his corse to the rampart we hurried;
> Not a soldier discharged his farewell shot
> O'er the grave where our hero we buried.

Mrs Bailey taught us Arithmetic too. We learned about columns for tens and units and how to do long division and we learned about fractions, pounds, shillings and pence. One night I lay awake in the dormitory for ages smiling to myself but puzzled at the name Vulgar Fractions and wondered what Marlow Grandmother thought about *them*, were they somehow bad, like Urchins, and not at all like Proper Nouns? I didn't dare ask; Mrs Bailey didn't invite questions.

Nevertheless Prep School was alright, I even almost liked it quite a bit of the time, we were all in it together, there wasn't a lot of homework, and we could get outside where the Teachers weren't watching us all the time. Once or sometimes twice a week we'd troop over to the Lower Pitch for a double period of Games. But once Summer Term came along we didn't go there at all it was so gloomy. And we didn't play cricket, not in Games. For Games, on a hot day we marched in a crocodile down to the disused Swimming Pool at the bottom of Bath Field, there wasn't much water, just a stream running through silt and mud at the bottom of the big square-walled empty pool, willow herb and plantain enjoying the sun and moisture, we stayed clear of a bed of nettles near the shallow end steps. Mrs Bailey'd watch us from her perch on her shooting-stick as we went down into the empty pool the stream running in a trough it'd carved in the sand and mud through the middle before it left under the sluice-gate at the deep end, she'd just sit and watch, making sure we didn't stray out of sight, weeds and thistles and grass and stuff growing in the mud and silt piled up by the stream over the winter, sometimes a cow had got in there and left a great cowpat, if it was close to the stream one or two of us'd try to ease it in so it'd wash away it might even float, we'd scrape little paths in the sandbanks and the mud for the water to flow and we'd build dams and play pooh-sticks and just soss about wading, as usual someone'd slip in the mud and fall full length in the stream, sometimes land on a stone on the sandbank and before long everybody'd be chucking water about, once or twice a couple of kids had old seaside pails they'd remembered to bring, or if we could get away with it fill a paper bag with water to make a bomb, but *No!*, Mrs Bailey'd say, *You mustn't waste paper!* and it wasn't till after the War that we learned to drop water-bombs from the dorm windows onto daykids or any other deserving victim but not on another boarder if you could help it, mud'd fly everywhere, bits of cowpat with it, noisy horseplay lots of shouting, all of us soaked. Mrs Bailey'd just sit there on her shooting stick in her tweeds and cloche hat. She never got wet.

  The water was quite deep, a couple of feet anyway, where it went through the sluice-gate, it hadn't been closed for years but the stream rushed through there on its way to the culvert under the canal, if we got at all close she'd call us back, and after a couple of trips to the pool some of us discovered that with innocence or absentmindedness all over your face you could with a shifty sort of sleight of body sneak out of sight at the shallow end upstream where she didn't look, the water quiet and shallow as it flowed through the entrance to the pool, she kept her eye on the depth at the sluice-gate, the current, I'd quietly wade upstream through the gap in the walls, the stream banks quite sharp just there and once past the wall she couldn't see me, what a pleasure that was, to be out of her sight, in the shade under the hawthorns hanging over the stream, soft muddy bottom dead twigs all waterlogged caught in it perhaps a few thorns here and there tread carefully but nothing much, dappled light, behind me a trail of muddy smudges in the water from where my feet'd been, just the slow sound of the stream, it only sped up at the sluice-gate, branches a faint shush I could hardly hear as they trailed along the water, I really had to listen hard, their faint background noise almost hidden by the steady in-and-out of my breath my heartbeat getting in the way, slight gurgle of water round my legs, the sounds of the other kids talking and laughing and splashing back in a bright sunlit world, goosebumps at the sudden chill of shadowed breeze. I quietly splashed up the stream, little eddies with long-legged boatmen scooting across the surface, midges and gnats maybe a dragonfly or two, tiddlers and even sticklebacks here and there as well as tadpoles or frogs, perhaps a bird's nest but you had to know where to look, minnows by the hundreds scooting off at my cautious step or at my shadow, there might even be a cow on the bank having a drink, deep muddy hoofprints at the water's edge crushing tufts of grass and filling with water, mixed cool smells, rabbit droppings, a thrush or blackbird calling, or the wonderful chittering mellow song of a robin, so tuneful some kids we scoffed at thought it was really a nightingale *As if a nightingale would sing in the daytime!*, and if you got missed then a shout, your name faint on the air.

If you'd got any sense you went back down the stream, you could say you were just round the corner not really out of sight, but not if you came back along the grass you'd be in for it *Where have you been? How dare you go up there!* But she was less forbidding even then, there wasn't any danger and she knew it, but there I was one time looking to left and right at the jungle undergrowth my pistol a forked twig in my right hand just above my waist *Got to keep it dry* looking out for the German spies in their pith helmets and rifles, there were two of them the fat one who slobbered and drooled a lot and the thin brutal one with a monocle *Achtung! Wir da?* with a curl of his lip cold and contemptuous, I'd better make sure their Overseers didn't see me with their huge bullwhips, could I get through and rescue Algy and Ginger *How did they get into such a mess this time?* can't wait till dark got to get back to camp by then *Must check Dusky's alright, that's a nasty wound in his leg* and as I silently crept up the Orinoco the ground gave way beneath me *Quicksand!* I floundered back waving my arms dropped my stick huge *Splash!* I went right under, *uuuurgh* my hair all wet Mrs Bailey'd be cross we weren't supposed to get our hair wet, I turned back my heart pounding away *I bet it really was quicksand* my foot hadn't touched bottom just really soft soft mud just like water really but squishy *There was no footing at all!* I'd lurched my weight onto my back foot *Horrible way to die* grabbed at a branch over my head *sluggish heavy bubbles bursting through thick ooze pith helmet sitting on smooth mud slow ripple as a finger broke the surface then subsided into the glop a desperate heave then everything flat and still* Good Job I'd missed, it was hawthorn, that'd've hurt, and when I got back to the Swimming Pool all in a rush I was still a bit panicky somebody said "Did you go very far up the stream then? Herrick said there's lots of potholes up there, they're not deep but they'll give you a start if you tread in one, pebbles and stuff in the bottom, nothing nasty," and I grinned, a bit quavery, but I didn't say anything.

Nor did Mrs Bailey, sitting there in the warm sun. The deep lines round her mouth softened a bit, her gaze drifted as she let go a bit, she wasn't watching very hard, us out of her clutches mucking about in mud and water too happy to be squabbling, her settled on her shooting stick or even down on the dry and sunny grass, us larking about, none of us bothered by all the mud in our hair or on our trunks and shouting as much as we wanted down in the baths. But after a while I began to shiver a bit whenever a cloud hid the sun, I didn't want to go back to the water to wash the mud off, but when I looked at a couple of the others, standing in the shadow made by the pavilion I saw a muscle on Arnold's thigh jump a bit and suddenly I couldn't stop shivering and I wanted my tea, wanted the shivery walk to School to clean up properly, wet muddy towels damp hair hardly any of us with energy enough to run about, we didn't even have to march in crocodile and we were allowed to talk.

Aside from PT the only times we ever got away from her were when we trooped over to Big School for Music, there was a piano there, or to the Art Room for painting and drawing, two or three times a week. Like Mrs Bailey, Moggie Morris, the Music Teacher, was simply hopeless, we endured him and his silvery long hair and his frayed grey chalk-stripe suit and his badly-polished shoes.

Once a week he'd teach Music Theory, there'd be a blackboard and easel on the Gym stage, we all had half-size notebooks, the right-hand page ruled like music-manuscript and the left just like a regular notebook and he'd tell us about music, how important "Grand Opera" was, the big room so empty and echoey we all heard "Ground Opera," and wondered what it was, "Is it because they stand on the dirt, Sir?" "NO, Boy!" he'd shout, "Pay attention! Don't be so rude!" or "Use the brains God gave you, Child!" Perhaps he'd scrawl it on the board but his handwriting was so bad and the board so pockmarked and battered you couldn't tell if he'd written an *a* or an *o*, he'd talk about great arias and he'd talk about composers whose names we'd dutifully write down, like Vargner and Showpan, some of the kids knew how to spell them but most of us didn't and we never handed our books in mine was all blots and smudges, but the bigger kids, the ones that knew what the names really were would bait him, all the years he taught at Brewood, they ragged him all the time because the classes were so dull, and unlike us small kids they got away with it. I didn't know where to look, couldn't rest my eyes anywhere but felt a bit cold and sweaty and cringed when they really got going, worrying that Moggie'd notice me. Or that *they* would. "When they sing, Sir, is it like the Walsall 'Arriers, Sir?" that was the name of a well-known local running club, and somebody else would chime in with a suppressed laugh "Do they run about while they sing their arias, Sir?" They had no fear of him at all, and certainly no respect, he didn't know at all how to deal with more than one child at a time and was unsure even then, he was useless as a disciplinarian, and to those of us who didn't take Private Lessons he was a figure of fun.

He was just as severe and erratic in my piano lessons. Once a week I'd go down to the Dining Hall in a free period or at the end of classes, the big room empty except for the mild clatter from the kitchen as Cook and Miss Butler got tea ready for all the boarders or lunch for the whole School, the tables all set up with plates and cutlery, cups and saucers, him waiting as I came in through the big double doors all us boys had to use, the whole length of the room between me with my music and him with a handful of music, sometimes an exercise he'd written out for me on music paper, my boots echoed round the room and he'd nod and say "Sit down." Just him and me. No other kids. I couldn't think of him as Moggie, he was Mr Morris. Nothing to divert his attention. The back of my leg shied from the cold wood of the piano bench, him at my right elbow on a padded chair he'd taken from High Table just behind us where the Headmaster and the Masters ate their meals, faint goose-flesh at the small scratch of his suit against my arm as he reached across to the music. He always made me adjust the bench, I never got it where he wanted it to be, "You're too far back," he'd say, or "you've got it crooked," and when I finished pushing and pulling and shuffling about a bit, my feet hardly reached the pedals never mind the floor he'd say "Now, play me your scales." I never did get the fingering right, except for C, I'd get terribly confused in A or D and especially in E, and he'd get very cross very quickly, he had a wooden rod or sometimes a ruler which he'd use as a baton and he'd beat hard on the misbehaving fingers, *snap!*, it hurt, "NO! Why don't you *listen*? D *sharp* in E, can't you *hear* it?" and he'd finger through it quickly "Like this! Use the *correct* fingering" or he'd bang me across the wrist, "Hold the hand like this, boy!" and he'd lean back and sigh, and I'd blink back tears, you should *never* cry in front of a Master.

But if Moggie Morris made the class sing then Music even became fun, twenty or twenty-five kids sitting on wooden PT benches up close against the stage, him sitting at the piano up there on the stage. He'd hand out song books and he'd play and we'd sing, "The Lincolnshire Poacher," that was a favourite, lively thumping good tune

>Oh it's my delight of a Friday night
>In the season of the year

or even better a song I've never heard since then but Our Kid still knows the words more than sixty years later, as do I, and we can both sing it with as great gusto now as we did then, carolling and chirping away at each other over the telephone

>There was an old man named Michael Finnegan
>He grew whiskers on his chinnegan
>The wind came out and blew them innegan
>Poor old Michael Finnegan!

We just loved the recital of his adventures and his downfalls, he climbed a tree and barked his shinnegan, and we really enjoyed those classes, exercising our lungs as the songs echoed and boomed round the big empty room along with the endless parade of military and patriotic songs sung with a lot of swozz. We sang *The British Grenadiers* so much that I still shudder over the inexorable "Hector and Lysander and such great men as these," I cannot drive them from my mind, but Moggie's great love was for genteel Victorian parlour songs and folksongs, the sentimentality of *Danny Boy* sung to the Londonderry Air, and of *Annie Laurie*'s "Maxwelton braes are bonnie," which he played again and again insisting we hold the notes properly and sing the songs "beautifully" because we'd be singing them on stage in front of our parents and visitors from the village when the School Concert came round. Rehearse and rehearse and rehearse again, "No No NO! You all start on the count of *four*! and you, Jones, you're terrible, is your voice breaking, at *your* age? you're no good, keep absolutely quiet until the second line!" Syncopation was completely alien to him, he despised it, I think I was an undergraduate at Nottingham and had joined the jazz club before I even heard the word. Once at the end of Term it must have been about 1945 when I was just over eleven and the average age of the Form was twelve-and-a-half, when he said he'd play us anything we wanted as a special treat, Music that year wasn't in Big School but in the Art Room, one of the older kids it might have been Bogey Butcher he was really big dark hair slicked back he had a lot of muscle he was just beginning to grow hair on his face he must have been nearly fourteen he had spots said from the back of the room "Play 'Home Sweet Home Again' Sir," you could hear the smirk in his voice and his spotty-faced pals laughed, it was a pop song on the wireless, Joe Loss and His Band, I didn't like it very much but it was the sort of song that stuck in your head whether you wanted it to or not, an earworm, we all knew the words, and Moggie shifted gravely on the piano bench and said "Good, you're beginning to learn something after all; you want 'Home Sweet Home' again" and launched forth:

>Mid pleasures and palaces
>Though we may roam,
>Be it never so humble,
>There's no-o place like home!

we'd heard him play it and'd had to sing it beautifully too many times all year, and we hated it almost as much as we hated "Come Into the Garden Maud" except *that* made us laugh it was so silly, and I wanted to pipe up "Please Sir that's the wrong song, he wanted the one that goes like this," but I knew my face'd be red and my voice a strangled squeak, I wanted to sing it to him to show the big boys in the room that I understood even if Mr Morris did not, I didn't want them to look down on me, they walked about owning the place, I wanted to be on their side I wanted them in their unruliness to be on my side, but I was, blessedly, too timid to interrupt him once he'd started playing the song and singing it to us, everybody in the room would've laughed at me he'd probably have walloped me if I'd said it. I started to say it but shut up and nobody noticed. I was frightened by Mr Morris, and they were not. And I saw more of him than they did.

Art was another refuge from Mrs Bailey. You never got bossed about in Art the way you were even in PT with everyone having to do the same thing at the same time, the whole class jumping-on-the-spot to the Master's count or waiting for their turn to vault on the horse or clamber up the wall-bars, and the pleasures of Art felt so very different from everything else we did. If you were lousy at drawing, well, it wasn't your fault was it, and nobody shouted "Pay attention, boy! Watch what you're doing!" the way they did in games and stuff like that. And we all drew stuff whenever we could anyway, we filled our Rough Books with doodles and made-up puzzles or something we'd snitched from the *Dandy* or the *Beano*. The Teacher'd help you if he could and if you asked, but mostly he didn't know how and just left you alone to get on with whatever you were doing so long as you kept busy.

"Draw this beaker" whoever it was'd say, or "Draw what you can see through the window" and just let us get on with it, and you could always say "I need to see it better" and move to look. A lot of us'd go over to see what Jake Bickerton was doing, he drew terrific pictures and you could talk to him about it or rubberneck your way round the room so long as you weren't too obvious, see what everybody else was up to. Jake could draw noses and ears and hands, his people looked like drawings of people as good as what we saw in books and his trees really looked like trees, especially when he had some proper paints. He could even draw animals, horses and cows, he didn't copy them from books, and some of us tried to do what he did. "I just look at them," he said.

The Art Room, sticking out into the Croft on its own the way it did, separated by a walkway from the other classrooms, beckoned the very first time I laid eyes on it. Perhaps the rule that we weren't allowed there without a Teacher or a Prefect to keep an eye on us had something to do with that, but I could glimpse its untidiness through the window, so *different* from everywhere else. The Art Room had so much stuff scattered about, desks higgledy-piggledy not in orderly rows, you just got to sit wherever you wanted and you didn't all have to face the same way, not all the time anyway, and a big grindstone just *waiting* to sharpen somebody's penknife, tins of poster paint begging to be *used* instead of tucked away in their proper place, little jars of glue you knew you mustn't waste, paper you carefully hoarded. It felt like you could get at *every*thing, books and pictures lying about on a table or two, leftover or abandoned bits of drawings some kid'd been doing pinned to the wall or even just lying there, broken chalk and smears of powder-paint all different colours everywhere, even on the floor. No secrets. Nothing hidden away. It looked *scruffy* and untidy, with small tables and wooden chairs scattered about, it looked *used*, a stack of drawing boards leaning over by the door, a stack of butcher paper, a dwindling supply of proper drawing paper. *That should be locked away*, a Prefect said, *Don't use it*. As long as you behaved yourself you could simply sit with your pals wherever you chose, you could even talk to each other, laugh together. We didn't lark about, not in there.

On Saturdays, right after breakfast the dayboys all at home with their mum and dad and us in the classroom all morning we had Mrs Bailey, nobody else. She was far worse then than the rest of the week, and after Break at 11:00 she'd drill us in Mental Arithmetic. "This is the most important subject you'll ever learn," she said, over and over, "you've *got* to be quick, it's no good if you're slow! And you must never make a mistake! *Never!*" and she'd fire questions at us. I'll never forget the first day, like the other new boys I didn't know what we were supposed to do. *You*, she said, *what's nine added to six? Quick now!* and after a pause not even long enough to catch your breath *you're too slow!* she hit her desk with the ruler. "I want to know *now*, right now, now! you can't stop and think, you've got to do it *NOW!*" and she turned to another boy, "What's twelve minus seven?" and waited a second and shouted "Too late! You're too slow!" and she hit her desk again, harder, and she turned to a kid in the front row and said "Multiply eight by seven and a half!" The kid looked blank and she hit his hand with her ruler, he flinched and went white, he didn't cry, and we all looked at him and quailed. "Sixty!" she cried, "Eight eights are sixty-four take away the four! Seven eights make fifty-six, add the extra four! You know your times-tables!" and we didn't dare look at her. As the class went on her face got redder and redder, she strode across the room and grabbed some child by the wrist, a barrage of *whack whack whackwhack**whack***, "You're just not trying! You're a very naughty boy." She looked at us all, "Why can't you get it right!" she shouted, "You're doing this on purpose! It's all very simple! You know your times-tables! We've done them in class, you've learned them." But of course we hadn't, not all our arithmetic books had them all the way up to eighteen-times, they stopped at twelve and most of them had pages missing or splodged illegibly with spilled ink, some pages in mine had bits missing and not just in the times-tables, and I had to copy out homework questions and all sorts of stuff into my Rough Book, someone had spilled so much ink onto my seven eight and nine-times that I couldn't read them any more than I could the ten-times, but that one was easy, all I had to do was count so there was nothing to learn, I didn't even have to think. We all copied the missing bits into our Rough Books, sometimes copying it down wrong, and as the book filled up I had to look harder and harder to find what I wanted, riffling through the increasingly tattered pages for my seven- eight- and nine-times tables. Perhaps that's why if I'm tired or have something on my mind I still get a bit hesitant or even confused where sevens or eights and nines multiply each other, I never really learned those stubborn factors but have to work them out. If I'm faced with "What's seven times nine?" the shortcuts in Mrs Bailey's mental arithmetic simply don't work for me, there's something too absurd about their devious ingenuity, they readily confuse addition with multiplication. Seven eights is fifty-six, add nine and you get sixty-five. But that's hopelessly wrong. Start again, *seven sevens is 49, twice nine is 18, So add 20 and take away 2, 69 minus 2 is 67! Mrs Bailey would be proud of me!* But that's ridiculous! *7 x 10 is 70, take 7 away and you get 63. Aha! That's the right answer!* How could I be so dumb?

My real confusion in Mental Arithmetic and the times-tables was that I never could remember, when I was trying to work out the next figure in those fuzzy areas of the times-tables, that 7 x 9 is the same as 9 x 7. Sir William Rowan Hamilton, him of the quaternions, would've loved me for that, but Mrs Bailey had no interest in telling us how numbers actually work and probably had no idea, I suppose she never imagined that there's actually a word, *commutative*, to describe the way numbers behave in addition and multiplication where the answer's the same no matter what order you put the numbers in. I didn't know that word myself until I was well into adulthood, but we'd've loved a word like that, it would have helped me anyway to remember, we all loved long words, we kept trying to learn new ones to baffle each other with, and of course it didn't matter if we nearly always got them wrong. How impressed we all were two or three years later when Henry Houston was giving out the books at the beginning of term in III A and asked us what sort of state they were in, most of them tattered and with loose pages but by-and-large complete, Ivor Williams stood up and said "Mine's indifferent, Sir" with a grin, I hadn't the faintest idea what it meant but it was such a lovely word, we all used it for weeks after, the way we learned to use "nondescript," mostly wrong.

Every now and again as soon as she came into the room Mrs Bailey told us to write out one of the times-tables *Do it right away!* we really did have to be quick, but it'd be all in front of your eyes as you did it so it was easier than reciting it straight off the bat, when you really did have to know. I can still remember a sunny winter morning a small fire in the fireplace writing the fourteen-times table. "This time you can do it in ink," she said, "It's time you started that. Take a page out of the middle of your Rough Book" and "Don't make any mistakes, you've *got* to be neat!" We got out our pens, I didn't know the fourteens table at all, I don't know that any of us did, I looked over at Adrian he was good at numbers he dipped his pen in his inkwell and started writing "1 x 14 =" "2 x 14 =" "3 x 14 =" and so on all the way to "14 x 14 =" down the left side of the page so I dipped my pen into the ink and started to do the same thing when I got to "2 x 14" I realised *oh! I can just add them up!* and I put down "28," *three times is twenty-eight and fourteen is forty-two, forty-two and fourteen is fifty-six, this is easy!* There were all sorts of little flecks in the paper shiny yellowish scraps of what looked like bits of straw your pen just skidded over them or a little string of curly thin hair, a tiny little scrap of wool likely, it'd catch in your nib you'd have to pull it off before it made a great big smudge, here and there spots of darker grey, some of them printed letters, we all knew the paper we wrote on was made out of old newspapers, it was Wartime Paper made of Salvage, it soaked up the ink in some spots, in other places it was thinner than tissue or even had a hole in it, you kept having to clean your nib off with a bit of paper you'd torn off another page, none of us had any blotting paper *Ink rots holes in your clothes*, Mum'd told me, and none of us'd ever heard of anything like a paper towel or paper hankies. Ink was beginning to get all over my fingers pale blue smears on the page *what would Mrs Bailey think? what would she do?* it was cold, *she'll use that ruler on me,* I shivered, don't make a mess, I dipped my pen in the inkwell it picked up a great fat glob of muck from the bottom of the inkwell a big fat blob fell onto the page a shiny wet blot of ink soaking into the paper a little hill of sodden fluffy stuff in the middle and I looked up Mrs Bailey was watching, her mouth sort of smirked a gash of lipstick, she said "I think you'd all better start again, and use a pencil," even Adrian had ink all over the place, everyone had ink all over his fingers and on the page. John had blue streaks on his chin and near his nose, he'd got some in his hair, "Neville, go round and collect all the papers and put them in the wastepaper basket. And be quick about it!"

But she wasn't often like that, she was too impatient, she thought if *she* knew the answer *we* should know the answer, she just made mental arithmetic too complicated, even now sometimes I still think of something like twelve minus seven as *oh yes 2 plus 3 equals 5* and I have to sort out the convolutions that got me there, the absolute rightness of ten as base. "How many pence in one pound thirteen and sevenpence?" she'd ask, and we'd be stumped, two hundred and forty plus twelve times thirteen plus seven, you really did have to know your times-tables, and the intricacies of money, "What's five pounds nine-and-eightpence from six pounds twelve-and-tenpence?" They were impossible questions. Except at Christmas and birthdays the most money we'd ever seen was probably half-a-crown, I was nineteen before I ever saw a five-pound note, that was at Nottingham we were going to the flicks at the Odeon and Brian Merrick had a five-pound note. It was as big as a bedsheet, we all clustered to get a look at it, they wouldn't take it at the box office even when he knew he was supposed to sign it, that was enough to live on for a fortnight. At Brewood pocket money was thruppence a week, and the questions Mrs Bailey asked were completely meaningless. Later in the War, and after, we'd sneer at Americans and Canadians who had the simplicity of decimal money at their fingertips and floundered away at pounds shillings and pence, our secret pride in the best and proper way of doing things and knowing how it worked scorned the ease of their spending. In the War I heard a bloke in the bus say "Overpaid, oversexed and over here!" and laugh, not that it was funny, later on when we lived in Rugby it was a favourite complaint of Gordon Jones's, I didn't understand all that, though the derision in the laughter was clear enough.

But one Saturday in Mental Arithmetic Mrs Bailey, pointing her ruler at Trevor, said "Take four and sevenpence-three-farthings from eleven and sixpence-ha'penny. Quickly, now!" He went a bit pale and his face looked blank, and he said, "Please Miss," and stopped. "What's the matter?" she said, "It's just subtraction. Get on with it! *Do it in your head!*" She raised her ruler, and I looked away. She got to her feet and stepped between of the desks and my eyes dragged back. *"You,"* she said, her wool-skirted figure hanging over him, *"Frank!"* he was one of the bigger boys, "Tell Trevor the answer. *Right now!"* and I recoiled a bit, thanking my lucky stars she wasn't looming over me, scared I'd cry if it was me. "I don't know, Miss," he said, in a small voice, "we haven't done fr–"and shut his eyes as she grabbed his wrist, lifted it high, *Whack!* Just once, hard, on the back of his hand, and then *Whack!* once more. A tear seeped from the corner of his eye. *"Haven't done what?"* she cried; "*your homework?* Why are you all such naughty boys?" The corner of her mouth turned down as she settled back to her chair. "Haven't done what," she said in a quiet voice, "Frank?" and he blinked, his eyelashes glistening in the light, "Fractions, Miss, we don't know how to do them." Mrs Bailey sighed, but even without farthings the questions didn't get any easier as the Term wore on. "How many pennies in thirty-eight shillings?" she'd bark, "That's nineteen times twenty-four! Quick, boy!" and if you took more than two seconds or came up with the wrong answer she'd take her ruler's edge to your knuckles, "Twice twenty-four is forty-eight times ten makes four hundred and eighty, take away twenty-four. It's *easy,*" she said, "You *must* pay attention!"

Sometimes she'd start class by announcing "Arithmetic dictation. Write out these numbers." She sat at her desk, looked down at a piece of paper, read out a number. She'd only say it once and she watched to see that you wrote it down as she spoke, clear firm numbers. "Don't forget to be neat!" The first time she did it we thought it'd be easy, we all knew how many noughts there were in a million and even in a trillion, and she said "This is the first one. Two hundred and fifty-four" and we all wrote it down, and then she said "thousand" so we all put in a comma, and she said "one hundred and sixty-nine" and we all wrote it down and looked up, her nod of approval, watching, and she gave us the next number. It started out easy but got harder and harder. "Next:" she said. "Four hundred and twenty-nine" she said, "million," she said, so I put in the comma, "Three hundred," she'd say, and I wrote down the "3" and looked up waiting for the rest, "and seventy-two," and I wrote *that* down as with hardly a pause she said "Next, four hundred and ten thousand." We were all caught flat-footed, and most of us scrubbed away at that "372" we'd just written in thinking it was going to be three-hundred-and-seventy-two-thousand, and tried to insert the three missing noughts. She smiled and moved on to "six hundred and fifteen" as your paper became a real mess as she said "Next." And without a pause she started a new number, and you didn't know where to put it. You didn't dare stop writing, if you did she'd reach for her ruler and start out of her chair, still dictating, so you wrote down what you thought you remembered she'd said, trying to get hold of the next number, it was always a complicated one and you listened very hard while you tried to remember the one you'd missed. None of us ever got all the numbers right, and our pieces of paper were always messed up, great smudges from the india-rubber. "Why can't you simply write down the numbers?" she'd say, "just do what you're told" and I suppose, looking back on it now, all these years later, that she thought she was teaching us to listen – to concentrate and remember – but it never occurred to her to tell us what she was doing or why she was doing it. How could we please her when she did what she did? Nobody escaped, and sooner or later no matter how hard we tried not to give in, we'd all've been crying *You're not trying hard enough!* welts on the bright red backs of our hands, "You're being *deliberately* disobedient!" Sometimes she drew blood, "Leave your hand alone, I didn't hit you very hard! You've got to learn!" the back of your hand puffy and bruised, so sore it hurt simply to ease your hand into your trousers pocket. But it could start to get warm once you'd got it there.

At lunch some kid down the table would see your hand as you reached for the salt, say "Had Mrs Bailey this morning did you?" There'd be just the boarders for lunch on Saturday Juniors and Seniors all mingled up at the same table, everybody else at home for the weekend, and you'd remember it all again, everybody knew what was going on, some of them would look up from their food or their conversation and glance at you and look away, back to their chatter with their friends while your cheeks suddenly felt a bit puffy and warm as you tried to smile. I couldn't really look at anyone who'd been with me there with Mrs Bailey, and they couldn't really look at me, we struggled to find something to talk about, how the Wolves were doing or who had last weeks' copy of the *Wizard*, but what talk we had simply petered out, I felt ashamed of my crying, somehow the others now knew too much about me, looked away at the merest glimpse of moisture round someone's eyes, dreaded to notice, fought back whatever tears welled up, blanked out the lively babble at the table, didn't listen. It helped to think of Biggles and Algy and their heroics fighting the Germans, but you knew that wasn't real, it was just a story, it didn't stir the hollowness. By the end of the meal, though, some piece of gossip, Basil Conrad sneaking out of the dorm late at night to go off for a midnight bike ride and getting away with it, or Fargo Hopkins somehow getting hold of an 1840 twopence-blue for his stamp collection, pushed your troubled bewilderment underneath, pulled you back into the world. After lunch you'd hold your hands under cold water making the skin redder a touch of blue and you'd go and watch the football game perhaps in the rain, you hadn't been able to dry your hands properly on the wet roller-towel behind the washroom door, a ring of wet round your shirt wrists, dank and uncomfortable, scuff your feet on the grass, your mac hanging down, its clinging wet edge heavy against your bare legs.

16

Dolly and Angus

Now and again on Saturday, and even during the week, starting in September 1942, my second year at Brewood, we'd go to class to find someone else in Mrs Bailey's place. The awful knot of dread in my stomach diminished, the load of her punishments eased, released. What a sunny holiday when Mrs Asprey turned up, or Henry Houston, to teach us Arithmetic. Being in the classroom was different, completely changed. "John," she'd say, Mrs Asprey called us all by our first names, Mrs Bailey never did, "Campbell Minor" *she'd* say, or "Smith Major." Mrs Asprey would ask "How many pence are there in a shilling?" and John would say "twelve, Miss" in a faltering voice, making his answer sound like a question, and she'd smile and say "Yes, that's good" and "Henry, how many shillings in a pound?" and Henry would look relieved and say "Twenty, Miss" she'd smile again and say "Then what is twelve times twenty?" and we'd all chorus "Two hundred and forty, Miss" and feel pleased. "William," she'd say, and she'd smile, "it's not your birthday, is it?" and when he said "no, Miss" she said "Well, let's pretend that it is, and you just got a Postal Order for half-a-crown as a present and you've gone to Mrs Roberts's to buy some sweets for five of your friends. How much does a sherbet cost, you know the ones I mean, they come in a little packet with a liquorice straw, they're tuppence aren't they? So you've bought everybody a sherbet, and one for yourself, how many's that, six? How much change is Mrs Roberts going to give you?" and we all worked it out in our heads, it was easy even if she had got the prices wrong, they didn't cost *that* much, and just as William said "one-and-six" Henry said in a loud whisper, "a shilling, she'll keep sixpence" and Mrs Asprey suddenly looked stern but there was a sort of amused dimple in one corner of her mouth, "Are you calling Mrs Roberts a thief, Henry? You can't go round saying things like that about people" and he went red and mumbled "No, Miss, I was just making a joke" and she said, "I know, but you shouldn't make that kind of joke ever." Henry looked chastened, she didn't say another word but looked at Alf and asked him a question.

She didn't put up with any nonsense and she wouldn't let you drift off into some sort of daydream, if you were looking out of the window she'd call you back, or she'd come over to where you were and look out of the window too, to see what you were looking at and you had to say you weren't really looking at anything, or you'd say "the rooks, Miss, they've found something" and she'd say "Yes but we're not here to look at rooks are we, you'd better try and answer the question. What was it?" and you didn't know of course so she'd have to tell you and you'd feel silly but you knew it was alright really, you could tell she enjoyed being with us she liked kids she didn't laugh much but she smiled a lot, she wore the same sort of clothes our mums wore when they dressed up to go out somewhere, good wool tweeds or twinsets and what Mum called sensible shoes, she was soft-looking and a bit plump and Mrs Bailey was thin and hard and all sharp angles.

Mrs Asprey lived in a great big house across from the village cricket ground, not that very much cricket was played there during the War; on our Sunday walks if we went down that way we'd look up the driveway and see the big shrubbery all dark green bigger than the one at Rushbury, twice as dusty looking, and the edge of a tennis court, we didn't dare go in, it looked far too posh for that, much later I heard that Before the War she used to run a kindergarten there, but there was no swank about it it wasn't at all splendid it looked lived in, but quiet, prosperous, and private, a bit like Chillington Hall I suppose but of course a lot smaller, not the least bit grand the way Squire Giffard's was, his grounds went for miles, the big Avenue crossing the canal by a Private Bridge with fancy stone balustrades, the Park'd been landscaped two hundred years ago by Capability Brown. Squire Giffard was chairman of the School Board of Governors and a magistrate, the only time we'd ever get to talk to him was when he came to the annual Speech Day at School, that was the only time you'd ever see him except at Church and you certainly wouldn't talk to him there, a lean old man with a slight stoop, always wore a suit. He was a bit aloof though the villagers liked him, he was the local gentry. Mrs Asprey wasn't like that, but she had the same sort of class about her, in the way she walked and looked at you and spoke. I think her husband was a major or more likely a colonel away in the Army, somebody high up anyway, if it wasn't raining she'd come to School on her bike, it had a basket on the handlebars where she carried exercise books she'd taken home to mark, or she'd walk, she liked exercise, but now and again she'd drive to School in her car, goodness knows how she got the petrol. But I don't remember her ever showing anger. She'd get annoyed by facetiousness and let you know she was irritated but she was always soft-spoken and polite, she didn't have any doubt about anything so far as we could see, she never shouted at us, she had a strong sense of her position and what was proper. We always knew where we were with her.

As 1942 stretched towards 1943 Mrs Bailey wasn't there as much as she used to be, and Mrs Asprey began giving us English lessons as well as Arithmetic, and one day she was standing there at the front of the room, she didn't like to sit down much when she was teaching, her right hand kept straying to her left wrist and then her left hand would reach up to her throat and she stirred about a bit walked to the window at the back of the room peered out towards the church came back to the front looked up at us, her right hand back down to her left wrist she sighed, she said "I can't see the church clock but it's not working anyway. I haven't got my watch, does anybody know the time?" and we all looked a bit puzzled, we none of us had watches, Dad had said both Phil and me were far too young to have a watch we'd only break them, they were hard to find anyway in the War, you couldn't even get the pocket watches Marks and Spencer's used to sell for five bob before the War, both Dad and Grandpa said they were terrific, unconditionally guaranteed for a year, but *What would a child do with a pocket watch anyway, besides lose it*? Not many kids at School had a watch, not that we knew anyway,

Dad said they were only vulgar show-offs, you don't boast by giving your *children* things like that, he'd say, that just *spoils* them, What do you want a watch *for*? And there could be no answer to that question. There weren't any clocks in public places so you didn't see one very often, we knew what time it was because people told us what to do or what time it was and she said "Who knows how to tell the time?" and nearly all of us put a hand up.

It was a nice clear sunny morning, a bit of a breeze, you needed a pullover if you were outdoors but better than in this stuffy room with all the windows shut small fire smouldering in the grate I wasn't at all sure I did know how to tell the time but I put my hand up with the others you didn't want to look ignorant, *I* didn't anyway, and I was pretty sure the big hand said the minutes and the little hand the hours or was it the other way round, and I was waving my arm about but I didn't say anything, other kids were saying "I do, Mrs Asprey" and "Please, Miss," and she looked at me and she said "Peter, you go. Do you know which is my car? It's parked round the corner just by the Science Lab, it's the only one there."

I must have looked a bit doubtful as I stood up because she said "Are you sure you know how to tell the time? the big hand tells you the minutes and the little hand the hour" and I nodded and started to leave. "Be as quick as you can. The clock is on the dashboard" and I said "Yes, Miss, just like on my Dad's car" and I clattered down the stairs and ran off. It was so good to be outdoors, I was all excited at having a special task to do, to move about, everybody else still in class, the whole Quad empty, the sun shining on the red flowers in the centre flowerbed, the Headmaster's front door open. Somebody was shaking a rug out of a window upstairs in his part of the house, dust and fluff flying out of a turbulence of blue and I suddenly got confused, *is the little hand the minutes, it must be, hours are bigger than minutes, no the big hand moves quicker so it's the minutes the little one's the hours* and I couldn't remember which and then I was at the car I suddenly remembered I knew how to tell the time I opened the car door and I looked at the dashboard and it was covered with dials there were so many of them *Which is the clock?* I couldn't find it, she did say it was on the dashboard didn't she but it wasn't there, in Dad's Austin it was right in the middle, a big dial, but not here, I couldn't see it anywhere, what was this, "Morris" it said. I looked on top of the dashboard, but there wasn't anything there I climbed in the car and sat down in the driver's seat, the dark leather hot on the back of my legs all crackly a yellowy-brownish light coming through the speckled windows, they were made of layers of brownish glass lots of cracks and flat-looking loops all yellowy peeling-looking it was just like the old car on the farm at Alcester a close dusty smell hot leather the car all closed up in the sun it was hot everything quiet I listened and there wasn't any sound at all somebody's voice droning through a window in the Science building there was a pair of soft leather gloves on the next seat a bit of screwed up brown paper a hint of her perfume and I looked and looked *Where's the clock?* all the dials looked the same everything was brownish and faded-looking the glass over the dials all dusty *Which one's the clock?* I could hear it ticking and suddenly there it was, right in front of my nose a small round disk just about an inch across, I had to count round the face the big hand was between the IV and the V and the little hand was past the XI and I climbed out of the car "*the little hand is past the eleven and the big hand is next to the five* it's nearly half-past eleven" and I closed the car door "*the big hand is nearly at the five and the little hand is next to the eleven* no no no it's the other way round it's nearly eleven thirty *the little hand is past the eleven and the big hand is next to the five* oh blimey which way round is it I can't remember" I rushed back to the car and peered through the window I couldn't see the clock clearly it was so gloomy in there so I opened the door again the handle hot on my hand as I pushed it down and peered in "I've been gone such a long time! she must wonder where I've been! she told me to hurry up! oh yes *the little hand's the eleven*" warm dusty air flowing out past my face smelling of car a mix of petrol and oil and dust and old scent and dry leather and I closed the door and ran like mad back to Rushall chanting *the little hand's just past eleven* over and over to myself a jingly little rhythm trying not to think *big hand* but knowing that I mustn't forget where it was and I got back, I stopped at the bottom of the stairs I walked carefully up at a proper pace Mrs Asprey didn't like noise and wanted us to walk properly everywhere but she *had* told me to hurry and I went in red-faced a bit sweaty and still out of breath I was sure she'd wonder why I'd been so long I'd been gone for ages I said "It's nearly half-past eleven o'clock, Miss" I was pretty sure I'd still got it right she'd be really cross if I hadn't but all she did was ask me where the hands were and I told her and she nodded and said "Oh, we've lots of time then, I thought it must be time to start English but we've a bit of time yet. Thank you Peter. Carry on, Patrick, tell me the answer" and she smiled so that was alright then and I went and sat down.

Henry Houston always knew what time it was, he was in charge of almost everything including telling people when it was Break, he'd send someone round from class to class to say it was Break, he was very stern, when he gave an address to the School which he did sometimes at the end of Prayers he'd say *you rabbits* or *you animals* in a fierce voice but you could tell he didn't mean it, there was a twinkle of mock in his eye but he was still a bit fearsome, he never promised a penalty he didn't give. He was always polite and serious in class, scrupulously attentive, he explained things to us as often as needed till we understood, he explained how Mental Arithmetic works so we could do it, and it became a kind of game *but you'd better be attentive!*, after he'd been teaching us for a while we'd try to think out ways to do sums, shortcuts, before he told them to us. "If you have to multiply by nineteen do it by twenty and then take one of them away; quick, what's nineteen times three?" and he'd show us on the board, tell us "take away the three from the sixty to get fifty-seven," and smile, if you got it wrong he'd simply say "No. You took away nineteen instead of three. Try it again" but he'd change the problem, "Twenty-seven times four" and see if you made the same mistake, urging you to be quick, friendly, attentive, he made it a bit of a contest so that sometimes we'd actually enjoy it, *ask how you did it*, we weren't terrified, we wanted to win, but he wasn't pleased if you kept making the same mistake. "Think, you rabbit!" he'd say lifting one eyebrow. We adored him, he was all bark and only bit if you deserved it, his bit had *bite*, his ability to lift one eyebrow much higher than the other terrified and fascinated us we quailed before it, he told us he'd been injured when he was a young man in the 1920s in hospital his head in bandages for months his right eyebrow immobilised he didn't say more except that was why he could lift the left one so high. It all sounded heroic, for weeks after that you'd see troops of small boys going round the School with one hand pressed firmly over one side of their face wiggling the visible eyebrow furiously up and down, we did it everywhere we went, we practised and practised but it didn't make any difference none of us ever learned how to do it, I didn't anyway. The villains in all the stories we read, like the Nazi air ace Eric von Stahlhein in *Biggles Flies West* or General von Scharnkamf or whatever his name was of the Gestapo in the *Wizard*, always had a supercilious look on their face when they shot a plane down or tortured prisoners or even talked to underlings, that's how we knew they were villains, enemy spies were called supercilious so we'd know they were spies, and the craze for wiggling one eyebrow and not the other came to a sudden stop when one of the older boys, I think he was in the Fourth Form, told Harold that *cilia* was Latin for eyebrow and *supercilious* meant raising one eyebrow higher than the other, "Why d'you want to look like a Nazi?" he scoffed, "That's bonkers." But of course you still raised your eyebrows, you can't stop doing that, and I still have a sneaking regard for people who can lift just one, wish I could do it, Phil still does it, beautifully, when he wants to look at you askance, it's terrific for dealing with kids, scornful and slightly comic all at once.

Henry wouldn't ever put up with nonsense and he never lied to us. When I was about twelve he spent a whole Geography class telling us what we were like inside, telling us how vulnerable to serious damage the bladder was when full, how it distends, little drawings on the blackboard, I haven't the faintest idea if they were even remotely accurate, "And if you ever raise your hand and ask to be excused to go to the bathroom I never say no. Now you know why." What a change from Mrs Bailey. We never abused that, he trusted us, he helped us to cope, he helped us recover. He must have known something was going on, but he was only the assistant Headmaster and she was the Headmaster's wife.

Like Henry Houston, Angus Beaton, our new Housemaster, after Mrs Bailey left in 1944, was a friendly face, even at weekends he was always in our sights, he ate all his meals with us boarders, chatted with us, told us about where he lived. We saw as much of him as we did of Henry Houston. We knew nothing about him really except that he lived in the Lake District somewhere and went home for the holidays, one time this elegant middle-aged woman turned up at School dressed to the nines she looked much nicer than anybody's mum she looked like somebody posh in *Picture Post* or *Illustrated* asking for him and we all fell over when we found out it was his wife, some of us didn't believe it, *"That's* Mrs Angus?" we said, somehow that was hard to credit he was so scattered sometimes and untidy seeming.

"I stay there all summer," he said, and when we asked what he did there he'd smile over what he called his good luck and tell us "I paint. That's what I like to do." About once a week or so he'd go over to the Art Room as soon as his breakfast was over, some of us still eating, and when we got to class we'd find him starting on the second of the two blackboards, he'd already filled the first, his greenish checked-tweed suit all dusty with chalk a propelling pencil clipped into his top pocket, he never wore a gown, the board speckled white from kids chucking things about the room over the years. There was no such thing as blackboard paint, not in the War. As soon as we'd all got the left-hand board copied *Haven't you finished it yet? Hurry up!* he'd wipe it off and fill it up again while we got on with the right, his suit getting dustier and dustier and looking baggier and baggier as he scrunched over to reach the bottom of the board and one of the daykids'd say, they could take risks we couldn't. "Please, Sir," we loved to tease him, "it says on the board 'Corot was born in Paris in 1796 at the age of 26.' 'Ow did 'e manage that, Sir?" and Angus would raise an eyebrow go a bit pink look at the board and as he turned to make the comma after "1796" bigger, and somebody else would ask "Was he born in 1770, Sir?" and he'd look a bit blank. "Is that a full stop after 'Paris,' Sir? When did he start painting in 1796?" and we'd all laugh a bit. He had a wonderful pixyish sort of elfin face, hooked eyebrows, not much hair, and he'd look a bit cross but he'd shrug as he gazed at that poxed blackboard and gesture vaguely, his pointed ears stirring as he swallowed, "You know what it says," he'd say, he didn't often get vexed, you could tell he was suppressing a tiny quirk of a grin even if he found putting up with us a bit tiresome and we knew enough not to go too far, we liked him too well for that. He was impatiently good-humoured, he was too courteous to say "Shut up, Jones, and don't be impertinent," too gentle, and in Art class he'd pay close attention to how you were doing, he attracted us in ways teachers like Moggie Morris in Music didn't and Mrs Bailey couldn't. He'd lean over your shoulder and sketch a line in, show you different ways to hold your pencil to get effects, his asthmatic wheeze in your ear, he'd been gassed in the First World War he'd been in the trenches like Dad I suppose but I never really made the connection for ages and ages, we had no idea at all what it meant to have been gassed though we knew mustard gas was a Terrible Thing, had no idea that chlorine gas even existed, yet of course we came across and met a lot of people like that and we still had no imagination of the War, didn't really know anything about it, couldn't begin to think what it was like. When I went to Nottingham in 1952 Professor Pinto had all the first year English students round to his house one evening, he'd been in the Artists' Rifles and knew Siegfried Sassoon, but I never made the connection there either, when he showed us all his books inscribed by Sassoon and carefully paged through his big Max Beerbohm *Poets Corner*, talking about them and explaining them to us. The War was remote, his gentle reminiscences of the people he knew made it somehow a bit glamorous, the stuff of books really, and it was a real eye-opener the year I got my B.A., even if we had read a lot of poetry by Owen and Rosenberg and Sassoon, to look at a pictorial history of life on the Western Front which Frank Gibbon had brought from home, all those photos of damaged and disfigured life in the trenches and death in the towns, bodies lying at the side of muddy roads.

Angus had a lot wrong with him not just his lungs, there were some things he couldn't eat, now and again Cook would make him something different, like herrings with mustard sauce, all bright yellow we thought it looked like custard only revolting instead of nice, and we'd watch him eat, lean over his food, "you put that on fish, Sir? *Eeyuew!*" He didn't really know how to talk to young boys and wasn't really at ease with us except when he could talk about painting and drawing and artists or show us how to do something, he cared enormously about that, and photography when there was any film, he loved to encourage us and we responded to him, he could always pick out the good bits of what you'd drawn or painted or modelled and he'd show you, make you feel pleased with what you'd miraculously done, he shared your distress if you'd worked hard at something and then it got ruined, somebody'd dropped a plaster-cast while moving it out of the way or torn a picture or spilled something on it or smudged their pastels. The Art Room was always an untidy dirty place, Nunc couldn't clean it properly, there was stuff spilled all over especially round the benches at the front, the gluepot forever boiling over, there was a big grindstone on a wheel with its assorted litter in the corner, and pencil shavings scattered everywhere, it smelled of chalk and powdered posterpaint and gelatine, glue and plaster dust, crunchy underfoot, bits of string littering scattered round the place.

As Housemaster, his bedroom was just outside the Second Dormitory. One winter we were all reading away under the covers with our torches after Lights Out pools of light traversing the ceiling a bit of whispering going on it was late he could see the ceiling through the ventilators high on the walls and he called out "Go to sleep! I can hear you, I'm not blind!" and then as he climbed to the second floor on his patrol we heard him chuckle to himself as he realised what he'd said and we all giggled our heads off.

It didn't occur to us that Art was something somebody could actually *do*. Then one breakfast after Angus'd left early to set up his blackboard and somebody at Matron's table loudly complained "I hate Art, we never have anything to do, I certainly never learn anything" Matron asked him "Why not?" and in the silence that followed that she said "Honestly, you lot! Some of you're forever drawing in your Rough Books! It looks to me that you really like drawing and painting. And look at the models some of you keep working on, think about Bud Flanagan and the models he made! Why don't some of you ask him for help? See if you can get Mr Beaton to open up the Art room after Prep or during the weekend?

Art isn't like Geography or French! You've got to tell him what you're trying to do!" She paused. "Honestly!" she said, "you can't expect Mr Beaton just to guess. Ask him how to design, oh I don't know, a good camouflage for somebody's bike?" "Oh," Mike said. "Yeah. How would you hide the Wolverhampton bus?" Matron's idea was so unusual that it took a good week to sink in, and of course some of the kids didn't really care much either way, not about anything to do with School, and Art lessons were just a break from being ordered about all the time, told what to do. But then one day in the Billiard Room Lionel Cooper asked Mr Beaton how he could make what he was drawing look shiny and Angus said "Here, I'll show you" and he sat down next to Lionel, "D'you see? try to hold your pencil like this – no, don't press so hard – let the pencil do the work it's supposed to do. There's a little trick to it, it's really pretty simple," and he looked up to find a bunch of kids'd crowded round. "Oh," he said. "You'll see better if you give us room, you know" and he looked pixyish as he smiled. "That's one way, there *are* others" and of course some of us wanted to see them too, and he said "No, not now. Save it for next time" and he looked at another kid. "Let me see what you're doing, show me" and suddenly lots of us wanted to show him, see what *he* could show *us*, and after that we began to like Art, we could actually *do* something. He said "You have to practise. You can make something look round and solid instead of like a dent or a hole in the paper, but you won't get it right the first time, you never do. You have to work at it, look carefully at shadows, see what they do." He showed us how to use a grid to copy a drawing accurately and shook his head as he said "*No*, you can't use tracing paper! Do it freehand! Everything takes a lot of practice," he said, "you have to train your eye as well as your hand," and more than once he told us "You don't need to draw with the *point* of your pencil, you can just lay your pencil down like this so you so you can draw with the flat of the lead, you get a nice soft shade that way. Try things out! Look at what happens when you rub your pencil over a piece of paper you've laid over something rough, on your desk lid for instance, or a brick" and that was quite astonishing, we already did that sort of thing, but I didn't know we were allowed.

17

Letters Home

We didn't know from one day to the next whether Mrs Bailey would be teaching us or not, but she was still an implacable presence, and we only got away from her on Sundays. What with no classes there wasn't very much to do, and with the full-size table in the middle and the lockers against one wall there really wasn't enough room in the Billiard Room for all us boarders at once and we certainly couldn't play boisterous games there, especially when Sunday was supposed to be a Quiet Day. Not as regimented as during the week, but we still had to watch ourselves. Breakfast was half an hour later, at nine o'clock, Matron would go up and down the dormitories as usual getting us up, Sunday was Cook's day off and Miss Butler boiled eggs for all forty of us in a great big saucepan. Some of them would be hard, some of them all runny hardly cooked at all, and any that'd cracked had rubbery swellings of white bursting variously through the shell, some streaked with yolk. Nobody'd be at the High Table, there'd only be Boys in the Dining Hall except for Matron and the Housemaster, and after breakfast we'd put clean sheets and pillowcases on our beds and stuff the dirty ones in a pillowcase to be sent to the laundry. At a quarter-to-ten we'd troop off with a Prefect to a classroom for an hour to write letters home before we went to Church, but nobody needed a whole hour to do *that* no matter how hard it was to find something to say. Sometimes the Juniors went to one room with the Housemaster or some other Teacher, and the Seniors to another with a Prefect, it was just like being in class, we weren't allowed to talk or anything, even if it was a bit more relaxed, we were there to write letters, you *had to* write one, and we had to hand our letters in in unsealed envelopes properly addressed. Mr Bailey would read the letters before he sealed them and stuck a tuppeny-ha'penny stamp on, they got posted in the village in time for the afternoon collection. It was hard to think of what to say because Mum and Dad didn't know who your friends were and it was much too difficult to explain, but now and again Mum'd managed during the week to send me and Our Kid a sixpenny postal order each, we could cash them at Mrs Roberts's shop and then tell what we'd spent it on, but that didn't happen very often *We're not made of money*. Some kids every week'd get something on top of what Mr Bailey dished out every pocket-money day, but with everything rationed there wasn't very much to spend your money on. It got to be a sort of standing joke we all recited to each other about writing home, "Dear Ma, 'ow's Pa, send dough, Dick" in a little chant, we'd giggle away at that, pretending that'd be enough, Mr Bailey made sure it wasn't and the Prefect or the Teacher checked that you'd written at least a page and that it was neat and tidy. Nobody escaped writing a letter home every week, we had to sit in that room until it was time to go to Church, and it didn't matter how fast you wrote your letter you still had to stay in that room and sit quiet. I suppose that was the only way to make sure we'd all be presentable when we went trooping off dressed in our Sunday Best, but the second or more likely the first Sunday I was at Brewood I didn't have any idea how to write a letter and whoever was in charge wrote on the board what to say, how to put the address, *The Grammar School, Brewood, near Stafford*, three lines properly lined up on the right at the top and then the date "You put the number of the day first, then the name of the month, and then the year, *21 September 1941*," and he wrote it out, "Day month year is the proper order, it's logical and it's natural." And then *Dear Mum and Dad* over on the left *You always put your Mother first*, and after that you're on your own, you had to decide what to write, and you finished "love from" and your name, just your first name. All I could think of was something like "I'm still here" *Of course I was still here, where else would I be?* but those three words looked terribly lonely on the page, *What else is there to say?* It was a long time, I mean a lot of years, before I realised that most of what we say to each other in love and friendship is the obvious and familiar, when I did find that out I chose for quite a long time to say nothing at all because I thought Small Talk was a complete waste of time. Writing letters on Sunday mornings was just like being in class, it was like doing a test. I looked at the kid in the next desk, what was he writing, we couldn't talk to each other, we had to be quiet, I didn't know the name of the boy on my right and when I looked over wanting to know what to say he just smirked and leant over his letter hunched his shoulder so I couldn't see, what he had to say was private and he wouldn't look at me, Dad'd get furious if you tried to read a letter of his, it was none of your business, so I looked at Andrew on my left he was writing about a Biggles book he'd got and he grinned at me, it was open on the desk in front of him, Biggles telling Ginger "I don't like being hounded about by these dagos" and I wondered what sort of scrape Biggles and Algy and Ginger had got into this time, the thought of Squadron Leader James Bigglesworth D.S.O. and his pal the Hon. Algernon Lacy stirring me in my seat, their adventurous heroics. I sat there I don't know how long, miles away, shivered a bit, I dipped my pen in the inkwell, you had to write in ink you couldn't use pencil, and I wrote "I'm enjoying my classes" and "There's a library here with a lot of books in it by somebody named G.A. Henty and there's some Biggles books" and "I'm in a dormitory with a lot of other boys," big round cursive letters like the ones we'd been doing in class. I didn't say anything else, the page was nice and full it was just letter-sized notepaper, blue with an envelope to match, I wrote "Love from Peter" and suddenly I had nothing to do, I just had to sit there being quiet and not move, I'd filled up the page and I'd written Mum and Dad's name on the envelope "Mr and Mrs C.P. Quartermain" and where I lived, "94 Solihull Road, Shirley, Birmingham" I could hardly get it all in, and folded my letter in half and put it in the envelope. The Teacher said that if I was just writing to Mum I'd still put Mrs C.P. Quartermain, but those were Dad's initials that wasn't her, Mum was Ada Bessie, and it was only after Dad died in 1954 that Mum felt at all easy about being addressed as Mrs A.B. and even then for a while she was occasionally a bit bothered.

It would be ages and ages till we could all of us together get up and go out to Church, there was a bit of sun outside, I could see the gate to the farm across the Croft and the hedge by where there used to be a tennis court, just a scruff of grass now, and my bum was getting numb from the hard oak seat. *Numb bum. Bum numb. Bumb.* Other kids were reading books, I didn't have one, hadn't known to bring one, didn't know what the time was, nothing doing, not even to listen to, except a bird somewhere outside or perhaps the faint sound of a horse on the towpath pulling a barge. *How much longer till we can move?* I hadn't been to church much anyway, Mum and Dad didn't take us to church, they didn't go, but when we got there there'd be prayer books and hymn books to read and in between the sitting-quiet bits I could stand up and kneel down and sing the hymns and give the proper responses, much better than just sitting, I could easily work out what I was supposed to do, read the responses in the prayer book or just mumble along, all I had to do was just watch everyone else in church bobbing up and down at the same time, some people didn't really kneel, there was a hassock to kneel on but they just crouched over, one person just leaned forward, you could tell, she wasn't kneeling at all, when I went home at Half-Term Mum said "She probably doesn't want to ruin her stockings, all those clothing coupons" *How could kneeling ruin stockings?* I didn't understand that. The Prefects made sure that we all knelt properly, a nudge and a whisper would go down the line "Kneel down properly, pass it on," the worn red hassock scratchy on your knees. All of us kids from School sat at the back in a special set of pews on the left, Juniors in the front rows and the Seniors behind supposed to keep an eye on things, while the Vicar maundered on and on, I could barely tell what the words were as he chanted "*Nnny*oh Lawd ohpen thou ower lips" but I could follow the funny spelling in the book and say back "And our mouth shall shew forth thy praise." If you were careful he wouldn't see you read the hymn book or the prayer book as he droned on during the sermon. Even a psalm could liven it up with its chanted bit at the end of every verse, we stood up to do that, stretched our legs a bit, and if we knew the tune we'd really belt it out.

But at Sunday letter-writing we were supposed to read Improving Books and Andrew wasn't supposed to have that Biggles book for after he'd done his letter, he could get away with it if he didn't make it obvious, some kids put homemade wrappers carefully folded with a real-looking title on the front to disguise their books *It's to protect it, Sir!* but I didn't have a book at all, I hadn't the faintest idea what I could do *I'd better bring a book next week! Get one from the library* and I sat there looking out the window, I tried counting all the pockmarks in the scabby blackboard stuck on the wall, I kept losing my place so I stuck my hand over one eye and put the other one out in front of me so I could only see one bit of the board at a time and a cross-sounding voice said "Quartermain! what *do* you think you're doing?" Everybody turned round and looked at me and a bigger boy said, "He doesn't have anything to read." The Prefect said "There's a copy of *Pilgrim's Progress* over here, you can give him that," and somebody sniggered, *How was I supposed to know?* and I got a bit hot under the collar my tie too tight my face too big for my head a tingle at the edge of my eye, nobody was writing any letters any more they shuffled and twisted round in their seats to look at me, the Prefect looked annoyed his hand held back as he looked at me down his nose and said "Settle down all of you. Yes, Jones?" and Jones, a kid a lot older than me he must have been about fourteen got permission and came over and whispered "Here, try this, it's a bit difficult to start, a bit slow, but it's a terrific story, it's really exciting. It's smashing once you get into it." I looked at him and I looked at the book with its creased red covers and hundreds and hundreds of pages with small print all very thin paper and said thank you, my lower lip sticking out a bit, hesitant and a bit grumpy, and I opened it up, the title page said *Oliver Twist* by Charles Dickens. Somebody dipped a pen into his inkwell and a pen scratched on paper, somebody sighed and the Prefect stretched out his legs, his chair creaked the cloth of his trousers sussurring, one leg against the other, somebody turned the page in a book, a shoe scraped on the floor, the room was full of little noises small coughs and throat clearings I could hear my own breath and I swallowed, whenever I have a drink Mum says I sound like a horse, "you must drink quietly" but no matter how hard I try that first swallow always makes a great big gulp, it still does, *I wonder what she's doing, where's Dad* watched a shadow creep along the wall *How long will it be till Church* I scratched my leg and Andrew looked across at me from his desk, pointed at his Biggles and grinned. *I wonder if he'll lend it me.* I turned the page, here I was at page four and I hadn't taken in a word, what did it mean "finding in the lowest depth a deeper still"? Some sort of sense glimmered there but I couldn't work it out not really, what was an "experimental philosopher" anyway, but I struggled on. Not many of the sentences meant very much but there were some lovely words in there, nice big ones like *engendered* and *stipendiary*, whatever they meant, and funny ones like *leathern* and *wurkus* and *fondlins*, I had a vague idea what a workhouse was, I thought there was one at the bottom of Dean Street but somebody had said no that's an almshouse and then there'd been an argument about the difference, but that'd been at lunchtime a day or two before, Grandfather at Marlow had once said terrible things about people in the workhouse and Grandmother had looked stern so I knew it was a horrible place, everyone looked down their noses at even almshouses and then the Prefect stood up and said "Hand in your letters, we have to leave now, get ready for Church" and somebody on the other side of the room looked at me and said "Did you get to Fagin yet?" I looked puzzled and somebody else said "Isn't it terrible when he can't have any more" and there was a whole chorus of "Please, Sir, I want some more" they all giggled and I didn't know what they were going on about, they expected me to know and they all laughed sharing a joke and I couldn't understand it, and Martin Mercer said "It's all in the story, didn't you get that far?" and I said no and felt stupid. "He's too young for it," the Prefect said, as though I wasn't there, "you should have done what I told you and given him *Pilgrim's Progress*," and we all trooped off to Church in a crocodile my hands in my pockets my shoulders hunched up hot and bothered, "Stop slouching and get your hands out of your pockets" the Prefect said, "you're not a Village Boy."

About a year later, sometime in 1942, we were all, us smaller ones anyway, sitting in the Art classroom, which was also IV B's Form Room, writing our Sunday letters, and Tom Hansen, about a year older than me, he was tough and wiry, had lost some teeth in a soccer game or a fight I don't know which it could've been a cricket ball or he fell off his bike he looked pretty intimidating to me raised his hand and said to Miss Merrit in his broad local accent "Please Miss 'ow d'you spell Chezlin A" and she'd never heard of it, had no idea where it was, she was new that Term, came from somewhere near London, she wasn't at Brewood very long anyway, though she came back again for a Term or two a year or so later, she wasn't fit enough for the Land Army, and it soon became clear that she thought he'd made it up, there couldn't be such a place, "Is it one word or two?" she asked, and Tom had no idea. "But don't you *live* there?" she asked, and he said, "Yes Miss" *of course he did!* and somebody else stuck his hand up and said, "It's somewhere near Cannock, Miss," and she gave in. I don't think she was too sure about Cannock either and asked us all "Does anyone know how to spell it?" and somebody said "It's c-h-e-s-l-y-n I've seen it on a bus" and we all started guessing, she wrote it on the board. Some thought the second word was simply the letter *A*, and that there'd be a Cheslyn *B* somewhere close by not that any of us'd heard of it and others thought it might be *e-i-g-h* like in neighbour or eight, or just simple *e-h*. There weren't any maps to hand or close by *Don't you know there's a war on?* you have to keep all local maps under lock and key so the Germans won't be able to find their way about. It was all a bit of a puzzle, you could still buy maps in shops if they had any and the shopkeeper knew who you were, and a couple of months before I started writing this bit Phil gave me an Allday's street-map of Birmingham Dad'd bought for 9d. in 1942, and I've got a *Bartholomew's Road Atlas* I look at now and again while writing this, "FIRST PRINTED 1943," but the only atlas that was any good at School was locked up in the Library, an ordinary School Atlas like we had in our desks didn't have any detail in it, and the speculative conversation went on and on. Nobody knew anything but we were all getting a wonderful break from the silent hour of letter-writing, they were enjoying themselves, they were laughing as they made their funny guesses, but I really couldn't believe that a Teacher didn't *know*. That was a bit of a shock, and I felt sweaty and wriggled in my seat as the talk went in fits and starts as people came up with different ways to spell "A" and fanciful anecdotes about what that strange second word, if it was one, might be. I kept quiet as I puzzled over it, Miss Merrit looked more and more bewildered and after a while she said "We just don't know, so I think you'd better write a plain letter A. It's *Cheslyn A*" she wrote it on the blackboard and that settled the matter. Mr Bailey took one glance at the messily addressed envelope when it was handed in along with the letter and scornfully said "It's Cheslyn Hay, *every*body knows *that!*" but none of us did. We do now, though.

Church was about a hundred yards down the road from the Gates past Mrs Roberts's tuck shop on the corner, the clock on the church tower stopped and the church bells silenced for the duration, they didn't ring to call people to worship, they'd only ring in an Invasion or if a paratrooper came down, except somebody not long ago told me they rang the bells in October 1942 to celebrate Montgomery's victory at the Battle of El Alamein, I don't remember that, though I do remember going to the pictures to see it, it must have been the Rialto at Rugby, that would have been right after, it was a full-length black-and-white film "Desert Victory" it was called, the guns blazing away dazzling the night sky in that strange sandy landscape of camouflage nets and tents, tanks and guns, the intense noise of artillery, men in helmets scrambling about, martial music, a lot of black screen, lots of flashes, but on Sundays at School somebody who had a watch had to keep an eye on the time and make sure we all assembled ready to parade off to Church in proper order, smallest in front tallest behind, at about ten to eleven, the rest of the village steadily making their way there, except for those who didn't go of course, not many of *them*, all of us in our best suits if we had one and our shoes newly polished *you'd better be wearing your cap!* Nosey Parker would tell us when he came to teach us Scripture, but that wouldn't be till 1944, that it was a sub-cathedral "That's why it's so big" and that the church at Wheaton Aston had had to be built at the bottom of the hill so that it wouldn't be closer to heaven than Brewood church, but he must have made that up there's no hill worth mentioning at Wheaton Aston. It helped put Wheaton Aston in its place though, we Brewood kids looked down on kids from other villages just as we boarders looked down on dayboys, secretly envying them.

But we boarders reserved our ill will for the kids at the Nash School just round the corner, you could see their playground through the orchard and the overgrown old tennis court across the street from the Gates, and even more for the kids at the Catholic School over on Bargate Street near Brewood Bridge just above the wharf, some of them lived at their school, they were boarders, but we never saw them they kept themselves to themselves, weren't allowed out very much so far as we could tell, and they had all sorts of silly stuff going on in Church, incense, and bells, and the service was in Latin. Nobody could understand what they did there, how could they be going to Church properly, they didn't even wear a School Uniform, none of them had a blazer, and their Vicar, only he wasn't called that but a priest, sometimes we'd see him wearing his weird black hat *It's to do with what goes on in their church* Ken said; *I don't know what it's called. He's not supposed to wear it outside.* Often on the way into the Square we'd go past the Nash playground bursting with energetic kids playing noisy games, they were a scruffy-looking lot all dressed in a whole range of cloths and colours, boys and girls all in the same school, corduroy and flannel, brown and blue red and green purple and mauve, some of the girls in dresses some in skirts, some of the small boys even in long trousers, wearing hand-me-downs mostly. They didn't have School Uniforms, some of them wore jumpers, none of them wore blazers and they didn't even have a School badge, boys and girls played together in a small paved yard just the other side of Nunc's orchard, two doors marked "Boys" and "Girls" in the building behind them just the way it had been in Wheaton Aston but the girls shared the playground with the boys. Now and again the ball the Nash kids were playing with would come bouncing over the fence into the street and we'd throw it back, along with an insult, they'd shout at us and talk to us and sometimes taunt us as we walked in pairs and trios down the street. We hardly ever went into the village by ourselves, I don't think we were supposed to, but if I did I always crossed the street before I got to the Nash. Some days we could hear them playing outside on their Break while we were still in class, their timetable wasn't the same as ours, their energy and noise reminded me of the kids I'd seen going down the air-raid shelters in Birmingham and even of the kids I'd played with at the seaside on our holidays before the War or the Townies at Wheaton Aston, we were always a bit cautious around them they were so unafraid. They knew what they were going to do when they left school, they'd leave a lot earlier than us after taking courses in machining and lathework and woodworking, stuff like that, become apprentices at Boulton Paul's airplane factory in Wolverhampton or the Goodyear tyre factory at Bushbury if they didn't simply end up working alongside their dads or as a farm labourer somewhere near. The bright ones might get to the Mechanics Institute in Wolverhampton or to Birmingham Technical College but they all of them, boys and girls, had a pretty good idea of what they were going to be if they weren't in the Army. Even if we weren't at all sure what we'd do when we got out of school, if we thought about it at all we knew that some of us'd be schoolteachers or even parsons. If the worst came to the worst we might get to be Civil Servants. No matter what, they'd be decent jobs, you could say you'd have a career even if you weren't at all sure what you'd be doing or even if you'd actually get to be anything very much, but not working with your hands, not manual labour.

Sometimes we'd come across Nash kids cycling about and shouting to each other, their school just round the corner from us. Usually we'd avoid them but other times we'd hook up and ride together and talk, they'd take us places we often didn't know about, down farm lanes and across fields where they knew the farmer, somewhere like Plant's Hagg or Cream Pot, I never believed those were real names till I saw them on a map a lot later.

Once in the twilight Jim and Ken and I sped into the orchard across from the Gates hunting for apples, we loved the excitement of scrumping and we were always hungry, Ken was a little bit ahead of me and Jim and *Ssssh!* he said as quiet as he could, *Listen!* one of the trees softly thrashed about a little and another voice whispered *C'mon, hurry up!* as we crept forward, we were all on edge it was just like our war game in the cornfield. We might get caned if we got caught scrumping. Jim pointed at a silhouette against a tree, the clothes were all wrong it wasn't one of us at all it was a Nash kid, one of the Conklins. "*Thieves! Thieves!*" Ken shouted, and behind us we heard their mad scramble as we fled back to the safety of School and Nunc came blundering out of his cottage waving his stick and shouting. "I'll larrup the hide off you, Sam Crutchley" he shouted, "I know it's you, you young bugger!" Once we got back to the Quad Jim said between heaves of breath "That can't've been Sam, he lives out in Penkridge" and Billy said "It was one of the Conklins." We'd got no apples, but Nunc can't've seen us he'd got the culprits so wrong.

But we never went over towards Bargate, there was real hostility between us and the kids at the Catholic School, we viewed Catholics with real suspicion anyway, we knew all about Titus Oates and the Popish plots, I'd learned about them in Prep School or even at Wheaton Aston, just as I'd learned about Guy Fawkes, and every morning in Big School at the end of Prayers the door down at the front would open and a handful of kids would come in, they were the Jews and the Catholics, they'd stand by themselves at the side up near the stage where the Masters all were, we all knew who they were and there'd be a lot of coughing and shuffling of feet, all of us standing waiting for them to get into place all of us bored and eager to get out now Prayers were over so we could run off and chase each other to class get rid of some energy shout a bit, and once the shuffling was over Mr Bailey'd say what he had to say. "Mr Burnett the Chemist came to see me yesterday," he'd begin, "and told me two of you had thrown mud and dirt at his shop sign," and he'd look round Big School for the culprits, he hadn't the faintest idea who they were, and we'd all look accusingly at the Jews and the Catholics.

But we played games with them, we helped each other with our Prep, they had runways for marbles in their desks just like we did, we made friends with them, and for a long time I didn't really know why they didn't do Prayers with the rest of us, they just didn't and that was all there was to it except that sometimes I envied them, even if they did have to wait quietly outside the door nothing to do until we'd finished Prayers, and they had nothing at all in common with the kids who went to the Catholic School in the village, *those* kids really were different, they dressed completely different from us, somebody said they learned Latin and Greek so they were terrible snobs, snotty-nosed, pretending to be learned, everyone knew they didn't have any money, worse than High Church, they never laughed, never paid any attention to us, if you had any business up at that end of the village you didn't go by yourself, you went with four or five others, after all they went in groups if they ever went about in the village, they made a gang. It didn't occur to us that they sought safety in numbers because there were so many more of us than of them, and we certainly didn't learn anything in History about Protestant persecution or anti-Catholic legislation, except that the Catholic James II was a villainous fool who betrayed his trust. We had absolutely no idea of the long suppression of Catholics in Protestant England and the desperate devices old Catholic families had been driven to to preserve themselves and their property. We never heard a word about any of that in history lessons even though all sorts of people in the village boasted about King Charles in the hidey-hole at Boscobel or hiding in the Royal Oak. There can't have been more than about twenty kids in the Catholic School, more than half of them boarders and all ages, there were nothing like as many people going to the Catholic Church on Sundays as at our church and some of them lived outside the village, most of the teaching was done by the Priest and nuns from the convent, you could see him now and again cycling in the village, string webbing over the back wheel to protect his priest's robes, *skirts* we called them, a funny-looking hat on his head, he was a bit fat and always looked very stern, had a frown on his face and scowled at us as he went by. He lived in a small house with a housekeeper, the Catholic School a gloomy-looking building next to the tiny Catholic Church. We had absolutely nothing to do with him at all, I don't think I ever spoke a word to him or ever heard him speak except for the time he came to address the whole School. Some of the older kids would occasionally jeer at him or not get out of the way when he went past.

Then one Saturday afternoon just after lunch, it was my second year at Brewood, I was fishing something out of my tuckbox in the passage just outside the Billiard Room when someone came running and said "You've got to come to the Croft, quick! You've got to help, we're having a war, come on, it's a real one. Hurry up!" and I rushed out with a couple of others, a clump of about twenty kids just inside the Croft by the iron gate next the belfry and as I went through some of them turned and ran towards me to get out of the Croft *Look out!* one of them shouted and covered his head as he ran, behind them facing the other way the other kids had their hands full of stones and clods of earth and as I looked Pongo Ruddick took a few quick steps and hurled a stone well over an inch across toward Dirty Lane, I couldn't see what at, but a shower of stones and lumps of dirt fell around Pongo as he was throwing and everyone crouched down, I peered round the corner of the building at the far end of the Croft, just as it went into the lane by School Bridge. About a dozen kids shouting and jeering had a hefty supply of rocks and stones and stuff they were getting from the field the other side of Dirty Lane *That's a School field, it belongs to us!* some of them coming halfway across the Croft to let fly and retreat, they'd got more ammunition than us, "It's the Catholic School" somebody said, "They're invading," a mad scramble of kids at this end of the Croft, all of us, even Pongo, more timid than them, scattering about to avoid the flying stones and all at once one of the Catholic kids came running up real close and let fly before turning tail, a complete half-ender sailing through the air we all scattered, when it hit the grass it bounced weirdly as the square jagged edge of the half-housebrick turned, and it popped up and out a raggedy bounce and hit Paunch Chatterton on the forehead, cut it open, he fell over as he lifted up his arm, and a couple of our kids shouted "Truce! Truce!" but the stones kept flying a bit and we all did a lot of shouting back and forth while someone took Paunch to Matron to get his head seen to. The Doctor gave him a couple of stitches, I went with him I wanted to know if he was alright, he was a friend of mine a year older than me, like me he hated Sports, we collected stamps together gave each other duplicates swopped stamps a lot, told each other about books we'd read and liked, read each other's comics talked all the time. I don't think anyone ever sorted out how or why that fight started, but when it was over, Mr Bailey gave us all what for and punished all of us. On Monday he and the Catholic Priest talked to the whole School at Prayers, they were both very angry and the whole School got punished, we all got Detentions, some of us thought it wasn't fair but Henry Houston told us in class that we'd been let off lightly, if he'd had anything to do with it it would've been much worse, and the Priest had Gated the whole Catholic School for a whole week, they couldn't go anywhere, not allowed even to talk, their punishment much worse than ours their School was so small. Of course nobody could get to the bottom of that fight, nobody could find out how it started, but we couldn't get over the idea that we'd lost the fight, of course we were better than any bunch of Catholics, villagers all of them *How could we have let them win?* and on Friday after Tea about ten or fifteen of us were complaining in a corner of the Croft that we hadn't given the Catholics what they deserved and we should've and could've, and if we had we wouldn't've got Detentions, Paunch turned up with his black eye, his face still bruised and in bandages and he asked what we were talking about. Somebody said "You lost us the War! Why didn't you get out of the way of that brick?" and somebody else said "Yeah, you're too clumsy!" we called him Paunch because he had one, he was a bit of a flabby kid, looking back I realise he was a very gentle bloke and generous in spirit, I admired him without knowing, and somebody else said "Blind! That's what you are! No wonder you got hit in the head!" and suddenly we were all shouting "Blind! Blind! Blind! Blind! Blind!" and "It's your fault! It's your fault! It's your fault!" and we all stood in a circle round him booing and jeering me as loud as the rest and with a splotchy face he turned, tears in his eyes, holding his grey jacket close to his ribs, and walked carefully but determinedly through the edge of the circle and away, our catcalls following him. It took me a long time, over a year, to make up to Paunch for that betrayal, we were in the same dorm and that night he told me I was a coward and should've stood up for him it didn't matter how young I was I was supposed to be a friend, and after that I couldn't be comfortable with him for ages or look him in the eye, and for a while he went home every weekend, his mum and dad lived in Wolverhampton, he didn't have any brothers or sisters. I began to see how strong he'd been when I'd been so terrible. But it took me a long time, and I still wonder about it, and him, and me, it wasn't like what we did with Birdie when he first came, we'd been trying to find out about *him*, and we'd settled something, Birdie'd been alright, but we didn't give Paunch a chance.

18

Bike Riding

It was the boys that we knew in the village, not the girls, who kept mostly to themselves. In any case we boarders could get into trouble if we talked to girls. But in a spell of mild weather in early March 1943, I was still eight, Myrtle from the village, she'd left the Nash the previous year when she reached fourteen, began hanging around Dirty Lane and the entrance to the Croft most evenings, after we'd done our prep. Mum would have said she was "amply provided for," and always short of breath but strong as an ox, you could really hear her breathing through her nose the way some people had adenoids, her face always a pale gleam in the twilight as we went back to the dorm. I think she was the only girl I ever had a conversation with on my own before I left Brewood in 1951 when I was seventeen. She tagged along behind us as we walked over School Bridge after we'd done our prep, I said to Brian and Dennis "I wish I knew how to ride a bike" and "Then perhaps I could get one" and they both laughed *What kid could ever afford to buy a bike? You'd be lucky to find one!* "I could teach you if you like," she called out to us, "I've done it before." Dennis nudged Brian and grinned, as I said "Really?" "I could teach any of the others too," she said. "If they wanted." And there she was, next day at the usual time, standing on School Bridge, and she'd brought her bike along. Every day after that she tromped up Dirty Lane in the evening with her bike, panting and slow, "It doesn't take very long, "she said, "just a couple of sessions really. You've got to learn how to fall off, then it's easy to learn how to stay on." I'd been begging Mum and Dad for a bike for ages and ages, Our Kid had one, but Mum said "You'll have to learn how to ride one first, won't you!" and everybody smiled, me included, without a bike how could I learn to do that, I'd never been able to find anyone to teach me, not that I'd really asked, most kids couldn't be bothered.

The first time I rode solo on her bike, it was our second session her all out of breath puffing and panting along, her weight and mine leaning together the bike steering every whichway, with a great heave she got me and the bike upright and pushed, "I'm holding on to the saddle" she said her feet thudding as we went along. I pedalled my wobbly way along the edge of the field I couldn't hear her breath and the bike went much more freely my ears beginning to sing through the air as the bike began to go in great uncertain loops wobblier and wobblier till I got my balance, it was breathtaking, but I was so busy hanging on I couldn't really see where I was going, I was aiming down the slope for the gate into Dirty Lane the grass more and more tussocky the trees and the hedge at the side of the lane a blur, the handlebars and front wheel all I could focus on, the sound of the tyres on the grass the thumping of the bike over the tumpy lumps, her thudding footsteps behind me growing fainter and fainter I couldn't look at the ground rushing by under *"The brake!"* she shouted, *"Put the brake on!"* a wobbly turn to keep from falling off and a big bump the ground was falling away it was hard to hold on, I loomed so far over the handle-bar I couldn't pedal at all, down through bushes and scrub *bumpety-bump bump* right down the embankment towards the canal, the slope steeper and steeper I had to miss that tree and there was another one, a shiny greyish blur dead ahead down through the bushes "Don't go in the canal!" she shouted, it was all I could do simply to hang on, "Fall off! Mind my bike! Fall off!" she screeched, "My bike!" and I clutched even more tightly, twigs and leaves and stuff brushing and whipping round my face and shoulders sounds of crashing crumpling deadwood breaking I didn't dare close my eyes there wasn't time to do anything not even that, I couldn't loosen my grip enough to grab the brake lever with my fingers and a bit of wood just a stick jounced up as my front wheel went over it and jammed in the chain and I fell off whump, the bike sliding all messed over me I'd only gone about halfway down the slope, maybe ten lurchy yards, she rushed up and looked at her bike, then at me, crossly told me to bring it back up,

"*Carry it!*" she said, led me to the middle of field and made me try again. By the end of the week she'd given me lots of practice telling me I was hopeless then suddenly something settled me riding off by myself away from her in the field and tazzing my slightly wobbly way up and down Dirty lane, leaving her standing there a bit annoyed waiting for me to come back she said "I need my bike back, you'll have borrow somebody else's to practise, I need mine." In the evenings after supper I'd see her pushing some other kid along on her bike in the twilight, distant calls, a small wobbling figure cautiously pedalling away as she stood motionless, an unattended silhouette.

For once, in 1943 we were at home for Easter, it was so late. Mum and Dad'd moved to Lower Hillmorton, a small village two-and-a-half miles out of Rugby on the Northampton Road, the road always busy, but there was lots of countryside for Phil and me to go wandering off in, Dad cycling off to work every morning. He and Mum really liked it there, hardly ever any Air Raids, and we lived in a flat, *9 The Croft, Hillmorton, Rugby* is what Dad wrote in my Report Book. That flat really was too small for the four of us, and gloomy along with it, but it meant we could all enjoy a walk in the fields and lanes on Sundays. Phil and I had to go through the kitchen and the bathroom to get to our bedroom in that flat, *not enough room to swing a cat* Mum said, but by the time we came home for Easter we'd moved into Flat 7, a terrific place just like a real house, with two floors, the bedrooms upstairs along with a lavatory and a small room where Dad stored whatever we weren't using at the time, like Mum's dressmaker's model and our prewar picnic basket and all our suitcases, he called it a Lumber Room, room enough for Our Kid and me to use our Meccano sets and Minibrix.

The next time we were home, nearly three weeks after my ninth birthday, Mum said at breakfast "Don't go anywhere, Peter, later on you're going out with your father" and I wondered where, we usually went for a walk on Sunday down towards Lower Hillmorton and through the long tunnel under the railway line, that was a fantastic echoey place a cow-track mainly, just a farm lane all roofed over with brick, the slightest noise boomed and scattered back at you and around you for ages it was fun to throw stones along the tunnel as you went through it booming and rattling noises magnified all round you millions and millions of bricks arching over your head dank and musty air sometimes, water loudly dripping, gloomy and cold, puddles in the unpaved ground, but it was always all of us Mum and Dad and Our Kid and me on those walks. But I didn't think much about it, Easter was always a bit special, Dad'd brought a ham from the farm or Mum'd got a small one from the butcher *that'd be lucky!* and we'd have that for dinner, there was lots of things for me to do I liked playing indoors anyway with my Dinky Toys or my Meccano set, Our Kid and I didn't share our Meccano sets at all but we shared a terrific set of wooden bricks and boards Dad'd had when he was a kid, Phil and I loved it, we played with it for hours and hours making roads with houses and bridges, airfields and harbours, for our Dinky Toys, or we'd build great tottering towers almost as tall as we were, twelve solid two-and-a-half-inch cubes and twelve triangular shapes made by cutting cubes diagonally in half, five boards as long as four bricks and five as long as two bricks all of them snugly stored in a solidly-made wooden box all the corners beautifully morticed that itself became part of the games we played.

After a while Dad came in bringing all the fresh and cool outside with him *Peter I've got something to show you. It's in the garage* and Our Kid looked up from his Minibrix and grinned, we all trooped down, Mum came along too. I knew something was up. Dad heaved open the garage door and there leaning against the wall next to the car with a bit of ribbon and a card on it was a bike *Happy Birthday!* the black paint all fresh the saddle worn, it was a Hercules, no gears or anything, but everything clean, polished up it'd even got a bell, a smooth trace of rust on the handlebars and spokes. "We're sorry it's late," Mum said, "but your father had a terrible time finding one, they're very scarce nowadays and he had to fix it up a bit. Didn't he do a lovely job." They smiled at each other. "Now you can ride a bike. I hoped you thanked that girl properly who helped you, what *was* her name, Myrtle? From the village?" Of course just like in every other year I'd had my birthday at School, when I got home there'd be birthday cards and things from Aunt Kath and Aunt Mabel and everyone waiting for me, Mum had sent me a birthday card with a one-shilling Postal Order, she was ever so good that way she always managed to post it so it arrived on the day, Mr Bailey'd dish it out along with all the other letters at breakfast, every week Mum'd write two letters, one for each of us, Dad never did things like that nobody expected him to, if he were to write to us we'd know it was over Something Very Important, and this time Mum'd said I'd get my real present at home at the beginning of the Easter Holidays. I'd been wondering what it was but you weren't allowed to pester. Our Kid'd been bursting to say something that morning before we went down to the garage, goodness knows where Dad had managed to find a second-hand kid's bike in good condition but he knew a lot of people through the Chamber of Commerce and the Masons, not that I knew anything about that of course, but we knew Dad was a Mason he went to lodge meetings every now and then in the evening, he'd showed us his regalia once. He was dead keen on the Masons, I remember him once telling Mum all about how if anything happened to him the Masons would look after her and make sure that Phil and I could finish school, they'd help pay hospital bills and things like that if he didn't have a job any more, "Masons look after each other," he said, "That's what they're for." Our Kid told me they have a secret handshake so they know each other but he wouldn't tell me what it was, and it never occurred to me till years and years later that people looking after each other like that tend to form a pretty closed exclusionary bunch, preferring to buy things off each other instead of at ordinary shops the way other people did, look after each other instead of just anybody in real need, it was all very complicated, and by the time I went to University in 1952 Dad'd dropped his membership, I think he found the jockeying for office and the smug closeness of it all a bit irksome, though he stayed friends with the men he knew there.

Of course I was desperate to take the bike to School but Dad said it was far too much trouble, far too difficult, to send it to Wolverhampton on the train and then somehow get it forwarded to

Brewood, "You won't be riding your bike anything like well enough to be able to cycle it from Wolverhampton Station to Brewood," he said, "through all that traffic, it's terrible until you've got through Ford Houses and Bushbury, far too dangerous. It had better stay here till you come for the Summer Holidays, you'll want it here then. Let's see if we can take it in September. See if I can use the car." I was just itching to take the bike out but Mum and Dad weren't at all sure how good I was on one, they'd only let me ride it in the courtyard there was plenty of room there I could cycle in big circles and do figure-eights but I soon got tired of that, the same thing over and over round and round, and I wasn't half pleased when Sunday came round and Mum and Dad said we'd go for a bike ride down through Lower Hillmorton and the railway tunnel, all of us, we'd go further afield than we would on a walk, *Good practice, you've only had the bike for a week,* stay off the main road wherever we could and cycle in close convoy when we couldn't, all of us riding sedately, or get off if the traffic's bad. On the way back, as soon as Dad said Phil could go off by himself tearing round Cordles Crescent, "can I go too" and begged and begged, it was obvious Phil was just dying to get a move on after Mum and Dad's cautious pace, *It won't take me long, honest! I'll be back at the road before you get there.* Mum and Dad weren't at all keen but I kept on at them Our Kid fidgetting away anxious to be off. "Alright," Dad said, "but you be careful, make sure you go slowly," the words hardly out of his mouth before Our Kid zoomed off you couldn't see him for dust. "Don't try to keep up with your brother" Dad said as I turned away, "Be careful!" I wobbled a bit till I got up to speed, just a little hill, nothing much to it at all, brick houses on either side, gardens with walls, over the top the road sloped down, I pedalled like mad *See if I can catch Phil* the wind rushing through my hair the tyres humming away on the blacktop smell of dust in the sun. Up ahead the road forked *Which way did he go? I'll go left* it was a sharp turn and as I got close I saw it was just a cul-de-sac with a round area at the bottom for cars to turn round, pedalling away *I'd better turn right!* and rushing right at me, right in front, the kerb's big heaving *bump!* didn't let me even catch my breath, not even a wobble as the bike leapt up all of it so fast a low brick wall behind it no more than a foot-and-a-half high a whole lot of daffodils behind it the bright yellow and green tumbling under me the sky round my ankles I somersaulted the bike left behind landed on my bum flat on my back all shaken up, ornamental chain looping between brick posts of the wall, no one in the house nobody to see what I'd done curtains and furniture painted front door more flowerbeds daffodils flattened under my back my heels gouging the bright lawn dirt scattering up my short trouser-legs grit in my hair it was all so fast I didn't hear anything at all of the crash breath right out of me but it must've made a lot of noise the bike lying there against the wall bright sunlight the back wheel ticking its slow spin, and when I climbed back over the wall and picked up my bike, the handlebar was all twisted to one side. I knew how to fix that, I'd seen other kids do that, just put the wheel between my legs and turn the bars back again, but the wheel was really smashed up, all buckled and warped, I'd never be able to straddle that misshapen mess it wasn't anywhere near round any more a great wedge bent into the rim, spokes splayed out the wheel couldn't go round at all, surge lurching my stomach my breath caught short all over again, a cold shiver, no air in the tyre anyhow *Oh crikey! what'm I going to do?* nobody about, I shivered, *It's wrecked!* Quiet Sunday afternoon not even any kids around, a touch of breeze smarting the graze on my knee, pungency of a privet bush stirring by the driveway to my left everything sharp and clear in the light *what'll Mum and Dad say? What'll Dad do??* but I couldn't think in words at all, it was just an empty fluttery sinking feeling my heart thumping away with shivery me looking round wanting help and at the same time hoping nobody was there, my ears burning eyes desperately watery I tried to straighten out the wheel a dog yapped over behind a hedge somewhere *Did anybody see me?* I couldn't carry the bike all the way back to The Croft by myself it was too far *What else are you going to do then?* Our Kid's voice sounded in my head I turned around half-carried half-dragged the bike scraping sounds off the pavement onto the road splayed spokes sticking into at my leg, heavy pulling slog up the hill start home shaking all over tears streaming down my face socks down around my ankles shorts runkled mucky, me catching and bumping against the pedal as I tried to stay clear of the spokes, my shin then my calf *Lean the bike further out* but that didn't work it was too heavy and kept sliding I'd fall over or I'd have to drop it *Move the pedal out of the way* but it was jammed against the frame grease all over my socks I'd grazed my knees, big bruises but they didn't hurt much I could hardly feel them everything numb but for the *bump bang* as my leg hit the pedal sweat trickling everywhere my arm getting tired switch to the other side *Stick my arm through the frame put the front of the bike on my shoulder* ache in my back it was too heavy I couldn't get it up there *bump* the leg *bonk* stop take a rest start again pick up the bike the sound of tyres. "What on earth did you do?" Dad's voice angry and worried, "Give that to me! You can just walk with me, don't even try to say anything!" He stomped off before me, his shoulders all tense and rigid his head looking straight ahead I didn't dare look at him, his bike on one side, my bike hoicked on the other, holding the ruined front wheel clear of the road, my blubbery trudge, my shaky legs. Shivery. "You don't really deserve a bike do you" Dad said when we got home. Mum was no help either, just gave me a look. Next day Dad was at work, he'd taken the bike in I don't know how perhaps he used the car. Mum said "It probably can't be mended. If it can't you'll have to do without, won't you" and when I got back to School the day after that I was worried, sorry for myself. And I didn't have a bike. Didn't tell anybody anything. Nor did Our Kid, and nobody asked.

All Summer Term I borrowed other people's bikes if I could, that wasn't very often, other kids wanted to use theirs when I did, and you could only really expect to borrow a bike from one of your friends, after all I wouldn't've lent mine to someone I didn't know very well, or like much, either. Now and again a bunch of us hanging about the Avvy Bridge, someone might turn up on a bike and you might tool around a bit on it cycling on the grass while the others stood around and talked, we'd take turns I suppose but it was all pretty idle and easy, better than aching about to get through the afternoon but not like riding a bike, not really. Some weekends and evenings though we'd have slow bike races from the belfry to the gates, you could easily borrow somebody's bike for those, you could only have two or three kids going at a time, there wasn't room for more at the starting line, you had to go in a straight line and you couldn't put your feet on the ground, you had to keep moving, the last one in won. Other times we'd have free-wheeling contests, there'd be a whole lot of us two or three bikes between us, but you could only go one at a time, you'd pedal like mad across the Croft towards the Quad and as soon as you reached the tarmac you had to stop pedalling. As your bike got slower and slower you'd stand up on the pedals and try to magic the bike forward by swinging your body forward but of course that didn't work, *Don't you know any physics?* someone in the Fourth Form scoffed, you had to be terribly careful not to move the pedals while you did that everyone watching you closely and if your feet touched the ground that's as far as you got, you'd mark where you'd got to, and then you'd have to take the bike back so somebody else could have a go. Some kids'd crouch down on the bike streamline themselves try their feet on the handlebars or lie face down on the saddle their legs straight out behind them, contort themselves *flat*, but I couldn't do that I knew I'd fall off, break something, or land on my head. Once Ken Hatton made it all the way outside the Gates and halfway to Mrs Roberts's tuck shop before his bike stopped but nobody else got that far and he only managed it the once. About a week after I came home for summer Dad took me into Halford's, a serious look on his face, and said "We're here to get your bicycle. You're very lucky" and the bloke behind the counter looked at Dad, Dad in his suit from work, then walked into the back, came out with my bike, he had on a brown overall its edges all stained and frayed, he didn't look like anyone we'd *know*, he looked at Dad and "Good thing we didn't 'ave to replace the spokes" he said, "can't get 'em" and "That'll be ten bob to you, guv." He gave me a hard look "You'd better be more careful next time 'adn't you!" I scuffled my feet and blushed and didn't know whether to grin or not. Dad said, "Thank you Jack, that's really good of you" and I thanked Dad in a strangled sort of voice I felt so daft at what I'd done. Ten bob was nearly five months' pocket money, more than I'd ever had, I wondered if the man was one of Dad's friends or something, giving him a special price the way he'd said, I didn't dare ask, but he'd served Dad right out of turn, before all the other people already waiting in the shop and nobody seemed to mind. Dad sent me home on the bus, he got a local deliveryman to bring my bike to The Croft, he told me "That's your Christmas present, you won't get anything else."

So I had to think about the bike and what it meant to me. I'd have to leave it at home when I went back to school. I had to practise to get better at riding it. At school, I could borrow one of the old boneshakers from the bike sheds, nobody knew whose they were, but you had to get permission from one of the Masters to use them, you had to tell where you were going. If I could I'd go for a bike ride with some other kids on a Sunday, I could get to places I'd never walked to before, they were too far away, perhaps out past Somerford or the other side of Bishop's Wood or even into Codsall where I might find some of the dayboys, though they all felt different outside School, hard to talk to.

The wonderful thing about having a bike was the freedom it gave me. Myrtle showed me a side of village life, and village people, that in my school habits I had always ignored. She was so completely outside my class and my experience. Other Brewood kids didn't think she was real. Oh Myrtle, she's such a pest, what on earth were you talking to her for? they'd say. It took me a long time to see that she was somebody to admire and to take pleasure with. She was faithful in her companionship. It was not just the hunger of a lonely person. She enjoyed teaching kids how to ride. She enjoyed going for walks with us. The narrowness of village life drove her to us kids.

Bike riding took me outside the confines of boarding school and respectability, outside the realm of books and the classroom. Grandfather Marlow always put us on our best behaviour. *Never forget you are a Quartermain.* But I discovered that Brewood Grammar School also bred snobbery, it bred my timidity, the necessity to be correct and to lord it over others, so unlike Grannie and Grandpa in

Spalding, who laughed and played with kids, and didn't mind mucking in with the workers to clean up the flood. So too, bike riding allowed me to enjoy myself and village places like the Nash school, bursting with rambunctious kids full of life and energy.

19

Sundays

Sunday was nearly always a problem for us boarders. We'd written our letters, we'd done all our prep, no fire in the Billiard Room, the heat turned down, all the classrooms shut up tight. You couldn't get at the old carpentry benches at the back of the Fourth Form the way you could in the evenings after Prep, nowhere to spread out to work on your balsa model plane or even get at your stamp collection, too many kids around for that. All the grown-ups insisted on their bit of peace and quiet as they sat before *their* fire, even the kitchen maids and the cook, except for Miss Butler, most of them'd gone home anyway, it was their day off. So we all had to go out, do our Sunday Walk, and the Prefects were there to make sure we did, they wrote down where each of us'd go and who with before they went out on *their* Walk. *You can't just stay on the Croft! You've got to go somewhere or do something.* But you'd been everywhere and you'd seen everything, you'd even, if they were still legible, read the gravestones in the churchyard so many times you knew where the oldest one was and who was under it, what it said, you'd climbed most of the trees, even the big one with all the initials carved on it in the corner of the Croft. We were completely at a loss if we met any of the Masters when we were out on our Sunday Walk, and there were some places, like the village, where you couldn't go unless you had permission, you couldn't even visit one of the dayboys at home without a written note *how can I know where I'm going until I get there?* It wasn't often that we went where we'd said we'd go, we just went, and it was a bit of a shock to come up against one of the Masters, the way Ken Hatton and I did about a week after Mr Evans came back from the War, he'd been an interpreter in the Army and'd come back to teach French, that was his old job, and Ken and me'd climbed up the embankment to Avvy Bridge, scrounging for beech nuts, sudden cigarette smoke as we climbed over the stile onto the Avvy *Oh, somebody got hold of some fags, I bet not in the village. He'd better not get caught!* and I started to say something clever like *I wish we could get into the pub like him* but choked it back, *Crikey! It's Mr Evans!* Ken and me didn't know what to do with ourselves, I couldn't really look at him standing there keeping two small kids company as they rootled about under a bit of broom. We lifted our caps off to him, neither of us could think of anything to say except "Hello, Sir," *had to do that*, and he shifted his weight from one foot to the other and nodded and gave us a tiny smile. We skedaddled as quick as we could and hoped he wouldn't know who we were.

When we'd said where we were going we would simply name somewhere like Bishop's Wood or even White Ladies, not too far away from School or near heavy traffic, no fun going along the Watling Street even if you'd got permission, and we'd end up on the Avvy, same as always. We certainly didn't want to meet Mr Evans, or any other Master for that matter, we didn't want to be part of their private lives any more than we wanted them to be part of ours. We shied away from the notion that they had a personal life and could be real the way Mum and Dad were, Teachers were just part of the landscape you wanted to get away from. Stay out of trouble, get out of their sight before you get spotted, don't get reported for being where you'd not said you'd be. *As if they have lists of everything* Dickie Hampton scoffed, *and remember what's on it!* But in the anxiety of being caught it was hard to remember that, or to think that if they asked anything at all it'd most likely be "Boy! What are *you* doing here?" and you'd have to explain. If you got challenged you'd be Remembered, so you'd steer clear, you didn't want *that*.

A lot of Sundays especially if you were by yourself all you wanted was to find a quiet corner somewhere, keep yourself to yourself. You'd sneak back early, or even not really go anywhere at all but hang about, tuck yourself away somewhere until everybody else'd gone. You could *feel* the emptiness of the School so palpable you could almost touch it, the silence so strong you could *hear* it, Matron nowhere to be found, the Housemaster nowhere to be found, the kitchen closed down, tables and counters clean, all the dishes on their shelves, the clock quietly ticking, everything in its proper place, no one round the bike sheds, all of us left to fend for ourselves, the only sign of life Mr Hawkins bringing the cows in across the Croft to the School Farm to be milked. One time I quietly opened the Billiard Room door to get something out of my locker, desperate not to be seen, and heard faint shuffling as Billy Crawford's face peered cautiously over the back of the sofa and dropped out of sight, *What are you doing?* I whispered, and he held up *In Dangerous Waters* by Percy F. Westerman, his finger marking his place, *Oh, I haven't read that*, I whispered, *Where'd you get it?* and *It's mine, I keep it in my locker* he kept his voice down, *My dad gave it me for my birthday*. We both knew that a Prefect'd be on him a ton of bricks if he caught him, *Why aren't you out on your Walk?* confiscate his book till the end of term and probably give him some lines to write as well. That's what Prefects did, including me when I got to be one a few years later, it was a very tempting power, but why shouldn't Billy sit and have a quiet read, have some time to himself if he wanted.

It was hard to find a hidey-hole where you could do that, or do something quiet like draw something without being interrupted, nobody checking it for skill or silliness or something to be proud of, you couldn't listen to any music there wasn't a wireless or anything like that in the Billiard Room, eventually Derek Leigh got a one-valve set he'd built at home and put it in his bedside locker, he had to listen on earphones, and that started a craze for crystal sets. But crystal sets were more trouble than they were worth, you couldn't take one with you anywhere they were so cumbersome, the only place you could listen at all really was in bed, and even then the slightest movement joggled the cat's whisker and you lost the signal, it felt like if you even breathed it'd drift off, and there all of us'd be, hunched up trying to find a signal when we couldn't even see or even hear as we stifled under the covers, nobody talking to anybody, all of us so fagged out in the morning, a crick in my neck my nose scrunched up against a dead earphone, a crooked furrow on my cheek from lying on the earphone-wire, we couldn't even talk to each other until we'd somehow got some food down our gullets. So the only music we heard except for what we sang in School was some kid practicing the piano off in the Dining Hall and of course what hymns we sang every Sunday in church.

On a really wet Sunday, once or perhaps twice a term, some of the bigger kids'd get permission to open up Big School for the afternoon with a Prefect to keep an eye on things, it wouldn't be a quiet time, and you'd find yourself running and clambering about with everyone else, shouting and hiding, getting into places you weren't most times allowed, rambunctious excitement and show-off dare-deviltry, Big School with its big stage where the Masters sat at morning prayers, a trapdoor under the chairs, Big School with its seven-foot-tall wall-bars lining three sides, gaps in them for the five doorways, hard to negotiate as you went right round the room without touching the floor and harder to do here than in the First or Second Dorm where you could swing on the door to get across the gap *But watch your fingers!* In Big School we couldn't use the heavy equipment like the beams or the vaulting horses or even the box. We'd get the gym mattresses and coconut matting out of the dark pokey room where they belonged, and like the others I'd clamber up the wall-bars as high as I dared and jump, but none of us could get onto our feet at the very top, the wall crowded you too much as it leaned out to start the ceiling, nobody dared. So like everyone else I'd jump and then climb a bit higher to jump again until at last mostly because it was so same-and-same-again I ventured into the gallery at the top of the belfry stairs to jump down to the Big School floor. I'd been at Brewood three or four years before I dared make that jump, I was about ten by then, but the whole of Big School and the corridors round made it a wonderful place for Releasio and Fishes-in-the-Net, run like mad down the corridor and through the door in the corridor outside the Gym, rush up the twisting belfry stairs, the gallery parapet at the top nine feet or more above the Gym floor. When I got big enough I jumped like everyone else right over the parapet straight down *Watch out for those below!* it was another way to fly, I'd land on the mattresses clouds of dust billowing round, or the rough smell of coconut matting, but before I was big enough to do that a bigger kid'd galumph up the stairs with me, lower me at arm's length over the edge and let go, then jump down himself, the kids in the net all left at the top looking over. To catch you the unbroken net had to touch you and if you got caught you became part of the net. As the net got longer and longer catching a fish got harder and harder, got to be *work*, and we all preferred being a fish, fish could always run up the stairs faster than the net, I'd scramble over the frenzied edge and stretch the two-and-a-bit feet along the wall to the bars *Hurry up! Hurry UP!* clambering over each other *Get out of the way!* I'd pretty well fall down the wall-bars in delicious panic at being caught, we'd bruise ourselves and scrape our shins in the wonderful hysteria of the chase, shouting and whooping, getting greyer and greyer as cloudy grime puffed up, more and more breathless, still running like loons, legs wobbly or not, steamed and sweaty by the time we got to Tea. If we could we'd have a shower in the Changing Room first, but a Prefect had to be there for that. We drank gallons of tea till the milk ran out, warm and wet and weaker and weaker, until there really was none left, and no hot water.

Life changed when Mr Redhead, the Chemistry Master, moved to a flat just off the Square in Speedwell Castle, the red-brick folly built two centuries ago on the winnings from a horse race. This let him live closer to School, and he put his old radiogram in the Billiard Room for us to use. Some of the valves were burnt out or missing, and after the War you still couldn't buy any, so the wireless part didn't work. It took quite a while to add any records to the four or five that he gave us with it, we played them so much that we knew every note by heart, we endlessly whistled "Hora Staccato" and "The Flight of the Bumblebee," and sang Hoagy Carmichael's "Old Buttermilk Sky" and "Huggin' and Chalkin'" again and again, I can still sing along with those word for word. Mr Redhead told Mr Page what he'd done and Mr Page, he taught Agriculture and Biology, set up a music club, him and his wife had a big collection of classical records, heavy 78-rpm album sets, really brittle shellac, lp's hadn't been invented yet and he'd bring an album in most Tuesday evenings after supper, he always gave us a cautious little lecture on how to change the needle *No need to spend any money, a thorn from a*

hawthorn tree works fine! and play a whole album, a complete concerto or symphony broken up into however many sides it took, he'd say what he liked in it and get us to talk about it. When he asked us to name our favourite composer I said Tchaikovsky because he was the only one I could remember except Beethoven and Mr Page raised his eyebrow and said "Ye-e-es, he's very good at arrangement, isn't he, orchestration's his great strength" and that took me aback, led me to wonder, I'd never heard that sort of judgement before, not about music, and he'd given me a new word. All that Term and a bit after, until Our Kid said "Oh, for gosh sakes put a sock in it" I'd somehow stick "orchestration" into whatever I said, how good somebody's was, or how dramatic, or how smooth. When he asked which conductor we liked best, Malcolm Sargent, Adrian Boult or Sir Thomas Beecham, the only name I knew really was George Weldon, so I didn't say anything.

I knew George Weldon because after we moved back to Birmingham from Rugby Mum started taking us to concerts in the holidays, and I liked him, he was the permanent conductor of the Birmingham Symphony Orchestra, with his hair flopping about more and more as the concert went on, a sheen of sweat on his face more and more visible as he pushed the orchestra through its paces. The first time we went I was really shocked to see a big chamber pot sitting up there on the rostrum, it was so visible, no attempt at all to cover it up or hide it, and I felt embarrassed and apprehensive, really uncomfortable, I was afraid he might be going to use it and I didn't dare imagine that, I was shocked because nobody except me seemed to be at all bothered, I cringed at that and at my disconcertion, but when George Weldon got up to the rostrum he took a drag on his cigarette and then dumped it in the pot as he turned to bow to the audience. *Don't be so barmy!* Phil told me afterwards, "It makes sense if you think about it. Practical. He's a heavy smoker, a lot more than Dad," and that made me think. The three conductors Mr Page asked us about were always on the BBC, but as soon as we were asked who we preferred Our Kid straightaway said "John Barbirolli," hardly anyone had heard of him. Phil was showing off a bit, but Mr Page said what a great job Barbirolli had done in Manchester rescuing the

Hallé Orchestra, I'd never heard of it, nor had the rest of us. But for a few kids from there none of us'd think anything from Lancashire could be any good, they didn't even speak proper English did they. That's why I knew that the Hallé couldn't be any good, I didn't know how anyone could tell. Phil could, he was absolutely mad about music, he'd kept slogging away at the piano with Moggie Morris after I'd given up, I hated Moggie so much, and he even practised at home, just the way Mum did. For quite a bit now he'd been spending what pocket money he had on records, not that he could afford much. One of the first he got was "In the Hall of the Mountain King," the way it built up from the quiet sinister pace of the start to the mad whirl at the end made me wish it lasted a lot longer, I loved it probably as much as he did, but he wouldn't let me play it even when he was in the room with me, he wouldn't let me touch it at all, *You might break it!* so I almost enjoyed his discomfiture if the gramophone began to run down and he frantically wound it back up to its proper speed.

I can still see Phil in the Billiard Room, jammed solid on the settee between other kids, Mr Page in the only armchair, the rest of us mostly sitting on the floor, me nodding to the rhythm of the music, others Phil among them quietly tapping it out on their sleeve or their trouser leg, if it got a bit of swozz in it his whole body'd start to sway and rock, he'd get up from the settee so he could wave his arms about, and every week he ended up leaning against the radiator under the window flapping his arms about, completely carried away as he conducted the whole orchestra, grand sweeps of his arms, lips pursing and unpursing, his hands in quick little gestures signalling the percussion or the brass or the bassoon to come in he'd nod in approval, his eyes closed, his whole body telegraphing sheer possession, and Iain Clarke sitting on the settee nudged his neighbour leaned over and whispered they both smirked and laughed as Phil in his extravagance got carried away. I couldn't pay attention to the music any more, stuck in an uncomfortable mix of loyalty and anxious embarrassment *How could they laugh at his enthusiasm?* as waves of orchestral sound flooded the room, *He's my brother! What makes* them *so superior and know-it-all? They're just dayboys!* Iain was in the same Form as me, and he played in the Junior Eleven at cricket *and* football and was always sure of himself, he never noticed the likes of me. But Phil knew how to listen to music, and when we were home for the holidays he started borrowing miniature scores from the Birmingham library "We should have them at School" he said, "in the library," he following the score on the wireless or in concerts at the Town Hall and eventually, this was after he'd left School and was working for a living, he bought them, pocket scores published by Hawkes or by Penguin. He knew how to read them the way I read words, he could finger things out on the piano, or even just sing or whistle bits straight from the score without even having heard them.

We always felt hungry, even during the War, when we got lashings of spuds and plenty of bread, but it was not appetizing with the gravy all gone, and no butter or marge left. I suppose dayboys felt hungry too, but they lived in houses with gardens to grow stuff in, they were bound to get more to eat, us boarders couldn't get at the School garden, Nunc defended it so fiercely, that was where some of our food came from, as well as the School farm, we copped it if we got caught scrumping, we were always on the lookout. One Sunday after Church Sam nudged me with his elbow and said "Niffy told me yesterday," Niffy Bosworth was a village kid I didn't much know, I'd only spoken to him a couple of times, "that clamp at the top of the field just across Dirty Lane from Pussy's garden, it's full of swedes! Somebody opened it up and then didn't seal it up properly," and he grinned. "Probably hungry." We often got swedes in school dinners, orange-yellow turnips boiled soft, mushy and faintly sharp but pretty tasteless with nothing but salt to put on them, perhaps a bit of pepper, we none of us liked them and I still don't, but "Better'n the beetles," Victor said, and the three of us laughed.

The trees on the canal bank next Avenue Bridge always had beech nuts lying about to pocket as we prowled around, eat while we walked. Not many boarders knew about them and we wouldn't tell about them or there'd be no nuts left, it was bad enough having to search as hard as we did when there'd not been many in the first place, lying there dampish in the leaf-mulch under the trees, small and delicious but finicky to peel. Sometimes the cases would be completely split, glossy little black bugs inside, minute against the rich brown case and the delicious white they made so bitter. We knew a few hazelnut trees too in a hedgerow, good filberts but everyone knew about them, the supply didn't last very long at all. We'd crack them open with our teeth while we walked, but sometimes there'd be a bad one, all black inside, bitter and mushy *Uurgh!* you'd spit it out crack the next one with your shoe to make sure it was alright, eat it to take the taste away. You had to pace your eating or your mouth'd get so dry you go bonkers wanting a drink. "Those swedes'd fill us up a bit." Sam said, "get us through till tea. Niffy said you can eat them raw, he says he did that on his uncle's farm, tried one out." I looked at him, and he looked at Victor, there hadn't been all that many spuds at lunch. "Nobody'd notice if we took a couple," Victor said.

We took our School caps off so they wouldn't show if anybody was looking out of the dormitories or from a window in the Headmaster's House, you could easily see the clamp at the edge of the field from there, and I hung back a bit till Victor said "Oh come on, what's to be afraid of? Nobody's going to be standing there watching out of a window especially upstairs to see if anyone's doing anything all the way across the garden into the lane. They've got better things to do!" And it was easy. We just had to shift the straw a bit it was all wet and muddy and loose, it was easy enough to put back, and we tamped it down with our feet. The swedes were absolutely huge, I thought much too big to carry, but "we only need one," Sam said, "pick and choose." They were heavy with wet. Some of them still had bits of stems and soggy leaves to get a grip on, all of them dirty, great heavy clods of earth and stones clinging to them. "That's all wrong," Sam said, "they'll rot if they've not been cleaned up." We all had our gloves on, mine were just wool, Mum had knitted them, and before he picked one up Victor said, "I'll get covered with mud" and took his off. "It's so heavy," he said, and while he held it we tried to brush the dirt off, the mud clinging to the swedes and the stones clinging to the mud.

I couldn't budge the stones with the edge of my hand, that hurt, our hands got colder and colder, I'd put my gloves in my pocket so they wouldn't get all wet and covered in mud, but the mud didn't dry out at all on our hands, it just stuck there, where it was thickest, the swede hard to hold. Victor tried scraping it off with his shoe and that didn't work any better than what Sam did, rubbing it on a clump of long grass, that just smeared the mud around made the swede dirtier. "I've got my knife," Victor said, "we can scrape it off. It's in my trouser pocket" but his hands were so muddy he couldn't pull his mac to one side to get at it, our hands just as mucky. "Here," said Sam, "I'll do it," he wiped his hands on a clean-looking tussock, and after a lot of groping and wriggling about undoing buttons and two of us pulling his mac back and doing the buttons up again after, the belt flopping in the way, all of us getting colder and colder and more and more narked as we got even wetter, Victor at last opened up his penknife. *It's only for sharpening pencils* he said, it really was a bit titchy, didn't look very strong, Sam tried carrying the swede with one hand under, the other on top holding it steady, but it was too heavy that way so we carried turn-and-turn-about. We were going to wash it in the canal but when we got to School Bridge the water looked greasy and mucky, skims of dirty oil reluctantly glistening, "No!" Victor said, "I'm not even putting my *hands* in *that*. We'll have to go to the stream."

By this time I was getting a bit fed up, I think we all were, but we couldn't just throw the swede away or leave it for someone to find *That's food, can't waste it!* and by the time we got to the bottom of Bath Field and the stream in the old Swimming Pool, we'd all almost *had* it we were so cold and wet and dirty. I'd been traipsing along clutching this swede to my waist, every step I took jogged more mud onto my mac in splotches the streaks all a bit paler round the edges but not really drying off, and my nose was running like billy-oh, I couldn't wipe it and I had an itch in the middle of my back. The others didn't look any happier than I felt, and when we got to the steps at the shallow end we just dropped the swede *Thud!* four feet onto the skim of mud on the sandstone floor and it just lay there. It didn't even bounce.

My right foot skidded as I went down to look at the stream on the far side of the Baths, it'd cut a channel through a sandy bank, the small cliff can't've been more than six inches above the water, grass and scraggly willow-herb on the bank downstream, ragwort and dandelions and thistles and stuff, a plantain or two, but all bashed about from the winter, an old cowpat or two further down the sandbank. It was easy to get to the edge of the stream. It was my turn to carry. I went back for the swede while Victor and Sam washed themselves off a bit, the swede slipped, a cold splash into the wool of my sock, and I stuck my hands into the stream to get them clean, so cold I couldn't clench my fist properly or flex my hands. We all crouched down along the edge, a corner of my mac trailed in the water, we scraped at the swede with the back of the knife-blade, the dirt didn't much want to come off and we sloshed the swede about a bit holding on to the stubs, wrists and sleeves getting wetter and wetter as they got a bit less muddy as we took turns scrubbing away. "No, it's too hard," I said, "that'll have to do."

As I clambered upright my right foot plumped down towards the stream a sudden lurch as the bank collapsed my shoe just touched the water and I jumped back a bit but none of us laughed, not even *Oo-er*. Both Victor's feet slid down *whoosh* the whole bank collapsing under him *splosh* one shoe almost right in the water, he pulled it back real fast and jumped clear, we scrambled up the steps and slogged across to the stinky old pavilion and sat on the two wooden steps, looked at each other and shook our heads, the swede so impossibly hard, we couldn't even stick the knife into it, so huge we couldn't get at it with our teeth, not even gnaw at it. Sam walked back to the shallow end of the Baths lifted the swede above his head and smashed it down with all his might onto the top step, but it just bounced a listless bounce and rolled down onto the mud, a long dented bruise where it'd hit the edge of the step. After a couple of tries we took Victor's knife and hacked away again, the big blade so short it could only cut a small wedge. We didn't want that mushy bruised bit and Sam said "That's no good. Give it me!" and he went halfway up the steps, raised the swede up above his head and threw it down as hard as he could, all his might and main, against the sharp edge of the top step and the swede just bounced and then rolled down a step, he nearly lost his balance stepped back a bit and stumbled, picked up the swede *I've had enough!* he shouted, *More than enough!* and threw it down again, his face all red. A big crack appeared across a big squodgy bruise. Victor grabbed at it, stuck his knife and then his fingers into the crack and strained to pull it apart, discoloured bruises, and *My turn!* he said, smashed it down and again smashed it down, and suddenly the swede split, four or five muddy gritty-looking pieces a bit mushy round the edges tumbled down the steps. "*Bugger it!*" Sam said. "I don't know that I want to eat *any* of *this!*" My nose running like mad, more mud smeared over my mac from trying to get a hankie out of my pocket, we grabbed three bits of broken swede, a long stretch to where the bank wouldn't crumble and we washed them off in the cold cold water yet again, all of us shivering and laughing, our funny desperation, all of it a bit too much in its strange mix of misery and accomplishment, so shrammed we couldn't curse properly or even talk much at all, my lips a bit floppy and numb. I used Victor's knife to trim dirt off the edge of my piece and bit, I bit hard, a good solid bite.

And it was horrid. It clung to my teeth pushing the gums back and away so they hurt, and it was so cold I really had to get it away from my front teeth, but when I tried to bite so I could get a bit to chew my teeth wouldn't meet, the wedge was too thick, it just pushed really solid into my gums and was stuck there *my teeth'll come out if I pull on it!* I jiggled the swede from side to side with my fingers back and forth saliva running down my chin my mouth watering like mad and there it was, lumped damp gritty woody roughness against my tongue, rubbery tough and stringy it tasted of nothing at all nice in its slightly sour half-solid resistance, as I worked it clear of my teeth it tasted like field, a great wodgy piece, I nibbled and chewed away at it and as it softened a bit did begin to taste faintly like it did when it was cooked. But the more I chewed the more it turned to a sort of sawdust dry as dry the way raw carrots sometimes do when they're old and woody, I tried to swallow what I could, a rough and scratchy plug just sticking there halfway down, I spat out what I could, a greyish pale yellow mess, just as Victor shrugged and said "It's not that bad" and took another small bite, so I took another small bite, and so did Sam, each of us gnawing away all the while the three of us trailed back up toward Dirty Lane, "Oh yes it is," Sam at last said, "What?" I said, "That bad" he replied, and I looked at him his hands were empty "Did you finish yours already?" I said and he shuddered and said, "I threw it away," "Oh," I said, and Victor and me threw ours away.

When we got back we could hardly wait for tea it was only ten minutes away, anything to take the taste away, *oh for a cup of tea!* but of course we had to clean ourselves up, Matron was really cross about our macs and a Prefect had to watch over us while we scrubbed at the mud, had to find us a nail-brush to borrow, all narked because we'd made him late for his tea as well as ours. Then when we said where we'd been Martin Tudge said "What! That's not swedes, that's mangolds in that clamp. Mangel-wurzels! You can't eat *them*, no one can even if they cook them. That's cattle feed!" and laughed and laughed till he folded over, "Worse than sugar-beet!" he crowed, "horrible stuff," and made sure everybody knew what we'd done. "Bet you get a belly-ache" he said. But we didn't.

That wasn't the only time my clothes got really messed up, but it looks like it only happened when we were on our own, loose ends on a Sunday. Ray Shaftbury and Barry Wallace, a kid in Second Dorm I hardly knew at all, ended up together with me one Sunday Walk, we went up Dirty Lane to the field at the top just to get out of everybody's way, and as we climbed over the five-barred gate to go towards Hockerhill Farm I looked back and we still weren't out of other people's sight, there was a Prefect coming up behind us out on *his* walk, we'd said we'd just follow where the School marathon goes but we'd never go all the way round *who'd want to do that* so we struck off to the right towards the woods, somewhere new, ducked under the barbed wire fence and got among the trees, we'd none of us ever been over there before, when I turned round in the bracken and ferns I could still see a Prefect's cap bobbing across the field behind us but not in our direction, I pointed at him, and we walked on through bits of bush and scrub as fast as we could, there were a lot of bluebells about, the tall and spindly trees all spaced quite far apart, and the ground stretching away all round us was all bluebells and green fleshy leaves bulbs of some sort small white flowers. We just stood and looked, all you could hear was the sighing of the trees in the wind, quiet creaks as they swayed, there was no sign anybody else'd been walking in here, we kept our voices down, wondered if we weren't supposed to be in these woods *What if there's a gamekeeper?* When I looked up I saw the treetops swaying against intense patches of blue, white puffy clouds scurrying across, everything smelled clean and fresh, there weren't any birds about that we could hear, not even any stirrings in the undergrowth, so unlike School it was just smashing, and the dew and last night's rain soaked up into our socks the skirts of our macs got wet in the long grass and suddenly Barry said in a low voice, he was about twenty yards in front of me ankle-deep in dark-green leaves, Ray off to my left, "Hey, come over here, come and smell this, it's terrific!" but I was looking back to see if the Prefect was still there and Ray was drifting off somewhere he wanted to go. Barry said "No, no. Come 'ere! Come and see!" so we walked over, and as we walked our feet scrubbed through the dark green leaves and crushed them the most wonderful pungent smell more aromatic than any flower we knew, good enough to eat except you wouldn't find anything like that in the middle of the woods, we hadn't the faintest idea what it was, not lily-of-the-valley or anything like that, and Barry got down on his hands and knees and started digging with his hands, "Have a look!" he said, so the two of us got down too and started scrubbing at the soft wet soil between the plants they smelled smashing close up and we stuck our noses down and breathed it in, little clusters of bulbs, and our clothes got damper and damper we wandered round among all these plants leaving a great trail of crushed wreckage behind us, our clothes picked up more and more of the scent my socks were just dripping with this juicy pulpy stuff and then I said something I don't know what but Barry pushed me a bit and Ray tackled him and we all fell over and started rolling around larking about, after a few minutes we were just covered with juice we all smelled of it our clothes smeared with damp stains rain water and dew mingled up with bluebell juice and whatever this stuff was it got on my face and lips it didn't taste anything like as nice as it smelled. Ray licked his lips. "Blimey!" he said, "I bet it's a kind of onion," and Barry said "Go on, there's no such thing, not in the woods!" and we teased him for thinking onions only grew in gardens the way some town kids think milk only comes from bottles. Barry told us "Don't be so ignorant!" and we started to push each other about some more. But the sun went in, the air suddenly got cool, and we looked at each other. "Enough's enough," said Barry. "We've been out long enough for a good Walk," Ray nodded, "we should get back."

When we got back to School everybody was already in the Dining Hall having Tea. We started to sit down and a great cry went up, *Where've you three been? Poooh! Stay away from me!* and *Go and get out of those clothes!* Matron came in looking annoyed and *Ugh!* she said. She told us "Go into the scullery and get washed before you sit down!" and in the kitchen Miss Butler took one sniff and said, "Have you been up at Little Hyde Rough?" We said where we'd been and she scowled "That's just as bad. You've been rolling around in the garlic, haven't you. I don't know what Mr Bailey will say. Those woods are full of it. Go and get changed, you'll have to clean up your clothes as best you can, talk to Matron. You'd better have baths" and then she said "Come back here afterwards, I'll have to see if I can find you something to eat. You certainly can't stay in here in that condition." Matron sighed at us and shook her head. "You'll have to let the smell wear off, especially your macs" she said, "I can't get that out, and the laundry doesn't go till Wednesday." But she couldn't help laughing either, and we got ragged about it for weeks after *Here come the garlic boys!* people holding their nose. Going where we're not supposed to, daftly getting caught, a scornful *Why don't you three advertise?*

20

Self-Help

That was just before the weather began to warm up or at least started to dry up a bit. The Head Prefect stood up at tea the next Saturday and announced, "We're going to clean out the Swimming Baths." I thought of the three of us struggling with that swede in the oblong stone-lined pit, the stream running through the muck, the big dressed sandstone blocks lining the walls, the mud-covered sandstone slabs across the bottom. The Baths'd been derelict since before the War, barbed wire fence on the far side to keep the cows in the pasture, just enough room to walk the narrow strip of grass between it and the empty pool. "We've got permission," he said, "and if we get it done by the time the weather warms up we can start swimming. We'll start tomorrow, and we'll keep at it every Sunday until it's done." Pussy Bailey must've fallen on his knees in thanks, it gave us all something to do instead of just going for Walks, and I know it was a relief to most of us, including me, we'd no longer be forever casting about for somewhere to go, it'd keep us all busy for weeks. Next day after church and we'd all had lunch we trooped down to the Swimming Baths, we'd changed out of our Sunday best, a raggle-taggle of Juniors keeping the Seniors company and getting in the way, most of us in gym knicks and pumps, shouting and laughing and chasing about, asking questions and wanting to help, the bigger kids pushing a wheelbarrow or carrying shovels and spades and a few buckets, most of them were Nunc's, I suppose Mr Bailey'd told Nunc to lend them but he wouldn't've been pleased about that, he always kept a sharp eye on you if you went near his tools, he'd shout "Leave 'em be!" if we even went near them. At least two of the buckets had come from the room where the maids stored the cleaning stuff, "We've got to be absolutely sure to take everything back," somebody said, "and *clean*. How many things've we got?" and there was a bit of argy-bargy as that got sorted out and one of the Prefects made a list, some kids'd got their wellies on but Gatley'd said "Not me! trying to shovel out all that muck'd ruin them, they'd *leak!*" and then "You can't buy any more, you know, there's none in the shops. Wear your pumps." Quite a few of the Seniors had really old ones, Stevenson'd found an old ratty pair on top of a locker in the Changing Room, cobwebby canvas full of holes, a big split halfway up the heel, bits of string for laces, and he told us Ticker Ranson's got "dozens of pumps, old ones, all beaten-up, different sizes. For emergencies. He keeps 'em in a locker. That's where I got mine." Some of us laughed, "I was going to go barefoot, but my feet wouldn't last long, worse'n wellygogs, so I asked him" and somebody laughed again.

As I sit here, well over sixty years later, I can't for the life of me work out how we used the wheelbarrow, you couldn't push it up the stream bed it'd bog down as soon as you left the Baths and none of us, no matter how much help you got, could've pushed a loaded wheelbarrow up a four-foot rise from the bottom of the shallow end to the top of the wall, not even Mr Hawkins'd be able to do that, not that we had any planks anyway. I think we simply trundled the loaded wheelbarrow from the middle to the edge, where it could be thrown up onto the grass. Of course once all that muck'd been tossed onto the grass it had to be moved again, and I do remember me and another kid struggling a pail of dirt over the grass, one on each side, and dumping it under the trees on the canal embankment behind the pavilion. I expect the wheelbarrow was used for that too, though it wouldn't get far in all that scrub. Long before we'd finished we'd made a huge pile of dirt back there, and of course mud trailed everywhere *Never mind! It'll grow back in.* What with all the larking about we were all covered with it, it was a wonderful excuse simply to soss about and make a terrible mess, though what with all the stones and old cowpats the Prefects soon stopped us throwing stuff about. All in all it was a wonderful event, the Seniors so single-minded about it *Get out of the way! The way you're going we'll never get it done. Go play in the Spinney or somewhere!* they were absolutely determined to go swimming once the hot weather came along, and we Juniors, even if we were just as determined to have a wonderful messy time, were equally anxious to learn how to swim. It's amazing nobody got hurt in that spasm of spontaneous good-humoured frenzy, and that the job actually got done at all, let alone in something like three or four weeks, everybody simply fagged out from it, and ravenous all the time.

But Matron began to make rules, and insisted, "I can't clean your clothes up, and the laundry won't take them all muddy. You'll have to deal with it. Wear your gym knicks, take your shirts off. *And* your socks. Or else!" And I wondered what she'd do. "Might make you wear damp and dirty clothes," Sam said, "or get Angus to give you Detention." I knew I'd never get my school clothes clean if they got muddy trundling all that mud about, and most of us did do as we were told, just once Taffy didn't and we saw him stuck in one of the bathrooms trying to get his trousers clean *She wouldn't let me wear them in the shower* and Brian told him "Of course not! They'd shrink!" Harrington frowned, he was the Prefect on duty, "The mud'd clog the drains! Then where'd we be?"

Some kids gave up, it was all too hard, even before we'd dug the shallow end out, but there was still a boisterous clump of red-cheeked kids, sweaty but scrubbed of mud, clamouring in to the Dining Hall for tea Wednesdays and Saturdays full of their job-well-done, their clattery satisfaction not even ruffled for more than a couple of minutes when somebody said "Hey! How're we goin' to get the gate down? The sluice-gate?" and somebody else asked where the doofus was, does anybody know. The Head House-prefect said, "Not to worry, everything's under control, I already asked" and looked all superior. It turned out Henry Houston knew exactly where it was, up in an apple room in Rushall, big black-iron crank called a key, a little bit of rust on it. And of course when the job was done we all trooped down on the Saturday to watch the gate get lowered, pretty well all the kids from the village along with some of the grown-ups as well as all us boarders, somebody'd gone down the day before with Mr Hawkins to loosen up the screw with a mallet and a dollop or two of grease all down it and turn the key a bit to get it started, see if it worked, but it still took a couple of big kids a lot of work to get the sluice-gate snubbed all the way down, they had to use a trowel to clear its way, scrabble the small stones out. For the next few days on your way down to see how full the Baths were getting you'd meet other kids coming back up shaking their heads "It'll never get filled! It's running out as fast as it's running in!" But it wasn't, it was just with so much water leaking through the sluice-gate it didn't seem to be filling up at all. Some kids'd get down in the stream bed on the outside of the sluice-gate to see it if was seated in its groove properly, but the water was just spouting out in great sprays between the planks as well as round the edges worse than it did in the lock gates on the canal. Henry Houston and Ticker Ranson both told us "Don't be so impatient!" it'll settle down and fill up nicely once the wood gets really soaked and swells up to fill its frame, and after a few more days you could see they were right. The Baths were filling up and suddenly there was a whole lot of new rules and regulations about when you could go swimming and who with, not that many of us knew how to swim anyway, and the Prefects were given the job of making sure nobody got drowned, you couldn't go in the deep end until you could swim all the way across *and* clamber out the other side by yourself, and of course nobody was allowed to do anything till the pavilion got cleaned out for changing in, after all these years sitting open and idle it didn't half stink.

 A lot of us'd splash about in the shallow end shouting and larking about, squirting water with your fist, scooting spray into somebody's face with the flat of your hand, stuff like that, and one day soon after we'd got the Baths going there I was in a splashing contest with somebody or other, both of us hanging on to the edge of the pool kicking away like mad there was a great chorus of "One! Two! Three!" down by the deep end, that wasn't very far away the pool was only about thirty yards long I looked up and there was this kid flying out in midair towards the middle a couple of Seniors waiting there in the water a huge splash and all at once there we all were in the bright sun crowding round the big kids clamouring "Me! Me! Me next!" I can remember it almost as though it was yesterday it was so amazing, getting down on the grass between these two big kids, the sun hot on my face, *close your eyes* one of them said, one had my arms the other my legs, the damp grass faintly prickly on my back a nubbly bit from a worm-cast or a small stone then the shock of cool air as they lifted me, a cooler patch where a bit of mud had stuck, my feet a bit cold, firm hard grip round my ankles, big hands warm and wet solid hold on my wrists, sound of his breath faint goosebumps the quiet *slap* of water at the edge of the pool me sagging in the middle *Will my bum hit the ground?* the rush of air first one side then the other as they swung me *One!* "Just relax!" somebody called, "go limp!" *Two!* "Hold your nose!" *As if I could do that him holding my wrists!* and then *Three!* and as they let me go I snatched a big breath and grabbed my nose closed my eyes tight turning in the air just sort of hovering there for a split second the air absolutely motionless and *floosh!* the delicious shock, cold water all round me my ears filling up little popping bubble noises dull roaring like when you hold a seashell to your ear the steady thump of heartbeat, arms flailing a bit and then hands under my shoulders, head above water, take a breath, a laugh behind my head and there was the edge of the pool in front of me, a hand under my bum boosting me up onto the grass the worn cement rim rough on my belly as another kid plunged *splash!* into the pool behind me, take a big breath, wipe your eyes, find your soaking-wet towel, get rid of the shivers, shake the water out of your lug 'oles and run round for another go, invariably returning in a direct line just like the big iguana Charles Darwin chucked over and over again into the sea in the 1830s on Albemarle Island because it kept coming back for more.

I must say that seemed a funny sort of thing for a grown-up to do, but just like Darwin's iguana us kids couldn't get enough of it, all those amazing contrasts, your swimming trunks all clammy clinging cold, sun hot on your back, a patch of muscle twitching against the goosebumps just under your shoulderblade, the sound of someone coughing back at the water's edge *Told you to hold your nose!* wet muddy grass squishy underfoot, cool trickle of water running down the inside of your legs, the sheer friendliness of it all, but one of the Prefects a day or two later said it was too much work. "You could jump off the diving board if you learned to swim" he said, and he set about teaching us. I've no idea who it was, all I can remember is a lanky kid telling me to find out if I was scared of the water, he had a bunch of us stand there in the shallow end and stick our heads under, "Don't hold your nose" he said, "and open your eyes once you're down there," all that mucky water. And then he had us float on our back, "nothing's going to happen if you sink," he said, "you know that." It wasn't long, just two or three days, he had us all dog-paddling the thirty or so feet right across the pool. He was really painstaking and patient, worked hard to build our confidence. He was really itching to join the other Seniors in the deep end, dive in, perhaps race across, try a bit of underwater swimming, play a scratch game a bit like water polo, or just simply muck about, but it's equally clear though I didn't see it at the time, that he wanted to be sure we could all swim so he wouldn't have to worry about us, and he enjoyed teaching us. I don't suppose he actually spent more than half-an-hour with us at any particular time, and I'm pretty sure that one or two others of the Seniors came along too, it was all of a piece with the great communal effort to get the Swimming Pool opened up again in the first place. I can't remember any more how long the Baths lasted, but it was a couple of years at least, till well after the War anyway, and when I asked Phil about it he said "Oh blimey, I'd forgotten about that, haven't thought about it for years. What I remember most was the cowpats," he said, "you'd be swimming along and there'd be a bloody great cowpat floating down the stream towards you." I didn't remember that especially though now and again there might be a bit of one, or more likely a dried-up one, you'd splash at it to steer it towards the overflow, mostly they just broke up and dispersed. "You wouldn't be *allowed* to swim there nowadays," Our Kid said, and we both laughed, commiserating with each other over how times have changed, "But none of us got any infection from the Baths." And that's pretty surprising when I think about it, the water really was pretty bad what with all the silt and rubbish from the stream, leaves and twigs and goodness knows what else, to say nothing of what the cows sent us, it was so cloudy you couldn't see the bottom at even the shallow end, you couldn't even see your knees. Every autumn, around October, somebody'd open the sluice-gate to drain the Baths, and they'd stay empty till Easter, there wouldn't be much digging out to do. I found out from Michael Horowitz's book, *Brewood: Some Notes on the History*, that the Baths were probably fitted up with their sandstone lining some time in the middle of the nineteenth century and had first been dug as a fishpond back in the Middle Ages, carp and bream mostly I'd think, so the stream had been dug out and widened a long time ago. But we none of us had any idea of that sort of history at all, nobody in the School ever told us anything about local history, they probably didn't know; in the War at any rate almost none of them were local people, and if we thought about that sort of thing we simply didn't think there was any history at all except for the Crusaders' effigies in the church, and Giffard's Cross, but no big battles or important events. History wasn't what went on in the village, that was just the village.

Once the Baths started filling Mr Hawkins had to put a couple of hurdles across the stream to keep the cows out and by the time School started again after the summer he'd always got the sluice-gate up, it was super to be back among your friends in September to tell about your summer, Phil and me always spending most of it at the Farm in Alcester. There wouldn't be many kids kicking a ball about on the Croft, we were no sooner settled back at School than there'd be knots of kids, especially on your Sunday Walk, clustering under some chestnut tree or other, there was a terrific one in the corner of a field out on the Somerford road, chucking sticks up into the branches or even stones, trying to knock chestnuts down, leaves and twigs fluttering and tumbling, now and again a soft chunky wavering clatter as a chestnut dislodged, the soft green cover with its sharp spikes thumping away as it bounced through the branches, sporadic rattle *thunk ... thunk-thunk*, and you'd listen for the pause after it cleared the lowest branch, a suspended quiet *thunk!* as it hit the ground perhaps a limp bounce, one or two kids their caps fallen off scrabbling among the leaves and debris to grab the loot, *Bags it! Bags!* or *'Ey that's mine! I knocked it down!*, arguments and shouts, sticks, twigs, leaves, and perhaps stones and even a conker or two falling on them a bit prickly perhaps, it didn't hurt if they landed on you you didn't want to look up but of course you always did, running towards whatever was falling through the tree, scrambling in the clutter, negotiations and swops in the patchy barrage, strong smell of bruised leaves and damp soil, sometimes a lovely sharp frost your breath a misty cold cloud around your face, you'd huff and blow it out in front of you but it'd still settle all clammy. I can still taste that glossy brown smell the shifting woodpattern glow of a fresh conker as you peeled the green case, your hands staining with juice, you'd inspect it for bugs especially borers they'd ruin a good conker, sharp disappointment if a conker split the way big ones sometimes did, sometimes two conkers huddled together both with one side flat from sharing one case.

The ones you knocked down weren't as good as the ones that'd fallen on their own, we all thought windfalls were harder because they were riper, but us boarders couldn't be out there early in the morning to get them before anyone else got up, we weren't allowed, it was terrific to find one under the tree its cover split open the lovely brown sheen of the conker eyeing you from the bottom, the snug green case with its dull cocoa splotches fighting your fingers as you peeled it away, juice getting under your nails and dribbling down your hands getting muckier and muckier, your clothes, the smell a bit sharp at the front of your nose. You couldn't wait to get back and show everyone what you'd got so long as you'd got some good ones, but of course no one was interested in what you'd got, they'd got their own, it'd be dead quiet in the Billiard Room, you'd poke and bore away with a compass-point to get a hole right through the conker, the compass-point wouldn't reach all the way through and you had to bore from the other side after you got halfway, you had to be terribly careful, the brown skin of the conker split ever so easily and you knew it'd be no good but you'd finish anyway, sometimes a conker that looked all cracked'd last ever so long. Daykids had it all over us, there was no such thing as a school bus, they walked to school or came on their bikes some of them four miles or so from Codsall or Bilbrook, they could scavenge like mad on the way, get really good ones, and their dads had tools they could use, augers and drills made lovely straight holes right through, there'd be bits of string all over the place and a skewer or something in the kitchen to poke the string through. Some kids even got their mums to bake their conkers in the oven to make them hard and dry, there were two schools of thought about that, bore the hole before or after you'd baked it, and one kid I can't remember his name but his dad worked in a chemist's shop even tried pickling his conkers the way soldiers toughened up their feet in a mix of potassium permanganate. We boarders were scrounging all the time for string, if you got a parcel from home you could let other kids have a bit, "For a consideration of course" one of the others said, you'd get a conker or a sweet or even money, a farthing or a ha'penny from somebody really desperate, "More money than sense" a Senior said, or you'd give a piece away to your mates, there was a lot of trading going on, swops, muttered curses as kids struggled to thread the string through, cries of anguish if the conker split. In the Billiard Room or in prep there'd be little heaps of conker innards, flecks of brown conker skin, shreds everywhere, they clung to your socks got up your sleeves and stuck in your leg hairs till you brushed them off, sometimes you'd find some in your belly button when you went to bed. You soon discovered or remembered that any old string wouldn't do, it had to be strong, white was best though some kids said binder twine even if it is rough, it had to be stout so the knot wouldn't pull through the conker ruining it, and you didn't want the string to break there were all sort of rules about that.

You'd go outside with a conker or two in your pocket and you'd challenge somebody for a game, didn't have to be one of your pals, and if you'd both got new conkers you'd sort out who got first go, there were all sorts of ways to do that, one of us hiding the string behind his back and other one calling *short* or *long* was what most of us did, or you could toss a coin, I'm amazed nobody cheated but of course if you got found out then nobody'd play with you, and if you lost you'd hold your conker hanging about nine inches down real steady from your clenched fist out in front of you about chest height, you mustn't move, and your opponent'd hit it with his conker, he'd have three goes, his conker in one hand the end of the string in the other, the string stretched tight, and he'd swing the conker down hard he wasn't allowed to hold it too close, if his conker didn't hit yours really square on it wouldn't break at all, it'd just swing round wildly till you steadied it and he had another go, and of course it might be his conker that broke anyway. As soon as you started to play there'd be a small cluster of kids standing round to watch, and at Break there'd be bunches of kids huddled in groups round the Croft, somebody shouting *Strings!* when a conker missed and the strings got tangled, the first one to shout it got to have a new go, three tries at the other conker, and every time your conker bashed another one to pieces it counted, a sixer would've demolished six other conkers, or perhaps it was a brand new conker that smashed a fiver and so became a sixer, the conker with the highest number always went first when you started. A week or two into the conker season there'd be large clusters of kids standing round while someone with a fifteener or more defended a challenge from another big conker, perhaps a twenty-five-er or more, the winner becoming a forty-er or whatever, and one memorable day Jeff Whitcomb held his beaten cracked and scabby old conker up in front of his Geography class just as Henry Houston walked in, he was in IV B, and announced that after class, right before school lunch, he'd retire his hundred-and-seven-er. Henry gave him a look and said, "Where will you break it, Whitcomb?" Jeff looked a bit startled. "On the Croft wall, Sir." "Let's have a look at it," said Henry, and "Yes, that looks like a wise decision. You'd all better go and watch, see he does it right." Of course we all heard about it, it must've been half the school I'd think, more than thirty kids anyway, trooping across the muddy grass of the Croft to watch Jeff whirl his conker round his head and then smash it to smithereens, a ragged cheer, a nine-days' wonder. It was funny, that, we all felt a bit self-conscious and daft, I know I did, and Jeff looked all proud and a bit awkward and unsure of himself, some of the older kids standing round looking smug and above it all and talking together in a superior sort of way, but they still came out to watch. And they played conkers too.

You had to be a good shot, it was ever so easy to hit your opponent on the knuckles no matter how careful you were, it hurt, the conker whizzing down on the back of your hand, if you got hit you'd shout *Knucks!* before the other bloke and he'd lose his go, but if he shouted first he'd get to keep going. You weren't allowed to flinch, that'd make your conker swing a bit on the string so your opponent'd get another go, and that'd be three more hits, it was really hard to hold your hand out steady as a rock as the conker came plummeting down especially when you'd just been swacked a good one, every time you flinched they'd get another three shots. If you kept hitting people's hands then they'd make sure they'd hit you back, and they wouldn't play with you any more. We all got to be pretty good shots, but it wasn't long before we all had red and chapped-looking hands, bruises round the knuckles and on the back, your hands didn't half hurt when you wrote anything down in class, and your prep got pretty messy. But we were mad for Conkers, it was obsessive, and at the end of October once the conker season was over, one or two kids might store some conkers away somewhere to use next year, nice and hard they'd be, and tough.

January was so cold in 1947 that at Break and at lunch a lot of us slithered across the ice-bound Croft to see what the canal was like, the ground so slippy it took ages to get back up the embankment if you went down to the towpath. Break was so short we'd never get back to class on time and for punishment we'd be stuck in a classroom forever at the end of the day. Even the Teachers got grumpy at Detention, so at Break we'd stick to School Bridge and wait for a barge to struggle through the heavy ice. With everything frozen the towpath was really perilous, you slid all over the place, *Stay away from there!* we were told, and *You won't see any horses, not in this weather.* "If a horse fell it would break a leg," Mr Page said, and we all nodded wisely, especially the farmers' sons, "it would have to be destroyed." It wasn't long before the ice got so thick not even the ice-breaker could get through, even if its engine roared away like mad and two rows of men in heavy gloves rocked it side-to-side, sometimes to a shanty sung by the bargee, as they clung to a chest-high rail that ran the length of the boat. Their breath rose in cold clouds and we loved to see its heavy steel bow lurch up on top of the ice and then slump back, the crunch of the ice collapsing under all that weight, a narrow ice-strewn path of black water stretching behind. We'd watch a thin skim of ice slowly span its path as the barge went on to the next bridge, and as soon as lessons were over after the ice-breaker stopped coming we'd send one of the small kids out to test the ice, the water was only about a foot deep at the edge, the ice would creak and groan as someone gingerly stepped down to it, sometimes a whole sheet tilted a bit as water seeped up from a crack you didn't even know was there.

After a few days the canal was frozen solid even under the bridges, Mr Page told us it was easily six inches thick and perfectly safe, and once the barges couldn't get through the whole landscape got quiet and still, the only sounds someone working in the fields, the shouts of kids running and sliding on the ice the other side of Brewood Bridge, the air so dry and cold, the clear sound of the bus from Wolverhampton out near Giffard's Cross or even a car miles away in Coven or as far as Bishop's Wood. "Just *listen*," Broggie said in class, "listen *hard*, pay attention to the world! The sounds bounce, the way Wordsworth says they do. Hear the skaters, really *hear* their skates on the ice. In winter the world really *does* ring. That's what cold *does*." And after a pause he said, "Go and ask Mr Hutchings *Why* in Physics." You couldn't help but notice the way things now sounded, and we loved the adventuresomeness the cold gave, kids sliding and skating and playing on the canal at the other end of the village and beyond, all of us boarders sticking closer to School, stumbling and stoitering on the jagged and jumbled ice alongside the dark frozen track the ice-breaker'd left, rear-ups of small slabs. When you hurled a stone along the ice, the way we did playing Ducks and Drakes in the summer, it'd end up in its clatter miles off, the sound bouncing about like mad as it faded in the distance, a lovely strange diminishing music. But you had to scrabble about to find a stone under all the ice and snow.

The snow was really super, so heavy and persistent that when Malpas went scooting across the steep slope under the trees in the Spinney his feet went out from under him and he slid all the way down, breakneck speed flat on his back with his mac ballooning up about him the snow jamming all the way up his trouser legs. "It isn't half cold," he laughed when he got back to the top all breathless from the effort, and he immediately turned round and launched himself down the slope again, same place, but this time he hunched down and kept on his feet all the way to the bottom. That afternoon when classes were over we slogged over to the Spinney with two or three kids from the village, they'd got a sled or a toboggan they'd dug out from the garden shed or somewhere at home it hadn't been used since the last big freeze, years ago, or they'd cobbled together with scrap wood with their dads. You had to scramble *Get out of the way!* as they clumped down the slope at you heavy but flimsy impossible to stop and too flimsy to steer, exhilarating and ungainly. Then on Saturday Gavin Frost turned up all chuff, for some reason we called him Olive we none of us knew why, he was a big bloke, one of the Seniors in the Third Dorm, he'd gone down to the Vicarage and somehow, he never said a word to let on how, he got the Rev Broughton-Thomson to lend him his Norwegian toboggan. He'd carried it through the village up to the School, we none of us had a clue how he'd known about it, he had strict orders to take good care of it but we could all use it so long as Olive stayed in charge, not leave it out all night, clean it properly at the end of the day, oil the wood to preserve it "He gave me some oil" Olive said, not bash it about. *Some hope!* It was not at all like Olive to be so insistent. "He's all right, really, " he said, "a very kind man. But if we damage it he'll take it back and never lend us anything ever again. It's very precious. We scrabbled it out of his cellar, him and me together, it's been there for years and years, we cleaned it up, well, me mostly, while he watched. He remembered it last Sunday. He's never lent it before, not to *any*body."

What a surprise that was, the Vicar was ages old, as old as Squire Giffard, tall and thin and frail looking, pale flat face, and when we asked Olive told us the Vicar'd used to do a lot of winter sports, in Switzerland and Norway, that was before the War. With its thin varnished oak frame it looked quite fragile but it was tremendously strong, springy, and really light, any of us could easily carry it, it had narrow metal runners shaped like an upside-down U, and by the time Olive'd pulled it over the Croft with a couple of smaller kids on board the runners were jam-packed with ice, give it a push and it just scooted along, it held four small kids easily, the back one had to do the steering dragging his feet, it stood up above the snow on its slender frame, you sat on narrow wooden slats running across the top or you could lie down on it. It was ever so light and when a couple of the bigger kids got on and slid it down the Spinney slope we couldn't believe how fast it went they had to tip it over to stop it before they ended up in the canal, they came back up the slope all breathless and grinning like mad. "It's smashing! It's ever so fast, it's hard to steer and you can't stop it" but we all wanted to have a go "Let me! Let me!" and while we were arguing about it Olive was so busy deciding he let go of the rope *Oh no!* the Vicar's toboggan slid straight down the slope so fast we didn't even have time to move, down between the trees and up over the three-foot ridge into mid-air at the edge of the canal and it didn't even wobble it went nearly all the way across and ended with a clatter up against the tow path. It wasn't long before we were all piling onto it and slamming down the slope and out over the canal a great *whoosh* through the air that roaring rush miles better than downhill on your bike you'd hang on to the kid in front, you had to sit upright and not move about at all or the toboggan'd start to tip, and *slam bang* you'd go as you hit the ice *bang wallop* you'd all jostle together as you landed, your feet up off the runners out to the sides so you didn't land on *them*, the toboggan would pitch it'd tip over if it hit a sticking-up lump of ice and you'd all spill out in a great jumbly fan of arms and legs wet raincoats and gloves. We all got soaked to the skin, we built a ramp of snow on the other side of the canal so it'd slide up onto the towpath if it was going fast enough the breath'd *whump!* out of you and the toboggan lurch up to a wonderful stop perhaps you'd fall off it was the most exciting thing we'd any of us ever done, nothing remotely like it in our lives not even in a fairground, we all got obsessed with it couldn't stay away, laughing and shouting building snow forts in between rides having snowball fights, that night we all fell into bed so tired we could hardly talk to each other at all and next day when lessons were over hands chapped clothes still wet prep not finished, we did it all over again, we got into trouble for that but we didn't care, until a couple of days later after supper Olive went down the slope as fast as he could, he'd taken a couple of pals over with him *I want to try something out* he told them, the rest of us still in prep, he didn't tell us what he was going to do, the toboggan run was solid ice by then and he held up the toboggan in front and ran a few steps till he reached the ice launched himself forth onto the toboggan as fast as he possibly could lying flat his head sticking out in front "I thought I could get all the way across" he said, and halfway down *crunch!* straight into a tree, knocked himself out, *so fast I couldn't steer at all, no time!* Next day he had a huge red and blue lump on his forehead, stitches under a bandage, a bruise blotching down over his face, two black eyes and a terrible headache. The School Doctor, called in from the village, made him lie quiet in sick bay for a couple of days the blackout curtains closed in case he had concussion and that was the end of it. The Vicar took his toboggan back. We were all cross with Olive for wrecking things, no thanks to him for getting us the toboggan in the first place, but as soon as the snow and ice began to thaw a day or two later we forgot it. We all marvelled at that toboggan though, and argued about it, *had the Vicar been in Winter Sports before the War? Had he been an Arctic explorer trekking to the North Pole?* It was the most exotic thing we'd ever been close to. Yet none of us ever wondered how come the Vicar, that thin, mild, gentle elderly man, had something as exotic as that, no matter how unexpected it was that he had it, and how right it was that we should have the use of it. We simply knew that if the Vicar hadn't had what we wanted then somebody else would've, not that we even knew what it was that somebody would've had that we might've wanted anyway.

21

Wartime City

No matter how much in the early years of the War we might've looked forward to school holidays in Brummagem none of them was at all easy. If we were going anywhere except the Farm we had no idea what it'd be like, we didn't even know what sort of neighbourhood it'd be in, it'd just be a place to visit, not where we lived. All we knew really was that it'd be in easy reach of the Woolworth's store Dad managed at Sparkhill, but we moved a lot and for the life of me I can't remember much difference between whatever house we lived in when we went back to Shirley and the one we went to in Moseley. Let alone which came first. One of them had an Anderson Shelter in the back garden, Dad had it put in, but I certainly don't know where, the sequence of events at Shirley and Moseley all blurs into a blended and more-or-less featureless landscape where city parks, air raid shelters, bus stops, and static water tanks, everyday and local things, stationery shops and greengrocers and shoe repairs, all shift from one side of the road to the other as I cast back to them in memory, the roads themselves ill-remembered and shifting too, our time in Birmingham jam-packed with ever-repeated undifferentiated stuff we saw and did, day to day, moment to moment.

When Dad started working thirty miles away in Rugby because the manager there'd got called up, Phil and I went home for the Christmas holidays, two years into the War, to a village we'd never even heard of, we didn't go to a house. We'd never lived in a flat, and to Mum and Dad it was an unhappy step down in the social scale to be living in a place you'd never be able to buy. The Croft, which is what the building was called, had been built as a block of flats, the only place like that in the whole village, but housing was in desperate short supply. Phil and me liked it well enough even though the flat itself wasn't anything like as roomy as the houses we'd been in before, a bit pokey and crowded with four of us in it, but we were all under one roof again, the old village green with its stub of an ancient market-cross and a few labourer's cottages across the street, alongside a pigsty with a couple of pigs in it. The Blitz was nowhere near as bad as at Birmingham, and Lower Hillmorton was two-and-a-half miles outside Rugby, still pretty much in the country despite the number of factories in Rugby itself. It was a milestone in our lives. The very next morning after we arrived Mum took me and Our Kid straight across the street to meet Auntie Woods, "Come and meet the pigs," she said, "they're coming along nicely," and her stooped figure, she wasn't much taller than me, strode over to where she put the swill together, "D'you know about pigs? They're going to eat your kitchen scraps, your mum says you'll be bringing them over twice a week. We've got a few chickens too." Mum told us we might be getting some of our vegetables from Mrs Woods when they get ready, "she really knows how to grow her garden," and as we crossed the street back to the flat I wondered if Mum had known Auntie Woods for a long time, they looked so friendly together. "She cleans the stairs and hall floors at The Croft," Mum said, "She's there every day, so you two had better not track mud through that front door. She's got enough to do as it is." When he came home Dad told us that she knows everybody, "she loves to talk. So you'd better be polite, treat her with respect." Whenever we saw her she'd stop and talk to us. "What are you going to do today?" she'd ask, or "Have you seen such-and-such yet? You'd not want to miss that." Mum told us how much she and Mrs Woods liked to have a good natter together whenever they could, most days she'd come in for a cup of tea after she'd done the floors, and Phil and me liked talking to her, she always wanted to know what we were up to. Every day we'd see her busy about the cottage and the garden, Mr Woods most of the day away at work, he pottered about the animals or the sheds when he was home, fixing things for other people as well as them. What with seeing Auntie Woods every day and hearing about some of the neighbours at The Croft, we all began to feel a bit settled, Phil and me pretty sure we'd be living at Rugby long enough for us to meet a few kids our own age and start to make our own friends. If the War kept going Dad wouldn't be moved again any time soon, so at last somewhere might began to feel like home.

When I started writing this Phil and I spent a lot of time on the phone trying to figure out the details of where we'd lived for the first two years of the War, we went through whatever papers we've got and tried to reminisce, but there wasn't much to go on, fuzzy recollections, no photographs because nobody had any film, just a few scraps of envelopes and addresses from our old stamp collections, a couple of broken Dinky Toys, a wooden box of wooden bricks and boards we'd endlessly played with and hung on to for our own kids. Not much else besides our School Report Books, we'd hung on to them even though to anybody else they'd be nothing but quaint museum pieces, they tell us something about who we are and where we came from. Remembering takes a lot of *work*, and what I've got to go on is what memory struggled to find in its twilight, inventing more than it knows, lots of shadows, overcast with occasional patches of light, a lot of it simply blank. I expect that's true for most people, and I must say that Phil and I laughed with derision when in 1999 I applied for my Canadian Old Age Security Benefit and the application form insisted in its heavy boldface type that I list "all the places you have lived from birth to present" from "day month year" to "day month year" *What century do they think this is?* the task so impossible and the assumptions about how people live so completely bonkers. "The bureaucratic mind!" Phil snorted, "It's the same everywhere, isn't it?" He told me he'd once totted it up, he'd lived in more than thirty places since he got his first job in 1949, "more like forty." But where *did* we live once we got to Wheaton Aston? Did we go back to live in Shirley, in *another* house on Solihull Road, or did we go to Moseley? I'm not sure, and neither is Phil, but we've spent quite a few phone calls blathering about it, and now and again I get daftly obsessive, I fret in the small hours because I want to get it *right*. In my old stamp collection there's an envelope postmarked November 1941 addressed to Dad in Shirley, but Phil's

School Report Book says that's when we were at Moseley. There's contradictions everywhere. And in any case those School Report Books aren't very reliable, the addresses on the title-pages obviously added who knows when by who knows who, and at some time amended by Dad after he noticed it. But they're not *reliably* unreliable, not *always* to be mistrusted. Phil's Report Book gets our street-name wrong, it says *Blomfield* when it should be *Bloomfield* Road in Moseley, and mine, when I went to Brewood eighteen months later, in an unidentifiable hand gets our Rugby address right, but it looks as though it was written some weeks before we actually moved there, as if it could've happened before it happened. But memory isn't reliable anyway.

I was thinking about Moseley, we weren't there very long, and about the Anderson shelter which I think was behind the house. Did we ever have the cat in there, how could we have managed that, so I asked Our Kid on the phone, he had to think about it, the phone line was clear as a bell as though he was in the next room instead of seven thousand miles away, I could hear him scratching his head the way he does, his hand up over his forehead his forefinger rubbing where his hairline used to be, "No," Phil said. "We never had a cat at Moseley." And he paused, I started to say "That's what I thought," and he said "First we had Fluffy and then we had Sooty, but that was before the War, I don't suppose you remember Fluffy you were so small," and I started to say something and he said "I remember that very clearly because I named Sooty, I remember that, he was still a kitten, he was a long-haired cat, dark grey, we got Sooty after Fluffy'd gone, I can't remember Fluffy very well though" and I said "That's funny, I'm sure you've got it the wrong way round, because I remember Fluffy. She was a long-haired grey Persian, a Silver Persian Mum called it, I remember once a spark flew out of the kitchen grate and burned her, a smell of burning fur and suddenly she wasn't stretched out asleep in front of the fire but hissing and licking furiously at herself as she moved away. I didn't know whether to laugh or cry," and I thought of Fluffy cautiously emerging from a box when Mum or Dad, but it might have been Alice, brought her home for the first time, and in memory it feels like the house on Solihull Road before the War, there we used the kitchen grate. "But you know," I said to Phil, "I don't remember Sooty at all. Might that've been a cat we had at Rugby? Did we have a cat there?" and a vague memory popped into my head of Mum telling me once when I was home from Brewood that I had given Fluffy her name, I suppose we'd been talking about cats, Hermy and Ginger stretched out in front of the fire, it must have been Lichfield then that she said that, and I said so to Phil. "No, Pete," he said, "I don't think so. We got Fluffy when Florence was our maid, long before Alice, and Alice came along when you were only three," and I said "Oh? You must be wrong, I can't really remember Florence at all except she was a big woman wasn't she? wore black? But I can clearly remember when we got Fluffy," and as we talked we began to sound a bit peeved, we were both so certain the other was wrong, his absolute certainty that Sooty came after Fluffy really got to me, my older brother putting me right, an old irritation. But it was such a totally daft thing to get cross over. "I'm such a Great Aputh," I said, and we both laughed at ourselves. I thought with a grin how I used to think an Aputh was a baby Ape and how surprised I'd been to find it meant ha'pennyworth; even now that word conjures a fleeting Abominable Snowman sort of figure lumbering vaguely through a corner of my mind. The limbs of Osiris. Memory. Scraps of words clinging like barnacles along with other bits of flotsam and jetsam. You can't decide what you're going to remember at any given moment, you're just going to remember it, "this way, that way," a poem by Robert Creeley says, "just because / it was in my head today." The details conflate, pour together, confound. How apt, that Latin word confundere. In the 1960s a friend asked me "What don't you know?" and I didn't know what to answer, so he asked, "What do you know wrong?"

Probably everything.

So it's impossible to tell whether we went back to live in Shirley before or after we were in Moseley, and no matter what the Security Benefit might think, it really doesn't matter to anybody except me. Memory doesn't work by dates, it works by events, it works by what happened. When Phil started to think we went to Rushbury before we went to Wheaton Aston, we were both a bit bothered until we realised we could use getting my tonsils out to sort that out. Memory tells us who we are, and the mind conjures up a set of complex feelings connected with what you *know* happened, that's why Phil and I got so cross with each other when we argy-bargyed about the sequence of cats. Some memories are indelible indeed, even among a confusion of dates.

 I can remember Moseley alright, with the searchlight at the Merton Road end of the street, the barrage-balloon post with its big reel of cable and the sandbags round it the next street over, and the ack-ack gun near the Yardley Wood Road, but I'm not sure about the Anderson Shelter Dad put in the back garden, that might've been at the Shirley house, the second time we were on Solihull Road, but I can remember the shelter clearly enough. At Moseley we slept downstairs in the dining room, that's where we had chicken pox, it was supposed to be safer than upstairs if the house got hit. Once the Blitz really started, Mum and Dad talked about getting a Morrison shelter, that was just a heavy steel table with a hefty cage round it underneath, you could use it the way you'd use an ordinary table, eat meals off it, sit round it, play games like Ludo or snakes and ladders on it, or just put books or embroidered table runners or vases of flowers on it, and in an Air Raid you could hide under it. You could even go to bed there, there'd certainly be plenty of room for a couple of children, we heard stories of as many as six people sleeping under one, and if a blast from a nearby bomb hit the house and wrecked it they'd be able to dig you out safe and sound. But the whole idea was just a bit too potty, to say nothing of the table being too heavy for most house floors, it'd take two well-muscled men to move it, so we didn't get one. *What would it do to the carpet?* Mum wondered, *all that weight!* Bombed-out houses we saw nearly always had their chimneys still standing, and 9 Bloomfield Road was a pretty solid house with a really good brick chimney running up the outside behind the dining-room fireplace. Mum and Dad brought the mattresses down from our beds and Our Kid and I slept with our heads in an alcove beside the chimney as far away from the windows as possible, the windows all criss-crossed with three-inch wide bands of yellow-ochre blast-tape. I've got no idea really if the tape actually prevented the window, if it got blown in, from cutting people to shreds, or if it just reduced the size of the shards. In the back of my head there's a vague glimpse of shattered glass held together by dirtied splinter-tape bulging in a window-frame, hanging there above the windowsill. But that could easily be something I saw or even dreamt.

Way past everybody's bedtime, one night, Our Kid and me in bed on mattresses on the floor, pitch-black outside, I woke up to find Our Kid watching as he sat in bed against the chimney, Mum and Dad standing in the window the blackout curtains wide open, looking out into the night, the barrage balloon from the next street suddenly loomed high above and then vanished, the slightest glimpse as the searchlight at the end of the road swept over it, fires in the near distance, the houses all round getting in the way so we couldn't really see, *How did I sleep through all that racket?* the heavy dull pulse of German planes heading for targets somewhere in town, ack-ack guns banging away somewhere not too far, Mum and Dad quietly exclaiming together as the noise of the Air Raid, it was a big one, moved away from us towards where the factories were, and we wanted to get up and look the same as them but they wouldn't let us, "No, it's too dangerous" Dad said, "It's not there just for you to *watch*!" but I wanted to see, so did Phil, *No! Go back to bed!* and I expect they were just as much afraid we'd think of it simply as some sort of spectacle or some sort of wonder as that we'd get injured by bomb blasts and flying glass. And if I thought about it at all I did think of an Air Raid as an adventure the same way sleeping under the big steel table of a Morrison Shelter might've been; the War wasn't real to me or to Our Kid the way it was to Mum and Dad, it was slammed home to them by the wounded and the dead, realities not evident to us kids.

What sticks in my mind is the uncertainty of it all, the way everything kept changing. You'd go to bed at night in Brum and get up the next day to find rubble all round, bricks on the pavement and on the road, you couldn't go round the corner because there was a great big crater right across the road, wooden road barriers like long sawhorses blocking it off, in places the edge would be so clean-cut you'd see the layers, thin black paving on top of gravel and then sand and below that yellowish stony dirt, or if it was in somebody's garden bits of roots hanging out of dark topsoil, the end of a pipe sticking out into the crater, perhaps a bit of water trickling out as it ran down from further along the pipe, or a gas pipe sticking out perhaps now and again a bit of soft yellow flame but not very often, the gas got shut off, that was the first thing they did, but there'd still be a bit of its smell hanging round, there was always a pool of dirty water in the bottom, a bit of an oil slick on it, sometimes a crater might not get filled for as long as a week if a main road had been hit nearby, that had to be fixed first so the important traffic could get through, army convoys and stuff. But there'd usually be at least one navvy, more likely two, shovelling dirt back into the hole, or perhaps a couple of soldiers, once we had a whole platoon of Canadian troops about twenty of them filling in a crater and working in the street on Bloomfield Road, they were friendly and talkative, gave us sweets and even chewing gum we'd never seen before, flat strips wrapped in silver paper.

Sometimes you'd get on the bus to go into town and the bus would go every which way because roads were blocked off by fresh craters and repair crews, slow down to less than a walk to go over rough bits, even lean so steeply one side or the other at the edge of a filled-in crater that you could look straight down onto the street from your upstairs seat, there'd be pictures in places like post offices showing how much a bus could tilt without falling their centre of gravity was so low. You'd go past houses which had been bombed and you'd see a school satchel hanging on its peg on a bedroom door right up in the sky it seemed like, or a bathtub sticking straight out of an upstairs wall held up just by its pipes, no floor underneath it, towels hanging on a rail, flannel on the edge of the sink just like in our house, or you'd go past a house where the front and one side had been blown completely off and you could see inside just like a doll's house, all the furniture still there, pictures hanging on the wall a bit askew perhaps but still there, frilly bedspreads on the bed, flounces and frills, so *not* like home you'd feel a bit funny seeing it, like looking into somebody's really personal things or reading a private letter. Plaster and rubble, peeling wallpaper, shreds and bits, glimpses of lives. A whole row of shops and houses you saw every day, perhaps you'd bought something at the newsagents yesterday, had simply gone, a long pile of bricks and wood in their place, a craggy desert, fitful smoke and dust, people clearing up, directing traffic, keeping the kids and the sightseers off, and as it crossed the end of the street the bus carefully picked its way, bumping over and through the scattered debris. "I can't look," one person said, others stayed silent. "Close your eyes!" one woman told me as she shifted the shopping basket on her arm, "That's houses, that's where last night people were living," and a quiet voice said "I wonder if they got away. Hope nobody got killed" and the friendly chatter on the bus briefly stopped. But the intense strangeness of that sight, and the quiet talk around you, tempered the shock into curiosity and wonder. Other people's lives, but unreal.

Everybody who wasn't actually in the War, in the Army or Navy or Air Force, had to be in the Civil Defence in some way, all the men, anyway, and Dad started out in the War as an Air Raid Warden, some wardens'd go round checking people's blackouts, tell you if you had any light showing, and somebody told me, this must have been when we were at 94 Solihull Road, that Air Raid Wardens could come into your house when there was a light showing and if your blackout curtains didn't work properly and you refused to switch your lights off they could shoot the light out, somehow I got to believe that they could shoot *you* instead, in fact they didn't carry any sort of weapons at all but I didn't know that and I was glad that what Dad did as an Air Raid Warden was be a fire watchman, he'd spend the night on a roof looking for fires, trying to see where the incendiary bombs fell and then calling someone to tell them about it, probably the fire brigade. Not many places had telephones, there were hardly any in people's houses, perhaps he had to go and find a call-box down the road somewhere, it must've been cold work in the winter. For much of the time I think he was on the roof of Woolworth's at Sparkhill, it was taller than the other buildings round, he was on duty one night a week, most likely Tuesdays since Wednesday was Half-day when the shops closed early so he could do with less sleep. When we were at Moseley and even at Rugby later on he was in the Home Guard and when he was on duty or on drill wore a rough wool khaki uniform almost as heavy as felt, he had a rifle which he kept in the wardrobe in the bedroom during the day and in the cupboard under the stairs at night, he had six rounds of ammunition, if he wanted any more he had to go to the drill hall. Everybody was afraid of incendiary bombs, and we all had to keep a lookout for them wherever we went, sometimes they didn't go off, if you saw one lying somewhere you should get a long-handled shovel and put it in a pile of sand or smother it, or even just move it where it couldn't burn anything else, but it wasn't long in the War before the Germans made them so they exploded after they were well and truly alight. You didn't dare go near, you'd call someone, but we knew that the thing to do was smother it in sand if you could.

Everywhere you went there were galvanised buckets of sand, we had three or four around the house on Bloomfield Road, one morning we got up and found a burnt out incendiary bomb in the garden, another time we heard this clatter on the roof of the house and Dad got up and looked out, an incendiary bomb burning away on the edge of the slate roof over the porch, and he got a rake or a broom and knocked it to the ground and smothered it, it made a bit of a sooty mess on the cement path up to the front door but it didn't do any real damage. That night the buckets were full of sand again, but I don't know who filled them or where the sand came from. He might have used the stirrup pump as well, everybody had one or two of those, you stuck them in a pail of water, the pump straddled the side of the pail so you could hold it down with your foot, work the pump with one hand and aim the stream of water with the other, they'd have been wonderful in a water-fight but we weren't allowed to play with them, they were too much a matter of life and death.

Once, when we were sleeping in the Anderson shelter in the back garden, that must've been 1941, I woke up to see Dad standing in the door of the shelter Mum just behind him both of them intensely listening, the All Clear sign hadn't sounded yet and I said what's going on? *Sssshhhh!* they both said, and then I could hear, a loud crackling popping noise coming from the other side of the houses, fire glowing over the rooftops and Dad said "I'm sure it's HQ, that's the ammunition going up, I'd better go down" he'd go down on his bike but Mum said "There's nothing you can do. If they need you they can come and get you," the Home Guard had a troop lorry and a motorbike for running different sorts of errands, so we all went back to bed, next morning we found out a bomb had hit the Rialto cinema and what we'd heard was the film burning, the stink as bad as the noise.

In the mornings grown-ups would carefully pick their way round craters on the way to the shops, or coming back, shopping baskets over their arms, I'd stand and watch, or even go on down to the shops myself, a scrap of paper "Business As Usual" on a boarded-up shopfront, gritty brickdust and scraps of glass underfoot no matter how much they'd swept, the boy perhaps sweeping the oiled wood floor yet again, gloomy, sometimes a bit of candle or a kerosene lamp, the till not working, everything written down and added up. As you went down the street, terraced houses, some mornings women with a big handkerchief round their heads would stand there in the sunshine polishing their brass doorknob and letter-slot on the front door, or they'd be cleaning the front step, red-bricking or whiting the worn stone, or washing it, pails of soapy water and big scrubbing brushes, pausing to gossip, chatting away to each other, "There was some tinned peaches at the Co-op yesterday, they didn't have many" and "Too many points, duck, jam lasts longer, that's what we get if we can, in the big tins," talking about how hard it was to get the clothes dry on the airing rack when you didn't have enough coal for a kitchen fire, "did you see Johnny Franks, he fell off his bike yesterday, terrible mess of his face," and they'd cluck their concern as they swooshed the grey soapy water into the gutter and you'd walk by, like them enjoying the sun, dawdling along, a street where everybody knew everybody else's business, with all the rivalries and alliances and squabblings of a village, and a few days later you'd walk by again and they'd be gone, a whole row of houses one side of the street, nothing left after the clean-up but the odd bit of fire-blackened wall, heaps of bricks, timbers, the messed up front step now chipped and cracked leading nowhere, its red-bricking still bright with its polish, the boot-scraper all bent but still there.

People would talk about the raid as they waited in the long queues outside the butcher's and the baker's, the greengrocer's and the grocer's, you might join them yourself, there were rumours about new German bombs that'd split into lots of smaller bombs and flatten a whole row of houses one at a time, sometimes one of them wouldn't go off but might go off later, that was terrible, nothing was safe, parachute mines, they blew up before they reached the ground, people called them Land Mines, the blast did all the damage, "it was one of them flattened a whole row of houses in our Elsie's street, she was in the shelter with us so she's alright." Mum had sent you out with the rationbooks, "Don't forget to ask the butcher if he's got any lamb, tell him it's for Mrs Quartermain and don't let him take too many points or charge you too much. If he hasn't got lamb try and get a bit of brisket," or "Make sure you speak to Mr Harding when you get the potatoes, he knows who we are and he's got a new girl who doesn't, you don't want to get potatoes with wireworm or with a lot of mud on them. I don't want to pay for three pounds of dirt," not that I'd dare say anything if there was, you just had to take what he gave you. Fish wasn't rationed, but if you wanted some you had to get there very early, people would start queueing up a couple of hours before the shop opened, because there wouldn't be much in the shop, some days there wasn't any. The fishmonger would only sell you a bit *Make sure there's some for other people*, and sometimes he'd run out of fish before you got any and you'd been waiting for ages, a chalk sign "No fish today" on a sandwich board propped open on the pavement. It was sometimes like that with bread, and if you left your shopping till the end of the day you likely wouldn't be able to get anything.

Shopkeepers, especially butchers, had enormous power, you had to keep on the right side of them, everybody wanted a roast for Sunday, you'd eat it cold on Monday which was washing day, Shepherd's Pie on Tuesday, leftovers on Wednesday, spin the food out make it last, rissoles perhaps sausages if there were any for Thursday, fish on Friday, whatever you could scrape together on Saturday, and then on Sunday you'd start again. So you didn't want the butcher to give you a bit of tough old mutton full of fat and gristle that you couldn't eat, and you had to make friends with the butcher and the grocer you couldn't shop anywhere else, that's who you'd registered your rationbook with and you couldn't shop anywhere else for a lot of stuff like meat and what Mum called staples, but some things, like tinned fruit, used up points in your rationbook, you could get that sort of stuff anywhere so long as they had some and you'd got the points. But you had to be careful. You didn't dare offend the butcher or the grocer. You might be standing in line at Jones's and someone in the queue would say "Didn't I see you in Smith's yesterday when I walked by?" they'd likely been in there themselves for that matter, but they'd got their oar in first and you had to ingratiate yourself with the shopkeeper all over again and even, if you had been in Smith's, lie about it. But you'd better not get caught lying was a tricky business, because if one person in the queue had seen you there you could bet so had somebody else, denial was no good so you acquired a repertoire of strategies, "I went to ask about young Millie's mother, I heard she'd been poorly" or "I heard he'd got some Kolynos toothpaste, *you* don't have any do you Mr Jones?" knowing full well nobody had seen any of that stuff for months and it tasted horrid anyway. Everybody knew what was going on but your status with the shop would be safe and your dignity more or less intact. Tobacconists had the same sort of power, *and* their favourite customers, but they weren't so possessive, cigarettes weren't rationed just endlessly in short supply, and sometimes you'd see people going from shop to shop looking more and more despondent as they tried to get hold of a packet of ten or even a packet of five, they'd take *any* brand, it didn't matter, you learned not to be fussy. You learned quickly, too, not to be la-di-dah about anything, but to chat with other people in the queue about where you'd found things, or who hadn't got any what and how much you missed it. If a posh person came in, excessive politeness lording it over everybody *Aym not at all suah you will hev what aym lookin for, would you be so kaind as to see?*, there'd be a lot of loud remarks as soon as they left about how they'd been seen popping in and out of shops all over the place all over looking for stuff like anchovies or "Gentleman's Relish" whatever *that* might be, "You can't expect those sort of people to pay attention to the likes of us and Mr Jones, that you can't, can you?" and heads would nod and wag under the bandannas. It wasn't just buildings that the War levelled.

That process went on at Brewood too, we'd picked up a bit of Staffordshire there, and it was all very well the Masters at School saying "Speak properly, boy. B*ah*th, not b*a*th, and don't drop your aitches" but if you were talking to your mates or to someone in the village, some big tough from the Nash, you didn't want to come over all hoity-toity with a BBC voice, so at something like *Eh our Ma did y' 'ear what Mr 'Arris's did? It didn arf make me laff?* Mum and Dad would get cross even if you were just larking about, "Where did you learn to speak like *that*? Pronounce it properly, you're not a labourer's child!" How you spoke *mattered*. Mum and Dad both insisted, Dad in particular, that we not call Birmingham "Brummagem" *We don't talk like that*. "Brummagem ware" was tasteless showy rubbish, nobody with any sense liked that vulgar worthless stuff and calling it Brummagem seriously betrayed your origins. What a revelation, then, to find the name "Bromwicham" when I was looking for Birmingham on a seventeenth-century map in the library, *Oh! That's why it's called West Bromwich!* I don't think any of our Teachers, not even Henry Houston, knew that. At the start of one Term in the middle of the War Miss Merrit went through the usual ritual of "Where do you live? What's your father's name? What does he do?" and as usual none of us had the slightest idea what she wanted to know for, filling in a great big form, some kids actually didn't know what their fathers did, "'E works in Wolver'ampton Miss." When she got to Jeff Hayward he said in really broad Staffordshire "'e's a Wairta Squairta in Wairsle Wairta Wairks, Miss," she didn't understand a word he'd said he said it three times and she still didn't get it and we all sniggered away at both her discomfort and Jeff's ingenuity in inventing a job description, whatever his dad did he didn't work in Walsall, that was miles away from where he lived in Codsall, and he didn't work at any waterworks. She was at a complete loss, kids have long memories and *Cheslyn A* had told us where *she* came from and what *she* didn't know, and after about five minutes tormenting her somebody translated for her, Jeff putting more and more of a nasal whine in his voice and getting more and more incomprehensible each time he opened his mouth. So gossiping in the queues in Moseley with the women I'd drop into a Brummagem accent, I didn't want them sneering at *me* once I'd left the shop, as it was, my School blazer if I was wearing it was a dead giveaway that I didn't really belong. We all had at least two languages or more, the speech you used talking to Vicars, Schoolmasters, Policemen and the like, when you were on your best behaviour, and the speech you used elsewhere, yet we despised and laughed to scorn the Yanks, they simply didn't know the language at all, in their abysmal illiteracy calling the flicks *movies* and trams *streetcars*, not knowing what *petrol* is, and forever boasting about the size of things.

Grandfather and Grandmother in particular were very severe on the way we talked, they were deeply shocked by people like Wilfred Pickles reading the BBC News in his pronounced Lancashire accent, it was a sign he was uneducated, probably a red-eyed scavenger. After I'd been teaching in Vancouver for a few years we got a new Assistant Professor, his Lancashire accent broad enough to boil tripe, and it took me a couple of years or even more to pay him any real attention even though we talked together a lot, he was friendly and garrulous and what a shock it was to discover that he was a lot brighter and better educated than me. For years and years after I started working for a living if I got nervous or felt shy especially if I felt threatened or challenged I'd fall into a terrible snobby voice, a pebble in my mouth, swallowing half my speech, hoity-toity strained aristocracy. I couldn't help it, but whatever strangled voice it was it wasn't my own, a pompous Delphic screen reverting to a class I'd never had but'd probably learned from the wireless and films as well as social superiors, all condescension, not at all the voice I'd adopt in the street or down the pub or with my pals, involuntary caricature. I think we all developed great ears for mimicry, mine was largely unconscious, and it's still true that when I'm talking to a friend like Danielle with her definite French accent, within three sentences I've got one too *I speak to Danielle like zis*, and then we both parody it, *she speaks to me like zis too*, both of us enjoying our comedic conversation. When I was a student I prided myself I could go into a pub and talk to anybody, "make them feel at home," I said to myself, "being matey," but I also knew that I was snottily hiding my origins the way I did in the queue at the butcher's, condescending, and looking down my nose at them *What's the matter?* Colin Simms once asked me, *Your vowels are all over the place!* But I didn't know how else to behave. No wonder it took me a long time to take poets like Paul Laurence Dunbar or Joseph Skipsey at all seriously. Or even Robert Burns.

Early one afternoon in Moseley we'd just had dinner and Dad had gone back to work, a nice warm day, Phil was staying on the farm at Alcester, it was just me and Mum at home, and I went out to get something for her, a loaf of bread or something like that we'd just run short of, the shop wasn't all that far away but I often used to take my time, mooch about a bit looking in shop windows, a couple of pennies burning a hole in my pocket but unable to decide what to get, if I'd got as much as thruppence I might buy a stamp magazine if there was a new one at the stationer's, I was crazy about stamp collecting by then, and as I was walking up the slope back home I saw the old lady who lived two or three doors down past our house struggling along with a string shopping bag full of groceries so I speeded up a bit and said "Hullo, Mrs Stewart, can I carry your bags for you?" all I'd brought back from the shops was a small paper bag, and she said "You're a nice little boy, are you one of the children at number nine? What's your name?" and I told her Peter and she said "My aren't you big for your age" and we walked up the road a bit faster now that she didn't have anything to carry and she invited me into her house, there was a big bowl of fruit on a shiny polished dining table, winter apples mainly, of course, a bit wrinkly and soft but perfectly good eating, and there were some lovely big red ones as well and my eyes went wide and she said they'd come from Canada she'd bought them in Harding's yesterday she'd been lucky to get them "but now I've got too many, I can't eat all that fruit, would you like one?" and as she picked up a red apple to put in my hands the Air Raid siren went off and she said "You'd better stay here, you can't go out during an Air Raid, why don't you eat your apple?" She took me to the corner where she always went during raids and we sat there and we sat there and we sat there, we couldn't hear much, there was a plane buzzing somewhere, and then we could hear quite a few planes in the distance, they were German planes, Heinkels probably, you could tell by the engine sound, German planes had counter-rotating propellers, and I finished my apple and she had a cup of tea and then quite a bit later on the All Clear went off and she said "You'd better get home, while you can. Run along now," so I said thankyou for the apple and ran the three or four houses home to find Mum half out of her mind *"What happened to you?* Where've you been? Didn't you know there was an Air Raid? Did you get into a shelter? I know you were too far from one!" and I smiled up at her and said "Mum, I was alright I was with Mrs Stewart in her house, she gave me an apple and we sat and talked" and Mum wanted to know why I hadn't run home and I told her it was perfectly alright I was safe I'd sat with Mrs Stewart in the safe corner of the house "Where she always sits during an Air Raid." Mum had tears in her eyes and she made me promise "Never do that again! You *must* get to a shelter or come home! Run and be safe," she said, "we've got the shelter in the garden. I was in the shelter and I kept going out to look for you. I was so *worried*, Peter, what if you'd never got home?" she'd been peeling potatoes in the shelter doorway a bowl on her knee "I kept looking out for you" but I didn't know what to say except "Mum, I'm alright." I don't think it occurred to me even then that I was in any real danger and I didn't quite understand her anguished mix of relief and anger, fear and urgent need, desperation and release all at once. There was a big Air Raid a couple of nights after and a couple of bombs fell in our street one of them on Mrs Stewart's house and even then, her house gone, it didn't sink in.

22
Air Raid Shelter

In the mist of these wartime realities, we had the usual childhood ailments, like chickenpox. Our Kid had that a lot worse than me, but we were both pretty sick, itching like mad, we had high temperatures and were stuck in bed all day feeling really ill, on mattresses crammed up next to each other on the dining room floor, Phil in his blue-striped flannel pyjamas and me in my red-striped ones, the flannel all pilled up from being washed so often but still pretty thick and heavy, they were too warm and we were too hot, the air didn't circulate much in that corner of the dining room, the first week was horrible I kept getting new spots and they'd itch and I'd scratch and Mum or Dad would say you mustn't scratch, you must leave the ones on your face alone, they'll leave a scar, and they'd reach for the calamine lotion and put a drop on the worst bit. Calamine lotion was scarce *There'll be no more once it runs out* and instead of cotton wool we dabbed it on with a bit of rag that could be washed later. After the first week I didn't get any new spots and my temperature was going down, Phil was still covered with them and had a terrific fever, the doctor prescribed aspirin for him, and he simply felt ill all the time, didn't want to eat, just wanted to sleep, he couldn't even read a comic like *The Rover*, the doctor said we had to stay in bed until we were completely better, no fever, no new spots. But I was beginning to feel better, beginning to be a bit chirpy.

Mum brought me some stories and comics to read but I wanted to do a jigsaw puzzle. "Don't be daft," Mum said, "You can't do that in bed, you've got to be quiet, Philip is still very sick." But I wanted to play, I wanted to talk, I wanted to be up and about and I'd prod him and poke at him and tickle him and he'd retreat away from my mattress across his and try to sleep and Mum would come in and she'd tell me to leave him alone but I was restless and bored what was there to do why can't we play I Spy or make shadows with our fingers or play *Snap!* and Mum came in more than twice and said "I'm going to talk to your Father when he comes home, now STOP IT" but after five minutes lying down trying to be quiet my seven- or eight-year-old body stirred about yet again I clambered round my half of the bed *Where's my dinky toy?* I stood up and flopped down, bounced on the mattress, kneeled on all fours, tried to stand on my head, and Mum yet again came in she was really angry "You'll get a spanking if you don't stop this this minute!" and I'd stop and then I'd plump up my pillow and sit up and lie down on my back and twirl my pyjama-trousers cord about "wheeeee!" and then I'd flump down again half under the covers laughing and singing and asking Our Kid questions and riddles, "Hey! Our Kid! How do you make a Maltese Cross?" and give him a poke in the ribs I felt just wonderful "Light a match and stick it up his jumper!" and I'd laugh out loud and bounce up and down and give him another poke in the ribs, "Get it? See? Isn't that funny?" chortling my torturer's childish guffaw into his ear, poking my way into trouble. Dad came home from work and put his Home Guard uniform on and before going on duty he came into the room, I'd heard him talking to Mum and Mum talking to him, he looked very stern and serious as he leaned his rifle against the wall and he said "Peter. Come here" and I said "No, Daddy" and he said "Come Here" and I shrank away but crawled in spite of myself out of bed towards my Father's beckoning hand, "No, Daddy!" and he hoicked me up with his left hand and bent me over his knee and gave me a thorough walloping, four of them, hard, really hard, the severity of his disapproval a profound shock, I think his hand hurt as much as my bottom, but I flinched anyway and he didn't and on the third blow I let out a cry, desolate, isolated and completely sorry for myself, and when he stopped he said in a low voice, "There! Get back into bed and leave your brother alone" and I snivelled my way back to my half of the bed and Dad said, "Goodnight, Philip" and Our Kid smiled, a quiet weak smile, the first time that day.

It was the only time Dad ever hit me, and I hurt a terrific lot more than when I was formally caned at Brewood by Pussy Bailey my very first Term. Four of the best across my pyjama-clad bottom with a cane hurt a lot more than anything Dad's hand could do, of course, but this was serious stuff. "You had to be taught a lesson" Mum said the next day when I was allowed up for a couple of hours while Our Kid began to recover, and Dad asked me when he came home for dinner if my bottom was sore and I said, "Not *very* much." I looked down at my plate. "And I'm sorry for what I did."

But the real trouble was of course the War and its anguish, how could the children be safe? I think that crowding us together in the dining room, hardly a refuge for any of us in an Air Raid, was bad enough; the chicken-pox was the last straw, and I'm sure that was why Dad soon after that got the Anderson shelter installed, covered with about six inches of dirt and sod, he rigged up an electric cable from the house to the shelter so he could plug in a space heater, an electric one, a brown metal tube which stood on end and worked by convection, if you left it on for very long the top would get too hot to touch but it wouldn't set anything on fire, it was perfectly safe so long as you didn't put a book or clothes or anything on top of it. He and Mum had a wide double bunk about six inches above the floor, a wooden duckboard alongside, Dad on the outside with the heater right next to his head, he'd turn it off before he went to sleep, and Phil and I shared a three-quarter bunk which jutted out like a shelf about three feet above theirs, Dad couldn't quite sit up in their bunk, there was no electricity in the shelter except for the heater hooked up to a flex from the house, we went to bed with a dim electric torch, there was some sort of ventilation system I don't know what it was but we all slept there with the door closed, Dad lying on his back snoring away, he had a really loud snore, Phil up top against the wall which curved over to make the ceiling and then came down to make the wall on the other side, it was corrugated metal of some sort, and me on the outside, neither of us could sit up up there and it must have been terribly hard for Mum to make the beds every day and keep it clean. When I asked, Dad said we wouldn't be safe from a direct hit, but then neither would the big shelters in the street, it'd be alright with all that dirt on the roof if the house went, and it was shrapnel-proof. As a rule Our Kid and me would both go to bed at the same time, we might wake up sleepily when Mum and Dad came to bed, it was a tiny place, if we didn't have the heater on before they came to bed in the winter condensation'd make it a bit damp, and if we did it got really hot and stuffy.

One night I turned over sleepily moving away a bit from Our Kid's warm body I had my leg hanging over the edge of the bunk I'd thrown the covers back I was turning from my right to my left I was all woozy with sleep I just reached out with my left hand to heave myself up to turn over again it was suddenly cool and I'd hardly realised I was in the middle of the air I'd just begun to stick my hand out when I landed with a great soft shocking *thump!* almost on my back on top of Dad he was snoring he was lying on his back the way he always did and *Whoof!* I think the top of my head hit the edge of his chin it was a bit sore the next morning, he thought the roof had fallen in a bomb had hit the house a great clatter as he sat up in a tangle of arms and legs him and me straight out of a deep sleep him and Mum woozily groping to find the torch somewhere near a pillow I tried to sit up stuck my elbow in his ribs didn't really know what had happened at all what was going on Mum cried "Leo! Are you alright? what happened?" and I was all stunned and surprised still not fully awake and didn't weigh very much thank goodness but Dad was really shaken up shocked and spluttery and out of breath he shook himself a bit it took him a while and he said "I never thought that would happen, I didn't dream of it, you've never fallen out of bed in your life that I remember" and Mum said "Not since you were about three" and Our Kid woke up and said "What's going on? Is it an Air Raid?" We were all in the dark, it was the middle of the night, Dad was all winded he groped for a torch and turned it on I'd landed smack in the middle of his belly and he said "You're not going to do that again, we can't have that" Mum said to me "Are you alright?" and Dad gasped "I think I am, but he stuck his elbow in my stomach" and he rubbed himself as he struggled for a good breath, "Thank goodness you didn't hit your head on the stove, it could have killed you!" I didn't really believe that but I knew it would've hurt terribly, "You're lucky you landed on your father." Dad grunted it was a good job he was soft and climbed up into the top bunk, it was a bit of a struggle for him to get there the space was so narrow and he was so sore, and I spent the rest of the night next to Mum in Dad's place, Dad snoring right into Phil's ear.

Next day when he got home from work Dad stretched a long elastic band he'd got from the stockroom at Woolworth's along my side of the bunk from one end to the other, and I said "Dad, I'll fall right through that. It won't stop me falling out of bed, what are we going to do?" and he laughed and said, "It'll tell you you're too close to the edge and wake you up," but I didn't think it would. And then he said "It had better! I couldn't stand you falling on me again, I still hurt." I didn't think it would work at all but it did, I can still feel the reassurance of that bit of rubber band, tied at each end to the chains that held the bunk up, I'd cautiously nuzzle up to it staying under the covers to keep warm so I'd know where the edge of the bunk was before I dropped off to sleep, I could smell it as well as feel it, a bit rubbery and slightly sticky-feeling, it became a comfort it helped me drop off to sleep. But I don't think any of us was ever what you'd call comfortable in the shelter, some nights if there was an Air Raid Mum and Dad would stand in the door listening and watching, so long as the planes weren't directly overhead or really near, watching for incendiary bombs as much as for anything, worried, but also caught up in the sheer peril and anxiety of it all.

We got caught up too, of course, and not just with falling out of bed. Some mornings if there'd been an Air Raid we'd go out hunting for bits of shrapnel, twisted lumps of blown-up and burnt metal, sometimes it was all honeycombed like that chocolate we got on the barge ride, and even if it was as big as your fist it was quite light, all hollow inside. If you saw one you had to scramble for it because some other kid had seen it too *finder's keepers!* but you quickly learned not to get into a fierce argument about who saw it first or whose it was, while you were arguing other kids would come along and find a lot of other bits, possession was possession, and we scoured the streets for stuff, some kids even climbed up into the teetery shells of bombed out houses but that was dangerous, testing a flight of wooden stairs going halfway up a wall, scraps of carpet flapping, any grown-up would stop you so would some of the bigger kids, and if the police saw you you'd be in real trouble because that was still private property and you could be accused of looting. But we were all of us dab hands at clambering over the piles of rubble where a house had once been, bricks shifting under foot, sometimes you'd catch a glimpse down into the cellar's dark black part-filled with rubble, faint sounds, perhaps a slow drip of water. I'd look away scamper clear as fast as I could my heart pounding my breath all short *What if there was a dead body down there*? but not wanting to miss a piece of shrapnel, all those cats prowling around coming out of unsuspected holes in the heaps of rubbish, sometimes great timbers sticking out over your head, splintered doors lying on piles of bricks or half-buried, someone on the street would give a shout and the kids on the bombsite would just vanish, every which way in a blink. We all had collections of stuff, metal army badges, bits of bomb casings but sometimes you couldn't tell them from shrapnel, cartridge cases mostly from rifles more rarely from Bofors ack-ack guns, some kids had got the vanes off an incendiary bomb all twisted and black with soot but I never managed to find one I could keep, other kids always got there first or Dad took them away, we were supposed to hand in the solid brass cartridge cases, scrap metal to be melted down and used again; some kids liked to polish them up to a real shine, some of their dads did too, but I liked mine to look mucky and used. "Been through the wars, that 'as," I'd say proudly to what pals came to see what I'd got, we all guarded our collections jealously, called them our museums. Some kids tried to swop things but I was too ungenerous and only wanted things I'd found myself, that really made them mine. Knowing that someone else had been the one who found it in the first place, even if he was a pal, took the edge off the pleasure of ownership, not that that stopped me wanting more and coveting theirs.

It must have been about that time, I think we still lived at Moseley but it might've been Rugby, that people began talking about kids being blown up by things they'd found lying in the streets and on the grass in the parks, bright and shiny things that looked like toys, dropped by the Germans in the middle of the night said some, planted there by German spies and fifth columnists said others, a three-year-old had been killed in Wales was what I heard, and Mum and Dad got more insistent than ever that we not collect things we found in the street, especially if they looked like a toy or like sweets, "never play with *any*thing you see lying in the street," they said, I remember Mum being very particular about what we might pick up in the park "Don't even pick it up! You leave everything alone!" and other kids' parents told them the same thing, so our collections began to tail off a bit. But we had to be told, later on, when the fields and woods and lanes began to be speckled with strips of silver paper a bit shorter than a wooden ruler, shiny one side and all tissue on the other, that we mustn't pick them up, they'd been dropped from planes by our side, we didn't know what they were for and nobody would tell us it was all a secret but they were part of the War Effort. We came back from our Sunday Walks anyway with damp bedraggled strips that were losing their shine, we put them in our lockers or our desks, but who'd want to come over and look at your collection of one-sided-silver paper scraps, everybody had one, they were everywhere and they were all the same, and it wasn't long before you'd see little bunches of kids, bulging pockets in their shorts, furtively trailing down to the bike sheds to dump their silver paper in the school dustbins. But there was always a new edge of excitement when you walked down the road, you had to be extra alert in case something happened.

We all collected souvenirs and stamps and old cigarette cards and foreign coins. We collected everything. Bommy Rogers had a huge collection of football pictures he cut out from the *Express and Star*, he glued them in a scrapbook, and Our Kid collected pictures of ships and naval battles he glued in an old telephone book, goodness knows where he got that from. After the War long after I'd lost all the bits of shrapnel and shell-casings and what all else, I discovered that some people collected leaflets dropped by the Air Force over Europe during the War, there was a stamp shop that specialised in Air Post, Francis J. Field in Sutton Coldfield, and issued a catalogue listing some, I couldn't afford to buy any, they were much too expensive, so

I wrote to the Foreign Office in London, how I knew to write to *them* I can't imagine, asking if there were any left over from the War, this was in 1950 and I was still crazy about stamps, and they sent a fat envelope, three dozen propaganda leaflets, all in French but for three in German, a dozen of them with "North Africa" written at the top in light pencil, along with a typed letter,

    FOREIGN OFFICE
    S. W. 1.
    27th October, 1950
    Sir,
        In reply to your letter of 24th September regarding leaflets dropped by the Allied Air Forces during the war I am directed by Mr Secretary Bevin to enclose, herewith, spare copies of such leaflets as are available in this Department.
    I am,
    Sir,
    Your obedient Servant,

and a carefully legible signature in washable blue ink, "E.J. Passant," it looks as though it's been copied out, not like a real signature at all.

    Bits of speeches by Allied and Axis leaders; reprints of stories from *The Times*; leaflets aimed at Belgium carrying the same before-and-after pictures of a bombed-out factory in Cologne and of a flattened street in Lübeck in leaflets aimed at France and Africa; photographs of de Gaulle in the back of an open car in Beirut; crude cartoons printed on pink newsprint of Mussolini stabbing *La France* in the back on *Le 10 Juin 1940* and of *Le Touriste*, a caricature Nazi in civilian garb smirking and spying his sinister way through a North African town. Quite a few of the North African ones exhort the civilian population to *Defendez L'Empire – Chassez Les!*, with labourers, commercial travellers, and tourists as the explicit target, but there's also a safe-conduct from 1943 for German troops in Tunisia, it's printed in German, EINGEKESSELT it says in large type, and in a ruled box it says in English, "To British and American Outposts: Any German soldier presenting this safe-conduct is to be disarmed and made prisoner," the same message in French. I'm sorting through all these as I write, there's an exquisitely printed India-paper pamphlet just over an inch square to hide in the palm of your hand, *Si on l'avait écouté*, General-then-Colonel de Gaulle's speech of 26 January 1940, five months before the French set up the Vichy Government through the armistice of 22 June, thirty-two minuscule pages people could be shot for hanging on to or even picking up at all, like the first issue of *La France Libre*, November 1941, with a London speech by Jacques Maritain and an essay by Charles Morgan, "*distribué par la R.A.F.*" And there's a wonderful bit of newsprint, *Un pilote de chasse de la R.A.F. a pris ces photos*, "Flight-Lieutenant Gatward" and his machine-gunner "Flight-Sergeant Fern" some time in 1942 flying their Beaufighter the length of the *Champs Elysées* at third-floor level and shooting-up the GHQ of the German Occupying Army in the *Place de la Concorde*, a snapshot of the Eiffel Tower seen over the wing of the plane, another of a domed building taken from about thirty feet away, a poster stuck outside the front door proclaiming *La Vie Nouvelle* in block letters, photos taken before they hedge-hopped back to England, picking up a hapless crow in their engine on the way. I'm amazed that I didn't look very much at these extraordinary scraps of paper when I got them, just glanced through them and shoved them in a box with the rest of my stamp collection. I actually forgot all about them until much later, when I bought a 1946-1947 run of *Alphabet and Image* sometime in the nineties, a graphic-design and typography magazine. In the fourth issue an article by Harold Keeble, he'd been involved in their production all through the War, told me a lot about how propaganda leaflets were produced and distributed, sometimes millions of copies at a time dropped over Europe, at first simply bundles held together by rubber bands and shoved out of the plane and breaking up in the slipstream as they fell, later with sophisticated leaflet-bombs designed to target really small areas, such as "those 800 men in that wood" as he puts it.

That article was a bit of an eye-opener. I'd never thought about those leaflets at all or how they'd been used, they were simply something to *have*, the way we set up small museums on a shelf in the bedroom, the kind of thing Marlow Grandfather encouraged us to have, or collected birds' eggs and stamps. I was secretary of the School stamp club, what the school magazine when it came out again after the War would posh up a bit, calling it The Philatelic Society. I don't see that I learned anything at all from those leaflets, I'm not sure that I even showed them to anybody else, and it took me a long time to develop a sense of public life which let me notice, as I explored them forty-five or fifty years later, the ironic parallels between the occupying German army's slogan touting *La Vie Nouvelle* in Paris and George H. W. Bush proclaiming a *New World Order* on 11 September 1990 – that was in the run-up to the first Gulf War, in a speech to a joint session of Congress. Back in 1950, five years after the War was over, I still hadn't the faintest glimmerings about the political necessity for propaganda and its nature. Yet there's a leaflet dropped over Northern France urgently explaining with accompanying news photos that the disastrous commando raid on Dieppe in August 1942 "was a surprise attack and not an invasion," a piece of spin-doctoring that passed right over my head. And there's a remarkable little newsprint pamphlet celebrating the arrival of the great relief convoy lifting the siege of Malta in August 1942 *At the very moment our ships entered the Valletta roads, German radio proclaimed that "The Maltese convoy is no more."* And I remember reading that, my amusement at Axis mendacity, but how come it never occurred to me that the Allies might equally be guilty of telling lies in those fragile and once dangerous bits of paper. They were a bit like all those soon abandoned bits of Air Raid rubbish, slightly sinister and extremely evocative, they were another kind of stuff of war to hang on to for no reason I can fathom except that I had something the others didn't, they stirred my curiosity not one whit when I got hold of them, and I *never* talked about them.

About the middle of the War an Army sergeant came and gave a lecture to the whole School about booby traps and different kinds of bombs and what they did and how they worked and what they looked like and what to do if we found any. He showed them to us, hand grenades and sticky bombs that exploded "along the line of greatest resistance" he asked us if we knew what it meant and I was sure I did I'd read it before somewhere, I racked my brains and thought of "least resistance" I couldn't explain it to myself but I still knew that really I knew, and then he explained *Oh yes of course!* I wasn't half glad I hadn't risked it, hadn't put my hand up in front of the whole school to show how clever I was, I'd never've lived it down getting wrong what most of the kids would've known anyway, and he showed us shells and bullets and all sorts of stuff, we were all fascinated and excited. One weekend a bit later the Brewood Home Guard and the Territorial Army had a mock war down at the Show Grounds, with smoke bombs and tommy guns loaded with blanks and Armoured Personnel Carriers, motorbikes and what we'd later call jeeps, field radios and despatch riders, lots of smoke and noise, false explosions throwing sandbags up in the air over on the other side of the field. There'd been a story about despatch riders in the *Rover*, heroically scrambling their bikes through enemy lines to get their message through, lying flat on their bikes and ducking under wires stretched between the trees, for a while we all wanted to be one. The whole village turned up as well as all of us from School, quite a crowd, we made a day of it, people brought sandwiches and fruit, had a picnic, "just like a fireworks display before the War," I heard somebody say and somebody else said it'd be nice when we had Brewood Show again the War'd be over, but it was fun, we knew it mattered, bikes and jeeps and lorries churning the grass into muddy ruts, soldiers in uniform handing messages over to Officers in peaked caps, men running across the field in a crouch behind fake hedges and fences, intervals of quiet and spurts of noise and bustle as men boiled out of personnel carriers to run across to attack a place across the field, people emerging from smoke with their hands up above their heads.

Though we weren't allowed to, I loved watching the searchlights at night in Birmingham when there was an Air Raid on, the air heavy and oppressive with the sound of dozens or even hundreds of German bombers droning overhead on their way to some target, Liverpool perhaps, or Cardiff, we didn't really have any idea where if it wasn't us getting bombed, but if we weren't already there Mum and Dad always chased us into the shelter as soon as it started, there'd be shrapnel pattering down from the ack-ack if the raid was close, you'd hear it all round, and Dad was the only one of us who had a tin hat so we had to stay under cover or we'd get hit. It wasn't till we moved a good safe distance away from the raids that we could stay out and watch without danger, the lights tracking back and forth across the sky. Sometimes you'd catch a quick glimpse of blurry planes as they flashed through the beam of the light, you'd wonder if you'd really seen them. Sometimes it'd be our own aircraft we'd hear and see darkening the sky and you'd still shiver a little as you first heard and saw them. One of those propaganda leaflets I collected eight years later says that on Monday the 1st of June 1942 one thousand-and-thirty-six bombers raided Cologne, the sky must have been heavy with planes, bombers and their fighter support, I remember the sky at Rugby some nights black with planes, Wellingtons and Lancasters, and later on American Flying Fortresses, on their way to Europe to bomb the Nazis in France or in Belgium or in Germany, perhaps it was the raids on Berlin, a loud insistent droning roar as wave after wave of planes flew overhead, for as much as forty minutes it must have been, the sheer weight of endless growling roar hanging high up, people'd go out and look, there were too many to count, insistent battering of noise right across the sky in all directions it seemed like, a persistent assault on our ears making any sort of talk almost impossible, planes so thick you'd think they shut out the stars, there was nothing to point at, just the dark outlines of plane after plane, squadron over squadron, a solid mass of unbroken sound rippling in waves, into the bones, and your heart would lurch a little as you lifted your face, stupefied with a kind of awe uneasily proud to see us Fighting Back, but frightened too, the worry of all those planes, Our Bombs going to drop out of the sky, tanks and guns, lorries and Nazis, factories and dockyards going to be blown up and burned, and just like us, gardens and houses, front steps and door-knockers, mums and their kids, streets filled with rubble, give them a dose of their own medicine, and a couple of weeks later you'd go to the pictures and see *Gaumont British News* or

Pathé Pictorial with photographs taken from one of the planes of a big raid on the docks at Rotterdam or Hamburg, the pilot's head and shoulders filling half the screen, bombs dropping out of the plane in front or alongside, or the camera pointing out of the bomb-bay as the bombs fell away, puffs of smoke on the ground where the bombs fell, tracer bullets and searchlights patterning the air, searching for British and American planes, sometimes you'd see a plane falling out of the sky, or you'd watch a German fighter zoom over the camera held in the pilot's cockpit, a fast dark blur spitting white lines of tracer, or a picture of a Wellington or a Lancaster alongside the camera, its engine on fire, and the news announcer saying the plane got home alright, stirring military music hovering in the background waiting to surge out as the bombers got met by Hurricanes and Defiants sent out to provide fighter cover on the way home and waggling their wings in salute. Our minds were filled with pictures of men in helmets and sheepskin coats huddled over bombsights on a windowed fuselage floor at the front of the plane, or hunched with pens and pencils and rulers over the navigator's table or crouched over a tailgun watching for the enemy, everything in dark black-and-white, sharp contrasts, gloomy and cramped, heroic and horrible.

In those black-and-white films grotesque and frantic figures silently ran for planes or fell out of the sky, or attempted impossible tasks in desperate urgencies, always someone in the air or on the ground getting killed. A reassuring world, but nevertheless filled with menace. We'd see one of the Princesses in Land Army uniform ineptly tossing hay, or the Queen, armsful of flowers, clean and fresh and tidy, nodding and smiling, opening a jumble sale or visiting the wounded, some legless man smiling and smoking a cigarette showing how well he could manage his crutches, not much reassurance for Mum and Dad, the dangers too close, too many houses demolished every Air Raid, people they knew and spoke to suddenly gone in eruptions of fire, collapses of bricks. There could be no holiday from this even with the heat of summer nearly here. Before the War we'd gone to Newquay or to Swanage, explored the ruins of Corfe Castle on the hill above the town, pleasure for Dad away from work, time to lie in the sun, eat meals made by somebody else, play with the children, spend all day with Mum, on the beach at Swanage we'd play French Cricket, grown-ups and children laughing and running about together, talk and muck about in the sand with your bucket and spade, paddle, look for shrimp, scratch about in tidal pools or just watch, play with other kids urchins perhaps but how could you know, you'd never seen them before and'd never see them again after the two weeks were over, throw seaweed about and lose your sun hat, toss a rubber ring back and forth like the frisbee that hadn't been invented yet, Mum and Dad in deck-chairs reading, gossiping with the folk in the next beach hut, "Oh, you come from Birmingham do you? we live near Watford," kettle hissing on a primus, "Have you read this book by Ngaio Marsh? Her Inspector Alleyn is ever so good, better than Agatha Christie," cups of tea and biscuits, "Why don't you try a bit of this cake?" wet towels hanging everywhere, "Did you get to see *The Dancing Years* while it was on?" "Ooh, I do like Ivor Novello, yes," sand in everything, a sudden damp chill as you came out of the sun back into the beach hut to get back into your clothes, the wet slats of the duckboard floor cold to the feet and gritty. Goosebumps. Every night when you closed up your beach hut you swept out all the sand, a bit shivery from the sun on the skin all day, you'd walk back to the hotel, salt on your lips and in your hair, full of talk and sand, chatter chatter chatter.

But now? You couldn't go to the seaside if you didn't live there, you wouldn't want to anyway, girders and traps, land-mines and obstacles all over the beach, forts and pillboxes, concrete and barbed wire everywhere, everything closed down, there were even big concrete posts sticking up out of the grass strip on the divided carriageway on the Wolverhampton-Stafford road to stop enemy planes landing there, and one morning in 1941 in the house at Solihull Road and then again at Moseley, Dad was getting the car ready and Mum was packing things in suitcases, Phil and I were sorting out our toys and books and we were off, we never knew how long the journey to the farm would take, it wasn't far, only about twenty-five miles but it might take a couple of hours to get there what with all the traffic and the War. Dad had enough petrol ration to do about one return trip a month, he saved what coupons he could, you couldn't spend them in advance and you couldn't save many up, that'd be hoarding, and he'd say as we turned off the road from Knowle to Hockley Heath "Wouldn't it be good to stop at Henley-in-Arden?" Before the War, on the way to the south coast, we always used to stop there and get ice cream cones at the dairy, triple scoops on triple cones or even foursomes, "the best ice cream in the country," Dad called it, and me and Our Kid would say "Why can't we?" and chorus our "Please?" and then we'd remember, no more ice cream now there's a War on, they don't make it any more, and they haven't made it since, not as good, and so we just drove on through to Alcester, right turn off the Stratford Road, up the long drive, a dogleg round the two-and-a-half acre home field, hollybushes, gates, outbuildings, barnyards to the right, and then Kinwarton Farm house, big, Mum and us two kids there for six or seven weeks, Dad coming down at weekends and spending his two weeks' summer holidays to help bring in the harvest.

I can remember once driving down in the dark, I must have been pretty young and I expect it was before the War because I can remember the headlights of the car stretching ahead of us, you wouldn't've seen that in the War with the headlights painted over or all masked the way they were, they couldn't make a great big cone of light stretching ever so far in front of you, and as we came along between the hedgerows, tall bosky shadows rushing by, I began to glimmer a pattern of small red lamps *Was it a triangle* glowing in the dark, wondering what it was for. *Of course!* "HALT MAJOR ROAD AHEAD" said the sign, and as the front of the car got past it all the little lights switched off. I turned round and looked out of the back window but the back of the sign was just a dark blur against the trees and by the time I turned back we'd gone round the corner onto the main road. Pairs of tiny white lights stretched out in front of the car to mark the middle of the road, they lit up as we got closer and you could see them far ahead if the road dipped down and then up again, when I looked behind us I couldn't see them at all *They've all gone out!* and as I looked in front the lights kept turning on as we came closer, and as I turned round to see if they really did all go out as we got past, there was a car behind us and I couldn't see them even *then*. Mum said "They ought to put cat's eyes on all the roads. Do you know why they don't?" and Dad said "Costs too much I expect, but it's a good idea" they kept on talking quietly together and when after a while we met a car I turned round to look and all the little lights'd turned on as that car came up to them and then turned off again after it went by, magical and enchanting, and I asked "How do they get all those lights to go on?" *Were there little men sitting somewhere turning them off and on as cars went by?* it was like the wireless, I used to clamber up and look in the back to see the orchestra playing but it was just small lights in warm dusty-smelling gloom, a low buzz coming from a lot of wires. It was like holding the *Picture Post* or *Illustrated* up to the side of your face to see inside the picture, I kept on doing that, I might have done it even as late as after the War, trying to see further down the street, it was Mr Attlee going somewhere I think, or getting out of a car, something like that, a street scene at any rate people in macs and trilbies somewhere exotic like New York or Washington *Can you see the Empire State Building from here?* and I cursed myself for being a daft Aputh as I tried to squint round the edge of the photograph I remembered you couldn't do that with pictures, it was just marks on paper it wasn't a window, how disappointed I was, and I didn't dare tell anybody what I'd just been doing wanting the magic, certainly didn't want to get caught doing something so stupid I'd never live it down. Mum told me the cat's eyes weren't lights they were mirrors but I couldn't quite sort that out in my head, *Why don't they break?* and she said "Why don't you have a look at them when we get to the farm? They're set in little rubber bumps that don't break when the car goes over them" Our Kid said "They're square ones, Pete, you've seen them all over the place" and I wondered how I'd see them on the farm, there weren't any there and anyway we'd be too busy. Dad said we could walk down to the Stratford Road and have a look tomorrow if we wanted but of course I'd forgotten all about it by then, the farm was so interesting and different.

23

Wartime Farm

First thing every morning before anybody else was up I'd hear a dull regular *cheunk-bonk cheunk-bonk* like a ticking clock but not quite as fast, the first time I went to the farm it must have been late in the autumn I wondered what it was and Uncle Tom said "Why don't you get up and see?" and everybody grinned and nobody said anything, and ever so early one morning all the curtains still closed, I went down all sleepy-eyed in my pyjamas and dressing gown and slippers the light so dim I could hardly see, the noise was coming up the cellar stairs, at the bottom the glow of an oil lamp and the noise much louder as I stood in the doorway but just as regular, and I went carefully down holding my hand along the white-washed wall and there was Uncle Tom standing next to a black-iron pipe running through the floor to disappear through the ceiling, moving a wooden handle back and forth left to right, right to left, *ktch-lunk ktch-lank, ktch-lunk ktch-lank* his right arm steadily moving back and forth, "Want to try it?" he asked *ktch-lunk ktch-lank* and I said "what are you doing?" and he said "Pumping water. There's a well under your feet, and there's a tank at the top of the house. Want to try it?" and I put both hands on the wooden handle and pushed, I could hardly move it, "The water's got to go a long way," he said, "all the way up to the attic, it's a deep well, been there a long time" and he chuckled, "it'll be a year or two before you can do it, and it takes half-an-hour to fill the tank." He told me he had to be careful not to let the tank overflow *I did that once, you can see the stain on the ceiling in one of the apple rooms*, that'd be up on the third floor. A couple of years later I tried it again, Tom watching, and I didn't even last five minutes, my arms got so tired.

There was always work to do, we all had chores, and the second wartime summer, after breakfast on the first morning, Uncle

Tom said "Peter, I've got a nice job for you, you can feed the chickens," and he gave me a zinc bucket half-full of corn. I knew what to do, I'd done it the last time I'd been here, and really enjoyed it. You went out the back door and opened the gate into the back barnyard, past the pig mash cooking up in the shed next the pigsty, all the potato peelings and kitchen scraps cooking up with a mess of feed in a great big pot like the wash-copper in the scullery at Wheaton Aston only bigger, a small fire underneath, if I did a good job feeding the chickens then I'd have time to stand on my upended bucket and give the pig-swill a stir with the wooden paddle sticking out of the top. The swill smelled like nothing else in the world, a mix of garden and kitchen peelings, haunting and delicious, compost mingled up with all the dust of a granary, I loved the smell of the granary and years later in Lichfield walking to town I'd linger by the corn merchant's and simply sniff at it it was such a warm and comfortable smell better than a bakery any day, the smell of seeds and hay and all the different kinds of corn like barley and wheat and oats, fields and harvest and cattle feed, livestock, horses and cattle, but underneath that blend of garden vegetables and grain the swill had a sharp almost vinegary sourish edge, just a hint, the whole thing just filled you up, not just your nose but your mouth and your lips, it was in your clothes and your hair and even your skin, almost my favourite of all my favourite smells, and along with all that the scent and heft of the corn in the bucket, hard and golden, shifting and adjusting as I carried it, little cascades patterning corn over corn, slight swirls of corn rubbing against itself like the wind in the fields just before harvest and with a faintly tinny sound along the galvanised wall of the bucket. Last year's corn, smelling like this year's summer.

    Before I reached the gate I'd set the pail down and dive my hand into it, run grain through my fingers, take out a fistful and let it trickle back a hissing pitter-patter, light dust rising, and as I opened the gate I'd take out a fistful and scatter it broadcast ahead of me with a sweep of my hand across and away to keep the chickens back from the gate the way Aunt Dot had taught me the last time I was here, a lovely golden curve in the air as the grain scattered and then bounced on the ground, the hold of the grain and its smoothness rustling over my hands and between my fingers, a little sharp rattle as some of it fell against the side of the bucket, the softer patter as grains fell on the mass of grain underneath, and the colours, it wasn't just golden brown, but flecked pale and dark bits, shifting as individual grains moved, bits of dust, a touch of white where a new plant would sprout, and cool, always cool on the skin, on a really hot day feel the tiny currents of warm and cool as you gently moved your hand about in it. I'd take the bucket and open the gate, swinging a fistful of corn out before me in an arc, the chickens running towards me, "here chick chick chick c'm up here chick chick chick," be careful to shut the gate so they don't get out, take the hasp and hook it in the eye, turn the wooden catch, and parade around the yard scattering corn broadcast before me, lord of the hens as they all settled here and there to peck away, every one content including me, clucks and occasional flurries among the birds as they scrambled about again, I'd watch to see that every one got a fair share, and march round and round till the bucket was almost empty, my nails scrabbling on the bottom as I tried to get a last handful, I couldn't pick up any more in my hand so I'd stand and fling the last bits in a great wide circle out of the bucket swivelling like mad, the grain rising in a high loop right across the chicken yard.

  The second summer when Tom asked me to feed them I couldn't wait, I cast a handful of grain as I opened the gate, and *blam!* an explosion of great black cockerel flung himself at me, beak thrust out bright red comb puffed up erect wings outspread fierce black eyes starting out from his head *bang! bang! bang!* on the bucket the eyes as I lifted it up in front of my face, *slam!* went the beak so hard I thought it would break, *slam! slam! slam!* and I wanted it to break, this huge fierce bird screaming and charging at me in the air and on the ground I hoisted the bucket and lowered it again the bird everywhere round and round determined to get at me, it was going to get my eyes it lunged up in the air toward me clamouring its screams as it clattered against the pail *slam! bang! slam! bang!* beak and claws after me the gate not shut properly the pail a useless shield, I didn't think to cry out I was here to feed the chickens and I took handful after handful of grain and flung it with all my might at the bird I thought I could hurt it that way or make it see that I'd brought it food and it would leave me alone it's so hungry I thought but it left the grain alone I never got away from the gate the chickens all scrambling about in front of me after the grain I was throwing at the cock and it kept coming at me again and again *bang!* it went up against the bucket *slam!* and I was afraid it would break its beak *What am I doing wrong? What'll happen if it hurts itself so much it dies?* I wanted it to be dead and I was afraid it would be, what would Uncle Tom think that I couldn't feed the chickens and the fierce cock died what would he do claws rattling down the side of the pail beak upthrust at me *bang! slam!* and *slam!* again I reached into the bucket and flung grain left and right as fast and as hard as I could left and right for the chickens and the cock flew at me again and again huge and fierce, me with this bucket of corn in *its* yard. I hardly noticed the chickens they were just clucking and pecking away at the corn and this big black frightening outpour of sheer menace got more and more fierce and more and more clamorous till I simply upended the bucket all over it and fled back through the gate, fumbling at the catch behind me opening it as little as possible and slamming it closed as I got through, *blam!* went the bird at the gate I'd hardly got into the chicken yard at all, I'd not even begun my grand parade of goodwill and generosity. All out of breath and sweaty I shook so much my legs all wobbly, arms tired from shoving the bucket about to keep the bird from me, my hair falling over my eyes my socks round my ankles one sock torn, a bit of blood where he'd pecked me. I went over and stood by the mash cooking for the pigs and simply smelled it till I got my breath back, I don't suppose I'd been in the chicken yard for as much as two minutes, one of the farm cats black with a white bib and two torn ears came over and looked at me and had a wash, paws round its face, Hullo, I said, but I was still afraid and breathless and he paid no attention to me and I knew better than to pet him. If he wanted some attention he'd come rubbing up, otherwise I knew to leave the cats alone.

    When I took the pail back to the house Aunt Dot was in the kitchen and she said "Oh! Did you feed the chickens yet? Don't go in the chicken yard, we got a new black cock and he's so fierce I daren't go in there, Tom will, but I feed them over the gate." I must have looked pretty tousled because she took a longer look at me and said "Oh! he pecked you didn't he" and got an Elastoplast and some TCP for my leg, and I was pleased, secretly proud that I'd done something she didn't like to do, I still had the shakes. "We'll probably have to get rid of that bird," she said, "perhaps we'll eat him, but Tom wouldn't have that, he's wonderful for the chickens, they're all laying like mad, we'll have lots of chicks," and I was glad. I didn't want to eat that bird that had tried to eat me, there was something funny about that idea, a bit creepy, just the thought made me feel a little bit sick, a bit like wanting to eat something that's still alive, a leg kicking and twisting in your hand as you bit into it. Perhaps I looked a bit funny. She said that since I'd already got the pail I might as well go into the orchard and see if I could find any eggs, the chickens got in there yesterday so there might be a few, look carefully, and if Brenda turned up she could help me before we went off to play. Don't go into the henhouse, she told me, or the chicken yard, until Tom's locked the black cock up in his own coop, and "then you can get the eggs," she knew I liked doing that. I hadn't when I first went to the farm, I was afraid of these big feathery creatures, I didn't like to touch them, and once there'd been a hen got in the kitchen when we were there and Tom said "Catch it, Pete" and I chased that hen about, bent over my arms stretched out in front, a clumsy doubled-over waddle waving my arms from side to side, I got the hen in a corner *Got it!* but it scooted between my legs, it was so very alive I was afraid to touch it really, didn't want it to peck me, I thought it might make its mess on me, I was just too squeamish, and everyone sat around the kitchen laughing their heads off, Dad and Our Kid as well as Uncle Tom and Aunt Dot and Brenda, Mum not so much, she was a bit afraid of chickens and couldn't stand them really, shied away from it, I capered about until Aunt Dot simply walked over and picked it up holding its wings to its side, tucked it under her arm, a terrified but quiet and motionless hen, out the door. Brenda started to jeer at me but Uncle Tom soon put a stop to that, "You're no better at it than Peter is," he said, "and you're two years older than him."

But now I really enjoyed handling the chickens their lovely warmth and getting the eggs, there was something quite magical about going into the twilight of the henhouse, breathing through your mouth because of the sharp ammonia of the droppings, most of the birds would be outside but there were always two or three hens roosting on their perches, you ducked under them pretty quickly, and you'd see the dim shape of a hen in a nesting box, you'd slide your hand underneath, it'd cluck a bit grumpily and sleepily mutter away at you, sometimes quite annoyed but only half-heartedly pecking at you, they were used to us, all that lovely soft warmth under the birds, feathers enveloping the back of your hand, everything placid, perhaps you'd brush the firm roughness of its claw, the firm warm roundness of the egg almost warm enough to eat, it felt alive and welcoming, you'd check to make sure you weren't taking the china egg by mistake, sometimes your hand got into some glop under the bird too, but you'd fold your fingers round the egg and gently take it away, lay it in the pail with the eggs you'd already got and go round the other nesting boxes. The smell in the chicken house was pretty awful really, but so long as you weren't there too long you got used to it, nobody liked cleaning it out. They laid their eggs all over the place, Uncle Tom told me to watch out for the broody hen over there, under the hedge. "She's got eggs there but she won't let you have them, she'll protect them, she can be pretty fierce. They've been there too long anyway, and we'll have to let them hatch, I don't think they're addled. And we could use a few chicks anyway, we're getting plenty of eggs."

Mum didn't go near the chickens, and she never got the eggs, not even from the ducks, she was terrified of birds the way some people are terrified of snakes, the way I used to be revulsed by spiders, the great big ones that'd climb up the drain into the bathtub to get away from the cold of autumn, but Phil and I never really understood that I think until one day in Lichfield, this must have been in 1953 or even after that, Mum was doing the dishes in the scullery with the back door open, I was in another room and I heard this crash as she dropped a plate, broke it, and she was standing there frozen perfectly still this funny look on her face, I came in and said "what happened?" and in a strangulated voice she said "bird" and gestured, just inside the door was a sparrow almost as motionless as she was, trembling minutely and trailing a wing, just outside the door was one of the cats.

After I'd shooed Herman away and rescued the bird – as soon as I picked it up and put it down again it flew away – Bess and I sat down over a cup of tea and she told me that when she was about six or seven, this must have been around 1910 or so, her father had decided that this nonsense about being scared of birds and hating the way feathers feel had to stop. One day he brought a couple of chickens home from the butchershop, called Mum to come here, hid behind the door and when she came in leapt out at her rubbing these dead fully-feathered birds all over her face and neck and shoulders and then chased her all over the house with them, her screaming in fear and him shouting "See? they don't hurt you!" He'd lie in ambush around the house and then jump out at her until after about a couple of weeks of torment everybody else in the house prevailed on him to stop, all he was doing was turning her into a hysterical wreck, she daredn't go anywhere in the house, Grampa upsetting the other two girls and the maids and generally getting the whole place in uproar, "It's not at all funny, Albert, so you can stop laughing," Grannie had said, "Leave the poor girl alone!" And even after that, every now and again he'd leap out from behind a door or out from under the stairs waving a dead chicken at her. It was just the shock of seeing the sparrow there inside the door, all of a sudden just like that, that had made her drop the plate, usually she was okay, but on the farm she never had to do with the chickens, she couldn't pluck them or eviscerate them, it was the feathers that bothered her, not the bird itself, and much later when she was living by herself on the Isle of Wight, she belonged to the Royal Society for the Protection of Birds.

Work never seemed to let up on the farm except on Sunday afternoons, but we all loved being there, it was never dull but it wasn't an easy life and it toughened us up a bit, the fact that we always had plenty to eat must have had something to do with that, not like in the city or at School where you only got one egg a week and that often ruined and there wasn't much fruit. In the summer everybody got busy bottling plums and cherries and making jams, they'd be there to eat all winter there were so many of them, and the house would be filled with the smell of plums cooking in a big black pot in the scullery to make jam. Everybody'd saved their sugar ration for weeks and weeks, wasps everywhere, buzzing away at the windowpanes trying to get out, crawling across the tablecloth towards the milk jug or your plate in the kitchen, sitting on the butter muslin draped over the milk jug to keep them and the flies out, a bit of gauzy cloth embroidered round the edge with heavy beads to weight it down, they'd just sit there a bit and then take off, looking for plums and cherries, damsons and greengages.

Making jam was supposed to be a job for the women and the kids but nobody could stay away from it, the lovely stickiness of it, the thick sugary smoky smell if it boiled over, crusty and caramelised down the outside of the pot you could pick it off if you did it sharpish. Not a lot of the work got sorted out that way anyway, if a job needed doing then it didn't matter who did it so long as it got done, but Uncle Tom would find a lot more things that could only be done in the house when it was jam-making time, and we'd stand round the pot. I had to stand on a chair so I could see and reach, when it was my turn. One of us would skim all the junk off the top of the cooking fruit with a big flat spoon, plum stones, skin, a lot of thick off-white froth, and wasps. We'd flap our arms about to keep the flies off, how Dad hated flies, but we'd let the wasps alone, if they wanted to get cooked that was their business, and every now and again you'd just dip the spoon in, let it cool off a bit, and eat the jam off the end, sometimes it was terribly sour so you'd let it cook a lot more before you tasted it again. I'd only do it when I thought nobody was looking, until Aunt Dot simply dipped the spoon in and then licked it off while she was talking to me. But of course we couldn't spend all day standing round the scullery watching jam, there were still all the usual jobs to do, we had to go out into the orchard to pick the fruit, we'd send a lot of it to market but we kept quite a bit back, and we'd be at it pretty well all summer. We didn't have any apricot trees so we'd sometimes exchange a chip basket of greengages for some, and there was always a bowl of fruit on the table when it was in season, but things like damsons were so sour you had to stew them first, I loved their dark intense flavour, like all the best plums in the world all rolled into one, a sharp rich taste, if they were really ripe you could eat them raw but they made your mouth pucker and you'd get a tear in your eye, sometimes a bit of a shudder as it went over the back of your tongue on the way down. They were worth it, the taste lingered on and on in your mouth after you'd eaten one. Once Brenda gave me a damson to eat and it was so sour I couldn't eat it at all, it furred my teeth as soon as I bit into it, there was so little pulp it was like a thick skin and my teeth straightaway hit the stone and I hated it, a horrid taste for ages after, dark and bitter, and she laughed and said she'd given me a damseen, harsh and concentrated and impossible to eat without being made into jam with lots of sugar and lots of cooking. They made the most fantastic jam though, but there was never enough to make more than a jar or two, very precious stuff. Mum said you had to be terribly careful not to put too much sugar in, lose the flavour, not that there was much danger of that in the War.

Us kids all liked picking fruit, if there weren't enough ladders it was a lovely excuse for climbing trees, cherries were best for that but you had to be terribly careful not to break any branches, you could sit up there in a fork or straddle a thick branch and reach around you for the fruit, you'd get to eat some of it but you'd better not get caught too often, a basket hanging from a hook on the branch under you, if you looked down at the bark there might be a line of ants trailing in the cracks between your legs on their way somewhere, probably to a lump of sap leaking out of the branch, but they'd leave you alone so long as you weren't all sugary or juicy, sometimes your trousers would stick to a gob of sap you'd sat on, you could never wash it off afterwards and our clothes got really messy, I liked that, it meant I didn't have to look after them so much,

I could never keep clean anyway, later on at School I was called *Hesperus* but only till Roy Beasley came along he really did look like something from Longfellow's poem and we called him *Wreck* for years. Aunt Dot said Brenda was too fastidious but I didn't know what that word meant and she said "she's too fussy, you can't do any work if you don't want to get dirty" and Brenda said that wasn't fair, she liked to get into clean clothes afterwards, but I didn't care, I knew it was hopeless me being neat and tidy, why bother trying. I'd come in from the barn or from the rickyard with bits of barley or oats sticking out of my clothes, sometimes my socks would be almost yellow, solid with prickly awns, they were so barbed they were almost impossible to get out, you had to get them out one at a time, tease them or they'd break, it was easier to turn the sock inside out and pull them through, that was too much nuisance, I'd just put up with the scratchiness and hope they'd fall out of their own accord but they never did and eventually out of all patience my legs all sore and scratchy I'd sit down and get rid of as many as I could, Mum hated them, said how horrible it was trying to wash socks when they were like that.

It'd get terribly hot up there in the trees and your arms would get tired stretching for the fruit, especially if you were picking apples or pears, sometimes if I was up a ladder I'd lean over for a bunch of cherries or a plum or two and I'd feel the ladder lurch sideways a bit, once it really started to slide and I stuck my arm through between the rungs and grabbed onto the branch and hung on like mad, the ladder must have slid about three feet and if it had gone much further it'd have fallen, I'd have run out of ladder. I let go of the fruit in my right hand and worked the ladder back along the branch till it was upright, it was very hard to do and I dropped the fruit from my left hand, I didn't have time to put it anywhere, and in my haste I knocked the basket off the branch its hook fell too. After I'd got the ladder upright again, no one was looking but I had to go down the ladder to get it back, put all the spilled fruit back in, and Our Kid said "I saw that! You dropped it didn't you" and Aunt Dot looked over and grinned and I went red, I think she might have seen the ladder slide but she didn't say anything. I suppose she thought you had to make your own mistakes and no harm done. I'd look at how much everybody else had picked and I was always dismayed, I'd been busily picking away and half-filled a basket while Uncle Tom had moved his ladder four times and filled six or seven, the other kids had picked much more than me and I always thought they'd eaten more too, "You've got to do better than that," Tom would say, but he didn't seem to mind as long as you weren't really slacking off, and if you really did get too tired you could always lie down in the long grass in the shade for a while and look at the patterns the leaves made against the sky, or watch one of the big black beetles that lived down in the grass, or simply listen to everything growing, the tiny faint noises always down there in and on the ground. What a delicious shock of recognition later on to read John Clare, that wonderful Northampton poet, he'd lie and listen to the cracking of corn stubble in the sun and the "bounce" of the grasshopper. The intensity of harvest-time. Or if it was cloudy you could go in and stir the jam if there was a pot going, sometimes we'd take turns to get a rest from picking fruit.

At about four or perhaps half-past, if we were all out in the orchard or harvesting, Aunt Dot would go in and make tea, it was my favourite meal of the day in the summer, we'd sit at the kitchen table in the sun up against the window looking out into the orchard, white chintz curtains ruled off with red lines into squares, window wide open for the wasps to get in and out, gauze half-curtain flapping gently in the breeze, plates of bread and butter, cake, honey from somebody local and jam we'd made, the sun streaming in the windows across the table, some days. The farm didn't have a butter churn so I don't know where the butter came from, another farmer likely, in exchange for eggs or feed or fruit, there was always enough. Even now, whenever I eat bread and honey, more than seventy years later, I can taste those teas in that sunny spot, all of us sitting at the table, soft grit of the granulated honey so stiff you could hardly spread it, it would bunch up towards the edge of the bread pushing the butter before it, or it would push right through, you'd eat it in uneven lumps with the crusty white bread, your teeth worrying away to get through it the butter flooding into your mouth, the honey clinging a bit to the roof of your mouth just behind your front teeth sweetness trickling down, clover honey was good, tasted the way honey ought to, heather honey with its brutal pungence, a sandy sort of melting across your tongue and down toward the back of your mouth, you'd chew at the resistance of the crust and then wash its sweet paste down with hot tea and take another bite. There'd be last year's rhubarb-and-ginger or greengage jam, and fruit, egg-plums perhaps, or – if they were cookers – Victoria or Belgian Purple sitting in a deep lake of their own juice, sometimes sour as sour, a bit of Bird's custard to help them down, and we'd sit around the table waving our hands at the odd wasp or two and talk a bit before going back to work. We kids would run about a bit, we didn't have to do anything really after tea, but we'd often end up back in the orchard, letting the cows out into the field again after milking and shutting the gates behind them.

A couple of Italian Prisoners of War came to work on the farm when I was about eight. Mario was the one who knew most English, liked to talk to us *Learn English more*, he'd say, and Giuseppe who we called Joe kept pretty quiet, didn't even say much to Mario when they sat together at meals and could talk in Italian, he'd laugh a bit once Mario got him going, but didn't laugh the way Mario did. But they both liked it on the farm even if they did sleep in a room out in the barn somewhere, locked up for the night, "better than prison camp," Joe said, Mario smiling. *Much better than getting shot at on the Front, more like* said Uncle Tom, *the War's over for them*. He didn't like them much, *Almost more trouble than they're worth, lazy devils, both of 'em*. They're *not going to run anywhere*. But he kept them at it, made them work and work and work. "I suppose they're alright," I heard him telling Dad one day, me in the kitchen all ears, "but they're like all bloody Eyeties, they're so bloody lazy. Don't know how to do anything, you've got to watch them all the time" and Dad murmured something about how glad Fred must be of their help "With the other hands all off in the War, couldn't manage at all without him." Fred lived in one of the farm cottages down on the Stratford Road, the only real farmhand to speak of because of the War, a couple of extra hands coming in at the right time for haymaking or the harvest. "I been on this farm man and boy," he told Phil and me, "since long before your uncle took it over," he showed the Land Girls obscure little places chickens especially sometimes strayed, or even tools, usually mattocks or sickles or pitchforks, he showed them what to do and how to do it. Fred was the only person Tom'd let feed the threshing machine on its yearly visit, and he knew how to thatch the hayricks so they'd keep dry through the winter. He was older than everybody else and Uncle Tom got in the habit of asking him what he thought about the plans for the day's work. "Those damn Eyeties," Tom said, "at least they're not bloody Germans, you can't take *their* word for *any*thing, *nobody* trusts *their* parole. Kill us *all* in our beds."

He complained the way he always did about the extra work PoWs caused, *make sure they don't run off!* The Eyeties weren't likely to run anywhere, even with the Eighth Army fighting its way into Italy and us busy with the harvest. "They're on Easy Street, and they know it" Dot said, but of course they had to be fed and we did get ration books for them. *Nothing but work.* They weren't supposed to eat at the same time as we did but when the Land Girls ate, Aunt Dot looked after all that, but it was so much trouble making separate meals that most times the PoWs simply ate when we did, at their own corner table in the kitchen, the same food as us if there was enough to go round. They were pretty harmless. But during the day you couldn't leave the both of them alone anywhere, inside the house or out, if they weren't locked up in their room the way they were every night then somebody all the time had be around them, they were *prisoners. We* were at war and *they* were the enemy, and Fred couldn't be dragged away from his work just to look after *them*, could he.

Uncle Tom fretted that he had to keep his 12-gauge hidden and locked away somewhere along with the 4.10 instead of hanging the bigger shotgun on the wall in the kitchen, the ammunition locked up in a different part of the house. It got to be quite a business to go rabbiting. He'd just go out of the room without saying anything, Mario and Joe locked away for the night, and we'd hear him rummaging about somewhere, down in the cellar as well as upstairs, and then he'd come back with one of the shotguns, ammunition in his pocket, *Evening's best for rabbits* he'd say, but of course it wasn't, not when you couldn't drive round the field in the old Morris eight freezing them in the headlights the way he did before and after the War, Uncle Tom or Aunt Dot driving and us kids after the War sitting on the bonnet as the car jounced across the field, one of us usually Brenda clutching the 4.10 and potting away at them. She was a pretty good shot, but they were hard to miss, you didn't really need to aim, the rabbits just sat there absolutely still in the lights their eyes shining as though there was a light bulb in them, looking at the car just waiting to be shot, and one of us would shoot two or three they wouldn't even run away from the noise and then Tom would switch the lights off, stop the car and the other rabbits would all run away, and whoever didn't have the gun would go and pick up the dead ones. We ate a lot of rabbit in those days, just as we did during the War.

But in the War we went rabbiting on foot. Tom was a really good shot, like most farmers he'd been doing it for years, and we could only go rabbiting in the evening, curfew time for the Eyeties, we double-checked that the farm showed no lights in the blackout, and in dark clothes we'd go tramping across the fields in the gathering dusk, boots getting a bit wet from the dew, and he'd nudge me and whisper "Stay here, just wait," rabbits just sitting there near the hedgerow, vague little greyish patches and then a blurry little movement and the white scut would show clear against the dark of the hedge *bob-bob-bob*, ten or twelve of them or even more, thirty yards or so away, I hadn't really seen them at all till he whispered, and I'd stand stock still and he'd carefully raise his gun and creep forward in slow little clumps of motion, he'd move a bit and then he'd stand still and then he'd move a bit again not making a sound that I could hear, he'd try to get about ten yards or so from them and then he'd let both barrels go swinging the gun between shots and all the rabbits would vanish to the flat thuddy *blam! blam!* the sound echoing back from the woods a bit flatter, and he'd motion me forward, I'd pick up the two rabbits he'd shot, and we'd go on to the next field. Sometimes you could see the rabbits all the way across the field, their scuts gleaming in the dusk, but as soon as you got over the stile and started across they'd scatter and we'd often turn back, not worth the wait. Sometimes we'd simply stay put after he'd shot them and I'd picked them up, usually by the hind feet sometimes by the ears, their bodies still warm and alive feeling even if they didn't move, I'd put them in an old sack, and we'd squat down on our haunches and wait for the rest to come out of the warren again, we knew where all the warrens were and sometimes we'd set snares, but none of us liked that, the wire'd dig so far into their necks it was hard to get out, blood all round, their eyes bugging out so cruel they looked terrible, but I wasn't very good at waiting, I'd get little cramps in my legs and stir a bit or I'd need to scratch or I'd start to say something and Uncle Tom'd get cross with me and we'd move on. Sometimes the ones he'd shot weren't completely dead and he'd have to club them, and when we got back to the barn we'd have to skin them and clean them, I hated that job but the fur always felt wonderfully soft and warm except where there was blood all stiff on it, and we'd wash the skinned and gutted carcasses and then take them in to hang in the pantry next to the kitchen.

24

Farm Girls

Tom never shot more than four rabbits, that was all we needed, but if he only got two then the Eyeties would have to do without, the pair of them sitting at their separate table hunched towards each other in their PoW clothes with the big red patches on the back, jabbering away in low voices, gesturing softly in our direction, us eating the rabbit they couldn't have and laughing quietly or sometimes looking a bit angry, we never knew what they were talking about, now and again they'd catch your eye, and I'd worry *What are they plotting?* That question came from all the stories we read in the *Wizard* or the *Rover*, all of us at School would go on about how some stranger who'd got off the bus from Wolverhampton was really a Spy. Our lives were filled with suspicion of strangers, we made excited guesses, and if we heard anyone talk in any sort of funny accent we'd follow them around as much as we could and report back to each other, make notes on scraps of paper, sometimes we'd even tell one of the Masters but they'd tell us not to be so daft *Leave commercial travellers alone!* Aunt Dot just shrugged if she saw me looking at the PoWs, "Stop worrying! *They're* not going to run away, they're in clover." Even Uncle Tom, for all his complaints, was glad they were there, having to help, they gave us a bit of a break, Tom to go rabbiting, Aunt Dot to go off by herself for an hour or two. She began a couple of times a week to put her jodhpurs on and ride one of the cart-horses down the drive, the PoWs standing by to look, its stately clop-clop clop-clop, its great big feet looking too ungainly to get up to much of a trot, but it could move pretty fast if it wanted and so long as she let it, securely sitting with no saddle to speak of, a long way to the ground from its broad back, and she'd ride it down the drive and into the pastures near the Arrow River, get back a bit later relaxed and smiling. *Want to try?* She hoicked me up in front of her but I wasn't really big enough and didn't like it all the way up there with nothing to hold on to except the mane, the horse's back wide and smooth and my legs too short to get a good grip and she had to lower me down when I wanted to get off. *It's not as far as it looks*, me dangling at arm's length, *just let go!*

A few days before, with just me and Daphne the Land Girl in the kitchen, everyone else off doing their chores, I'd been standing by the table eating an apple, she'd got one too, and she took a bite of hers and said "This one's no good, it's full of worms," and she chucked it in the coal scuttle as I said "Mine's alright, just a bit bruised." She took a look and said "Ugh! That's not bruise, that's maggot eggs! You're eating all those maggot eggs!" and she laughed and laughed, "Don't you know the difference?" pointing her finger at me, I could feel myself going red and I said "I know that," her all neat and tidy in her Land Army uniform, a cold and forceful soldier, still laughing at me, "I don't mind maggot eggs, I always eat them." I felt all righteous in front of her jeering, I wasn't going to let on I didn't know the difference, I'd always thought the brown grainy firm bits of apple were just a different sort of bruise than the soft squishy brown ones, they were more sort of tasteless than they were anything else, they just didn't taste of anything very much, there was just no juice in them. I took another big bite of my apple her watching me and laughing. I didn't dare not eat it now, but it didn't taste the way it had. We all carefully ate our way round the really wormy bits, deep little holes with a dark black rim winding their way down into the core, or we broke 'em off with our teeth and threw them away, and Daphne just stood there, she watched me and watched me, a superior grin on her face till I turned away and went outside, holding the apple carefully so I could miss the maggotty bits as I bit into it, and when I got out to the back of the scullery I threw the whole thing into the pig-swill bucket just outside the door, hating her for what she'd done, not knowing really whether it was rubbish or not, what she'd said.

A few months later at the beginning of 1943 Mum and Dad sent Our Kid to the farm for six weeks he was so poorly, the doctor in Rugby said he was really run down and must get lots of rest and fresh air, not go to school but concentrate on getting better. I don't know who the doctor was, perhaps a specialist, he wasn't Dr Pike, Dad's friend as well as doctor, in Birmingham, so we knew it was really serious. When we lived in Brum Dad would once in a while come home chuckling away "I saw Charlie Pike this afternoon, that's why I'm so late, I was with him for about an hour" he'd say, and Mum would want to know if Dad was alright, "Oh yes," he'd say, "but there were a lot of people in the waiting room so we just sat there for a bit and told each other stories, we both needed a break" and Mum would look a bit cross because he hadn't told her he was going, and a bit relieved there was nothing the matter, "Oh Leo you are awful, you really should have some consideration for all those people waiting," and then when we were out of the room he'd tell her some of Dr Pike's off-colour jokes and we'd hear her laugh a bit. But anyway the Doctor in Rugby said Our Kid had to have a long break, fresh air good food and exercise, he was away from School for most of the Term. I'd pretty well forgotten all about this, don't remember being at Brewood without him, but then I didn't see much of him in Brewood, he was in the Third Form and I was still down in Prep and we were in different dorms anyway, and it wasn't till I showed him those paragraphs about picking fruit that he reminded me. As usual we went to the farm in the summer of 1943 and Our Kid took me through the orchard and across the field to a place he'd found when he'd been there for so long by himself.

Phil loved going off exploring by himself and then telling us what he'd discovered, it was easier by road but a lot longer, and when we got to the other side of the field we had to find a way through the hedge, it'd grown over a bit since he'd last been, "There's not even a stile," he warned me, and we had to find a way over it, we couldn't really go through, that'd break it down. We got into a narrow country road, he was all knowing about it but not cocky, he wanted to share this new thing he'd found, show it to me, pleased with himself and it, and he pointed off to the right and there on the side of the road it felt like a hundred yards away but I don't suppose it could've been more than fifty, was a tiny little country shop, a couple of rusty tin signs sticking out on both sides above the window, a battered enamelled Wills's Capstan Cigarettes sign in a strip along the bottom, a jumble of stuff through the dusty glass, half-empty sweet jars, Dobson's, and Mackintosh, and Maynard's Buttered Brazils with who knew what inside; placards for Oxydol and Lifebuoy Soap; advertisements for cigarettes and Smith's Potato Crisps, tobacco and Huntley and Palmer's biscuits; packets of ribbon and pins. Climb a couple of steps push open the glass-paned door, its jangling small bell, a card of Carter's Children's Aspirin in little packets hanging just inside the door next to a card of hairpins, swept dark floor smelling of linseed oil, everything on the shelves here and there a little bit dusty. Our Kid said, "Hello, Mrs Jenks. I'm back. Have you got any Tizer left, can we have two?" and she said, "Wait a bit," she went in the back and came out dusting off a couple of bottles of orange-brown pop, and Our Kid paid her, 3d. each no deposit because we were going to drink them here, it was the most wonderful pop I'd ever tasted, "Tizer the Appetizer" it said on the bottle, it was what one of the signs said outside the door, we couldn't think what it tasted of, rich and sharp but not sour, perfect for a hot sticky day. Mrs Jenks said there wouldn't be any more after this lot had gone, these were from the last case she'd got, she hadn't been able to get it for ever so long, almost before the War she said, "They don't make it any more" but there was somebody in Stratford or Leamington, local anyway, who still made Dandelion-and-Burdock and she'd got some of that. She might even have made her own.

Like a lot of people round there she made her own ginger beer when she could and that's where we spent our pocket money whenever we got the chance. I'd no idea that shop existed till he showed it me, and the Tizer didn't last very long at all so we switched to Dandelion and Burdock, we knew what it was of course, Mrs Spencer used to sell it at Spalding, and Mrs Roberts in her shop at Brewood, but you couldn't always get it. Years later, in Connecticut, I'd be reminded of it when I first tasted root beer but it was better than that. Our Kid was eleven, he'd be twelve come

September, I was just over nine, Brenda'd been away at school when he was away from Brewood for six weeks, so he'd sort of had the farm to himself and knew a lot more about the place than I did. He told me when he reminded me about his six-week stay at Alcester that when he was about four or perhaps five, at most I'd have been three-and-a-bit, before the Thomsons had moved to Alcester and were still at Hunt End Farm near Redditch, he and Brenda had misbehaved and Florence, who was our maid then, punished him and Brenda by sending them to bed early, in the same room, and once they got there they climbed into the same bed. "It must have been Tom and Dot's," he said, "it was huge," and they took all their clothes off and happily found out about each other, played doctor and nurse, cuddled up in bed, just the two of them. Phil says I was sent to bed too, in the same room, but I can't even remember Florence, except as a vague large presence at 164 Solihull Road always dressed in black. She was a big woman by all accounts, but I was so young when she went away and Alice came along as the new maid that it's hard to sort out what I've been told from what I genuinely remember, and even Alice is a pretty dim figure after all these years.

But the night after Our Kid told me on the phone about him and Brenda I woke up at about three o'clock with a sharp picture in my mind, his tale had triggered it, of a girl a little bit older and a little bit bigger than me, before the War, standing in a back garden with a couple of other small girls, I don't know what her name was any more, but Shirley or Felicity sound about right to me, we did play with girls with those names, they were standing on a small rise it might have been a heap of builder's sand with their backs to the house and there was me and two or three other boys my age, I can't have been older than four, and we were all giggling and laughing away keeping our distance from each other but only about a couple of feet away from them and Felicity, she had dark wavy hair that came just below her ears, she had a blue chequered dress on with short sleeves, it was a warm sunny day, she gave a great big smile and opened her eyes wide you could see the white all round the iris and she lifted up her skirt in front of her, she wasn't wearing any knickers and the other two girls, they were smaller than Felicity, lifted their skirts up too and they weren't wearing any either and the three of them laughed away, I goggled away at them, I'd never seen anything like it, they were so different there was nothing hanging down in front of them at all just a thin dark slit up and down in front between their legs *What do they pee with?* they looked all bare and strange they must have been very uncomfortable like that *Does the pee just trickle down their leg?* I thought a slit like that must hurt and I was speechless, I don't know what the other boys did, we none of us said anything and the girls laughed and waved their skirts in front of us and then I started to say something but I don't think it was more than "Oh" and one of the other kids began to move and one of the girls said "you can't touch. Let's see yours." I didn't want to do that it was all very strange and uncomfortable and I still didn't quite believe what I'd seen the smooth skin of those pale tummies curving out above those soft and pudgy-looking cracks how could they manage to be like that and Felicity said "You've got to! We showed!" The loops of my braces went through small slots to hold up my underpants before they fastened to the buttons on my trousers, if I undid the quick-release I wouldn't be able to do it up again and Mum would know, I lifted my hands to my shoulders and pulled the braces down over my arms, we began to wriggle out of our trousers but ever so slowly I really didn't want to do it I'd get into trouble I knew we would the air was a bit cool on my bum and the back door of the house opened and her mum said "Felicity, come here!" in a stern voice, "you other children go back home," as the door closed behind them there was a loud slap and a cry and Felicity's mum's voice and we all ran away, me hoicking my trousers up as best I could.

Once, before this, we'd been playing Cowboys and Indians and we'd tied up a little girl much smaller than us, she was probably about three to our four and one of us had some matches and another of us had some string and we tied her up to a tree and took her shoes and socks off and piled some twigs around her legs and a bit of paper and tried to set her on fire, we were the Indians and the cowboys had to rescue her but the match was hot and burned our fingers the possibility of tiny yellow flames in the leaves really scary, much too hot to get close to, my own fierce flinch, she started crying and a grown-up somebody's mum ran out shouting "What do you children think you're doing?" and cuffed us away and picked her up and took her home sobbing, we all ran home and Mum was very cross, "You've been very naughty," she said. "See how hot a match is," she said. "What if I put it against your leg? You can't do that to other people. Not ever!" When she heard about us and Felicity she got even angrier, told me that if we couldn't behave properly I wouldn't be let play with any of my friends again, "not even Sammy Roe!" She sent me to my room. My bed looked strange in the broad daylight, it didn't belong to anybody, the sheets tightly folded down, the counterpane pulled up over the pillow, not a wrinkle even in the table-runner under my hairbrush, my teddy bear sitting rigidly balanced against the bulge of the pillow, not even my books waiting for me, everything neat and tidy and folded in its proper place, the curtains wide open so anybody could see in, nowhere really to sit, the bed far too tidy. Like everything else, I'd been put away. I waited a long time before Mum said I could come downstairs again.

After the War started Brenda was the only girl I knew to talk to or spend any time with until I left Brewood in 1952 to go to university. She was Our Kid's age, a month or two younger, and she was more his friend than mine, but sometimes I was there and he wasn't. One morning when I was about nine Aunt Dot shouted upstairs at us that breakfast was ready and was getting cold we'd better hurry up Brenda called out "Coming" from her room and I looked over, Phil wasn't in his bed he'd already got up and gone out somewhere, he'd gone off with Uncle Tom to do something, and Brenda came into the kitchen just as I sat down to my bowl of porridge, hers sitting on the table getting cold, and she whispered at me, "Hurry up, I've got a secret, it's a hiding place. You must promise not to tell," her breath hissed over the esses, she was bursting with wanting to tell me. I promised, and she leaned towards me "Do you swear?" and I said "Yes, Honest! I swear!" and we gulped our porridge and rushed outside "Wait here" she told me, "close your eyes and count to fifty, don't you *dare* cheat! Then come down the driveway and see if you can find me." When I got to forty-five I called out "forty-six forty-seven forty-eight forty-nine" as fast as I could, a quick pause to catch my breath and "Fifty!" at the top of my voice, and started down the drive peering about in the barnyard and the bushes I heard something rustle, it was just Moggy, one of the farm cats, and I whispered *Hullo* to it and then I heard a thrush stirring among the branches, no that wasn't her either, I was going quite slowly I had to see her I had to find her hiding place and I kept looking up into the trees a story in *The Wizard* said people always forgot to look upwards *Climb a tree if you want a good place to hide*, that still strikes me as a bit daft, it only works when whoever's hunting you is right under the tree you're in. I looked into the hedge on the right the home field hedge and I peered through the cowshed doors but she couldn't possibly be hiding in there, too many people about, no room for secrets there. My feet padding on the dirt and the grass patches and then crunching on the gravelly bits of the driveway. I got to the five-barred gate, it creaked when you opened it, and I hadn't heard it creak and if you didn't climb over it right next to the hinges it groaned a bit, Uncle Tom got really cross if you didn't climb gates next to the hinges "You'll ruin the gate!" he'd say angrily, "you'll make it sag!" and I hadn't heard it groan or anything, I stopped a bit to think, and I heard "Pssst!" *That was Brenda, it must've been!* But I couldn't see her. Listen some more. Look round, slowly. "Pssst!" again, over to the left *oh! the holly bushes!* A thick unbroken wall of prickly green. She wasn't there, the holly began to shake and *There she is!* wriggling sideways towards me her frock all ruckled and dusty under the branches, they reached all the way down to the ground, *How did you get in there?* "Come on, I'll show you" she said and scrambled over to the gatepost and squeezed carefully between it and the holly bush, once you were through you could follow a narrow little path, bend under one prickly branch and over another and there you were, a wonderful bushy cave, you could see everything that went past up or down the drive, you could even stand up in it, she had an old towel to sit on and some old plates and crockery for pretend meals and some pencil ends and stuff like that. I said, "This is smashing!" and she made me promise all over again not to tell anyone, this was her secret place, she'd set it up a day or two ago, and just as I promised we heard Aunt Dot's irritated voice shouting and shouting for us, and as we hove into sight she said "You haven't finished your breakfast! You can't go off like that and leave your food behind. Come in at once and eat it!" And when we got back to the kitchen, "What have you two been up to, running off like that?" and she handed us boiling hot plates of bacon and eggs, the eggs all hard from keeping warm under the grill, we told her we were full and didn't want any, "Don't be ridiculous, you've got to have a decent breakfast. As soon as you've finished that you've got work to do!" the contrast between that rubbery egg and the now-crisp hot fried bread and thick chewy bacon never to be forgotten.

Next day right after breakfast I went down to Brenda's hidey-hole and as I got close I could hear voices, and there she was showing Uncle Tom all round, and he said "You ought to have a newspaper down here to read," later in the day he brought one, Brenda and me sitting there *What a wonderful secret place!* and ten minutes after Uncle Tom had left us the paper Major Partridge came walking up the drive from the Stratford Road, I stuck my hand out through the holly hedge, it really was prickly and dusty, and I said *Pssst! Major Partridge!* and in a big uncly sort of voice he said "What have we here?" and bent over to have a look and Brenda was furious, "You told!" she hissed at me, "you promised!" and she pinched my arm and then she punched me in the ribs her knuckles in a point "I hate you!" and it hurt just the way it did when kids did it at School, made a bruise, I started to tell her that I thought it wasn't a secret anymore because she'd told Uncle Tom, but she'd run away before I could say it, why did I do it anyway it was her secret place not mine. I'd stolen her pleasure in telling, I felt all red in the face hot and ashamed, and I said "I'm sorry" in a loud voice just as she came back "Come and see it," she was saying as she led Major Partridge round through the path by the gatepost, "What are you sorry about?" he asked and I didn't say anything, Brenda was proudly showing him everything, I didn't know what to feel, nothing seemed to be the matter at all,

Major Partridge sat down and had a pretend cup of tea with us and then we all went up to the house, Brenda chattering at me just the same as usual planning what we could do next.

Life at Kinwarton Farm in Alcester was so different from life in Birmingham or at School, there was no electricity and the cooker in the scullery ran off Calor Gas, every two weeks or so the delivery man would come round and take the big dull metal cylinder away and leave another in its place, in the winter there was always a fire banked up with slack in the kitchen range to keep the water hot for washing up and baths, if we wanted a bath in the summer then Aunt Dot might light a fire in the kitchen or under the copper in the scullery to warm the water, or even take hot kettles up to the bathtub, but not if the weather was warm, then we'd walk over home field and across the busy Stratford Road, down to the River Arrow and splash about there, we had hot baths once a week just like at Brewood except that at School we had showers after Games as well, I couldn't swim and Our Kid had to keep his ears clear of water, he had a special pair of ear plugs, and he and Brenda would swim, and we'd all walk back up to the farm cool and tired and ready for a bit of supper before going to bed, but we didn't go to bed very early, what with Double Summer Time it was broad daylight till well after ten o'clock. There weren't any flush toilets that Our Kid and I can remember either, though I'm not too sure about that, Uncle Tom and Aunt Dot let the front part of the house off to Mr Partridge and his wife, he was not really a Major but he called himself that. We hardly ever saw them but I can't believe either of them would ever go traipsing out into the orchard to use the two-hole privy, they had their own furniture and carpets, they didn't always eat with us, sometimes Aunt Dot took their meals in to them, he said he had to have HP Sauce or tomato ketchup on every meal or he couldn't eat it but not at tea, we didn't get invited into their rooms very often, they were far too posh for scruffy kids who'd been mucking about on the farm all day, and if it was harvest time and there were oats or barley to be brought in from the fields, or wheat later in the summer, then we'd all be busy till dark and then it'd be bedtime. There was a washstand in every bedroom with a big china jug full of water and a china basin to wash in, soap in a soap dish with a flannel and towel hanging on the rail, and a water-glass by the washbowl. You had a cold wash in the morning when you got up, and if you'd used the chamber pot – what Grandpa in Spalding called a Guzunda – in the night then you had to empty it and wash it out in the morning, and when you emptied your dirty wash-water out you had to refill the jug yourself.

The two-holer out in the orchard was better than the Elsan at Wheaton Aston, emptied every Wednesday by the night-soil man, but it was just as cold. At Alcester we used old seed catalogues and pages from the *Farmer and Stockbreeder* and the *Farmer's Weekly* or the newspaper, the ink sometimes came off on your fingers, *Picture Post* was awful that way, and on your bum as well I expect but none of us looked. There was a nub end of candle in there too and some matches, the paper stiff and scratchy wouldn't crumple properly, much worse than the stiff Jeyes toilet paper we had at Wheaton Aston, *that* came in little boxes that you stuck on the wall, the boxes gave out one piece of paper at a time, smooth and shiny on one side and a bit rough on the other, ever so thin but tough, that's what you always found in Public Conveniences, trains, schools, places like that, and sometimes when you used it it *hurt*. Mum liked her toilet paper that way, it was the way things *were*, she hated the soft smooth stuff you get nowadays, and I never did understand that until, to my somewhat prurient amusement, in *Harper's* magazine I came across extracts from governmental memoranda between Sir Daniel Thomson and Sir Graham Wilson, who were working to revise the British Standard Guidance for Large-Scale Purchasing of Toilet Paper. Wilson, who was chief bacteriologist at the London School of Hygiene and Tropical Medicine, established via lab tests that "there is no question that the present government issue is superior to the soft toilet paper under discussion" and, no doubt, that the disinfectant permeating Bronco and Jeyes really worked. Even now that faintly carbolic smell of toilet paper conjures damp whitewash on old bricks and cold air, calling forth the sheer *wrongness* of the soft, of indulgent comfort.

One of our jobs on the farm was to make sure there was always paper in the privy, now and again we'd forget and you'd see Uncle Tom or Aunt Dot with a very annoyed look trudging across into the orchard from the house, a bunch of paper in hand, "You forgot again!" they'd say angrily, "and it's your job to remember! What if we forgot to milk the cows or cook your Dinner? What would happen then?" but we never did learn, if you didn't need to go you didn't think about the need for paper, and it didn't run out very often. Uncle Tom would hang the seed catalogues on a nail just inside the door, they lasted a long time and they were good to read, you could look at the pictures before you tore the page out and wiped yourself. Some farms had three- or even four-holers, mainly for the labourers, but Kinwarton Farm just had a two, you'd always knock on the door in case there was a woman in there, and sometimes there'd be two of us, Uncle Tom and me or me and Dad in there, and you'd sit and talk companionably about what you'd been doing or still had to be done, or even about the War, but the War was a long way away, the closest targets miles away, probably Birmingham, and I don't remember ever hearing an air raid siren at the farm. There was always a bag of chloride of lime in the corner and a bottle of strong-smelling disinfectant, but we didn't have to look after that at all, that was one of the grown-up jobs like topping up the Valor stove in the winter, there were two or three of those about the farm, sometimes one'd be used in a corner of the barn as a sort of incubator to keep the chicks warm, a tall black tin cylinder with a pattern cut in the top which cast shadows on the ceiling, flimsy looking things really, with a name like "Aladdin" or "Magic" stamped in the side or on the top, comforting warm paraffin smell when they were going, they drank up a lot of oxygen and threw out a lot of heat. Stanley Spencer's got one in his big double-nude painting done in 1937, the fireglow visible through the mica in the door, in the 1980s the instant I saw it at the Tate I had to shake myself, the farm at Alcester conjured into my head, the warm stuffiness of paraffin swelling the back of my nose.

What we did have to do was fill the oil lamps once a week and keep the wicks trimmed, that was a pleasant enough job, a bit smelly, you could do it sitting at the table but you had to be very careful not to spill the paraffin, not let it overflow, and of course it wasn't the sort of job you could do sitting by the fire. You'd spread a newspaper out on the table and take the glass chimney off, wipe all the soot out of it, turn the wick up to find out how much there was left, wicks weren't easy to come by and if you trimmed them carefully they didn't burn at all or hardly, but the ends often got ragged and then they'd sputter a bit and go smoky because you had to use too much wick so it wouldn't go out. You'd trim it carefully with a pair of sharp scissors, and then you'd take the cap off the brass tank at the bottom of the lamp and dip a bit of wood, a spill from the fireplace was best, to see how much was left, and then you'd top it up carefully through a little brass funnel, you'd do all the lamps, I can't remember how many there were but quite a few, you needed a really steady hand to pour, and then you'd check all the candles in the candlesticks, most of them highly polished brass, round with a little handle at the side, one or two with brass snuffs hooked on a peg on the saucer-shaped base, but mostly we pinched candles out, you'd learned how to do that without burning yourself the first time you went to the farm, it was a matter of pride and if you did it that way properly, licking your fingers, it stopped the candle smoking and smelling when you'd done it. And you'd clean off all the extra wax and trim the wick down so the candle wouldn't gutter and smoke.

Some of the paraffin lamps came with a fancy milk-glass shade that fitted over the chimney and a glass reservoir instead of a brass tank so you could see what you were doing, but we didn't use them so much, they were too fragile and awkward and went in the best room where they could look a bit posh. Major and Mrs Partridge had one or two, but they looked after their own lamps. It was a disaster if you broke a chimney because you couldn't get another one for love or money, if people had spares they hoarded them and there weren't any in the shops, even if people had electricity they always had candles and oil lamps for emergencies, even in the city, hurricane lamps in the outbuildings just in case. We saved the melted wax off the candles, but I've no idea what for, we didn't make candles with it, it must have been useful somewhere round the farm. Anything made out of oil or petrol was precious, you didn't throw it away, not in the War, any more than you'd throw away bits of string or paper, and I was absolutely shocked, I couldn't understand it at all, when in my last undergraduate year at Nottingham, in 1955, I read in some magazine or other a young American poet named Katherine Hoskins talking about how much she looked forward to "a world without monuments and where one didn't save string," a world of "present rationality and charm. Wherein the ego has learned grace and poetry and uses them." That still strikes me as witless arrogance, its arrant nonsense still profoundly disturbs me, catches my mental breath. Part of the job when doing the oil lamps was to keep count of how much oil and how many candles were left, and to make sure Uncle knew when to get more, he couldn't always, so you had to be careful with it, and the habit remains, deeply ingrained.

25

Milk and Apples

I was hanging about the barnyard, nobody about and nothing much to do once we'd brought the cows in and Fred came out of the cowshed. "Y'want to milk a cow, then? Y'been askin'." He nodded, his big gappy-toothed smile. I looked at him. I'd been nattering off and on about that for ages and ages but nobody'd said anything and I'd just about given up *I'm just being a pest*, I thought it'd never happen. "Oh!" I said, "Oh yes!" and thought he meant I could perhaps learn tomorrow, have a lesson, time to get ready for it. "C'mon, then," he said, and *that* was a shock. "You mean *now*?" "O'course," he said, "No time like the present," and he paused as I caught my breath. "Nothin' to be afraid of. You can 'ave Gertie. She's nice and quiet. She knows you, seen you lots of times," and right away I felt more at ease. In the pasture you could walk right up to that gentle plodding beast and give her a slap to get her moving, she'd hardly even bother to turn her head and look at you, placid dark eyes not even puzzled, imperturbable and somehow friendly. "She 'asn't been milked yet," he added.

As I walked with Fred towards the cowshed I saw Daphne through the door and my step faltered, but Mario came up to me Joe right behind him, *Where did they come from?* Mario grinned, he was tying knots in the corners of his hanky and shoved it at me, "Is clean" he said, he gestured towards his nose and fluttered the fingers on his right hand a bit, "Not used" and Fred said "Yes you'll need that," and took it from me, and put it over my hair as we went into the dairy to wash up. "I'll start 'er," he said, "and I'll 'ave to strip 'er, that needs practice. But you can do the middle bit. C'mon" and as we got to the big galvanised sink with all the hoses dripping he said "You've seen us wash the udders 'aven't you," he said. "You've got to disinfect your 'ands too," and he poured this stuff into a small enamel bowl it turned the water in it all cloudy and suddenly I was overwhelmed with that inescapable dairy smell I associated with just-washed tile floors, slightly pungent and completely unforgettable, redolent of udder-wash and milk, a bit like Bronco toilet paper, some sort of phenol, mild carbolic catching in the nose, "It's terrible on your skin, soft like yours," he said, "better make sure you wash it off proper when we're done," and I looked at his hands, I'd never really looked at them before, rough and scarred and deeply wrinkled, crazed, shiny skin between some of the wrinkles, and wondered if that was why they were like that. They didn't look sore though, just *used* a lot, calloused, dirt from farming ingrained into the cracks and pores, his nails all uneven, ridged and creased with black, *he* didn't worry about his cuticles, pushing them back the way Mum kept telling us to.

"Oh, ar," Fred said as we walked into the cowshed, "Daphne's started. I'll be off, then," and he turned, "I'll be about." And he just walked off, leaving me alone with her and all the cows, the other Land Girl milking at the far end of the cowshed. For a moment I couldn't breathe, I looked about me to see if anybody else was there. Daphne looked up with a smile and said "Good! You're here," sitting on her three-legged stool milking Gertie, a bucket propped between her legs, two or three cats hanging about along with everybody else *Oh no! they all know what's going on* and then *They all stayed out of the dairy so I wouldn't see them! I don't want them watching*. The butterflies started up in my stomach and I didn't know where to look. "C'mon you lot, can't 'ave you lurking about in 'ere," Fred said *He hadn't left at all!* "there's work to do" and he winked at Daphne, as Uncle Tom told the Eyeties to get on with something or other. Aunt Dot said she'd got to get busy in the kitchen, Fred said "I'll be about" this time he meant it, and he walked off. Almost at once there was just the two of us, me and Daphne, her as trim and neat as ever, and she looked up and smiled, a real smile all friendly, "Fetch that stool from the next stall and we can both sit. Don't come too close behind or she'll kick at you. That's what cows do!" and as I came back she got up and said "You sit here, then. There's nothing to it really, but your hands'll get a bit tired till you get used to it." I sat on the stool and hitched it a bit closer, as I shifted my weight the stool got a slight wobble and I hesitated a bit as I put my head against the Gertie's flank the way Daphne'd been doing, "Let it *rest* there, it won't bother Gertie," she said, "Put a bit of weight on it then you won't get a sore neck. Your hair'll be alright, that's what Mario's hanky's for." She reached round, her right hand close to mine, and there right under my face was the big dense curve of Gertie's belly, the close-packed bright almost-orange hairs brushed in swirls as the belly sloped down, tiny little patches of yellowy white hair getting wider and wider and then the bulge of her huge udder blotchy pinky-white, big blue veins threading and pulsing under stretched-tight skin I could almost see through, I lifted my head a bit so I could see her teats properly, all swollen and firm-looking from Daphne starting to milk her and there was a sudden little breeze wafting across my face from the door, Mario's shadow in it where he was watching, and the sudden cool made me realise how warm Gertie was. I'd never been so close to a big animal, my face like this, the smell of Gertie's hide, the prickle of sweat where my head rested against her, the sheer size of her, all *bulk*, the spattering of mud and stuff on her legs and sides, her back hoof looking so small under all that weight crushing the straw into a dimple like a saucer on the floor, the smell of the glistening straw, then a sudden catch of ammonia as Gertie let go a stream of yellow piss behind her, cats scattering, the air dusty with straw or hay but clean-smelling with it all, even the piss. I looked up and Daphne smiled at me, a grin really, and I reached my hand round one of the teats, smooth wrinkly softness a bit like an old woman's skin I couldn't believe how warm it was *It feels so alive!* and I let it go right away, it flopped about a bit even if it was all swollen with milk and firm it felt completely strange, and she laughed "It feels funny doesn't it? But you've got to hold it firmly, put your fingers round the top like this" and she put her hand over mine and squeezed a slightly rippling motion downwards as she pulled "Both teats, you ninny. But not at once!" and she laughed, I didn't mind her calling me that *of course you use both hands!* I'd seen cows being milked often enough, squeeze-pull one teat then the other, and out comes a squirt of milk! I flinched a bit and laughed as a stream of hot milk straight from the cow went all over my shoe. Daphne reached down and shifted the pail a bit and said "Hold it against your leg," some milk already in the pail *I mustn't knock it over!* concentrate like mad or I can't even begin to do it properly, *pay attention Booby!,* but the sound of the milk squirting tinnily against the side of the pail or even better into the milk making a light froth as it squirped and squelched a bit turned the whole business into a wonderful kind of music and I lost the rhythm of it as I listened, my hand slipped and Daphne told me "Switch to the other teats" my hands beginning to get tired I wondered if they were too small and she looked at me I was a bit out of breath and said "That's pretty good, that is. Keep going until it's time to switch and then let me take over, you can have a rest. You can do it again tomorrow. Well done!"

As I moved away my back and shoulders ached, I stretched and hurt and Uncle Tom *Where did he come from?* said "There's no need to get tense, you know. Gertie's a very contented cow" and Daphne looked up and laughed and said "Look!" and squirted a great stream of milk over one of the cats, "Want a drink?" and the cat shook itself and licked away at its fur. "Lovely warm milk!" but I wasn't so sure about that, a stream of milk straight out of an animal into my mouth I might choke. Brenda had a ladle from the dairy in her hand she dipped it into the bucket and took a sip, "It's lovely" but I still couldn't do it and turned away, Tom's voice making me jump "Yes, well, that's alright. I don't like hot milk either." *Blimey, they all really were watching!* that must have shown on my face and Dot said "That was very good, Peter; you've learned how to milk a cow. That's really helpful!" but of course I hadn't, I hadn't really done much at all, didn't know how to start or strip. Yet at least I'd started.

But whenever I went back to help with the milking the next few weeks Fred or Daphne kept a cautious eye on me and I got more and more uneasy and started to go less often, I'm not at all sure why, everyone keeping an eye on me, perhaps I was sick of being watched all the time, perhaps I was worried I was being more trouble than help, even a bit squeamish I suppose though goodness knows what of. And of course the milking had to be done, there was no getting away from that. Daphne said I should learn to start as well as strip, and of course I couldn't just go milking when I felt like it, Mrs Bailey's *You're not here just to enjoy yourself* sounding in my head, and it soon got to be a lot of pother. Mavis always kicked about when you started milking her, she loved to tread on her milkers or knock the bucket over and you had to be pretty sharp, such a big animal I didn't like to go near her at all, Fred or Daphne or Uncle Tom tried to look after her but couldn't always, even though in the cowshed I never got near her if I could help it, she always made me nervous. Yet when I thought about it, especially when I was back at School or back at home in Brum, I loved the idea of it, the thought of Gertie or Bessie or in memory even Mavis as I leaned up into them to enjoy their warm animal smell, their hide a prickly silk combination of smooth and rough, and that idea persists still. It doesn't take much to send me back there, even a whiff of warm milk, and when in the early 1950's I read D.H. Lawrence's description of, was it Tom Brangwen in *The Rainbow*, seeking comfort among the cattle in the barn, I was knocked for a loop it struck such a familiar chord. Even now as I write this I can feel the warmth radiating from that complete *otherness* of the cow, that flow of quiet energy profoundly indifferent to my own, the sheer uncompromising physicality obscurely disturbing no matter how familiar as I chivvied cows about in the fields or when I milked one, the idea of it, that mild oiliness building up on my skin as I pulled on those teats, it sticks between my fingers near the knuckle joints as I sit and think on it, the yellow inside of Gertie's ears, Fred calling them Alderneys and Daphne's odd rebuke "They don't call them that any more, they're Guernseys."

I suppose I gave up partly because I knew I was more a hindrance than a help, I thought Fred and Daphne kept an eye on me all the time because I wasn't doing it properly, they always made sure I'd stripped the cow dry, and they never thanked me any more or said I was doing alright. And I never did get up in time for milking in the early morning. And when milking was over at the end of the day, I hadn't finished when I'd finished, there was still cleanup, mucking out and hosing down the cowshed and dairy, and all the records to keep, what each cow had yielded, how many gallons of milk we'd got in the churns at the end of the day, what supplies were low. All of us mucked in to get it done of course, but that meant milking a cow wasn't something special any more, and neither was I. What puzzles me now is that I never got tired of other chores on the farm though of course I didn't have to do any bookkeeping, and people could leave us kids alone to get on with our chores, took it for granted we'd simply get on with them, I hadn't had to be taught but just shown once how to do whatever it was I was to do, any one of us could do it and we did, we were working together even when we weren't. Some jobs really did go better with two or more of us no matter who, thinning the beets one of you working on each side of a row, or haymaking and harvesting, tossing a sheaf of corn up to whoever's in the cart, making their job easier by chucking it the right way round, sweatily grinning looking at each other when the cart was fully loaded, almost too heavy for the horses, almost too high to get on or off, a hard clamber up the tailgate a helping hand reaching down, the ache of relief to lie on top of the load, the quiet jingle of harness, the smell of ripe corn, the plod of great big hooves, the whuffle of the horses' breath as they pulled us from the field, bumpety-bump along the lane, across the road, back to the farm, the adventure of hanging on as the load began to shift and stir, sharing a jar of cider or cold tea or even juice. The sharing.

And when we got to the rick yard all we had to do was unload the harvest, stack the sheaves properly, a nice steady pace, build a proper rick so Fred could thatch it. We didn't have to count, or weigh, or measure anything. We did a lot of counting and stocktaking anyway, eggs, apples, pears, and plums as well as milk, big set of scales in the barn but you couldn't trust the kids with that, the government kept its eye on everything because of the War, chickens, pigs, cattle, potatoes, sacks of grain, how full the granary bins were and how much hay. The farm had quotas to meet and needed to send stuff to market, so we had to keep records, a lot of paper work, sometimes the Ministry of Food or someone would send an official of some sort, never anybody local and always a stranger, to inspect the records, make sure you weren't cheating, Uncle Tom always behind in his paperwork, overflowing untidy piles on the big roll-top desk in his office under the stairs. If there was a big crop the records were especially important, but even more impossible to keep, and farmers swopped lots of things with each other to get round the rationing, cheese if they made any, or a bit of bacon if they'd managed to kill a pig without the Ministry noticing, fruit. You were allowed to kill one pig a year, some people managed to get away with two, but the Ministry was very strict about it, fined you a lot of money, you might even go to jail. If a pig just up and died on you then you had a ton of paperwork to do before you got off "They're not allowed to die!" Uncle Tom said, civil servants and inspectors pestering you no end, making it really hard to get any work done.

If fruit was spoiled or badly bruised you couldn't send it to market you had to preserve it or give it to somebody who would, or eat it, or feed it to the pigs. One of us kids' jobs was to go once a week to the apple rooms on the top floor of the farmhouse right up under the roof, sometimes two of us'd go together though there wasn't much chance of that with so many jobs to get on with, you'd find and clear away rotten apples and pears. They'd once been bedrooms, two of them still had flowery wallpaper, big pale frowzy blooms glimmering pinkly on the walls, faded patches showing where pictures or a mirror once hung. With the fireplaces closed off there was no heat up there, but it was dry, it never really froze hard, just a touch of frost on the inside of the window, scraps of curtain offering a bit of insulation, no water pipes to freeze and burst, the slight warmth from our daily life drifting up from downstairs. The rooms were filled with row after row of open wooden shelves, slats with gaps between them, stacked from the bare wooden floor almost to the ceiling. In the middle of winter you could pick up a slightly wizened apple, not much to look at, slightly soft and spongy and wrinkly all over, dry to the touch, pippins, Cox's Orange were the best, when you bit into one the skin dimpled away from your teeth little ridges in the skin opening up as they pressed against your tongue your lick tasted of apple you'd bite harder the apple yielding within its skin, the skin stretching a bit as it resisted and then your teeth broke through to the firm slightly doughy flesh underneath, not crisp and hard but a soft welcome, a quick little rush of juice mildly tasting of orange and apple. As you chewed it tasted better and better, stronger and stronger, much better to eat then than when just picked off the tree. Eat it slowly.

After apple picking we'd take buckets and trugs of apples up to the storerooms and lay them out carefully on the racks making sure they didn't touch each other, because if one went bad any apple touching it would go bad too, bruised apples would go in almost no time and so would some that had borers or other insects in them. I could just about reach the middle of each rack, the lower ones anyway, without standing on a chair or teetering over in this cold room, cold even in the summer, surrounded by the smell of hundreds and hundreds of apples. Whenever I opened the door to the attic stairs and started up I'd take a deep sniff, the scent of the apples getting stronger and stronger as I got higher and higher, sometimes quite a few of the apples would all start to go at once a penetrating fermenting smell heady and delicious, and I'd tell Uncle Tom and he'd come up and say yes, these'll have to be cider, I'll make arrangements. They'd be pressed into juice somewhere else, and a new barrel of cider'd join the four already in the cellars to ferment and age away all winter, they were about three feet across, and each year one of them would slowly empty through the summer, jugful after jugful of aged cider taken out every midday to the men bringing in the harvest. When we were big enough to wield a pitchfork, hard physical work, we'd get to drink it too, and those rooms upstairs smelled just the same as good aged cider, there was always a rotten apple or two somewhere in a corner, wizened and brown and smelly to flavour the air, and it was a precious weekly ritual, going up to inspect the apples, we were all super careful not to bruise the apples and pears or to mark them so they'd keep through the winter, and I remember seeing the same thing when I stayed at other people's farms, Robin Salmon's or Tom White's after the War. My memories of the apples there and at Uncle Tom's are all mingled up together as the body remembers the savour of it. I was cutting up an apple for lunch just the other day, the pleasure of insect prints round the stem, black borehole down to the core, dark shadows and cobwebby lace round the seeds, suddenly the apple room and the cider barrels emphatically before me as I cut, *if the insects like it it must taste good*. So much better than those Disneyfied apples that fill the shops with their bland perfection. All the farms with orchards had fruit-storage rooms and all of them tasted different, even the old disused one in the attic at Rushall House at School in Brewood. Mr Hawkins had another room for storing fruit somewhere on the School Farm, but he kept that firmly locked so marauding kids couldn't just help themselves.

Every year late in April when we got back to School after the Easter holidays we'd find the tiny apples and pears'd firmly set on the trees espaliered right inside the Gates along the walls of Rushall House and Prep School, and within the week once we'd all settled back into dormitory life a handful of bigger kids without fail'd sneak across the grass in the twilight, the grass in front of the trees totally Out of Bounds, they had to keep a sharp lookout, really in for it if they got caught, and with a pin they'd scratch NUNC in the smallest letters they could manage on those minuscule green apples and pears. They were so secret about it most of us had no idea when they were doing it or even what they were doing before it was done, though word soon got around afterwards. It was an old ritual, some mornings you might even see a Prefect, Prefects were allowed on the grass, look closely with one of his pals at some of the fruit, nod, say something quiet. Despite their knowing looks the rest of us stayed not in the know, we pretty well forgot all about it from one year to the next. You couldn't see the scratches at all without a magnifying glass, just a faint roughness on the skin catching the light if you were at the right angle. But of course as the weeks went by the fruit got bigger and bigger, and by the end of May if you looked at the fruit hanging there in full sight and knew what to look for you'd see over and over again the scratched letters, on dozens and dozens of apples and pears, NUNC NUNC NUNC NUNC NUNC NUNC NUNC endlessly repeating itself, here and there just NU and a straggly N or C trailing off where somebody nearly got caught, NUNC marching over and over up and down what branches were within a big kid's reach, growing and ripening fruit hanging against and over those walls. Then in Big School, when you'd think anybody with a pair of eyes in his head must ages ago've noticed NUNC written on all that fruit, the whole School still assembled after we'd finished Prayers, the hymns all sung and all the announcements yet to be made, the Masters standing alongside Mr Bailey on the stage, the Prefects at the side alert for miscreants, even Matron standing just inside the door, and that meant something really *was* up, the subdued furtive stirring among the kids died down completely as the door down by the stage softly opened to let Nunc himself in, careful tread in heavy boots, to stand next the Prefects. Without looking at him one or two kids scowled and shuffled themselves away, so did one of the Prefects. In the breathless silence Nunc glared crossly round at all of us the whole school assembled there, looked up at the stage and nodded just once, an abrupt jerk. Mr Bailey nodded back and leaned forward, his fingers splayed a little on the table before him as he looked down at us.

"You are outrageous," he said in a quiet voice, "and I'm ashamed of you. *All* of you!" We knew perfectly well what he was talking about. "*None* of you deserves to be at this School!" And from his lofty vantage he looked round the whole room, slowly. His gaze settled on a kid in one of the rows ranged below him. After a moment it moved on, paused again. Row after row. A head bobbed. A foot shuffled. "That includes you, Colbourne!" I didn't dare move, held my gaze on the back of the head in front of me, shifted my weight, held my breath as Mr Bailey's pale blue eye picked me out, down there close to the front row *I haven't even* done *anything!* His eye moved on. "Mr Whitehouse is worth the whole lot of you!" he said. "You *must* treat him with proper respect. I have told him," he said, and he raised his right hand and brought it down with the beat, "I have *told* him that without *fail* I shall strictly punish *any one* of you who does not treat Mr Whitehouse with proper respect. *Any*where. No matter *who* you are. And I am now telling *you*." I thought of the dorm raid when he caned us all, and I remembered Gravette. "And I shall punish you se*verely*." He said that the spoilage of food *That's what you're doing, writing on pears and apples* is criminal waste, *worse* *than shameful! Far worse!* especially when the whole country is fighting an enemy intent on destroying us all and everything England stands for. Nunc nodded again, his emphatic breath and his raggedy moustache, his compressed lips, his sharp blue eyes, he held at his waist the cap he always wore, and I turned my head and looked at him. His dark blue waistcoat and his collarless white shirt, almost his market-day best it looked like, but with his sleeves rolled up and dark trousers, a bit of baling twine tied round each leg just below the knee he suddenly reminded me of Fred, back at Alcester. I *liked* Fred, I liked his abruptness and his no-nonsense ways, I wouldn't dare treat Fred the way we treated Nunc, and I felt a bit abashed, a sudden rush of feeling, Nunc *belonged* here, one of *us*, in the School.

But that didn't stop me a couple of hours later as soon as Break started from rushing along with everybody else to look at what I'd already seen, the fruit with its burden of NUNC NUNC NUNC. A lot of the dayboys hadn't known about that, hadn't noticed it at all till Mr Bailey said what he'd said at Prayers, and I felt a kind of awed pride, a real sense of belonging, us boarders one-up on the daykids, *Look at this one, then! And hey, there's even more up there!* All of them done by we knew not who though we'd glimpsed their knowing looks, and Nunc not around to see us point the others through this wonder and lay claim to it, each of us secure in the safety of our numbers to claim a tiny share in the secret that wasn't really ours, to strut our smidgen of reflected glory, safe from Nunc's wrath and Mr Bailey's disapproval. But on the School grounds Nunc had no power of his own beyond his wrath, and we loved baiting him no matter how scary he was, that was a real dare. He lived with his son Alf, we called him "Young Nunc" but not to his face, in a cottage on School Road next door to Mr Hawkins, it belonged to the School and was part of the School grounds, but you couldn't get directly to his cottage from the School without going through the farm and then his back garden. His garden was *private*, it was *personal*, where *he* lived, not us. We'd all had *An Englishman's home is his castle* drummed into us since the cradle, you couldn't invade *that*. That's what the War was all about, and if we had a reason to go to his cottage, had been sent or invited, then we had to go the long way round, out the School Gates and up School Road. School Road didn't go anywhere except to itself really, whyever would you want to go there if you hadn't been sent? It ended halfway along Newport Street, no shops or anything, just cottages, village territory, not ours the way School was.

Every spring, even when the whole country was busy "Digging for Victory," assiduously planting vegetables and food crops on almost every scrap of available ground, Nunc bedded salvias, pelargoniums and forget-me-nots in the big round bed in the middle of the Quad. "Can't put cabbage and carrots there," said one of the Prefects, "In the middle of all that tarmac, that bed's for *flowers* and don't say it's for anything different," we all nodded in agreement, "there's lots of room for spuds everywhere else, all over the farm for starters." When somebody argued about that at tea, Matron scolded him "We've got to have flowers, especially there, that's the entrance to the School, the whole village can see it" which of course it couldn't if it didn't come walking by past the Gates. "What would people think?" she asked. "They'll make a brave show, all that colour, cheer us up" and that was an end to the fuss, and Nunc parked his wheelbarrow right by the main door to the Headmaster's House, the posh entrance, and spread sacking over the tarmac where he was working, it took him a week, he cleaned and tidied up at the end of every day. "It looks a bit untidy but it's well worth it," Matron said, and Pussy Bailey at prayers firmly told us to keep clear of the Quad and the flowerbeds. Nunc down on his knees and his hands busy with trowels and plants, right opposite the Masters' Common Room and right outside the Headmaster's front door, kids perpetually seized this golden opportunity for a really perilous dare, and at Break and at Lunch time one small kid after another'd seize it, a small knot of small kids clustered behind the holly bush in the corner of the Quad or sheltering in the open arch of the boarders' entrance. Loud whispers, giggles, the click of a loose steel heel-tip, the slap of a leather sole, stifled mirth *No it's your turn, you've got to!* followed by *He's looking!* or *I already did!* A flurry of leaves in the holly bush *Nicks!* followed by a tentative step followed by muffled quick steps on the sacking, a child's gabbled speech to the empty air, loud enough for all of us to hear, *Hey Nunc! You're planting that upside down* or *Nunc Why are you making such a mess?* and a quick laugh as the miscreant turned away and fled back to the security of his pals. A Prefect or more rarely a Master'd come along and break it up, but even if he recognised the others now long fled he could only punish the one he'd caught red-handed. As soon as he turned his back the others'd be at it again, more and more daring, they'd creep closer and closer to Nunc's apparent indifference. We knew he couldn't do anything to us, until at last out of all patience he'd shout "You, you young b–" and he'd bite the word off, "I know who you are!" But of course he didn't, not our names anyway, and we kept at it and kept at it, one eye always open for a Master or a Prefect, until at last he'd drop what he was doing sweep his arm round behind him in a great big sweep to grab, he never missed, and held on to his victim's jumper as the others melted away, got to his feet and transfer his grip to an ear *Ow!* he didn't shift it at all *Ow! Ow!* one small kid deserted by his fellows, at the mercy of that unrelenting grip. It *scrunched* like anything, his hard heavy thumb deeply creased and ingrained, and Nunc didn't say a word, but in his heavy boots simply marched his victim off to be Dealt With, by the Housemaster or failing that a Prefect.

And we still went scrumping, over the five-barred gate right across Church Road and into the old School Orchard, you couldn't really see into it from the Quad, but dead easy to get into, and dead easy to get out of, too, but for the iron palings blocking off the Nash School playground along most of one side. That all changed when they demolished the Nash School a bit later, and that sealed off some of the escape routes, it didn't make much difference with the abandoned tennis court at the bottom of the Orchard, behind the hedge opposite the School Gate, you could scramble out in no time, escape routes almost everywhere and hardly any houses overlooking it, just as easy to get out as to get in. Once you'd got over the rickety wooden fence half way up the Orchard, which was always so noisy it made scrumping at that end especially risky, you'd reach the best trees, up at the top of the Orchard, right across from Nunc's house. You could see right through Nunc's windows, him perhaps talking to someone by the fireplace or just sitting there, if he looked out he'd easily see you, you had to be silent and you had to be quick, you'd better not be stuck halfway up a tree when he came belting out to get you. He'd shout, "I know who you are" which he would if it was a village kid, but not always us, he didn't know our names, but if he came out of his house we'd scramble like mad, frantic not to be caught, fall over each other or over big tussocks between the trees, blunder into low hanging branches, burst like mad back over the rickety fence down through the Orchard to the safety of the bottom end and then over the five-barred gate or through the hedge back into the School exhilarated and breathless with our daring, only as often as not to be caught by a Prefect who was waiting for you, and *he* knew your name alright.

What was best about scrumping was getting more apples than anybody else, no matter what they were like, and baiting Nunc into the bargain. Two or three kids'd come back into the dorm just before Lights Out, shirts and pockets stuffed with hard green apples, and once we were all in bed, lights turned off, you'd hear quiet counting *Hey I've got more than twenty*! And then *I've got lots more than that! Who wants some*? And one of them'd chuck two or three tiny apples, hard as a raw potato or even harder, at least one of them bound to rattle on the floor "You'd better pick that up, get it out of sight before Matron or somebody sees it" and for the next half-hour or so you'd hear the sound of a rock-hard apple bouncing and rolling over the floor, the soft swish of a sheet or blanket thrown back, the quiet slap of bare feet on the lino, someone on his hands and knees groping in the twilight under a bed or over by the washbasins. And once we'd all settled, everyone with four or more baby apples, we'd struggle to scoff them down, most of them so completely unbiteable that you had to mash the terrible harsh sourness between your teeth, shrivelling and furring your mouth before you could urgently spit out the sour gritty lumps, as intractably unpleasant as the swede Sam and Victor and me'd snaffle and throw out a year or two later. But we loved the excitement of it all, we weren't famished and the apples had to be got rid of somehow, and we could chuck those inedible little green horrors straight out of the dorm window for Young Nunc to find when he next raked the Headmaster's lawn.

Scrumping was like Nunc-baiting, it wasn't a caning offence unless you persisted, and the Prefects were left to deal with it. There wasn't much they could do besides dish out some lines or dragoon you into doing something useful that always needed doing, all year round, that no kid in his right mind'd ever want to do, unpleasant or just plain tedious. Like rolling the cricket pitch, the roller so heavy it'd take a whole gang just to budge. You couldn't go off and roll the cricket pitch without somebody in charge, like a Prefect, and you certainly couldn't lark about pulling and pushing that roller back and forth, a five-foot stone cylinder three feet in diameter with a six-foot wooden frame sticking out in front and behind. It took six or even eight of us to get it going, especially when the ground was wet and the roller had settled into a shallow trough of its own making. One afternoon Brian Henderson turned up late at the roller, he was the Prefect in charge, most of us shifting our weight from foot to foot on the wet grass and fidgeting about, anxious to get on with it, when Walter Jenks said "I've got better things to do than wait here all day, I bet nobody's coming, they've forgotten" and bogged off over School Bridge back to the Croft. A couple of others shrugged and began to follow him but Henderson turned up and sent them back, and we all got cross, we only had an hour to ourselves once we'd finished the rolling and we all had stuff we'd rather do. When we got ourselves ranged round the roller, Daniel and Ben pushing like mad inside the frame in front of the roller, not much room for more than two but you could see where you were going, everyone's favourite spot, and we all heaved away, we really *had* to get it moving, up and down the pitch fifty times *Keep count!* and Ben's right foot skidded back towards the looming roller, he went down on his left knee, that roller'd've crippled him for life it it'd run over him, Henderson'd just finished tucking his notebook into his pocket, he was right next to Ben, it all happened so fast and somebody at the back shouted *Tip the frame!* just as somebody else at the back heaved away to lift it so it could dig down in front, Ben looking scared *there isn't time to do anything!* and Henderson just leaned over the frame and reached down, his weight pushing the frame down in front Ben clinging madly to the frame, pale sweaty face, and Daniel scrambled like mad to get out of trouble but the frame got in his way, he couldn't move it with Henderson's weight pushing it down, the roller kept trundling its inexorable weight over the grass, kids clinging in their effort to stop it and Henderson grabbed Ben and simply heaved him up and over the frame loud *Ow!* from Ben as his knees banged on the frame and scraped over it *Get out of the way!* Daniel frantically clambering to the side as everyone else heaved like mad and the frame groaned as it dug firmly into the cricket pitch, and the roller stopped. We looked at each other. "I'll have to report this," Henderson said, he was covered in sweat, trembling a bit. "Say what happened. I'd better write your names down." He took out his notebook and pencil, it took him some time to get everything down. "I shouldn't've let that happen," he said, "and neither should you. I'll see what Mr Houston has to say. But we're all at fault, you as well as me. From now on," he wagged his finger, "*no one*, absolutely *no* one, gets inside the roller frame. Not in front, and not behind. It's far too dangerous. Ben could've been hurt, even put in hospital. Now get the roller out of the way and leave everything alone. Mr Whitehouse'll have to repair the pitch, and that'll take time, I really will have to talk to Mr Houston," and he wrote something down. "Now, get back to School."

26

Punishments

Prefects always had notebooks in their pockets, full of lists of kids and their punishments and duties, they had to organise things, they had to find enough malefactors to do whatever tasks had to be done, make sure delinquents got to do their jobs on time and did their work properly. They had to report delinquents to the Master-on-Duty, whoever that was. "When it comes to stuff like punishment," one of the kids said, "the Prefects don't have any more freedom than the wrongdoers, they have to keep an eye on us all the time." And he laughed. "They punish themselves every time, even when they dish out lines." I didn't think that was quite true but I got no pleasure from that idea, and then of all people Ticker Ranson said, as he was telling us something about *The Shadow Line*, that *responsible* has two different meanings. "One of them points to shame," he said, "and the other points to honour," and I all at once realised that Prefects take pride in their doings, they please their Masters by giving orders. *Clear up that litter!* or *Make sure the gate to Bath Field is closed properly!* or simply *Sit Down And Shut Up!* For want of anything else they could simply set you an Imposition, amending your manners. "Write out a hundred times *I must not make fun of Mr Whitehouse*, do it *neatly*, and bring it to me before Lights Out." Of course, the Prefect'd have to enter it in his notebook to make sure he remembered, and when it'd been done he'd have to check that it'd been done properly. "Prefects behave responsibly. That's why we're Prefects."

Nunc did most of the gardening and groundskeeping, except for cutting the grass. That was Young Nunc's job. "You'd better ask the young Mr Whitehouse," Matron or a Master would say if something came up. "He's the caretaker." During the day we'd see him trundling wheelbarrow after wheelbarrow of coal the two-hundred-odd yards to the furnace room from the heaps in the ruins of the old Fives Court in the far corner of the Croft. "That's not coal, that's anthracite!" Cedric Penfold scornfully said, "Can't you *tell?*" But how would *we* know. *Coal*'s what Young Nunc called it, so did pretty well everyone else, including me. But not Cedric, he was a know-it-all, he *had* to be right. And when Young Nunc swept out the classrooms after Prep, with a pail of sand along with his broom and the shovel he used as a dustpan, he'd scatter the sand round the room and between the desks, and then sweep, and for a couple of weeks Cedric led his pals in baiting the imperturbable Young Nunc. "What're you doing that for? Aren't you s'posed to be cleaning it up?" Cedric'd taunt, and even after an older kid rebuked "That's so he can see where he's swept, you doofus!" Cedric still kept at it and laughed along with his little gang; they were all a bit posh. Young Nunc was so stubbornly unresponsive, we thought he was genuinely a bit daft and that that made him impervious to our baiting. He never spoke to us kids, we never saw him chatting with someone in the village the way we occasionally might see his dad talk, perhaps to Mr Burnett or even someone like Miss Butler, he never smiled, never reacted to anything we did, except when mowing the grass. Young Nunc'd gesture us out of the way; he certainly wouldn't stop or change course, he just kept going, and you had to scramble out of his path. He didn't even grin, or look cross, or anything, and his unresponsiveness made baiting him riskier than a dare, but such a dead loss that most of us simply couldn't bother, we had better things to do. Just the same he presented such an easy target to some kids that they persisted long after the rest'd lost interest. They'd try to turn it into a real dare by jeering at him "Hey, Alf, why are you doing that *twice*? That's daft, you've already done it once!" The rudeness made for a bigger risk, if a Master heard you you'd really be in hot water. And you'd really have to pay if you got told to help Young Nunc sweep the classrooms and corridors or clean the bogs, and baiting Young Nunc sputtered to a halt when Cedric complained about a punishment he'd got. Trigger Bradbury gave Cedric two hundred lines to write, "Neatly, no mistakes, no blots, nice and clear, *in ink*: 'Without fail, I must always treat Young Mr Whitehouse with *proper respect.'* Hand them in to me tomorrow morning immediately after breakfast!" Cedric complained, his pals hanging along with him, "That's not fair! He's only the caretaker!" and Matron really gave him what for and reported him to Mr Houston. "How dare you dismiss Mr Whitehouse like that! He's worth *ten* of you snobby little weasels. Learn your manners!" Henry's disapproval mattered, Matron's disapproval rankled, and they all got Gated for two whole weeks. It was just as bad as writing NUNC on apples and pears, if not worse.

"Confined to barracks!" Basil Harding called it, but he *liked* the Army, and couldn't wait to get in, they'd be bound to make him an officer, and with relish he plonked his favourite big word alongside. "Insubordination!" he said. We all hated being Gated, and only a Housemaster or the Headmaster had the power, it really was a punishment, you couldn't leave the School grounds or even go to the playing fields or the Spinney, you certainly could not go to Mrs Roberts's shop on the corner or to the village except to Church on Sunday, and you ended up aching about the place while everyone else was free to go off and enjoy themselves, the School library'd be closed, the only place you could go, really, was out on the Croft, and by yourself that was no fun, you couldn't even go down by the canal, and you definitely couldn't get into the Art room or anywhere like that, you couldn't work on your model plane or use any sort of tools without proper supervision. "You *could* turn it into a blessing," one Prefect admonished, "and use it to get your Prep done on time!" but any kid who'd think of doing that wouldn't've got Gated in the first place. Instead of Gating you a Prefect'd give you a job to do if there was one going, and most times that wasn't really a punishment at all so long as you didn't have to help Young Nunc. We never got sent to help Nunc himself, I expect he'd have flatly refused no matter who asked him, and we didn't often get told to help Young Nunc, it must've been as much of an ordeal for him as it was for us, an unruly resentful kid assigned to help him sweep the classrooms or Big School. Getting smothered in dust with Young Nunc for company really was a punishment, the other kids standing around outside the door baiting you instead of him. When a Prefect came along to keep an eye on things, and one always did, they'd skedaddle, what a relief, *they* didn't want to end up helping Young Nunc tomorrow, so you just got on to be done with it. Underneath his flat annoyance at the jeerers' tiresomeness Young Nunc intermittently smiled to himself, not saying a word, relishing your discomfort at having to work with *him*, and you'd get mad, you couldn't do anything about him, who was *he* to be giving you orders, telling you when you'd finished and could go, he wasn't really all there, was he. And you didn't have anyone to take it out on, so you just stayed cross for the rest of the evening.

Once Broggie became Headmaster, Prefects could send a bunch of you to wash dishes in the scullery after supper, some kids called it the still-room, I rather liked the unusualness of that, using this special name showed you weren't the same as everyone else, knew something special, but I didn't say so, most of the other kids thought it was too posh. Just before lights out the Prefect on duty asked, "Did one of you leave your pullover in the still-room? There's one sitting there by the sink," and the kid in the far bed by the door snickered "That's daft! They've got a still-room at Weston Park, that's where Lord Bradford lives, but you won't find anything like that here, it's just a scullery. My grannie in West Bromwich's got one of them, so's everyone else."

Doing the dishes couldn't ever be a punishment, not even close, and it soon became a regular duty, such a wonderful break from routine that quite a few of us volunteered, working just off the kitchen in the still-room hot and steamy from the lashings of hot water in the big metal sinks. Water splashed about all over the tiled floor, at the end of our shift we snapped our sopping dishtowels as loud as we could before we hung them on the airing-rack up at the ceiling, and the potato-scraping machine continually begged to be investigated. No grown-ups about, two metal sinks so big you could climb in, not that we ever, and a big trolley to move the piles of crockery about. It was even better if you had to help in the kitchen, the maids all gone for the day and just Miss Butler or especially Cook on the rare evenings she was there, no Masters about, not even a Prefect, no supervision worth noticing. Always a bit of food in the kitchen afterwards if you'd done the work properly, and you had time for it, that was a bit of alright, in that large echoing room with its red quarry-tile floor, square deal table in the middle big enough for eight people to stand and work at. We'd get the chance to turn the big heavy handle on the potato machine, lovely noise as it rumbled away, or there'd be peas to shell, or apples to peel, small tasks like that. You could always snaffle a bit, but mostly there was no need, Cook would usually smile at you and find a bit of cake leftover from the Headmaster's tea, Miss Butler too, but none of that happened till Broggie came, Pussy Bailey long gone. With all the changes his departure brought even Miss Butler softened a bit, found small treats to reward whoever had to stay and help in the kitchen. She still managed to look a bit grumpy, and with her, it never tasted as good as it did from Cook, I don't think she liked children very much, didn't know what to do with us, was probably a bit shy and caught up in what was proper. I think, now, that she was a bit lonely, middle-aged single women didn't have much to look forward to. But of course we never thought of that, what kid would?

When we went home at Easter in 1943 I didn't get my Report Book at all though Our Kid got his alright. I didn't get any marks from Prep School. Everything to do with Prep School was unsettled. My Report Book at Christmas had been almost blank, and Mrs Bailey ran Prep School almost single-handed, no other teachers but Moggie Morris twice a week in Music. She gave me the same mark, 85, in everything, Arithmetic, Dictation, Composition and Literature, the three divisions she'd devised long ago for English, and the only other subject I got a report on was "Football," where she said I was "becoming quite keen." But she didn't give any sort of assessment. From the gaps in my Report Book, I didn't get any French at all, nor History and Geography, nor any of the sciences either, but the whole School was a bit chaotic all that term. Mr Bailey wasn't even there, we didn't see him at all, he'd just *gone*, and nobody said anything, not to us Prep School kids anyway, and nobody I asked knew anything about it at all. That's what they said, anyway. All we knew was that we had no Headmaster at all for most of the Christmas Term even though we still had Mrs Bailey in Prep School. Henry Houston took over the rest of the School, he ran Prayers every morning and looked after everything, he was in charge. In IV B, two years ahead of me, Our Kid took all the usual subjects, but in that whole year he had seven different teachers in fourteen different classes, including the Chemistry he loved. Some kids left halfway through the Term and Prep School was suddenly a lot smaller. It's obvious now, though I didn't think so at the time, that the Prep School was closing down. No wonder Mum and Dad were a bit worried, and at the end of Term that December Mrs Bailey's "General Report" sounds a distinct farewell. "He has had a very satisfactory period in the Preparatory Class," she wrote, "and I hope he will make good progress in his new school." I didn't really understand that "new school" she mentioned, but I'd heard Dad say to Mum when we were home in Hillmorton for the summer that "the fees at Rugby, just for Philip, are more than I can earn in a whole year. Besides, he wouldn't get in, and Mum's quiet voice as they closed the door, "We'll have to keep looking, Peter's too young to get into the Third Form anyway." I couldn't hear anything more, but it did begin to look as though we might be leaving Brewood. And some time later, just before we went back in September, Dad said at dinner that "Mr Bramhall was at Masons last night," he meant the Freemason's Lodge, and when I looked a bit puzzled Phil said "The geometry master, you know, at Rugby, he gave me that amazing geometry set the school got rid of." "Yes," Dad said. "Mr Bramhall told me there's a very good Prep School connected to Wrekin College in Wellington, he's taught quite a few junior boys who went there, very well prepared, he told me." He looked at Mum. "It looks like a real possibility." Mum nodded, "Wellington's quite a nice town," she said, "could you look into it?"

But I didn't want to go anywhere new, not at all. *Brewood's where all my friends are, I'm there most of the year! I don't really know anyone here, not in Hillmorton.* "Well," said Dad, "the way things are in the War, teachers in such short supply and good schools hard to find, we *have* to find out," and early in October shortly before Mr

Bailey went away I found myself, extra pocket-money dished out by Mr Bailey, on my own on the bus to Wolverhampton and then the train to Wellington, to find out what it looked like. *A lot more than fifteen miles along the Watling Street* I thought when I got off the train, that's what Henry Houston'd said it was. *More like thirty!* I thought. But of course it wasn't, it just took ages because trains were so erratic in the blitz, and I bought a glass of milk and ate my sandwich in the station refreshment room before setting out for the school, tea slopped all over the counter, stale-looking rock cakes under glass covers, me carefully shielding my mac. I had to look about me going down the street, I kept checking the sketch map Mr Houston had given me, I had no idea how he knew what the route was, and after I got past a pub on the corner and stopped to get my bearings my breath lurched when a voice said *Excuse me, young Sir* a calloused hand reached out *Pardon me, Sir, bu*t a slightly stooped man, he looked older than Dad, a worn and creased raincoat, check cap on his head, red-rimmed eyes, grey stubble on his chin, a bench behind him near the closed doorway to the pub, as he smiled his face crinkled a bit next his nose and his eyes looked up at mine, "Here," he said, "I've got *this*" and thrust some slightly crumpled pages at me, "I've got this letter" he said. "Could you please read it to me?" and he bobbed his head, turned his face away, a big man, heavy boots like a navvy, a bit scary, but he smiled again as I worried that I might be late getting to the school. *How can I possibly refuse?* "I need to know," he said. Four or five pages of cheap letter-paper, ruled, four or five pages torn from the sort of pad they sold at Woolworth's, one of the pages from a different pad, faint blue and a bit stiffer, blue paper, the handwriting nice and round like Mrs Asprey's, easy to read, lots of little drawings scattered through the words, and I started to read, the letter a warm and friendly voice, clear and no nonsense, but worried and affectionate. It must all have sounded a bit odd to anyone who listened, my child's voice, clear and proper, reading the way I read aloud in Prep School, just words, no feeling or expression at all, this woman's patient friendly voice asking if he'd been working and had he found a place to sleep, illustrated with little sketches of beds, knives, forks, plates, and cups of tea, saws and spanners, money. One of the things I'd learned reading aloud in School was to let the eye run ahead of the voice so I could keep track of the sentence, and my heart sank as I moved to the third or fourth page and two lines down big letters, in capitals not joined letters, "STAY OFF" and an unmistakable sketch of a pint dimple mug, foam lapping over the edge, "BEER" near its handle, and for a fleeting second I thought that if I said "stay off the beer" or "don't drink" to him he'd get angry, punishment of a whippersnapper, *who was I to tell him not to drink?* I took a deep breath and I rushed on through, and when I'd finished he took the letter back and shuffled through the pages, pointed to that sketch and said "Yes" and I said, "I have to go" and turned away. He folded the letter carefully into his pocket and "I thank you kindly," he said, he bobbed his head.

The sign outside the school is really the only other thing I remember about that trip. Discreet dark-painted wood, small lettering, "Old Hall Preparatory School" followed in even smaller letters "Founded 1845," a coat of arms underneath, with the motto *aut vincere, aut mori*. After I said who I was I was turned over to a posh-looking kid, he might've been a bit older than me but I don't think so, he might've been ten, in a spotless dark blue blazer with the same badge that I'd seen on the notice-board sewn on the breast pocket, a sharp crease in his long grey trousers, neatly pressed like Dad's when he went to work. None of my pals wore long trousers yet, and I was a bit envious of Our Kid because Mum and Dad'd said he might get some next year, if they could find any and had enough clothing coupons, and my escort blinked a bit and sniffed when he saw my somewhat runkled green blazer with its Brewood badge, *virtute industria doctrina* sewn on its pocket. Once we were alone together he asked "What are you like in a scrum?" and I must've looked a bit baffled, "Don't you play rugger at School?" he asked, he sounded surprised, and after I explained that we played soccer instead he asked, "What's the tennis like? Do you like grass? I prefer a hard court like shale, but we've got both." I couldn't very well explain that all we had was a dank overgrown plot of grass and a rotting net beside the orchard outside the Gates, and said "we play cricket." And he sniffed. If I'd told him I didn't at all like organised team-games like cricket or soccer, with official scores and referees and such, and only enjoyed the sort of scratch games we played on the Croft, he'd've looked down at me, and we'd've ended up with nothing to talk about. Our conversation didn't improve when he asked me about Greek and Latin and I told him we didn't have either and we fell silent until we turned a corner. "There's the library," he said. "That building" and he pointed. I started to say "Yes" but that was so daft that I changed into a gargled sort of "Oh!" and asked him "What books do you like?" and right away we found we both enjoyed stories about the Navy, especially Percy F Westerman, and we at last began to chatter a bit. He told me about their Prefect and Monitor system, and their privileges, and about fagging for the older boys. "We don't have any bullying here, certainly not" but I didn't believe him. Our Kid and me'd read *Tom Brown's School Days*, Grandfather had given it for Christmas, one of his favourite books for boys, Flashman vivid in our minds, and of course we devoured stories about Billy Bunter at Greyfriars School, all of us at Brewood did, we knew all about the tyranny of the immaculate. Old Hall School was so tidy, so was the town, everything even in the War manicured and bright paint wherever my escort took me, everyone terribly polite and restrained, nothing out of place. I thought of Little Marlow, grandmother and grandfather.

As it turned out, Dad discovered we couldn't afford it anyway, and once Mr Bailey resigned, before the Board of Governors could dismiss him for "professional misconduct," things at School settled down more. The grown-ups, staff as well as teachers, began to insist we live up to the School's motto, especially the *Industria* bit, but Mrs Bailey's strict hand eased up a bit. Beyond the vaguest of innuendoes I knew absolutely nothing about Bailey's misdemeanours and trial, not then or after, and in 2005 Meredith and I scoured through old copies of the *Staffordshire Advertiser* and the *Express and Star* in the newspaper library at Colindale to find out. What a tedious process that was, us not knowing whether it was in 1943 or 1944. At School we all knew about his sentence, we heard that as soon as it was passed, but of course there was no way I'd remember the date, I only had my School Report Book to go on, and it turned out Bailey didn't go to trial until March 1944 when he'd been gone – he might even have been in custody – since the middle of October. Broggie'd been the new Headmaster since January and he'd been with us for the best part of a whole Term before Bailey's trial even started, but none of us knew any details or even what was going on at all. I didn't anyway, nor did the other younger kids like me. It's amazing how we were kept in ignorance. I've no idea whether villagers kept the newspapers out of our hands on purpose or whether papers simply weren't around, but we didn't see any reports at all. Newsprint was very short during the War, and newspapers very thin, sometimes just two sheets of paper to make eight pages, and there were never many copies of the *Staffordshire Advertiser* at the newsagent's, it didn't enjoy many casual sales, people mostly got it delivered or got it by post if they got it at all. After all, who'd want to read stories about soldiers home on leave or about weddings if *they* weren't mentioned, or all the reports of cattle prices? But all at once, with Mr Bailey out of the picture, people in the village shut their mouths when you walked into a shop, copies of *The Express and Star* not around at all when they usually were. And if a couple of us Juniors came in to the Billiard Room the cluster of older boys standing at the radiator under the window'd drop their voices and talk in hushed tones, carefully fold a bit of newspaper into their pocket. Somehow we knew it had something to do with Mr Bailey and the black market, perhaps they told us that, but us younger kids were kept in ignorance. The cover-up was pretty thorough, though some of the dayboys looked all knowing, they'd've heard their parents going on about it, hushed voices or not, and for a long time, long after I'd left School and started university, I really did believe he'd gone to jail for black market activities. I had no notion whether a seven-year sentence for Black Marketing was excessive or not, that story was part of the cover-up, it certainly made sense to me and my pals, all those cherries and other treats. But Mum and Dad were obviously worried and reassured when Henry Houston became acting Headmaster till the end of 1943, when a new Headmaster was properly appointed by the Board of Governors.

Quite a lot of parents threatened to take their kids away and even more must have tried to find somewhere else, Henry Houston must've found it all utterly dismaying, it was him really that as Acting Headmaster held the School together in that funny limbo time before Broggie took over in January 1944. Mum told me later that the Governors'd offered the job to Henry and he'd turned it down. He'd been at Brewood longer than anyone except Mr Bailey, the two of them had wrought "a remarkable change in the school," building it up from "no more than sixty boys" in the early 1930s when Henry arrived to well over a hundred in 1940 and it kept on growing after that, it was under Bailey that the school had managed just before the War to build the wooden classrooms on the edge of the Croft and the Dining Hall, and it may have been him that installed a proper Science lab with proper laboratory scales, a fume cupboard and multiple gas taps and Bunsen burners at every bench so the kids could do proper chemistry and physics experiments, there were even two or three decent microscopes. Mr Bailey must somehow've raised the money for all that. In those days Headmasters not the County Board of Education looked after School finances, and Bailey really did set the school on its feet again. "The school now justifies its place in the education scheme of the county," the Inspectors from the Staffordshire Board of Education and Whitehall said after they spent three days at Brewood in 1940, and those words suggest the school had been in real danger of being closed down. I got that quote from newspaper reports of Bailey's trial, and all parties at the trial seem to have agreed that Bailey, when he became Headmaster in 1933 after first joining the school in 1919, had damaged his health he'd worked so hard to bring the school up to what the inspectors called "Satisfactory organisation and adequate number of staff." His defence counsel painted him as a fundamentally decent man, Bailey hadn't tried to brazen it out or accuse the boys of lying and was obviously shamed, horrified and contrite at what he'd done, throwing himself on the mercy of the court. I think he turned himself in.

Not that any of this any more than the letters from parents and old boys written on his behalf helped when it came down to Mr Bailey's sentence, it looks like the judge threw the book at him, gave him seven years for indecent assault and two years for gross indecency, the sentences to run concurrently. Bailey, *The Express and Star* said, looked "stunned" by the sentence. I suppose he thought that with his counsel's eloquence and his own respectability, his good record, and his status in the village, he'd get quite a bit less, to say nothing of his turning himself in, but whatever privilege he might have felt owed him couldn't survive the thirty-nine counts in the indictment; he really couldn't wriggle out of twenty-five of them by pleading not guilty the way he did, the Judge in any case agreeing with the prosecution that these counts should be held on file because Mr Justice Mcnaghten had read the depositions, and there's no need to wash all that dirty linen in public. In any case he probably lost all chance of leniency when the police Superintendent informed the court that he could find no record at all of the B.Sc. degree Bailey claimed to have got at London University, that sort of lie would've been seen as a complete betrayal of the class he laid claim to, and that bit of information simply turned him into a fraud no matter what good he'd done. The trial, much like the newspaper reports, after getting the facts straight seems to have been devoted to character witnesses on Bailey's behalf, he'd "behaved himself with perfect propriety" up until the middle of 1941, that's just about exactly the time I first went to Brewood, Our Kid'd been there for eighteen months by then, and he did tell me, when Meredith and I were tracking down the details, that he thought he knew one of the kids who was involved but he couldn't be sure. Nobody talked about it, and I was far too young for any of it to mean anything to me, sex was so completely *terra incognita* that pretty well all I knew about it was from cocky Morris West back when I was seven telling everyone, after lights out in Dormitory One, that "your dad sticks it into your mum." There was nothing in our biology books or classes. I certainly couldn't ask Mum and Dad about it, I wouldn't've dared venture into that forbidden territory, a kind of universally enforced or obligatory dumbness that made me and Our Kid in later years completely stupid when it came to girls. "We didn't know what to do or how to talk to them," Phil reflected fifty years later when we talked about this on the phone, and we're neither of us much good when it comes to saying how we feel.

"You as Headmaster of the school," said Mcnaghten, "standing *in loco parentis* with regard to the boys entrusted by parents to your care, for the gratification of your own filthy lust debauched these boys." There were seven of them altogether, aged eleven to fifteen, and what lies behind those words haunts me, what his lawyer called "his terrible curse," I can't keep it out, the thought of those young kids with Bailey, what he did, how did it start, and his own torment, the terrible first step, the element of sheer terror on both sides, the pile-up of disgusted shame and no doubt revulsion at the body's sexuality, the utter sheer *criminality* of homosexuality, let alone of sex with a minor. The mortification. For Mrs Bailey too, who we all so hated, her wretched desperation and pain, the silence. What was the rest of *her* life like, I wonder, she too had lost her livelihood. I said quite a bit earlier that he must have been sixty when he went to prison, that's how old he looked to me when I was nine, as old as Grandpa, and I was completely astonished to discover when I read the reports that he was only forty-nine then, so he'd have been fifty-six by the time he got out, a seven-year gap in his life, the War well and truly over in 1951, him with nowhere to go and no job to go to. As his lawyer put it "he would come back into the world without qualification or commendation whatever, because the one calling for which, apart from these matters, he was well equipped, would be shut to him for all time." What a shock to realise that Bailey was almost the same age as Dad, just two years older, and a lot younger than I am now as I sit here working all that out. I still cannot actually imagine, from the inside, what it must have been like, what on earth it was like for her, not just the terrible sexual betrayal. She might have slowly become aware of his faithlessness, his growing appetite for boys surely beyond her imagining, but the abrupt loss of position in the village, the sudden silence of conversation and gossip as she went down the street, the speculative and pitying looks, forsaken, her husband no longer a man of substance and authority in the village, her social circle demolished, no more dinners with the local doctor and parson, no more visits with Major Swann in his lovely house down Dean Street, no more tipping of the cap from men she met in the street, no more automatic deference from the shopkeepers.

All that *gone*, and him in custody. Not a word of this came to my ears, or to Phil's, and I think now of what this disaster meant for the conduct of her life, her financial position too brusquely altered at a time when women swore to "obey, serve, love, honour and keep" their husbands in sickness and in health, that's from the *Book of Common Prayer*, the Solemnization of Matrimony, at a time when above all else you were obliged to keep up appearances and thus protect the privileges attached to your class, necessarily but surely not unwittingly involved in the cover-up, still running the Prep School until it closed in December. Impossibly difficult.

27

New Headmaster

In January 1944, I *still* didn't go to a new school the way Mrs Bailey'd predicted. But with a brand new Headmaster already settled in, the school was pretty new anyway, even with Our Kid and a bunch of others still there, Mrs Bailey gone without a trace, the Prep School along with her. That'd closed down completely, the door at the bottom of the stairs in Rushall locked up tight and that part of the building completely out of bounds. We weren't allowed anywhere near, and now we had to go to classes with all the other kids. On the first day of School, at Prayers, we met Mr Brogden the new Headmaster for the first time, though of course at breakfast us boarders'd seen him along with Mrs Brogden at High Table where Mr Bailey used to sit, neat grey suit, spotless black gown with not a single crease, crisp and new-looking, him a lot younger. He didn't have a moustache the way Mr Bailey had and his square jaw and the muscly way he stood made him look like Bulldog Drummond on the covers of books by Sapper, we all read *them*, he looked a whole lot younger even than Dad, he just glowed with energy and he didn't look anything like old enough to be in charge of *any*thing. Once the Catholic and Jewish kids had joined us at the end of Prayers, they'd been waiting outside the door the way they always did, he said to the whole School, "My name is Harry S. Brogden," and he paused. "You may call me Mr Brogden and will of course directly address me as *Sir*. I am here to act on behalf of your parents, *in loco parentis*, as well as to make sure you learn what we are here to teach you."

One of the kids behind me shuffled his feet and sniffed. "What's 'e going to be like?" he whispered, "'e's not even as old as my dad," and the Prefect standing at the side in charge of our row frowned at him. Mr Brogden looked down at our row and raised his voice a bit. "I am here, as are the other Masters, to teach you to be civilised, to treat others with *respect*, to *pay attention* to each other. I expect politeness and courtesy as a matter of course, and I expect instant obedience from each and every one of you. You *have to* obey orders, and we shall all be working together with willing spirits. With keenness and enthusiasm we shall accomplish what we set out to accomplish, and we shall learn what we are here to learn with interest and with pleasure." His use of *we* flew right over our heads, and no one said anything at all, not a whisper, not a shuffled foot, but as we came out of Big School afterwards to go to class the kid who'd whispered said "Some 'ope 'e's got. *What* pleasure? 'Ow can School be any *fun*? And my dad says we don't 'ave to obey *any*body till they've proved themselves." He laughed and kicked at a stone. "Too bossy by 'alf!" he said.

On the way from Prayers to my first class in the Third Form I stuck to the other kids I knew from Prep School, not many of us left from Mrs Bailey's time *I hope Mr Brogden's not* our *Teacher!* and thought about the room we'd be in. I'd never been in there much at all, the old woodworking room at the near end of one of the two wooden buildings right at the edge of the Croft, twice as big as the other classrooms, all the huge carpentry benches piled one on another to loom across the back, almost to the ceiling, dusty blackout curtains, old desks and unneeded wooden chairs blocking the gaps *Stay away from there! It's dangerous!* Close to thirty of us in one room and space left over, lots of room to breathe after three cramped years in the small, overcrowded Prep School. Big windows on opposite walls, one unfolding a view of the tall hedge blocking off the Headmaster's garden, the other, partly blocked by the Art Room building, looking out to the wide grass-and-mud expanse of the Croft where we played at Break. Not even a glimpse of the Quad or the Gates, and right outside the door a covered concrete walkway running the length of the building so you could walk all the way to Big School and through the Quad without setting foot on the mud or grass of the Croft and even perhaps without getting wet on a rainy day. But no apple trees espaliered against the walls, no neat mown lawn. Not like Rushall at all.

I wondered what we'd be doing that first class, I hadn't even got my timetable yet, and nobody'd issued me any books, I was a whole Term behind because I'd still been stuck in Prep School with half-a-dozen others my age or a bit older, stuck with Mrs Bailey, and I had a lot of catching up to do. We wouldn't just be doing Arithmetic in the Third Form but'd have to take Algebra and Geometry as well, and one lunch time those who'd got into the Third Form ahead of me last Term had kept going on about how hard Algebra is. "It's like Arithmetic," they said, "but it uses letters instead of numbers, you have to add letters up, A plus B plus C, or multiply X by Y and divide what you get by Z." But how could you do that, I wondered, it doesn't make any sense at all *A and B don't mean anything the way numbers like 4 and 5 do*, how could anybody understand when nothing adds up. I couldn't see how anybody could understand it at all, *any* of it, Algebra was so obscure. *How could there be an answer?* Phil'd never said anything about that at home, and over the Christmas holidays Dad told me "Stop worrying, you're just wasting energy." "Worrying'll never get you anywhere, it never does" Mum chimed in, "It'll be a lot easier than you think, and worrying will just make it harder." So what a relief to get to III B that first day and see Mrs Asprey at the front of the classroom, her familiar face, she told us she'd be teaching us Algebra, and we'd get Arithmetic and Geometry from Miss Small, she was new this January and none of us knew anything about her, didn't even know what she looked like, but Henry Matson said we'd all laid our eyes on her this morning at Prayers. "She looked alright," he said, but I'd been too busy watching Mr Brogden, hadn't even noticed. But how could anybody know, even Moggie Morris'd looked alright when we first saw him.

As it turned out, I came to *like* Algebra, it could even be fun juggling letters, a lot easier than Arithmetic where I kept making careless mistakes, I'd always got into trouble with mensuration, all my calculations forever wrong, but Algebra had something magical about it, you could apply those formulas and their letters to problems that didn't look as though there could be any answer at all and at first glance didn't seem to make any sense, but with *Let x be the gap between the trains* (or whatever) *and the distance y* you could make decisions, I could work it out. Mrs Asprey showed us that you could do anything at all to an equation so long as you did whatever you were doing on both sides of the equals sign, it didn't make any difference whether you added, subtracted, multiplied, or divided anything so long as you did it on both sides. That was amazing, a mystery with terrific freedom in it as well as power, even though it wasn't till the Summer Term that I began to see how in a given puzzle those operations could, applied step by step, actually resolve into an answer.

The average age of the whole class was exactly ten years, my age 9 years 7 months, the youngest in the class and still the youngest kid in the School. I wasn't supposed officially to be there, working away in the Third Form in a proper Grammar School, and one chilly January morning, first thing on a Saturday, Mr Brogden'd warned us the week before, me and the other kids who'd been in Prep School all got hoicked off to the old Prep School room in Rushall because of our age. Nunc or Young Nunc had lit a fire to warm it up for the occasion, and Mr Brogden sat and watched us while we wrote the new Eleven-Plus exam because we were too young to be in III B. We had to take the exam to show we belonged or we'd have to leave the Grammar School altogether and get moved somewhere else, to a "Secondary Modern School or a Technical School," like the Nash, only bigger and rougher, *They won't know anything at all! just noisy riff-raff!* Mum and Dad'd be horrified if I had to go *there*. After Mr Brogden told us a day or two later that we'd all passed and could stay at Brewood, Mrs Asprey told us it'd been a "single attempt" exam, "sink or swim," she said. "If you fail, that's *that*. You've *failed*." I was glad nobody'd told us *that* before we wrote it. "Good job you passed," Uncle Edward said later, "Your mum and dad wouldn't be able to hold their heads up, for the shame of it." It'd've meant working in a factory or being a Travelling Salesman, something like that, *a terrible step down!* But the exam wasn't difficult at all, even if I did have to scamper to get all the questions done. We didn't have to take two of the tests, in what they called "mental Arithmetic" and in "Writing," perhaps because we'd done so much of them in Prep

School, so we only had to take the Intelligence Test, that's what Mr Brogden called it, four big foolscap pages with "General Problem Solving" printed across the top of page one, and you filled in all the blanks, answer ninety questions in sixty minutes, and it turned out some of the questions demanded mental Arithmetic anyway. *Answer as many questions as you can* it said, and before he handed out the papers Mr Brogden said "You may *not* ask me *any* questions. And you may not leave this room." He frowned and looked grim. "After you have written your name on the first page, the *only* thing you can write is in answer to the questions. You may *not* make rough notes." He looked at his watch. "Now turn the exam over and start."

The first page hadn't got a lot on it, the alphabet printed across the page and the numbers 1 through 26 printed above it so the numbers lined up with the letters, and on a third line the alphabet again but in backwards order, those letters lined up with the numbers too. On the second and third pages as well as on page one you had sums to do, like multiply GFT by KF, or words to decode, like RHM'G GSRH XOVEVI, just like the codes we'd played with and read about in *The Wizard* and *Hotspur*, even writing our own names in secret numbers, spy story stuff. I wasn't at all sure we were allowed to turn back to page one, and looked around, I was in the front row, none of the others was checking back to page one, they were all counting things out on their fingers, and more and more I began to think we weren't allowed and I kept looking up wanting to ask. But Mr Brogden'd clearly said *No questions!* and I fretted all in a dither, I didn't dare be disqualified just for not obeying orders, I'd end up in the wrong kind of school and I'd never get *any*where. One of the kids was whispering away as he counted back so I tried it, without whispering, but it took too long, I'd never get the questions done that way, so I simply turned straight back to page one and looked it up. I looked over to see if Mr Brogden was watching, I looked between my fingers so he wouldn't know I was watching *him*, and he was looking down at his desk, he didn't say anything. I did that two or three times quaking in my boots, but that was still too slow and I simply flipped the page back and forth, keeping an eye on him as I did so. I tried to be quiet so he wouldn't notice, but the paper kept rustling as I turned the page and at last I gave up trying to be silent and just filled in all the answers as fast as I could, the pages flipping *whoosh whoosh* as I turned them *How could anybody not notice?* I was sweating terribly when I'd finished, my damp fingers leaving wet prints all over the left-hand page, my heart and stomach all twittery I was so sure I wasn't supposed to go back to the first page all the time, that'd be cheating, obviously it wouldn't be allowed *What would Mum and Dad think if I failed and had to leave because I'd been caught?* But I couldn't ask, I didn't dare, and I had to get the test *done*. Needless to say, though of course I didn't know it then, there's not many things more obvious than a small child trying to be furtive, and it's funny how we invent prohibitions when there are none, the unspoken making us stupid. I spent the whole exam in a blue funk, praying that Mr Brogden wouldn't notice *How else can I answer all those questions?* but Mr Brogden didn't say anything and didn't look at any of us in particular, he just kept his eyes open, looking round all the time without any particular focus, not really watching, me scrabbling away on a panicky edge, everyone else in the room whispering away and counting on their fingers and trying to do sums in their heads until Mr Brogden said "Alright, that's enough. It's time to stop, whether you've finished or not. Waltham, you can collect the papers and hand them to me." As it turned out I was the only one who'd done all the questions, but I didn't say I had, I was so worried that I'd got away with cheating, and when I said that to Our Kid he just laughed "Why'd they print all that stuff on the first page, then?" and I couldn't answer.

We hadn't got far into January before we began calling Mr Brogden *Broggie* when we talked among ourselves, he was clearly so very strict that we'd never dare call him that to his face, he'd've been so angry at such lack of respect, and one Monday morning right after Break we got back into class to find Broggie standing by the blackboard instead of Mr Miller, that was such a surprise I faltered a bit, so did a lot of the rest of us. Broggie wasn't supposed to be there to teach us Scripture, it was Dusty Miller did that, and Dusty'd been at Prayers that morning, nobody'd said anything about him suddenly having to go home or anything, but Broggie simply looked at us a bit impatiently and said "Come along, don't waste time! Hurry up and settle down at your desks, I'm teaching this class today, not Mr Miller," and then he said "Don't get your books out, we won't need them." He paused. "Tell me," he said, "how do we know the Bible is true? What evidence is there that there really *is* a God?" We all looked at each other, but nobody said anything *We're supposed to be doing Scripture!* "Oh, gather your wits," he said, "and *think*. Why do we think there is a God?" and we were all silent for a bit as Broggie looked round, a piece of chalk in his hand. Then Birdie stuck his hand in the air. "Yes, Prince? What do you think?" and Birdie said, "Well, the Bible says so, Sir, and that's the word of God, everyone says so." Broggie looked at him and said "I think we'd better leave the Bible out of this discussion, what you say is a matter of belief, and that's all very well but how do we *know*?" and he wrote "everybody says so" on the board. "Does that make it true? If everyone in this room says," and he looked round, casting his eye on us all, "hmmm, that Mrs Brogden is a better soccer player than any of you, does that make it true? If none of you have ever seen her play?" and we all grinned a bit as he paused, Mrs Brogden with her thin legs and delicate hands looking so fragile, shorter and smaller than even some of *us*, not a bit like gangly Mrs Bailey with her shooting-stick, but *slight*, yesterday Charlie Hammond'd said she looks as if a puff of wind could blow her away, and he was right. "What *is* there, from what our senses tell us, from what we see in the world, that tells us God exists?" More silence, and then a hand went up. Carey. "Well Sir, in big battles like in the last war some soldiers saw something in the air, spirits or something Sir, fighting on our side." Broggie turned to the blackboard. "The Angel of Mons," he said, and wrote it down. "Do you know about that?" Some of us nodded. "You can tell us later, Carey, those of us who don't know. What else can you all think of?" and more and more hands went up, and it wasn't long before we'd added lots of things to Broggie's list, *sudden cures to illness*, stuff like that, and Broggie said "Very good! That'll give us enough to go on with. Is all this enough to prove that there is a God? Tell me" and we all fell silent again, and a hand slowly went up, at the back of the room. I turned my head. Dan. He put his hand down again. "No, no," said Broggie, "say what you were going to say, Featherstone isn't it? I won't bite, you know." And Dan said "Well, everything has to've started somewhere, Sir, somebody *must*'ve made it," and Broggie smiled. "Yes," he said. "That's good. It's not proof, of course. We might want to think about what we mean by *somebody*, it can't be somebody like the people we might see in here, or anywhere else, can it?" and he wrote *Reason* and *Logic* on the board, "Let's think some more." A lot of hands started going up, and after about five minutes of different kids competing to speak, Broggie pointed to a boy in the second row. "We haven't heard from you, Trigg, not yet. What do *you* think? I'd really like to know," Trigg never said anything in class, not if he could help it, he wriggled in his seat a bit his face bright red and looked at his hands clasped in front of him on his desk, the other kids restless as they waited. Broggie frowned and gestured them into silence, and Trigg stuttered a bit and slowly said "There *must*'ve been a beginning, Sir, it's too frightening, there *has* to be a God. How can God not *be*?" "Yes," said Broggie. "Well done for saying that! that's very good, it's an honest response, and that's what we need. With questions of this sort you must always say what you *really* think, not hide behind a *lie*." And he looked at his watch. "This has all been very interesting," he said; "thank you. It's important for you to know what you think. Mr Miller will be back for your next class, but I shall be visiting you again. I hope you discuss what we did today among yourselves. Be sure to tell Mr Miller what we've learned."

That lesson'd been so interesting that at lunch we couldn't leave it alone, and other kids at our table, all of them in the Third and Fourth Forms, said he'd visited their classes too, in History or English, or Geography as well as Scripture. We heard he'd asked a Geography class in III A *How do we know the world is round and not flat?* and as soon as we heard Babcock and Jones going on about it as we waited for our spuds some of us started arguing about that too and the rest of the table joined in. Some of the kids at the other table, they were in the Fifth Form, scoffed. "Everyone knows *that*, it's a *sphere*, there's a Globe in the library! Go and look at it! Nothing to discuss!" But we argued anyway. "How do we *know*?" provoked us, we all had opinions, and that night as we were talking in the dorm after lights out the sound of a shoe in the corridor, a quick shaft of light as the door opened, intense in all that dark. *Broggie!* His quiet voice. "It's very late and you should all be asleep. You have to be alert in the morning, and you certainly shouldn't be chattering away as late as this! Now be quiet, or you'll regret it in the morning." We all fell silent, the possible threat of punishment hanging there, and as he quietly closed the door, "*Good night!*" Next day at breakfast Fatty Bullimore said "You know, he's always prowling about the place, he wants to make sure everything's okay. I think Broggie's going to be alright. He's not like Pussy Bailey was, he's going round all the classes, he was in the Fifth Form Friday, he taught a Geometry lesson." Bowcock looked up, "Yes," he said in his quiet voice, "he hasn't been here for more than three weeks, that's why he's visiting them all. He wants to get to know us, see who we are. Have you noticed he already knows our names?" And Fatty nodded, "And we can get to know *him*, too. 'Course he might be making sure that the teachers are doing a good job too, getting to know *them*," and as he laughed murmured something to Smethwick about teachers who'd gone away in the War and what *they*'d been like. Somebody said something about how strict Broggie was, he'd really lit into one of the dayboys for not doing his prep, "well, you can't blame him for *that*; you can't simply not do your homework!" and the talk drifted off to something else.

The next Sunday, or the one after, as we came back to the Billiard Room after Supper, the billiard table long gone, the kids in the front stopped dead as they opened the door and fell silent, the rest of us pushing away, crowding behind them to get into the warm. *Broggie!* Our chatter faded away. *Broggie*, sitting on the couch right in front of the fire? *What was wrong? What'd somebody done?* "No, no" he called, and waved his hand "Come on in! Nothing to worry about, everything is alright! I thought that on a cold night like this I might come in here and keep you company, talk to you a little." That was astonishing, Pussy Bailey'd *never* kept us boarders company, nor any of the kids for that matter, 'd *never* sat with us, not *any*where, the only times he ever spoke to me was when he was dishing out our weekly pocket money. He always kept his distance, and I really couldn't see why Broggie was here, nor could any of us, sitting on the couch in front of the fire, in *our* room. What does he really want? What are we doing wrong?

Once we'd all crowded in Broggie said "It's cold and dark outside, and I think the smaller boys should sit on the couch or near the fire." After a bit of kerfuffle we started to settle, a lot of us sitting on the floor. "None of you has any prep to do, not on a Sunday night, but you bigger boys" and he turned his head, shifted a bit so he could see them, "might have something you want to get on with, you certainly don't have to stay at *this* end of the room." Loud footsteps in the corridor outside, steel-tipped heels clipping on the tiles, talk and laughter suddenly louder as the door opened, the noise abruptly bitten off as the three or four kids coming in saw the room full of kids, hardly any talk at all instead of the usual babble. "I think you younger boys," Broggie said, "the Juniors, might enjoy what I've got in mind. Carry on, the rest of you, do whatever it is you usually do, enjoy yourselves, but try not to disturb those of us at this end of the room," and he turned back toward the fire. "I thought we could play a game or two," he said, "cheer us up, and warm us up a bit, too. Do any of you know *I Packed My Satchel*? or there's another one, called *I Like To*," and Pongo Jones raised his hand and said, "I know one called *I Packed My Suitcase*, Sir, it might be the same." Broggie nodded. "Why don't you tell us about it?" and Pongo explained, with a lot of stops and starts at first but fewer as he got going, that "one of us says I packed my suitcase with something, he has to say what it is, and then it's somebody else's turn, and he has to say what the first person said and then add something else to the suitcase, the satchel I mean, and the next person has to say all that and add something else." "Yes," said Broggie, "That sounds the same. Everyone in the circle takes his turn, he has to list all the items that have been packed so far, *you can't write anything down, you have to remember!* and then add something new, something that hasn't already been packed into the satchel by somebody else. But he has to start by saying *I packed my satchel with* and it can be anything at all, you can pack whatever you like, and if you make a mistake, if you get the order wrong or forget something, then you're o-u-t *Out*. When there's only one player left he's the winner," and he turned to Pongo, "Have I got it right?"

Pongo said yes and then said it's easy when you start, but it gets harder and harder as the list gets bigger. "It's easy to forget," he said. "I always leave something out." Broggie smiled and nodded and looked at the kid sitting next to him. "Chapman, why don't you start, and then we'll go round-robin," and Chapman packed his satchel with an orange, none of us'd seen any oranges for years, and when the next kid packed his bag with an orange and a tangerine, one of the kids, halfway round the circle, said "Please, Sir, what's a tangerine? Can you make things up to put in your satchel?" One of the seniors at the other end of the room looked up and said "Before the War we used to get tangerines at Christmas, they're a special kind of orange" and then "Oh, sorry, Sir!" as Broggie said "No, you can't make things up, they have to be real." And then he said "You know, I don't mind the rest of you listening, none of us does, but you shouldn't interrupt. And I do think, don't you? that you might better spend your time doing something of your own, not just *pretend* to be reading a book or drawing a picture. After the Juniors have gone to bed I'll be spending some time with all of you, you won't miss anything. Now," he said, "I packed my satchel with an orange, and a tangerine" and he pointed to the next kid, who added "an egg" to the list. One of the seniors muttered to his pal with a laugh that if the egg broke the inside of the satchel would be a real mess, and Broggie looked up, annoyed. "Jones, that sort of interruption really is not very helpful *is* it. You *must* learn to be more considerate. Why don't you pay attention to that book you're holding?" Jones went a bit pink, "Sorry, Sir." He turned away, back to his pals, and we all turned back to the game.

We hadn't got very far round the robin when somebody packed a whole donkey in his satchel, and very soon we all got giggly as we thought of ridiculous things to pack. The list got longer and harder to remember, we'd all had a turn, then all at once three kids in a row were o-u-t *Out* because they couldn't remember such a long list, one of them had taken ages to remember it and even then got the list wrong, and I was pleased, I kept reciting the whole list to myself just the way everybody else did, and by the time I'd had my turn another kid'd dropped out, and when Chapman got stuck at about the sixth thing on the list he kept saying "and, um, and, and, um, oh, yes, a kangaroo, and um, then…" and I heard my own exhilarated whisper, "*I* know, *I* know" bouncing up and down in my seat, a bit like scrambling for the last slot when we'd played musical chairs before the War at Sammy Roe's, and poor old Chapman looked at me as he took a deep breath and Broggie turned to me and exasperatedly said, he really did sound cross, "Be quiet!" he said. "Don't be so big-headed!"

Oh!

That took my breath away. I didn't know where to look or what to do with myself it was such a shock. "Give Chapman time to think," Broggie said. But he didn't single me out after that, or pay me any sort of special attention, he just left me alone as I sat on my hands and tried to calm myself down, I sat there and rehearsed the list over and over again and yet again my heart pounding away as I worried away at what to pack when it would be my turn, and when at last my turn came round I got stuck and I was o-u-t *Out*. Broggie treated me just the same as he did everyone else. The game ended soon after that, Birdie'd won, and to settle us down Broggie had us sing a bit of "There's a hole in my bucket," we all knew that song, and he told us Juniors, "Off to bed now. You're all staying up extra late tonight, so you'd better get to sleep right away. No talking!" Next morning at breakfast we heard that after we'd gone upstairs Broggie turned all the lights off in the Billiard Room and in the flickering firelight talked about a holiday trip he'd gone on before the War with an old school-friend, up in Suffolk near Lowestoft on the North Sea, I don't think any of the kids at Brewood came from there, and except for the fishing fleets we none of us knew anything about that part of the country. Broggie told about Harry Tate's Navy, the minesweepers in the Royal Navy Patrol Service, converted trawlers out of Lowestoft and Grimsby and Hull that we'd all read about in comics like the *Rover*. On the second day of his holiday Broggie'd stumbled across some old brickwork half-buried in the sand along the dunes near his hotel, and'd found an old whistle and cleaned it up, got all the sand out of it, some words he couldn't understand engraved on it *fur fla fle bis* he couldn't recognise them at all they weren't Latin or even Greek, and he blew the whistle to see if it worked. It sounded really strange when he blew it again, sitting on his bed in the hotel. "The sound came from an infinite distance" he said. And there came the comfortable thought, *Oh, he's telling a story!*

Of course, I wasn't there when Broggie said all this, I got it from Olive Frost when he told us what'd gone on after us Juniors'd been sent to bed. I can hear Broggie saying those things, even though I heard it secondhand, memory's really deceptive. Sometimes I can't tell the difference between what somebody told me and what I actually did, between what happened in a dream and what happened when I was awake, it's hard to sort out as memories blur and conjoin, what's told indistinguishable from what's done or even what's invented. All I can do here is write down what I remember from remembering all the different times we spent in the Billiard Room with Broggie. He came into the Billiard Room more than once to play memory games and tell stories, and we adored him for that. As he talked on the end of the couch, everyone huddled together in the warmth of the wavering and uneven firelight, he looked round at the kids to make sure that everyone was at ease and to make sure he'd got everyone's attention, and after he'd got someone to add a precious bit of coal to the fire he said "I had to take a huge deep breath to clear the sand and dirt from that cold brass whistle, it was horrible to touch, still faintly sticky no matter how much I washed it off in seawater, it wasn't just sticky with salt but seemed to cling it wouldn't let go, I couldn't get it warm, it refused to thaw in my hands no matter how hard I tried." Everyone settled more closely onto the couch or into each other, and as Broggie told how fierce the wind was that night, banging and clattering the entire hotel, whistling in the chimneys and crannies, *Oh! This is a ghost story!* He looked slowly round the room as kids' hair began to rise to the sound of that whistle tormenting Broggie's ears in the windstorm on the

North Sea coast, and suddenly he was backing and stumbling away from a frightful creature as it clambered from the bed and got closer and closer as it groped for him, him breathless and cold, cold, cold as its hungry face, a face made of crumpled linen, distorted and shifting, blind falters and sudden quick moves at times so very fast that in his startled panic Broggie staggered nearly fell, backwards through the window, as the door burst open, his friend rushing in to the rescue. "I blundered against the window frame," Broggie said, "I split my lip as I recoiled and the creature fled." In the Billiard Room fireplace a coal shifted and muttered, a wisp of smoke escaped into the room, and everyone stirred a little as the cold crept in. "That was some time ago," Broggie said, "before the War," and he paused. "If you look closely," he put his finger just above the corner of his mouth and we all peered, "you can just see where I hit the frame, a small scar where the doctor put a stitch. That's from when I nearly fell." But when I looked for it, later, I didn't see it, I never did quite see it no matter how hard I looked, except a very faint line, hardly visible at all, the sort of line most people have on their faces, even kids. "No real damage done," said Broggie, "I'm here, safe and sound. My friend and I threw that whistle away, as far as we could out into the sea. It's *gone*." And he looked at his watch. His audience stirred. He stretched. "Now," he said, "no talk. It's well after ten o'clock. You'd all better get to bed. Tomorrow is a School day."

The next week Jim Costley, he'd gone home on Saturday for the day, showed me a book his Dad'd had at home, *Ghost Stories of an Antiquary*. "Go to page 181," he said, and when I got there, "Oh Whistle, and I'll Come to You," the same tale Broggie'd told but a lot longer, and in old-fashioned prose, and we all marveled at that, *It hadn't really happened at all, perhaps he never even went to Lowestoft*, he'd got the story from a book, and when Olive Frost got hold of the book, he borrowed it from Jim, he said Broggie's version was much scarier, "it sounded as though he'd really been there. But it didn't keep me awake or anything like that," and a few weeks later it was really something, really smashing, to go into the Billiard Room after Sunday night's usual cold supper and find Broggie once again sitting on the couch in front of the fire, waiting for us. That didn't happen very often, perhaps twice a Term in the autumn and winter, but we all kept hoping, and it's clear to me now, as I look back, that Broggie worked very hard, and so did Mrs Broggie, to get us all interested in the world outside the schoolroom as well as in the world of books, to pay attention to what was out there.

One weekend when Robin and Jim and I got back from our Sunday Walk *Make sure it's a good long one* Broggie'd told us all, *and don't come back until Tea!* we were a bit late and we went straight to the Dining Hall, only to find that everyone else'd just started going in, the doors'd been locked till then. The whole room had been turned round, the chairs stacked neatly at one end, you couldn't sit on them, and the tables'd been pushed towards the middle, with all the food, doughies as usual, and one piece of fruit cake each, on two of the tables, big metal teapots and cups with milk and sugar ranged on High Table, and we could walk around the room. Photographs and advertisements from *Illustrated* and *Picture Post*, from daily papers like the *Express and Star* and *News Chronicle*, and various handmade notices and things, all of them numbered, festooned the walls, stuck there with drawing pins, some had captions and some didn't, and as we came in Matron gave us a small notepad with numbers listed down the left side, "Something a bit special today, there's pencils over there if you don't have one" she said. "Make sure you put it back. And be careful! Don't spill anything, don't drop any food on the floor, you'll have to clean it up if you do!" On the wall next to her was Number 6, the drawing of a butler leaning forwards offering a tray, an advertisement from *The Illustrated London News* or somewhere, with the drawing of whatever was in the tray carefully clipped out. Broggie pointed to it. "What we have here," he said, "is a quiz, and this is question six. If you know what this picture is an advertisement for, write that down next to the number six on your notepad. If you don't know, then move on to the next question," he gestured round the walls. "'Cigarettes' won't do, you have to say what *kind*." Mrs Brogden said "I'll start you off, so you get the idea clearly. Number six is an advertisement for Kensitas, so you can write that down. If you don't know how to spell that, well, do what you can." Then Matron spoke up. "But don't tell anyone else what you think it is, just write it down. You might have it wrong, and you don't want to mislead anyone. If it's just a picture, then say what it's a picture *of*; there's a question attached to the picture, then answer it."

I walked to the other side of the room, number 16, a picture of a biscuit tin with its printed caption "When we've beaten Jerry you'll see us again" and the name cut away. That was easy *and* difficult, it could've been Crawford's or McVities or Peek Frean's, you couldn't get any of them in the War, all biscuits the same "Utility" quality even if they were arrowroot or digestive or whatever, you couldn't know who made them. At home we never paid any attention to advertisements, "There's no point," Mum said. "They just make you miss things you can't have, I really don't need to be reminded I miss things like Cadbury's cup chocolate, thank you very much." But not many of the questions on the wall were about advertisements. One picture showed Clemmie Churchill and asked *Who is this woman married to?* Hardly any of us younger kids knew that one, but we all knew what Stanley Matthews looked like, he was *really* famous, so the question *What team does he play for?* was dead easy, like the one asking *Who are these people* written under pictures of Stalin and Roosevelt, we all got those, though the second question *Where did they recently meet?* stumped almost everyone. But the really hard questions were rebus puzzles, especially the ones encoding the names of towns. The one for Dublin baffled us all, it simply said "x 2." Broggie didn't let us see any answers at all while we were doing the quiz, so we couldn't find out what we'd missed until he gave them to us just before bedtime. He then told us we had to thank Mrs Brogden for it all, it was her idea, and it was her who'd put most of it together and hung it on the walls. What a far cry she was from Mrs Bailey! After Lights Out Birdie said "D'you remember when Broggie first arrived? He said we'd learn with pleasure, and we all scoffed? Well," he announced, "I enjoyed myself today" and Olive Frost on the way down to breakfast next day said "You'd never catch Pussy Bailey doing anything like that, not as friendly. He didn't *care* like Broggie seems to," and even the know-it-all seniors said they'd enjoyed themselves and'd had a good time.

28

Broggie's World

Broggie worked hard, he expected us to work hard too, and so did Mrs Broggie. There was a terrible shortage of teachers that year, worse than before, anyone who had the slightest knowledge of French or especially German'd been called up to be an interpreter for the Army, Mr Houston told us all the math teachers got called up because they knew how to do things, "They know how to calculate trajectories," he said, "how to use bomb-sights as well as how to navigate" and one of the senior kids said we were lucky to have any teachers at all, skilled workers were in such demand, "That's why we keep getting new teachers all the time, the beginning of every Term." Miss Small was one of three new teachers who came in January when Broggie did, she got to be Form Mistress of III B as soon as she arrived, and my Report Book says she taught us History, Geography, Arithmetic and Geometry, and she only lasted one Term, she left at Easter. With her teaching all those subjects, all of them more than once a week, I must've seen her quite a bit, but I don't remember her at all, I haven't the faintest idea how old she was or what she looked like, let alone what she was like as a teacher. "Things keep happening in a War" somebody's dad said, "and you can't tell what'll happen till it happens." When teachers left there wasn't much time to find replacements, and in 1944 there weren't many qualified teachers looking for jobs, some of them war-wounded coming back to civvy street. What with the battles in Italy and then in France almost anyone who wasn't "unfit for military service" was doing "vital work" on the Home Front, and lots of retired teachers got dragooned back into the classroom to fill the gaps. When it came down to support staff it was just as bad, kitchen maids and cleaners and even School Matrons, anyone who was able-bodied, had gone ages ago to work on the Home Front, or if they had any experience'd been given a nursing job, and a couple of the maids, girls from the village, hadn't lasted more than two weeks before they left. It might not've been their fault, but they left everyone in the lurch, Matron and the Cook all at once completely without help except for Josie who did the cleaning, a huge sloppy woman who wasn't quite all there, her adenoids so loud you could hear her a mile off as she waddled along with her broom and dustpan all out-of-breath.

School was always short of Matrons, we had so many one after another, none of them lasting more than a Term or two, that I simply can't remember them all. Our Kid says I've got everything wrong about when I first went there, for starters he says Matron's name wasn't Mrs Grant the way I said it was, and for seconds she wasn't the starched middle-aged woman the way I think of her, the School Matron in 1941 was about eighteen years old she was quite pretty and her name was Miss Molyneux all the older boys made up stories about her. I don't remember her at all, she's not even a glimpse at the back of my mind though her name vaguely rings a bell, and Our Kid agrees that after her came a plumpish middle-aged woman, the one I certainly remember as Mrs Grant, with her grey hair and crackly starched clothes and her friendly smile, but she didn't last long either, 'd been a nurse in a hospital, went somewhere else. After her we had a whole slew of Matrons in succession, among them Radish Wright's mum, we hated her sharp narrow face she had a temper to go with her bright red hair. I don't think she actually had any medical knowledge or training but was just somebody's mum filling in because she could. Forever telling us to behave ourselves she never smiled and we gave Radish a terrible time over her, cursing her and ragging him, I don't know how he stood it really except we couldn't blame him for what his mum did could we, and he knew that, it wasn't his fault she was such a dragon, but I couldn't imagine her giving him a cuddle and a biscuit and a glass of milk for elevenses not that you could do that anyway at School, him sitting on her lap on a green kitchen chair her bony knees poking, *how could* **she** *make a place feel like home the way Mum did*. Finding a motherly sort of woman able to live in and with some sort of medical training was a pretty tall order, and I suspect as I write this that Broggie drew on a pool of contacts he already had or that others helped him compile, because in 1944 things settled a bit with Mrs McGregor, she lasted a whole year, a small fierce Scotswoman with an accent that sounded a lot like Henry Houston's, she got to know all of us and we liked her. She was always available when something'd happened, and her mending basket was always empty at the start of every day. In all the years I was at Brewood she was the only Matron who managed to keep on top of that, we all ran through clothes like billy-oh, and goodness knows how late she had to stay up to get that done. "I've got too much to do to put up with your nonsense," she'd frown; "don't waste my time making a fuss, just get on with whatever it is you have to do." For the first time we had a Matron who knew what Matrons are supposed to do and who did them. She knew how to bandage Billy's wrist and thumb properly when he sprained it, "Of course it hurts," she said, "but it'll hold so long as you learn to be more careful. Don't you go climbing trees or fall off Croft wall" *how does she know we all do that?* "I won't be there to help you if you do." But she didn't smile. "You'd better not do PT till it's better. I'll tell Mr Ranson."

She left just before the War ended, and Joy Haydock arrived, a hefty young blonde with her hair done up in a French twist and wearing bright lipstick, not a bit like the women we saw in the School or even in the village, and she stayed on as Matron for something like two years or even more. Rationing of some things was even worse after the War than it was while the War was going on, and most of us had to have a weekly or even daily dose of something, vitamins, cod liver oil, or a tablespoon of concentrated orange juice, which I shuddered down in a single gulp, so pungent you couldn't make it *not* taste. "It comes from America," somebody said, "that's why it's so horrid." Every morning after Breakfast we'd line up outside her room to get injuries treated or dosed with whatever we had to be dosed with, some of us'd go again after Tea, Graham Newton going to both for almost a complete Term because of his boils. "They're really abscesses," she said, "They're very hard to get rid of," and on our daily sick-calls, morning and evening, she'd give him an injection, thick viscous stuff that made a lump in his muscle as she squoze the syringe, he'd rub and rub at it, grimacing like mad till the lump went down. He was in the First Eleven, both cricket and soccer, he never had any time for us younger kids, "Out of my road!" he'd say as he pushed through to the front of the queue, and afterwards he'd hang around her table and get in everyone else's way as he chatted to his pals, or he'd rummage through the mending basket next to Matron's armchair by the fire "No!" she'd say, "Leave that stuff alone, it belongs to other people. That's *work* I've got to do" and after a couple of restless days doing that he got into a way of pawing through her things on the table, him and his pals picking things up and looking at stuff and putting it down. "Leave that alone!" she said when he picked up an envelope, "That's personal! That's a letter! That's *private!*" and he didn't say anything, just lifted it close to his face and fingered its thick blue envelope, one of his pals murmured something and he smiled to himself as he put it back with a slight shrug. Ray Arnold was poking about a stack of papers on her table, copies of the weekly *Woman's Own* and stuff like that, he picked up a sketchbook with loose sheets of paper tucked inside. "*No!*" Miss Haydock said, "No! Put that *down!* You can't look in there!" she sounded really anxious she went a bit pink she was busy tying a bandage around somebody's sprained ankle "It's *private.*" Somebody said "Go on, Miss, can't we have a look? What is it?" and Graham simply reached round Ray and opened up the sketchbook. A drawing fell out, Miss Haydock with no clothes on, sitting down. "*Oh*" he said, and the clamour of kids fell silent as Graham nudged his pal and held it up to the light, "No!" she said, "Give me that!" And after a pause, "please." But the damage was done, we'd all glimpsed it, knew what it was. "I'll let you look in a minute, just a short look after I've finished this bandage, I'll show it you then but, you can't touch" and Graham put it down. I could feel my face get warm as I carefully didn't look but averted my eyes the same as a couple of others did, my clothes suddenly a bit heavy round my shoulders, but Graham made sure we all saw *him,* looking and nodding and tracing a line with his finger. "Mr Beaton has me pose for him," Miss Haydock blushed, "He says I've got a Rubens figure, it's interesting to draw" but I didn't know what to say and somebody else said "It doesn't look much like you" in a strangly sort of voice, and "How would *you* know?" asked someone by the door. None of us dared laugh at that, she went bright red and so did the bloke who'd asked the question, and that's the last we saw of that sketchbook.

Despite all the shortages, in 1944 we got a whole new set of teachers when we came back in April for the Summer Term, one of the village kids later said Broggie must've been scraping the barrel to get them, the only teacher we had from before was Dolly Asprey. Mum blinked a bit when we went home for the weekend and I told her, "It all sounds a bit make-do-and-mend," she said and then looked at Our Kid and me and smiled. "Nothing to worry about though, I'm sure it will be alright. I like Mrs Asprey, you've had her for a long time, haven't you, and you know her." Once Miss Small'd gone we got Dolly for English as well as for the Arithmetic and Geometry Miss Small'd taught last Term, and we didn't know from one Term to the next who'd be teaching what, everybody had to teach a bit of everything, teach stuff they really didn't know at all. When Angus Beaton came on the scene as the new Art Master, that was right after Miss Small left, he taught a lot more Science and Geography than he did Art, and that lasted all through the next year too, when I'd gone up to III A.

As Housemaster for Knightley, where all the boarders belonged, Angus had a small bedroom and his own bathroom across the corridor from the First and Second Dorms, he'd been gassed in the trenches in World War One, his breath whistling away worse than Josie's if he had to move quickly. He couldn't run for toffee, and near the end of Term, when he had to play soccer in the annual Staff Match against a School team because there weren't enough teachers to make up a team if he didn't play, the kids tried to make sure he never got near the ball so they wouldn't have to tackle him, they'd grin and lay off a bit. Besides Broggie he was the only teacher who lived in, the two of them along with Mrs Broggie and the School Matron the only adults on the premises, cooped up with forty-odd boarders pretty well twenty-four hours a day, seven days a week. He had a draughty little sitting room just inside the main School Entrance, if he turned left when he came out he'd go straight through the open porch out into the Quad, and if he turned right he'd be in the corridor leading to the Billiard Room, not much privacy with forty-odd kids clattering past half the time, not much time to himself if he didn't find a hideaway somewhere. If you went to see him he'd look up, sometimes with a sigh, always polite but not always agreeable, he'd smother his mild irritation if you saw it, smile a little. One evening I went with a couple of pals after supper to get permission to stay up an extra fifteen minutes, we were putting a model together and one of us'd actually got hold of some decent glue, he was plonked down in his armchair before the fire writing stuff down from the Physics textbook, a faded blue dressing-gown round his shoulders, "I'm teaching you Physics tomorrow," he said, and chuckled a bit, "You'd better be ready." Early the next week he gave us a written test that baffled us when it asked, "Why doesn't the air get hot when the sun shines through it?" and he didn't know the answer any more than we did. He went a bit pink over that, and we all grinned with him, he'd got the question from the end of the next chapter and we hadn't got that far yet.

We all knew he wasn't really supposed to teach Science, but he was a lot better at that than Ticker Ranson was at English. I still can't fathom why Broggie had Ticker teach it, he was so useless at it. Angus could've done a better job with his eyes closed, Ticker was so busy all the time with his PT classes or equipment to fix, like soccer balls or cricket stuff, but he still had to teach somebody *some*thing, Scripture one term and Geography the next, he taught it to more than one Form, and I got him two years in a row for English. In one of those, I can't remember which, the set book was Conrad's *The Shadow Line* and I certainly remember *that*. When we started he said he hoped nobody'd read it yet, "that would spoil the pleasure. *I'm* not in a hurry, and we're going to work slowly on this book. I want it to hold your interest, so I don't want you to read ahead. This is a sea story and Conrad tells it well, so we'll all have lots of time to enjoy it, and not reading ahead teaches you to practise restraint. That way you'll learn to control yourselves." And then he asked "What are the parts of speech? Do you know?" and of course we didn't, but as soon as he said "nouns, verbs, and adjectives, what are the rest?" we knew what he was talking about, but we spent the rest of the class going over all eight of them, and "No!" he said. "*The* is an article, and an article is not a part of speech, an article is an adjective. You *must* remember that, you must know the parts of speech by heart! I'll give you a test on it tomorrow to make sure." But next day at the beginning of English he told us to open our Conrad and start at the top of page forty-one. "Name the parts of speech in the first sentence on that page," he said, "Jones. Just the first word, then Smith, and then you," he pointed, and he took us round robin through the page until the end of class, and the next day he opened the book and wrote one of its sentences on the board, "The atmosphere of officialdom would kill anything that breathes the air of human endeavour, would extinguish hope and fear alike in the supremacy of paper and ink." He read it aloud and turned toward us. "Now, Williams. Tell me what sort of sentence that is." "Complex, Sir." "Rogers, what is the main clause?" "Oh, er, which, Sir? The main clause, Sir? Oh, um," he looked about him, eyes a bit blank, his head as usual full of cricket and football, waiting till he'd be old enough to be a sports reporter on the newspaper, and then, his voice all innocence, "There's two, Sir. Which one d'you want?" and we spent the best part of ten minutes trying to sort that out, most of us still confused when time was up.

Two weeks later we were still in the middle of Chapter One, we'd spent well over a quarter of an hour on what part of speech *inasmuch as* was in the sixth paragraph of Conrad's story, or even if it was one part of speech or two, and we hadn't got anywhere near the end of Chapter One. *The Shadow Line* and the white man's burden, such a strange tale to give a bunch of ten-year-olds to read.

Kids put up with a lot, and if Ticker was boring he couldn't help that, he was supposed to teach PT and Games not English, and he was good at those, enjoyed himself and we enjoyed him, we could even rag him a bit so long as we showed respect and didn't get too familiar. When Spotty Jenks missed a goal and the ball went into the canal and the game had to stop until we fished it out, "Don't get wet!" he said "don't fall in!" and when some of us threw stones and clods to knock it to the other side he shook his head and laughed "No, no no! You'll fill the canal doing that! The barges'd never get through" and that was such a daft thing to say that we all laughed as well. "Jones," he said, "run round to the other side, the breeze'll get it across" and by the time Wally got there the ball had got there too and we went back to our soccer. Ticker was a school fixture, he was always there, just like all the others he taught different subjects. The shortage of qualified teachers didn't end when the War did but got worse. "It's inevitable," Dad sad, "We've got to give people their old jobs back when they get demobbed, and that ties our hands. You can't hire new people and then two months later say you're sorry, you've lost your job because Mr Smith's come back." That's how Dolly Asprey got saddled with teaching French when she didn't know any at all, and it's how in January 1946 we got Mr Barnes to teach Science. And we absolutely hated him.

I can see now that he was just fresh, bright, young and up-to-date, probably straight out of Teacher Training College, he didn't look old enough to have been in the Army but we knew nothing about him at all, not even whether he lived in the village or somewhere else, and he never laughed, never had anything to say to us kids except what he was teaching, determined not to let us get away with anything. He simply *knew* that we were all good for absolutely nothing and had to be force-fed masses of facts to learn by heart. Dickens would have recognised him instantly, and so would we if we'd read *Hard Times*. He taught us Biology and Chemistry, all of it in the classroom, we never got near the Lab I don't know why, he just told us about equipment, made us learn from drawings and diagrams all about Bunsen Burners which we'd been using for ages, never let us near a microscope or a set of laboratory scales. We never got to use *any*thing. He wrote everything out on the board and we had to copy it down, he was a real terror, partly because with his very short blond hair he looked exactly like the Prussians we'd all been reading about in the *Wizard* and *Adventure* and seen in the pictures at the Gaumont and the Odeon in the holidays, and he hadn't been with us so much as two days before we were all calling him Belsen Bill.

We'd all recently been frightened, some of us enthralled, by the newsreels we'd seen of Belsen on *Pathé Pictorial*, some of us still had nightmares about those grotesques, all of us totally flummoxed by the emaciated swollen bony gaunt pale figures in those terrible shadowy photographs. In his single-breasted shiny grey suit and his shiny black shoes and short crew-cut hair he looked just like an American, that made us suspicious of him from the start, but after we'd seen him in class for ten minutes he was the living image of a Nazi Officer, rimless glasses and all, impossibly neat and scrubbed, half the time you couldn't see his pale blue eyes at all just the reflection like a mirror on his specs, and he had us all quaking in our shoes from the very first day. You couldn't hesitate for a second if he asked you a question, he simply loved giving you a Detention after School, and if you got your homework wrong you simply had to do *all* of it all over again, writing it out neatly and properly. What he wanted was absolutely different from what *any* of our Science Teachers had ever wanted. "No!" he'd say, "you don't draw glass tubing with a double line, you just draw *one*!" and he'd rip the page out of your book and screw it up and make you do it over, after School, and he'd cut your marks in half because you'd done it wrong. And heaven help you if you weren't neat. No blots or smudges! But you'd spent hours over the weekend or the night before carefully drawing in those narrow parallel lines the way other Teachers'd taught you, carefully using the compasses to get the curves right and the intervals exact, and then when you'd done it over again drawing all the tubes as single lines he'd contemptuously say "Why isn't this in *ink*?" and make you do it over yet again. He never smiled, he never joked, and he couldn't stand it if you fidgeted, didn't hesitate to give you a good wallop across the head, he knew how to make it hurt.

By the end of the Term he had us all properly trained his way, we were terrified of him, and when we got back after Easter lo and behold he'd *gone* and we had Hutch again for Science, Barnes'd gone and *Hutch'd* come back. We went back to doing experiments in the Lab and writing them up for homework. But the first time we handed in our Lab Reports Hutch took one look and said, "Where did this rubbish come from?" He was livid, bright red in the face almost purple and shouting at us, he'd always been a bit erratic and hot-tempered but he never struck us, he always apologised and he really did try to be fair. But "How *dare* you do this?" he shouted, "How *dare* you be so impertinent?" So John Parry told him that Belsen Bill had made us do it this way, only he didn't call him that he said "Mr Barnes." "Look at our books, Sir," he said, and handed his over, and Hutch leaned over it and skimmed the pages and said "Hmm" a lot and tut-tutted, "What a rubbishy mess all this is, the man should be shot," and "I see," and he looked up and said, "You'd better not do that any more," he looked very unhappy but smiled a bit so we knew it was alright, he knew it wasn't our fault, and when he gave us our homework at the end of class he grinned and said "Mind you don't do it the way That Man told you to or I'll be angry with *you*." We were surprised at his angry scorn of another Teacher, even if he had left. It was a bit bewildering, grown-ups never said anything critical of other grown-ups in front of us, it was unthinkable that a Master would say something severe about another Master, but Hutch got to be fond of using Mr Barnes as a scapegoat, used him as a sort of joke between us, and kept saying "He won't last long, that man, not as a Teacher."

I can't imagine Barnes sitting and gossiping and laughing in the Masters' Common Room with the other Teachers, I don't think he knew how to relax at all, his body always tight as if he was on the edge of the shakes but somehow puffed up along with it, perhaps he was one of the war-wounded and Broggie simply had to put up with him. We weren't half glad to get Hutch again, he so obviously loved mucking about with chemicals and showing off what amazing things he could do making loud bangs and smoke and flames, dramatizing the danger when he had to use the fume cupboard, laughing out loud when something went harmlessly wrong. He was probably the only Master we had that we actually *missed* after he'd gone, he was a character, we all knew him, and we all had lessons from him. And he cared about us kids, paid attention to us even if he did lose his temper now and again, "I'm sorry I was a bit short with you," he once told the whole class after he'd shouted at us, "Tuesday was simply not a good day, but none of you had done anything wrong and I should know better." There was a Periodic Table and Valency Chart on the lab wall, but he didn't tell us much about it, "You'll learn it as you need it," he said, and didn't bother to explain it.

But of course he still shouted at us when we kept making the same mistakes, "What you're doing can be dangerous," he'd say, "so you'd better get it *right*," but hardly any of us cared one way or the other. Once, he shouted *"Duck!"* as he picked up his jacket from the desk and threw it over a retort bubbling away on the bench, he moved really fast, *"Keep Down!"* ripped off his lab coat and smothered the retort as it exploded, evil smelling fumes, bits of hot glass and bubbly liquid scarring the bench. "Anybody hurt?" and we looked at each other as he said, "I think we'd better call it a day" and sent us away on an early break. If one of the kids showed interest then he showed interest back, it was because of him that Our Kid got into Chemistry. Hutch took Phil under his wing in the Fifth Form because he enjoyed Chemistry so much, showed him stuff he didn't show the other kids, taught him extra, and even gave him bits of equipment, flasks and test tubes, pipettes, and an old but working Bunsen Burner to use at home, there was a gas tap on the floor behind the kitchen door in the flat at Rugby and Phil hooked it up, tried to make soap just from a pile of ingredients he'd got at the chemist's, so Mum could use it. Phil told me once that it was because of Hutch that he got his degree in chemistry, doing it part-time at Birmingham Tech after he'd got a job, and then spending the whole of his working life as a professional chemist, eventually running his own small profitable company.

Some Teachers were completely useless, they had no idea how to cope with eleven- and twelve-year-olds and their energy. Mr Heiatt had a gammy leg and a big uncertain smile frozen on his face, all lips, he always looked a bit bewildered and tried to be strict but that smile gave him away, and he lasted just one year, I had him for English in III B. On his very first day when he came into class he even said, "Good Morning" and then took a long look and said "No! When I come in and say 'Good Morning' you should already have your English book and your notebook in front of you on your desk and you'll get on your feet, and you'll stay on your feet until you've said 'Good Morning' back. You'll say that *one at a time*, and you can only sit down after you've said it. You have to learn some courtesy, how to be civilised." We all thought that bonkers it'd take up so much time, and at Break Ken Larsen wondered if we have to stand at attention. "Next thing you know," he said, "he'll want us to salute!" Next day Bommy Rogers, his desk was at the side not far from the door, he didn't care tuppence for school and was completely irrepressible just the same as his best pal Jeff Hayward at the desk next to his, he said "Good morning, Sir" different from everybody else, humble and toady, he sounded really all meek and ashamed of himself, apologetic and a bit terrified, as if he meant "I'm ever so sorry, Sir, I couldn't help it, Please don't hit me!" And Jeff said "Oh!" but bit it down so it was almost under his breath I could hardly hear it, he looked up, pulled his shoulders back and loud and brisk, almost a bark, "Good Morning, *Sah*!" he sounded just like a Sergeant Major in the Army, any moment he'd click his heels and salute. A faint snigger from the back of the room, and Heiatt looked over and frowned, but the next kid was already saying "*Good* Morning, Sir !" all cheerful and perky, sounding all smiles *Isn't-this-a-lovely-day-to-be-here-in-this-classroom-with-you-Sir* and sat down with a crash. Heiatt looked a bit startled and opened his mouth but before he could speak the next kid said "G'morning, *Sir*" in a terribly feeble whisper he sounded as if he was at death's door and collapsed into his seat coughing terribly, almost drowning out the next kid's perfectly ordinary "Morning, Sir," but *he*'d left out the "Good" bit. Next day at the beginning of class we all did it all over again, same only different, and if Heiatt'd only said "I suppose you think this is all very amusing but it's not, it's simply tiresome and you can stop" we would've, but instead for a week or more it became a wonderful complicated game in which you couldn't say it the way anybody else had said it, all us kids standing up at the beginning of class grave and straight-faced, butter wouldn't melt, you couldn't laugh or even grin till you were sitting down and you mustn't let him see you grinning, that was one of the rules we all understood immediately without saying anything, we never talked about it at all really except perhaps at Break when you remembered somebody saying it in a really hilarious way or there'd been a really terrific sequence, the class starting with a progression of grunts and falsettos and wheezes and groans and anger and cheerfulness and misery and obsequiousness, always somebody sounding as if he was grovelling on the floor licking boots, somebody else imitating Mrs Mop or Valentine Dyall on the wireless, an ordered cumulation of suppressed hilarity. It was terrible if you were one of the last ones left standing while everyone else was bent over his desk chortling and grinning away pretending to read his English book, you had to keep your lips absolutely still and straight the goings-on coming towards you in an increasingly diverse cacophony, if you didn't you'd burst out in a great guffaw and you couldn't afford to do that, whatever you did you mustn't become a target for the Teacher's wrathful discomfort and helplessness, then it'd be your turn, you racked your brains how to do it. The best way was simply not to listen and to think about something else, but you *had* to listen to make sure you didn't say it the way somebody else had, and you couldn't help but pay attention to that wonderful harmonious sequence of squeaks and growls, terror and pity. "I don't know what I'm learning from Heiatt," Robin said to me and Jim on our Sunday walk, "but there must be something." "Like how boring he is," said Jim, "there's nothing there really to like or dislike. I don't think he's doing us any harm though." And we all laughed. Of course it wasn't long before the novelty wore off and Heiatt gave up his silly rule, it'd never worked. But when a few years later I came across the notion that the meaning of an utterance isn't in what the words say but in how they're said, the tone and the pacing, the silences, I instantly understood.

29

Nosey and Godfray

At the start of Easter Term, that was 1945, Nosey Parker came to Brewood. I was just on eleven years old, people said the War was nearly over. He was a curate at some coal-mining village out Cannock way and lasted the best part of two years, until he got a job as Vicar somewhere in the East End of London, we looked up to him a bit for that I suppose *Who'd want to be in a place like that, a missionary in the middle of all those London toughs?* but we were glad to be shot of him he was so erratic you never knew where you stood, and we wondered how long he'd last *there*, what he'd do with his temper, and we felt right to be rid of his intense do-good ways. He couldn't stand it when we whispered or talked to each other or fidgeted, all *that* did was show him we were full of sin, and he already knew *that*. He didn't understand our energy at all, and he certainly couldn't stand it. "Take a thousand lines!" he shouted at a kid the day after he arrived, and Roy Spark asked with his usual irrepressible fearlessness "What's he supposed to write then? *I must not waste paper?*" Nosey clenched his fist and went a bit pink, gestured with his right arm. "No," he said. "No," and took a deep breath. "But for the love of God behave yourselves! And don't you *ever* be so disrespectful."

He came to teach us three days a week, and his classes always dragged. After he'd greeted us he'd remind us that "This is a class in Religious Instruction, it is not a class in *Scripture* even if the School does call it that," but none of us could tell the difference. "You're all the wrong age for a class in Scripture," he'd say, "and my work here is to *instruct* you. Give you *Religious* Instruction," and most of the instruction came from the Old Testament. *The Lord killeth, and the Lord maketh alive* he told us, again and again. But we never understood, or at least I never did, and still don't, what someone like Samuel'd done to get rewarded, and what Eli'd done to die of a broken neck. After all, Samuel was only a child, and Eli an old man whose family was wiped out because he explained that God'd sent Samuel a message. That didn't make any sense at all. "God don't 'alf move in mysterious ways," Arnold whispered from the desk behind mine, but Nosey looked at him and raised his voice a bit, "The Lord giveth, and the Lord taketh away" he said, "That's how life *is*, and *that*'s why we must obey." In pretty well every class he told us stories from the Bible, along with the rewards and punishments they laid out "here and in the hereafter." His eyes bulged a bit as his Adam's Apple bobbed up and down and his voice gradually rose as he told us how to be a good Christian and learn to love our neighbours, and he'd quiz us. It was a lot like Church, only without the singing. "Have you learned that Psalm yet?" he'd asked, he gave us something to learn every week, a new psalm or the Apostles' Creed, that took more than a day or two, or we'd recite *The Lord is my shepherd; I shall not want*, the whole thing, as he marked the rhythm with his hand. "Woe betide you if you make a mistake," he said, "you shall not take the Lord's word in vain." Lots of "Save me" and "Heal me" and "Deliver me" to recite or read aloud. But not much *Jubilate*. He never asked us what we thought, he simply told us what we had to do or not do, and what we should feel about anything. "Oh!" said Uncle Edward, "He sounds like one of *those*. No jokes. Nothing in the Bible to laugh about." Nosey'd once told the Fifth Form that his greatest ambition was to be a slum missionary, "*That*'s where Good Works need doing" and "You *must* love God," he'd tell us. But Bob Lewisham chortled, "When Nosey says 'suffer little children to come unto me,'" his eyes flashing at his own wit as we sheltered from the cold rain during one Break, "'e really does mean *Suffer* doesn't 'e." The other kids laughed, and I didn't dare say that's not what the Bible means.

When I got into III A, that's when we got Mr Godfray for French, Nosey'd already been at School for a year, we had the Acts of the Apostles as our textbook, and after we'd all taken turns to read bits aloud to each other and he'd asked us what they meant he'd tell us St Luke had written the Acts, and how important St Paul was, he kept coming back to the story of Saint Paul falling off his horse on the road to Damascus and getting converted, and how terribly important "Paul's ministry to the Gentiles" is. But what he said didn't make much sense. That word *ministry* made me think of the Ministry of Food, everybody was always complaining about *it* and its restrictions, and a lot of us thought of ministers as being in the government, like Winston Churchill, he was Prime Minister and Mum and Dad worshipped *him*, but I couldn't see what that had to do with the Vicar, and none of us knew what a Gentile is. When Nosey told us a Gentile was someone who wasn't a Jew Billy Bebb said "isn't a Gentile the same as a Heathen, Sir? That's what it says here" and he waved his *Little Oxford Dictionary*. The only heathens I could think of were Umslopogaas and the spear-waving savages we read about in the Leatherstocking stories and Biggles books. *What does Saint Paul or even Nosey Parker have to do with them? Is gentile like genteel, sort of posh, like Squire Giffard's supposed to be out at Chillington Hall or the Earl of Bradford over at Weston Park?*

We were always passing notes back and forth in Nosey's classes, whispering, furtively playing Battleship or Consequences in our notebooks, perhaps from the back of the room a *tick-tunk-tock* as a marble made its way through a desk, shuffle of feet, Maurice or someone else at the back quietly chuckling over a comic under his desk. He just couldn't prevent our stealth, he'd clench his fists and splutter a bit, he'd stoop his tall bony figure at us, his hair ragged, no longer neatly slicked back above his ears, and dish out Lines by the hundred. But he was mostly a joke and we *couldn't* fear him, he hardly ever remembered what Lines he'd given and more often than not forgot who he'd given them to, or even that he'd given *any*, failing in his anger to write it down in his little notebook. But by the end of nearly every class he'd given somebody a Detention after school and he always remembered *that*, he'd sit in the front of the room reading and watching over you while you did it, writing your Lines or getting on with your prep, until Detention Period was over.

If you'd got a Detention you couldn't play with your pals or go off to the spinney or the village, you just had to sit there, and after the forty minutes he'd say in a tired voice "You can go now, before everyone's eaten all the Tea. Behave yourself in future, do what you're supposed to." Sometimes you'd miss Tea altogether, and he always threatened such dire punishments that we never quite knew what he could or couldn't do. Late in one rambunctious class, him shouting at us and all of us playing up like mad, he heard me say that St Paul must've been worse than Nosey he was always so busy bossing people about, and he went flat dead white and said in a strangled sort of voice "Quartermain. Stay behind after class" and everyone went quiet. After class he told me what I'd said was absolutely dreadful, "Think about Hell's fires, boy. What you said was truly wicked, You'd better learn what you've done. Learn about St Paul!" he said. "You have three days to copy out five chapters of the Acts of the Apostles, starting with Chapter Five. Write it in *ink*, no crossings-out, no blots, no mistakes, in your best handwriting, on good paper." *Not in my Rough Notebook, then.* "That way you'll get to know St Paul's conversion thoroughly, understand and *remember* it." He couldn't leave St Paul alone, always going on about the Epistles and how important they are. I thought the bits I understood sounded just like Marlow Grandfather, all *don't* do this and *do* do that. "Bring it to me at the Masters' Common Room on Thursday at Break," he said, and told me I could go. "Don't you *dare* forget!" And of course I didn't do anything about it at all, he'd never remember. But on Wednesday in class he scowled "Have you finished that copying?" "No, Mr Parker," I said. I hadn't even done *any* of it I'd been so sure he'd forget, but he bent his head down and peered at me his face close to mine, red rings round his eyes, uneven black stubble round his Adam's apple, "Tomorrow" he glowered, "at Break."

  As soon as supper was over I took myself off to the Third Form classroom, sat at a desk at the back of the room where people might not notice me, the inkwell good and full, pitch black outside, nobody about, I looked at chapter five of Acts, and my heart sank, it was huge, 42 verses and I looked ahead to chapter six, *Oh, much shorter, maybe I can get it done* but then I looked a bit further, it got worse, no better at all, chapter seven with its sixty verses *It's pages and pages! I'll never get it done!* And I wondered, *do I have to copy all the numbers too? Can I just do the words?* I blinked a tear away and wiped my nose, the only sounds the scratch of my pen and the shuffle of my feet and I listened to my breathing, *Gosh it's cold* and as I looked out, still pitch black out there and nobody about, I began to shiver *What time is it?* and I stood up and stretched, moved over to the radiator to warm my hands but it was barely warm, *Oh! Nunc must've turned it off* and wondered what was going to happen everybody must be in bed by now, Angus checking the dorms, he was the Housemaster, *What about the Prefects?* The room was freezing all those windows on both sides, I shivered so much I could hardly hang on to my pen, how could I possibly get all this done, it'll take me all night! I'd only done two chapters and a bit, and I slumped down trying to warm up, writing away, shaking my hand to get rid of writer's cramp, I kept having to stop to yawn and I thought about all the kids in the Second Dorm tucked up nice and warm in bed by now, *I've still got nearly all of chapter eight to do, let alone Nine and Ten* And the sound of footsteps, regularly paced, coming down the walkway and I looked up as the door opened. *Broggie!* I was too cold and tired to care much, "Quartermain. What are *you* doing *here*? Why aren't you in bed, it was Lights Out over an hour ago." "Please, Sir, I'm doing an Imposition for Mr Parker, Sir, he said I have to have it finished by tomorrow" and I had to tell him what it was and what it was for, I'd been very rude, and he blinked. I didn't know what he'd do, except I thought he'd punish me more, but I felt a lot better now I'd told him, and he looked a bit annoyed and surprised, perhaps a little puzzled *He's not even cross!* and I even felt a little bit warmer as my shivering began to take over, I began to ease up a bit, a tiny current of relief *I can't be in any worse trouble.* "Well," Broggie said, "you have *got* to get into bed, it's far too late. Put those things away and tidy up, it's long after nine o'clock and the Seniors are already on their way to bed. You can tell Mr Parker I said you should stop." He paused. "Don't worry about Mr Parker. Just get off to bed. Run, warm up a bit!" My breath coldly clouding as I went through the door he looked at me and shook his head, "Go along now. I'll have a word with Mr Parker." And next day at Break Nosey was waiting in the doorway of the Masters' Common Room, clink of coffee and teacups muffled behind him, air thick with cigarette smoke wafting round him, murmur of conversation, a quiet laugh *That was Dolly Asprey!* I didn't want them to see me as I handed him the bundled sheets of paper, their edges crumpled and curled, and before I could open my mouth he thrust out his hand and said in a low voice, a funny sort of lopsided smile on his face, "Yes, Mr Brogden explained. That's quite alright" and folded them up, stuffed them in his pocket. Not a glance, not a single word about what I'd done, just "Run along now." And that was the end of it. Not a word from Nosey, not a word from Broggie. It was as though nothing at all'd happened.

None of us was the least bit afraid of Nosey even if he was a bit of a fanatic in his desperate earnestness, he had an impatient temper but we couldn't miss the way he tried to hold himself in check and we knew he'd never hit us or do any real harm. We all knew it wouldn't make a scrap of difference if Broggie never found a properly qualified Scripture Teacher, anyone who was a Teacher could read the Bible and the prayer book, they'd know the Bible anyway, and could explain stuff to children even if they weren't Church of England but were Chapel or even Catholic instead, we didn't have to learn about Scripture the way we had to learn stuff like Science or Mathematics or even English, even if it got taught in schools everywhere. Almost anyone could step in to look after a Scripture class, even Matron or Mrs Broggie, if I thought about whoever it was taught Sunday School at Church even Mum or Aunt Kath could do it. Broggie's real nightmare was finding qualified people to teach languages like French, let alone German, Greek or Latin. Either somebody in the village or nearby knew one of these languages, or nobody did, and that was just a matter of chance. How could he find in a small village like Brewood someone who could *even read* the Greek alphabet, never mind teach the language? As more and more men got called up to fight and got replaced by new ones or by no one at all, our Teachers got older and older and fewer and fewer. In the nine School Terms from September 1941 to June 1944 I had three Terms with no French at all and five different French Teachers altogether. One of them had less French even than Angus had Physics when he taught us *that*, keeping ahead of us one lesson at a time and using a crib sheet. During the War a lot of schools simply stopped teaching languages at all, and by the time I got to University in 1952 you didn't *have* to have German or Greek to get in, and in some places you could even get by without any Latin. When Frank Evans came back to teach French after the War, he'd been an interpreter in military intelligence, he laughed derisively at Dolly Asprey for thinking French used apostrophes the way English did, her teaching us *Le fermier's vache. Le garçon's crayon.* "I can't believe she didn't know *that!*" he said. So Broggie must've been overjoyed in September 1944 when he got hold of Mr Godfray, who actually lasted heaven help us until Frank Evans got back in January 1946. By then we'd endured Godfray for four whole Terms. He was so bonkers they felt like four years.

This great big man, black shirt with a white dog-collar like the Vicar's, huge in his dark suit and untidy beard, taller and a lot older than any of the other Teachers, marched his heavy tread into class the first day of Autumn Term in his baggy trousers and clattery steel-tipped heels, a bicycle clip hanging from his top pocket. On that morning he had on a thick woollen cloak at least that's what it looked like but it was actually a herringbone overcoat he wore it like a cloak, and he didn't wear it in class after that but a teacher's black gown instead the way other Teachers except Dolly Asprey and Angus did. That morning everything felt new and strange, the first day in Form III A for all of us in that room, and he didn't look in the least bit pleased to see us, or even interested. His voice came through the open door before we could see him at all, a loud *"Debout,"* and we all looked up, a bit of a scramble as some of us stood up right away, desk seats clattering, some of us not so quick especially the two new kids, this was their first day ever at Brewood, it was his too and his face went a bit red as he scowled "On end, boy! that's what *Debout* means, *Stand up!* When *I* come into the room *you* stand up! Show respect for your betters! *You!*" and he pointed at one of the new boys still clambering to his feet, "How dare you not be ready!" Little bits of spit flew off his lips. I didn't dare look anywhere, his size so overwhelmed me, my desk in the front row, but with everybody so quiet the whole room felt *surprised*, nobody, not even at the back, whispered, not a single cough, not the sound of a single book being opened or got out, no faint creak of a desk lid opening or closing *How would we get on with him? What'd he be like?* When we were all on our feet and the whole room still he waited a bit then said *"Bonjour."* A couple of kids looked at each other. Some of us said *"Bonjour"* back, some were a bit slow, he curled his lips back I could see his teeth big and gappy, yellow and black stains, white flecks of spit drying out where his beard cleared the corners of his mouth, and he said *"Bonjour* means 'Good Day!' It is a greeting, it is a courtesy, it is good manners. When you see me you greet me properly to show respect *Bonjour* it is my due. I will try again. *Bonjour!"* and we all chorused *bonjour* back. *"Bon!"* he said, *"Asseyez-vous,"* clatter of seats at his gesture, and we all sat down. He frowned and said that we would do this every morning when he came in and that in English his name was Godfray, only what we heard was Godfrey. He said that this was a class in French and "in French my name is *Godefroi."* He wrote it on the board, and "Godfray" next to it. As he turned to do so I looked down, the hem of his trousers rose up a bit as he raised his arm to write, his trousers a bit short little threads hanging down at the back and he had a brown sock on his left foot and a black sock on his right, scuffed black leather boots and a big oily-looking stain on the back of his left leg. I wondered if it was off a bike, but how could it get onto his *left* calf? "You will always address me as *M'sieu Godefroi"* he told us, "you should say *Bonjour M'sieu Godefroi*. It is a famous name, I come from an ancient and noble French family, my ancestor led the First Crusade." He wrote *"Godefroi de Bouillon"* on the board, and the date 1096. "You will treat that name with great respect. It is an important name, and it is *my* name, and you will treat *me* with great respect. Write it down in your *cahiers*, your exercise books, so that you do not forget" and he came over and looked at what I was writing, it was the first page in my new exercise book, and as I was writing he stuck his finger down on the word *Godefroi* there was dirt under the nail it was black with it and all ingrained in the creases, a big hand, pudgy but strong looking, he smudged the ink, *"No, boy,"* he said, "B-o-u-i-l-l-o-n" he said the letters in French and he took the book and ripped out the page and crumpled it wasting all that paper that was shocking we were supposed to *save* paper it was *Salvage* and he said "Tidy that up, and start again! Do it properly! What is your name?" the smell of sweat and unwashed clothes stale scruffiness old man's pee, after the class was over Roger said, "Did you see all the food stains down his front?" In class I said "Quartermain, Sir" and he said *"M'sieu Godefroi"* and I said *"M'sieu Godefroi"* and he said "Your name is French, *Quatremain*, it means one of your ancestors had four hands, did you know that?" and he laughed, "You must have a coat of arms," and I said I didn't know, "How can you not know?" he raised his voice and looked round the room, "That is your family history, you have an important name, it tells everybody who you are. You should *all* know your family history, how can you not know *that*?" and I thought of Marlow Grandfather and his endless natter about the family, and Dad's genealogy book "by William F. Carter B.A. Inner Temple Barrister-at-Law. Prologue by Colonel Josiah C. Wedgwood P.C., M.P. Oxford University Press 1936" with the coat of arms in the frontispiece, "Gules, a fesse azure between four dexter hands couped at the wrist, or," and I didn't say anything, everybody would've laughed their heads off at me if I'd ever said anything about *that*, I wouldn't want to anyway, I'd had a bellyful. Godfray turned to the kid next to me and said, "What's *your* name?" He said "Cooper" and paused, Godfray lifted his hand I thought he was going to hit him, *"M'sieu Godefroi*, Sir" and Godfray lowered the hand. "No 'Sir,' boy, I am not a knight. Your name is *Tonnelier* you're a barrel-maker" and he made it sound like the lowest of the low, he told him how to spell it, he went round the room telling us all what our French name was but when he got to Arthur Wardle he made him spell it "What sort of a name is that? What does it mean?" and Arthur said he didn't know, it was just his name, and grinned a bit and Godfray just pronounced it with a French accent *Oo-arrd-luh* but looked as though it wasn't really a name at all.

That class went on and on, even after we'd gone through all the names, he wrote them all down on a seating chart he made, he said we would use our French names from now on. He told us he came from Guernsey, "Where's that, Guillaumes?" and Ivor told him it was in the Channel Islands, "the Boche are there now," said Godfray and he gurgled a bit when he said *Boche* the *ch* bubbling from the back of his mouth, "they are in my own home, where my family lives, our family house." Then he asked, "What is the French name for the English Channel" and nobody knew so he wrote *La Manche* on the board and made us pronounce it. "I speak proper French," he said, "the way it should be spoken. You will learn to speak with a correct accent" and he turned suddenly and glared, "*Vous!*" he said, "*Boulanger!*" and pointed, "*Dites moi l'alphabet!*" and Ron said "Me, Sir?" he'd forgotten what his French name was, he'd only heard it the once. Godfray said "You will not question me when I tell you to do something, you will simply do it. Say the alphabet, *en Français!* In this class we do everything in French." "Yes, Sir" Ron said, he was sitting a couple of rows behind me and Godfray threw a piece of chalk at him and said "*Oui, M'sieu Godefroi!* You insult my name!" Ron couldn't do the alphabet in French, and somebody on the back row snickered, Godfray threw a piece of chalk at *him*, he was a good shot and as the Term wore on we learned to put up with him. Sometimes he'd throw a book, the pages fluttering, some of them perhaps falling out, you'd put your arms round your head *thunk*, sometimes he threw the board rubber. But we got used to him, the way he'd parade into the room his big belly sticking out in front, we laughed at him more than we feared him, he was a figure of fun with his dirty habits. He'd pick his nose and wipe his hand on his clothes, he was smelly and unpleasant, always the bully, but we thought he was harmless. We hated it when he was the Master in charge at the head of the lunch table, his turn to dish out the food, none of us liked barley-kernel pudding but we never turned it down we were too hungry, made with much more water than milk, sometimes runny like soup other times like thick porridge as he scraped it off the bottom of the big enamel pan, a wodge 'd stick to the spoon and he'd slop it down on the plate *flop!* to get it off the spoon. When the wodge got so thick that it wouldn't come off the spoon he'd wipe it off with his big dirty thumb and lick what was left off the spoon, big red moist lips closing round as much of the spoon as would go in his mouth and suddenly there'd be a lot of barley kernel pudding left over at the end of the meal. He was totally unconscious of what he was doing. Looking back I see he was a coarse and physical man, sensual and immensely vain, blunt and belligerent, he had no idea at all how to handle a whole class of unruly kids, viewed them with a scarcely genial contempt, never missed a chance to put us right. "Call a spade a spade, boy, and not a bloody shovel!" he'd shout, and smirk at the effect of that *bloody*. His vanity over his ancestors led one of the older kids to look up the First Crusade in the *Encyclopaedia Britannica*, there was an old one in the School library, he read that Godefroy de Bouillon did indeed lead the crusaders of Lorraine to victory in Jerusalem, and Jerusalem fell on 15 July 1099 when "the blood of the conquered ran down the streets until men splashed in blood as they rode."

He couldn't stand it when we said *oo*, big and round and Staffordshire, sometimes nasal, instead of *u* or *eu* in French. "Say it like this!" he'd say, "No, boy, watch me!" and he'd purse his big wet lips all crinkly into a tiny round O and say it properly, the French way, "*tu es*," he'd say, "It's not *too ay*!" He'd drill us relentlessly, he was absolutely fanatic about pronunciation "Don't butcher the glories of the French language" and during Break or at lunch or at any other odd free moment some kid would purse his lips and go *u!* the way Godfray wanted and there'd be a whole chorus of us going *u! u! u! u!* falling about giggling helplessly and we learned from him what we learned from others, to look down on those who couldn't do what we could. "Don't you know better than that?" we'd cry, "It's not *oo-oo* it's *u!*" and thrust our faces close to each other and scream "*u! u! u!*" and laugh. "You sound just like a village kid! Say it properly," half-serious in our clowning and mirthfully convinced of our own superiority, until one startling day in Chemistry Hutch Hutchings brought us up short. He'd asked us all some question or other and Ivor Williams said "Please, Sir, you can only see that by an experiment in the *LAB*oratory" he said it like that, the stress on the *lab* and somebody snickered "You have to do it in the *LAV*atory? Don't be daft. You mean the lab*ORR*atory," and we all laughed away in derision, Ivor went red, and Hutch, he was in quite a good mood about it, said, and that was a surprise considering what he'd said to us about Belsen Bill, "Actually, Williams is quite right, so you can stop laughing. The proper pronunciation is as he says, *LAB*oratory. It comes from Latin, _labor_ it means _work_, a _LABoratory_ is a place where you _do_ work just the same as a _LAVatory_ is a place where you wash. Comes from Latin, just as _lef_tenant comes from French and should in fact be pronounced _lyoo_tenant – the Yanks know better than you do! Not many people know all that or even think about it, most of them get it wrong, it sounds funny to them, and you're all just as ignorant as they are! Williams knows better than you do. Now stop showing your ignorance and pay attention!" Ivor looked a bit chuff and grinned, his face still a bit embarrassed, and we were all left a bit confused. Of course you had to pronounce words properly _Don't be ignorant!_ you could never let on that you didn't know something, that just invited scorn. But none of us really believed Hutch and even after Paunch had looked it up in the big dictionary in the school library and found out Hutch was right we still pronounced it _labORRatory_ the way everyone else did. Language habits die hard, and it didn't make any difference to our snobbish belief in our own superiority to the village kids, our unassailable rectitude, any more than Godfray's endless drills in pronunciation made us feel inferior to _him_.

Godfray wore layers and layers of clothing always complaining about how hot the room felt, or how cold. "_Ouvrez la fenêtre! Refermez!_" he never once asked us what we wanted, we'd bait him when we thought we could get away with it, and once, when not long after the start of class he chuntered on and on with a book in his hand about his mother, Perce Watts stuck his hand up and Godfray stopped talking and scowled. "_Oui? Qu'est-ce que c'est?_" Perce faltered a bit, "_Excusez-moi, monsieur,_" and he stopped again, and he shrugged, the other kids round him smirking a bit, and then "Please, Sir, did you know your fly is open?" We all looked. A glimpse of greyish underwear. I thought Perce was pretty brave asking, interrupting like that, Godfray had such a fierce temper, he could be scary when he flew off the handle, some days he flew off it thoroughly and _fast_ and we'd have to be super-cautious. But today he was in a good mood, he didn't even move his hand to check the buttons, he didn't even tell Perce he should've said it in French, he merely said "I know, boy. It's cooler that way."

We couldn't take him seriously, most of the time his bluster just bluster. He wasn't real the way Henry Houston or even Dolly Asprey was, *their* displeasure *mattered*, but then you always knew where you were with them, they were predictable, and Godfray's conspicuous oddity made him a favourite target. He abominated electric lights, he dismissed them as *trucs* and turned them off whenever he came into the classroom, and that made him a sitting target for kids like Arthur Camden and Lanky Jones in IV A. Once, before class started they shorted the light switch with a sixpence so you couldn't turn it off, we all heard about this at Lunch, and Our Kid told me later how Godfray'd stood there flicking the switch on and off and getting more and more frustrated, muttering French more and more crossly under his breath until at last he told everyone to get on with their irregular verbs while he went off to get help. By the time he got back with Broggie Arthur and Lanky'd taken the sixpence out and the light worked properly again, Godfray baffled and uncertain-looking, Broggie a bit narked but an ill-concealed twinkle in his eye, all those butter-wouldn't-melt kids busy over their verbs.

When I asked Our Kid in April 2000 if Godfray was in fact a defrocked Catholic priest as we all believed even though he still wore a dog-collar, he simply chanted over the phone
  Godefroi de Bouillon led the First Crusade.
  He didn't use a shovel, he used a bloody spade!
the way we all used to chant it, but not when he was within earshot. I don't know who made that jingle up and I'd forgotten it anyway, but before the end of his first Term we'd learned to fear Godfray as well as laugh at him. When one of the kids in our dorm, Ray Shakeshaft probably, it was the sort of thing he would find out, the smart city kid from Willenhall or was it Wednesbury, his hair slicked back with Brylcreem, discovered that *Bouillon* meant *soup* we all laughed and laughed, but never dared even amongst ourselves to call him *Soup* outside the dorm or the Billiard Room, where Godfray never went, and we never gave him a nickname, *Soup* just didn't stick and neither would anything else. It's funny we never spotted the way he spelled that part of his French name he was so proud of, I suppose we never saw it written down except that time he wrote it on the blackboard,

but we made nothing of it at all. We had no affection for him or even contempt, he was just comic and unpredictable and occasionally very fearsome indeed. Just before Christmas in 1944 we were reviewing the irregular *-oir* verbs and he started listing them off, telling us to add to the list, *avoir* he started us off, *pouvoir*, and we slowly contributed others, *vouloir*, *s'asseoir*, *mouvoir*, and Arthur Wardle in fine humour at the back corner of the room whispered to the kid in the next desk *Godefroi* and we all laughed it was so witty, none of the rest of us had made that sort of connection, we all liked Arthur he was the class wag. Sitting at his desk for once, Godfray leapt to his feet bright red in the face, he simply leapt towards Arthur spittle flying as he shouted "Get out! Get out! Get out! Before I *kill* you, boy!" it was almost a scream, for a big man he moved terrifically fast. I don't think we'd ever seen anybody so angry in all our lives, certainly I hadn't, in his leap he banged into Henry's desk at the front of the room pushed Henry to the floor trying to get at Arthur, Arthur scrambled through a desk away from Godfray, ran for the door Godfray after him caught him by the hair dragged him slam bang against desks kids scrambling to get out of the way, desks jumbling together tipping this way and that, ink splashing about, books and papers everywhere, slammed the door open, *bang!* went Arthur against the jamb "Ow! ow! ow! ow!" he cried "And never come back!" yelled Godfray clenching the doorframe trembling, we were all pale as he turned back to look at us. Pale sweaty and out of breath, he closed the door, Arthur running away across the Croft clutching his head, "You'd better straighten these desks out and sit down, read your books, learn how to conjugate *savoir*" and between breaths you could see him trembling like anything. He asked Henry if he was hurt.

Next day instead of French, we had a free period with Moggie Morris watching over us and for the next couple of days we didn't see Godfray anywhere at all, not even at Prayers but got Henry Houston at French one day and Ticker Ranson the next to keep us out of mischief, but they couldn't do any French so neither did we. Everybody knew what'd happened, there was nothing else to talk about at lunch and at Break, and Wally Beasley told me and a couple of other kids how a week or two before Godfray'd really gone for Derek Elder, "didn't 'alf wallop 'im," chasing him out of IV B for using a six-inch ruler to underline his notes, "Mathematical implements have no place in the study of French," he'd shouted, "but that's not why 'e 'it 'im, not really. Derek was readin' the latest *Wizard* and 'e didn't bother to 'ide it, 'e just 'ad it out on 'is desk right in front of 'im. Got a real temper that man 'as." Him and Nosey Parker both.

30

After the War

As soon as the War was over Mum and Dad both said that Broggie must be really anxious as he waited for teachers to get back from the Forces, "*real* teachers" Dad called them, but "Don't hold your breath, it won't happen right away. It will take time to get everyone demobbed, that'll be difficult, getting them back to their old jobs or even finding them any work at all. Some jobs will have disappeared, and some of the troops never had a proper job before but went straight into the Army from school. They'll have to find somewhere to live too, all those houses bombed-out. Look at what it was like after the last war. It won't be easy." And he was right, it was a very unsettled time, and it wasn't helped by an epidemic of mumps in April and May, I was in the Sick Room on VE Day but went out into the village anyway, no one but Matron around in the school buildings, and a couple of weeks later, at the end of May, an epidemic of jaundice hit the kids in Knightley, me included, halfway through the Easter Term. And on top of that when I went home for the summer we found I'd got appendicitis. That's all just a blurred memory now, but when I came back to School in September 1945 I'd lost so much time I had to take III A all over again. With most of my pals especially Robin and Jim moved up to IV B, me left behind so I could do everything all over again, it was a bit frustrating, I'd read all the books for English, *Macbeth* so familiar I could recite chunks of it by heart, endlessly *Tomorrow and tomorrow and tomorrow*. And no matter how many classes I'd missed in III A last year French was dead easy second time around, I didn't learn much. At Christmas Godfray reported I was "Excellent: has shown great interest," but of course I'd already done all the exercises and I could look up what I'd done last year and get it right this time. I had a new English and History Teacher, he didn't know I'd done it all before and he praised me for "doing very good work." Doing Form III A all over again was pretty easy, "Jammy" one of the other kids said, and I romped through everything. At the end of term I came in first in Geography, French, and Science and close to the top in everything else, and Mr Bolton, he was Form Master, praised my "excellent result." But all the other kids were pretty much the same age as me instead of being a year or more older and it all got to be dead boring, I wanted to be with my pals so I didn't keep them company much at Break or after class, some of them thought I was a swot, everything was so dead easy, and none of us including me liked swots. But it wasn't all that easy being with my pals either, they weren't doing the same thing as me in English or in anything else. At the end of term Broggie reported my performance as "splendid." When I came back after the Christmas holidays I found I'd been promoted at last, the way I should've been, to Form IV B. I knew that had to've been Broggie's doing, he always paid close attention, especially to us boarders, away from our parents as we were, he took the role of *in loco parentis* very seriously indeed. Suddenly I had a lot of catching up to do, but I was back with my pals, me once again the youngest in the class, everyone else thirteen and me still twelve.

I needed that reassurance, because when we were getting ready to go home for Christmas Mum and Dad told us we wouldn't be living in Rugby any more, Dad'd got a new job and we'd have to move, settle into a new house when we came home for the holidays. Not that he'd actually got a new job, he'd taken over his old one at Spark Hill and it was all very sudden, the manager at Rugby'd been demobbed and come back to his old job in November 1945, he'd been a Major in the Army and had a lot of clout, so that same month Dad had to move back to *his* old job in Birmingham, Mum had to give up her job in Rugby, she must've been glad of that, but the two of them had to find a place for us all to live. That was a terrific scramble, so many people looking for housing all at once, Mum and Dad stayed awake worrying their heads off, not so much that we wouldn't find anywhere to live, there was no danger of that, but that we'd end up in a council house, or what was unthinkably worse, a two-bedroom prefab, badly-built more likely than not by German or Italian prisoners of war and crammed cheek by jowl with dozens of identical prefabs, so small that most of our furniture and everything'd have to go into storage, no room at all, paper-thin walls, no garden or anything else to speak of, and not our sort of people at all as neighbours. "Well, if that's the case we'll have to put up with it," Dad said. "I don't think it's likely. I'll have to see what I can do," and somehow he found us a house in Hall Green, a big step down from what we'd had at Rugby. "It took some finding," Mum said, "We're lucky. It's the only place there is close enough to the store." But in the three years we lived there, until I was fifteen, I never could think of it as home, a perpetual damp feeling about the place, "That's probably from the River Cole" Mum said, the river the other side of a scruffy bit of park so feeble you could hardly float a toy boat in it, "Best stay away," Dad said, "it can get pretty big at flood season, and that's every year," and even Our Kid said "Don't go *there*, it's not at all safe, especially once it starts to get dark." In his fifteen-year-old's restlessness Phil enjoyed exploring the big city, and soon after we arrived he got Mum to pack him a couple of sandwiches and a small bottle of milk and disappeared for the day. When I asked him where he was going he just said "Out," and when he got back at tea-time he said he'd spent most of the day on the Outer Circle bus, sitting on the top deck, "getting to see the city," he said. "It only costs sixpence, you should try it." But I didn't, I couldn't see myself asking the conductor if we'd be stopping long enough for me to go and pee, or even if I could get off the bus and catch another one using the same ticket, I didn't think it was possible anyway, and I wished I could be with Our Kid and Brenda on the farm or with Robin and Jim, but they wouldn't be in Brewood in the holidays and nor would anyone else.

Mum dragged me off to the Hall Green library where I could borrow books, and one day Phil went with me to the big library in Brum. "Come and see," he said. Big oak cabinets, small brass knobs sticking out in double or triple rows, the top one just above eye level, "Look" he said, and grabbed a knob and pulled. It slid out like a picture frame but glass both sides, on the side facing me a whole set of unused postage stamps, King Edward VII, and the caption with the dates 1902-1910 and all the stuff you'd find in the Advanced catalogue, the bright colours of a complete set, all the way from a ha'penny to a pound. I could hardly believe my eyes, and round the back, same frame pulled out, complete sets of the same stamps but overprinted "Official" and the name or initials of all sorts of government departments, like Army or Admiralty, I had no idea those even existed, so many of these frames that I came back day after day even after I'd looked at them all. "Aren't they smashing!" Phil said, and when I said "It'd be super to have something like that" he sniffed "What would you do with it if you had it? Wake up!"

Soon after that he led me along a wide hallway in another building, it must've been the Art Gallery, and pointed, "Look at the flow of that," he pointed and gestured, "It's called *The circle of the lustful*. Isn't it terrific! I wouldn't mind being able to draw like that, all that energy." On the left a fat rope like a snake, stuffed with what looked like naked bodies, looping up towards the top left corner of the painting while another fat rope, looking more like river-rapids flowing backwards up the middle of the picture, I could almost *feel* the stretch, and on the right side a fierce glow, people inside it. The weirdness bothered me, left me puzzled *Where's the story?* "It's a water-colour," Phil said. "It's by William Blake," but I didn't know who he was. "Oh yes you do," Our Kid said, and in a low voice he sang "And did those feet in ancient time" and I knew. "Oh," I said. I really liked singing Harty's tune, all that swozz, but I didn't like the picture all that much, I liked the one by Ford Madox Brown, a round painting called "The Last of England," a man and a woman sadly looking out of a boat at something not in the picture but outside it and behind *me*. That pulled me into the picture it*self*, everything so close, perhaps that's why it stuck in my head for years. Yet whenever I came home for the holidays it was the Blake, the flowing lines and shapes, the mysterious details, not the Madox Brown but page after page of Blake's illuminated books, they arrested me and haunted me as they somehow confirmed the sad loneliness evoked by "The Last of England."

When I look back at the years immediately after the War, when we left Rugby and moved back to Brum, when at School we at last got rid of Godfray and Nosey, what I remember most is the feel of endless instability and change. I've forgotten nearly all the people. When I look through my Report Book I can identify Belsen Bill Barnes alright, he was so arbitrary in his wrongness, but I don't even remember "D. Bolton." Yet Bolton taught me for two years, he was my Form Master in III A at Christmas 1945 so must've seen a lot of him, that's when he praised my "very good work" in English and History and three months later, after I'd moved back to where I belonged, in IV B, he said I "should do quite well." Then, like a lot of other teachers, he disappeared. That was the time when Broggie had teachers swop classes and teach each other's subjects, so far as I can tell that was just for one term, I got Henry Houston for History and Ticker Ranson for Geography instead of the other way round, and the only thing Ticker could say, as I came in twenty-fifth in a class with twenty-six kids in it, was that "Neatness is necessary for maps." The best Henry could say as I dropped down to eighth in History was that I was "untidy and careless." The unsettledness persisted for close to three years as teachers came back from the War in dribs and drabs, some of them, like Mr Embleton, for just one year, others, like Roy Leafe, for years, he taught Mathematics and eventually became Headmaster, long after I'd left for university. Embleton wore a leather support like a permanent bandage on his left wrist, we all believed a bullet'd gone through it in the War, and *that* along with his upright military bearing and officer's moustache made him a bit exotic *He must've been a hero!* He only taught Fourth Form and higher, and he fascinated some of us younger kids. In the autumn evenings he'd go out to the First Pitch and practise golf swings, most of us'd never even *seen* any golf clubs before and he had a full set, he'd brought them back with him from America. "Golf," Pongo said. "*Huh!* That's what rich people do," so strange to us that two or three of us'd go over and watch him, but he didn't like that *Your chatter disturbs my concentration.* The novelty soon wore off anyway, and we stopped, left him alone, and at the end of the year he went to another school, somewhere in Cheshire.

Changes came so thick and fast that Broggie must've been kept busy at the end of the summer in 1947, not just with old teachers coming back but with finding new ones like Mr Anderson who took over all the History classes, so solid in his chubbiness that we called him Tubby right away, that's what we called him behind his back until Horace said, "he looks just like the little jade Buddha that sits on our mantelpiece," and that was so spot on that most of us began to call him Buddha instead. He hadn't been in the Forces but had just come straight to Brewood once he got out of Oxford, we never again got Ticker Ranson for English or History and what a blessing *that* was. But the really big change came just before we went home for the holidays at Easter, we heard about it at the end of Prayers one morning, we'd finished the hymn and settled back, and Broggie said, "I have some very important news, it affects all of us. I have discussed matters with Mr Houston," and he looked to his right and nodded to Henry, "and very briefly with other members of the staff, and now it is time for me to share this news with you. At the end of term, which as I'm sure you all know will be at the end of next week," and he smiled, "you will all be leaving school for the Easter holidays, and I shall be leaving with you. I have accepted an appointment as Headmaster in the south of the country, and Mrs Brogden and I shall not be coming back." He gestured with both hands for us to keep quiet, and over our stifled hubbub a clear whisper from one of the village daykids, "My dad says 'e's surprised 'e stayed as long as 'e did; 'e must've got a better job," and Broggie frowned a bit and told us how proud he was to have been at Brewood. He looked to his left, then he looked to his right, this morning the whole staff up there on the stage. "All of you, collectively," he said, and looked at us all, "have made this school into a very good school, and I'm proud to have been part of it. I hope you are, too," and he said a bit about how pleased he and Mrs Broggie were with our progress and how he'd miss us and hoped we'd fulfil all the promise we've shown. And then he walked off the stage. Henry bristled his moustache *Quiet, you rabbits!* and stepped forward. "Your new Headmaster is Mr Finney, and he will be here in four weeks' time when you come back for the Summer Term. The nosey ones among you might have seen him when he looked at our lab equipment three weeks ago and talked to many of the Teachers. Mr Finney will be teaching you Physics. He's very strict," he said. "You'll still have to work hard, and you'd better behave yourselves." He paused, frowned. "To nip your ignorant rumour-mongering in the bud" he told us that Broggie was going to be Headmaster at the Brighton Hove and Sussex Grammar School, "It's a very important step for him, an unusually excellent school, big place, many times more Teachers than we have here, everyone a lot brighter and keener than you little weevils." His whiskers fluffed as he smiled and told us we should all be proud of Mr Brogden, and proud to have been at a school under *his* Headmastership. "Yeah," said Paunch, "but I wish he hadn't gone." Nods of agreement all round. And lots of wondering what Finney would be like.

With Broggie gone life at School felt a bit more bewildering. Broggie's departure was just a nine-days' wonder, we all talked about it for a day or two but like most kids I didn't have all that much to say, there was no point in saying that little over and over, that'd be dead boring. We all went home for the Easter holidays and by the time we got back at the end of April whatever shock or dismay Broggie's leaving may have given us had completely worn off. I didn't get Mr Finney as a Teacher in the Summer Term, so I didn't see any more of him than he saw of me, I was just one kid among dozens and he never came to sit with us boarders the way Broggie had. Stepping into Broggie's shoes must've been difficult, and he must've spent a fair bit of time learning the ropes, moving as he did with his wife and young child into a new place where they didn't know anybody and had to adjust to life in a small Staffordshire village. Yet of course by the end of term we'd all got fairly used to Mr Finney, we'd watched him play cricket against a School team and an Old Boys team, and he'd even been down to the village cricket ground to watch, he was a pretty good bowler, and I suppose he'd got more-or-less used to us, but it was a bit of a shock when it suddenly occurred to me that the end of Term was coming up, and some of the Fifth Formers and nearly all the Upper Sixth Formers, Olive Frost and Bud Harrison and Blondie Hall, they'd be leaving for good while we would still be here, Our Kid, he was in the Lower Science Sixth so he wouldn't be leaving, next year he'd be a Prefect, and when we saw the leavers again if we ever did, all half-dozen of them, they'd be Old Boys, they'd be grown up, they'd be a bit alien, working for a living, having to look after their own lives. They wouldn't be interested in what we were up to at School, they'd turn into strangers and they knew it and wanted to leave their mark. And they wanted to celebrate.

They'd all been at Brewood a lot longer than me, and they remembered better than me how the Leavers used to celebrate the end of the School Year under Bailey, all the Masters'd disappear into the village or cloister themselves in Mr Bailey's part of the building while we all played havoc before we went home for the summer, we called it a Rag, raiding each other's dormitories and grabbing people's clothes, taking their beds apart, pinching each other's pillows and mattresses. One year a group of kids had got together and somehow hung somebody's bed outside the window but while they were doing that somebody else came along with his pals and pinched all *their* mattresses and pillows. Kids competed like mad to get as much stuff as possible, but it was impossible to hang onto it all, and there *were* unspoken rules. The Headmaster's house was his private and personal place, completely out of bounds, and you had to keep clear of drawers and tuckboxes and lockers, that'd be like stealing, you couldn't take stuff out that'd been put away, and you couldn't damage or break anything, you always left personal and private stuff alone. Over the years, though, Ragging had pretty well died out, and the one thing that sticks out from that vague blur of Finney's first Term is the feeling of suppressed excitement as June turned into July, every day a small snatch of singsong somewhere, one of the leavers, *No more pencils, no more books, No more teacher's dirty looks* and a quiet grin, a half-suppressed and weirdly smug giggle somewhere in there no matter how tiresome the intermittent repeats, their relentless build-up of subdued excitement flavouring the air.

On the last day of Term as I was getting dressed, the clatter of kids running down the stairs a bit louder than usual, for once all of us in good time for breakfast, a few shouts I couldn't tell what welling up from down below and outside as I stuffed my feet into my shoes, and the dormitory door flung open, one of the kids from the second dorm *Come see! Come see!* all out of breath as we clattered downstairs. Lots of running feet. *Hurry!* A shocked sort of hush in the Dining Hall, kids standing round looking a bit stunned, restless shuffle of feet, a quickly-stifled quiet laugh, not a sound from the kitchen, not even a rattle of cutlery, Mr Finney glowering at Nunc's new second-hand garden tractor sitting where High Table should be, an oil smear along the handle, scraps of garden on the tines, tablecloth plates and cutlery set out on a board balanced across it, Olive Frost and Trevor Harrison carefully not looking at anything in particular as they stood among some other kids, smothering their irrepressible grins, school-leavers all. "Frost!" said Finney. "Harrison! You both have wristwatches. Wait outside my study door. I'll see you there in *exactly* ten minutes' time!" He looked at the watch on his wrist. "*Precisely* ten minutes," and he stalked out.

Trevor shrugged into the silence. Olive smiled a bit hesitantly and looked at the rest of us. "Nothing to worry about," he said, "no, not really," and he looked over at Nunc's tractor. "It's just a small Rag we did, you know, end-of-term Rag. So heavy it took a lot of us." And Trevor looked at Olive and nodded, "Science Sixth," he said. "We thought we'd put his car there, but it's too wide to get through the door, we measured it once we got into the garage. Had to take the padlock off and put it back when we got it out." "It'd be too heavy, must be," Arnold said, "you'd never get it up them steps." "Well, we tried," Olive said, "There was enough of us, and we *could* lift it. Only just, yeah, but we could. Glad we didn't, though, really, might've done some damage," and he looked at a scuff-mark on the floor. No harm here," and looked at it again, stretched his back.

But Finney was livid. He threatened to expel them, "I can, you know, and I should. You may think that you're safe from that because it's the very end of Term, but you could still be expelled, right now. It'd be a black mark on your record, it would affect your chances, it might even lose you the job you expect to be going to after you leave. It's not a question of punishment, but of your ability to behave like adults. This behaviour shows that you have no sense of responsibility whatsoever, you cannot be trusted to do the work any employer would pay you to do." He told them to come back at lunch time along with the whole Science Sixth, "I'll have to discuss what to do with you all with the Assistant Head," that'd be Henry Houston, "and the Board of Governors." Later in the morning at Break along with a couple of others I saw Henry crossing the quad and he didn't pay any attention to us, he didn't even look at us, he just shook his head and looked crossly at the entrance to the Masters' Common Room. As it turned out, nobody got expelled or even especially punished. And I suspect that was Henry's doing. "After all," Dad said when we got home, "there's really not much the School can do, they're all leaving, no real damage was done, and it was just a silly prank. Ill-advised, but not particularly serious on the scale of possible offences." So it all blew over, but not without consequences.

When we came back in September and I moved up to Form V A still in the same class as Robin and Jim we all saw how much Finney'd done over the summer, and at Prayers the first day of term Finney said he hoped we'd like the changes he'd made, and introduced a couple of new Teachers, one of them was Mr Illsley, he'd be teaching English. "We're all going to be busy this Term," he said. He didn't say a word about the shenanigans at the end of last Term and told us he'd very soon appoint several new Prefects and Monitors, "there'll be more than there were last year," but it was pretty obvious that no one in the Science Sixth last year would be among them, even if they'd had nothing to do with the cultivator incident. To check the details when writing this I asked Our Kid and he said "You know, Pete, it still rankles a bit that Finney didn't make me a Prefect that year, he didn't make anybody in the Lower Science Sixth one. He said none of us was responsible enough. I suppose it's a bit odd, that that still riles me after all that time, I mean, *seventy years* later! But it was so unjust. I had nothing to do with it, neither did anyone else in the Lower Sixth, we none of us even knew about it till it happened. It was just Olive and the leavers who did it, they made sure nobody who was coming back in September knew anything about it ahead of time, they were very careful about that."

Phil went on to say, as he'd said more than once before, Brewood was the only place he'd ever felt was home, even when he was a kid, we got moved around so much in the War. Nowhere else felt like home. "Not like being a Dayboy, they had a life outside School. But I was there from when I was eight until I was close to eighteen, close to ten years, and being a Prefect mattered, it mattered to all us boarders, it said something about how you belonged. Dayboys didn't' need that, they belonged somewhere else." Prefects had status, and it must've especially rankled when we came back to School in September and Our Kid found he hadn't been made a School Prefect when he had every right to be. And that was when among new appointments Finney made me and four others House Monitors, there hadn't been any before, and the other two houses didn't get any, they were just dayboys, and I still preened a bit when Jim laughed "Oh, that's a sort of Apprentice Prefect isn't it, I don't suppose you'll have to do much, look after prep and chivvy all the Juniors. And you'll have to behave yourself!"

At Prayers that first day of Term Finney told us "There's a lot to be done, and I expect each of you to take part. We are going to set up some new Clubs for you to join. We should have more than just a Stamp Club and a Chess Club, but it's up to you as well as the Staff to decide what. There's no reason why you can't simply start a club of your own. Talk to your friends, discuss it with your Form Master or your Housemaster. You don't *have* to join a club, of course, but you should be able to choose." From the end of the row, a loud whisper, "We could have a Farm Club, do a lot of Mr Hawkins's work for him," but a couple of kids, farmer's sons, looked crossly at him about to say something just as Mr Finney said "*No!*" and frowned. "Nobody will be allowed to do anything of that sort. This is what *you* want to do, not what I or anybody else wants. As I just said, membership in any of the new clubs will be *completely* voluntary, what matters is that there be plenty of choice. We should have more clubs, and you can choose whether to join one or not." He looked down in the direction of the kid who'd whispered, "An Agriculture

Club might be a good idea, yes, but if you're going to make suggestions you should make them to everyone, not just your neighbour. There's no reason to be secret. If enough of you are interested and the farmer is willing it might be possible to see some of the new equipment they're getting, how it works, and that would be the business of an Agriculture Club we might found, yes." As we left Prayers Horace Pugh walked a bit behind me, his dad ran a lawnmower factory, "it *belongs* to him," Horace had told us. "We could easily get a school visit to our factory, and dad knows a farmer near Church Eaton who's getting one of the new hay-dryers, I'd love to see that, bet it's smashing! It isn't half-expensive I bet there aren't many of them around." Roger said he knew the one Horace had said, he gave us an all-knowing look, "Y'know, it'd take at least half the day to get there *and* see it, all afternoon I bet, that'd be fun! Time off from School."

An hour later we met one of the new Teachers, the last class before Break, English with Mr Illsley, he paused as he came into the room dead on time and said, "I don't know any of your names yet, I won't apologise for that" and as he moved from the door to his desk, "I have a good memory, and will soon learn them. Meanwhile, you'll have to tell me what yours is. I'm Mr Illsley." We knew he'd spent a lot of the War in the Army and'd just got demobbed, and as he set his bag down he told us, the very same words that Buddha Anderson'd used a year before when he arrived to teach History, "I have high expectations, we'll have to work very hard indeed if we have any hope of meeting them." And then he added, "I won't put up with any nonsense. You're here to *learn*," and in our first two classes he tut-tutted over what he called our "spectacular ignorance" and the "rubbish" we all enjoyed in the *Wizard* and the *Hotspur*. "Adventure stories are all very well," he said, "but they don't last, you'll soon get tired of them. I'll see if we can get rid of all those G.A. Henty and Talbot Mundy books in the library and give you something better to read than Captain Marryat, they're much too old-fashioned. I'll talk to the Headmaster about it," and then he told us to write something, just a few sentences, about what we liked, "Just tell me about one book," he said, "a book you like so much that you want to read more by the same author, or even one that you might want to read again. It doesn't matter what the book is, I probably haven't read it or even heard of it," and he grinned. "I've not read *every*thing, you know, *no*body has, it's not possible. So you can just tell me about it, try and give me some idea of what you like in this particular book." He looked at the top of his desk, gave a little shrug, smiled. "This isn't a *test*, I'm certainly not going to give it a *mark*. I just want to find out something about you, what you've read, and what kind of story you like, what sort of book. You don't have to write very much, just a few sentences, say what you want to say as clearly as you can."

Next day at the end of class he gave us back what we'd written, all he did was put a tick at the bottom, he didn't even correct our spelling or grammar, but just wrote a few words, *That sounds interesting, I see you like cricket,* or *Do you know someone else who likes it?* something that showed us he'd read what we'd written, and he glanced at a piece of paper in his hand and told us "I'd like these boys, please." He read out seven or eight names, mine wasn't one of them, "to stay behind for a few minutes at the beginning of lunch Break. Thank you." That "please" and "thank you" was a bit of a facer, but *what on earth could he want to see them about? They can't be in any trouble, not with Robin on that list,* and as the rest of us went out to the Croft at Break I asked Trevor he just laughed, "Glad it's not me, whatever it is," and just behind me Geoff said "I dunno, who cares?" and ran off towards the old fives court. But that list was such a strange mix, some of the kids boarders, the rest of the kids from the village or close by, no one from any further than Kiddemore Green, an easy walk, and I kept puzzling *What did he want? What am I missing?* It wasn't till after Supper that I could ask Robin. "Oh," he said and he had to think about it. "Nothing much. He's read what we wrote and he thinks we might be good at English, thinks we might enjoy it. He wants to start a club, we could just call it the English Club if we want, meet once or twice a month, talk about the books we're reading." They were getting notebooks, he said, and keeping a list of books they'd read, along with what they thought of them. "Just for us, not for School. It sounds interesting, it might be fun to write stuff down, tell each other. We do that anyway, don't we, but then we forget. I do, any road."

A sudden little shock of dismay and jealousy *Why didn't he choose* me? I'm *good at English! I'm easily as good as you* "Why didn't you tell me?" I said, and "What's there to tell?" he asked back, "it's just something he wants. It doesn't matter," and I was puzzled, how could you forget that Mr Illsley thinks you're better than the others, "Couldn't you've told him," I wanted to ask, "that he should have put *me* on that list along with the rest of you?" but as soon as I opened my mouth I knew that was just plain daft, *no*body could ever say anything like that, you couldn't talk about your friends that way no matter what, and my voice stumbled a bit, suddenly a bit tight I had to clear my throat, "What sort of notebook did you get?" I asked him, such an odd question in such a strained voice that Robin must've noticed something of my bafflement and dismay at being left out, but he just shrugged and looked away. "Just a notebook, nothing special, fits in my pocket. Got it from Mrs Roberts's" and I wanted to see it. "You know," Robin said, "there's nothing to stop you from getting your own, it's only sixpence. You can keep a journal of what you read if that's what you want," and he turned away. "You don't need me or Mr Illsley to do that" but I couldn't let it alone, and after we'd gone to bed I lay awake worriting over how I felt. *Why did I have to be* noticed *doing something instead of just* doing *it?* It didn't matter that Mr Illsley'd called the *Wizard* and the *Rover* nothing but rubbish *just what you'd expect a teacher to say* but that "spectacular ignorance" really bothered me. It was all very well for Robin not to be bothered, he's so good at everything *Look at that page of sweet-coupons he drew in his Rough Book*, the paper had been all wrong but *Mrs Roberts'd never notice*, he could easily've traded them in and I really wanted to see if he could get away with it, but he refused, "You can't do *that*, it's dishonest. I just wanted to see if I could draw it properly." We all marvelled at that. "I did it for fun," he said. He made things look easy, how he told stories in the dorm after Lights Out, how he came up with the ball after he tackled someone in soccer, the knack he had of simply focusing on what he was doing "You've got a good ball-sense," Ticker Ranson'd told him when he put Robin on the Second

Team, and I wished I could be more like him. Once, me as usual moaning away about my clumsy efforts in Art when you put them next to his, he said "I *like* drawing things. When I'm doing it I don't really notice anything else, I just draw, it's what I see, and getting things to look *solid* when you put them on a piece of paper that's *flat* that's interesting, I want to know how to *do* that." He got really indignant when Brian Noakes said he did it to impress us. "Why should I do something just to please *you*? I've got better things to do with my time."

31

Robin and Jim

Things intensified after the summer of 1948, with Robin and Jim and me all in V A, School Certificate exams coming up at the end of the year, in July. Most kids'd be leaving school after that, Jim and Robin included, but if I passed and did well enough I'd probably do what Our Kid'd done a year ago and move up to the Sixth Form. Phil'd gone into the Science Sixth but I didn't want to do that, I really hated Science, I didn't like the mess and stinks of the lab in Chemistry, and when we got to electricity in Physics I got lost, it didn't make any sense at all, nobody could tell me what it *is*. I could *see* water, I could *see* how long an inch is or a yard, but volts and amps were incomprehensible and impossible. I couldn't for the life of me figure watts out, there was nothing to watch except needles on a meter or filaments in a light bulb, and all the terms in the textbook were simply defined by other terms. What use was it to say, "we obtain the number of watts by multiplying volts by amperes" when all I knew about a volt was that it's a "unit of potential" and an ampere a "practical unit of intensity." I knew I'd have to go into the Arts Sixth or go *nowhere*.

None of that seemed to bother Jim and Robin. Robin had his future mapped out for him on his dad's farm after he got through agriculture college at Sutton Bonington, and Jim didn't seem bothered by anything at all, he disappeared so many weekends that I began to think of him as a weekly boarder. But we still stuck together the way we had before, and we knew that whatever happened we'd still see each other after they left school, they lived close enough for that. Our School Certificate really mattered, you wrote not just one exam but a whole set in pretty well everything, it'd take nearly all week, one every morning, one every afternoon, two or three hours at a stretch. "What you'll be doing for the rest of your life, and how you'll get on, depends on that exam," Henry Houston told us, "so you'd all better pull your socks up and do some work, learn something before it's too late! You can't be young rabbits all your life!" *Munch, munch,* I thought, I couldn't help smiling to myself, *Lettuce doesn't grow on trees!* I remembered the eleven-plus exam I'd taken to get properly into Brewood when Broggie came, and I said how easy that'd been. Henry nodded as Prendergast said, "It won't be like that at all, will it Sir. You have to *know* things, how to *do* stuff." "Yes," Henry said, "what we've been doing in Geography. Map-reading, working out from the contour lines what you can see when you look along the coast or through a mountain pass, what's hidden behind a headland. Show you can *use* the map, and that you can *think.*" *Like maths,* I thought, *or French. My French isn't too good.* "You'll have to write an essay in French," King Evans had told us. "You have to take an oral exam if you take the Higher Certificate, and you'll need that if you go to University. You should learn some idioms anyway, it really helps to work those in," but he didn't tell us any. "You have to read some books in French," he said, "like *Eugénie Grandet,* that's the set book in the Sixth Form, make it sound like a language people *speak.* That always persuades the examiners." Of course King's advice, like Henry's warning, fell like water off a duck's back and I never did get down to reading that set book, not all the way through. Somewhere and somehow I came across a few idioms and got so proud of *fleur à* that in July I actually worked it into a one-page French essay *twice,* my essay effort concocting some sort of excuse for its presence and no doubt affording the examiner a moment of exasperated weary humour, and I did manage to get the mark I needed. But like pretty much everyone else, I left it all to the last minute. "It's a long way off," Jim said, "plenty of time before the end of the year." He looked round. "Besides, School Certificate won't really make much difference to me," and when I asked, "Oh. I haven't told you yet." We hadn't seen each other all summer, and he said, "After I've done the School Certificate we're going to move," and he lowered his voice a bit. "It's not settled yet, but we're probably going overseas, another country." That came as a surprise, we'd no idea. "We're keeping it quiet till it's settled, But Dad thinks he's got a job in Canada. So while we're here I've got to get whatever qualifications I can." I could hardly believe my ears *How could he do that? Terrible change, a bit frightening.* "Can't talk about it" Jim said, "not when it's all up in the air. There's a lot we've got to do, just simply so we can go, passports and stuff, lots to think about. It's not like just moving house y'know, the way Filo just did to Lichfield." He blinked as he said that, took his glasses off and wiped them, and I nodded. But what a shock! All the way to Canada! I didn't know what I felt about that *Where would he be? What sort of place?* Life'd be so strange with Robin gone from School, Jim all those miles away, and me still here in School, in the Sixth Form, all of us in different places, gone for good. I couldn't think what to say. All I knew about Canada was my stamp collection with its pictures of pine forests and combine harvesters and fishermen and it'd been a long time since we'd had to read in that Fourth Form book about sod-busting the prairie, I didn't even know if he'd be in a city. With his usual streak of practicality Robin said, "It must be a worry. I've heard you can't take more than five pounds out of the country and you won't get very far on *that*. Exciting though. Bound to be interesting." And I wondered. I'd heard Dad talk about currency restrictions but had no clear idea of what they might mean to anyone. "How will you manage?" Robin asked, "how can you move to another country if you can't take anything with you?" and Jim said "We'll just have to manage. But dad's looking after all that, says we might be able to get permission to take stuff with us so long as we can't sell it. Can't take anything valuable like antiques. You can't even take a stamp collection if it's worth more than five quid," and I thought of his dad's stamp collection, how proud he was of it, much bigger than Jim's, he must've spent years putting it together *How could you get rid of something like that?* "Will he have to sell it?" I asked, and wondered *What's the good of that if you can't take your money?*

"What about Griffiths?" Robin asked. "You should talk to *him*. He lived in Canada all through the War. He could tell you a whole lot," and Jim and I both nodded *Good idea!* We all knew Griffiths of course, how could we not, he'd turned up in 1946 as a new boy and gone straight into IV A, that made him senior to us, and I'd never even spoken to him he looked so American with his self-possessed air and his button-down shirt collars, Dad said Americans "don't even wear proper shirts, don't have our sense of dress at all" and Mum frowned, "Do they use collar-studs? I don't think they even know about detachable collars, I think they just take things to the laundry. Very extravagant." But a week later Jim said he'd learned a lot when they talked, and liked him. "He didn't tell me much really, hadn't lived in a big city like Toronto, made it all sound okay. Said it took him a while to get used to pounds shillings and pence and cars on the wrong side of the road but it's not much different from here. He's a nice guy, he actually listened to what I was saying. I feel a lot better about the move." And then he said, "Remember last year's Sports Day? How he just did it and looked pleased?" and Robin said, "He didn't boast, just did it. Like everything else he does," and who could forget those Sports Days, he looked slow and heavy, this new kid from the Fourth Form. Barnett on the First Eleven football team said Griffiths was a good middle-distance runner, "slow and steady, great stamina," but what did that mean, sorting runners like that. But it turned out Griffiths could really sprint as well. Every time his foot came down his head and shoulders slumped forward then straightened up, awful hard work, but he did better than anyone else at the Junior level, came in first or second eight times, from the hundred yards to the mile, sweaty and tired and pleased, just enjoying himself, big smile whether or not he won. We'd laughed in wonder when he won the Cricket Ball Throw, all of us lounging about in the sun, Barker as usual sprawled on the grass surrounded by his pals, a quick flurry and Morgan's indignant "Ow! That really hurt! *Quit* it!" as Barker pulled hard on the seedy grass-stem he'd twisted into Morgan's hair, "You drew blood! For Christ's sake *stop*!" Even Barker perked into attentiveness as Griffiths got to the head of the contestants' queue. None of us ever paid much attention to that event, the contestants standing about so much between throws nothing happening, but one of the kids from Codsall'd said, "You don't want to miss this, it's amazing!" so we eyed the contestants waiting their turn at the canal end of the First Pitch and five or six Masters acting as judges halfway down the field to mark exactly where the ball'd land. Griffiths ran up to the crease-line *Blimey he's fast!* drew back his right arm and unwound, a lovely smooth flow, and *Crikey! Look at that!* some of us speechless as the judges all suddenly scampered and scrambled, Buddha Anderson almost falling over himself to get out of the way as the ball landed and bounced right where they'd all been standing and only Angus stayed put, he didn't even move an inch, he'd kept his artist's eye on the cricket ball up against the sky watched it bounce then strolled over to plant a small white peg where it landed, dusted his hands together smiled his elfin smile and looked satisfied as the other judges sorted themselves out. Henry Houston and Ticker measured it off from the crease, Ticker said something, and Henry shrugged as he wrote it down and smiled his tight little smile. Griffiths'd thrown the ball miles better than the winner of the Senior throw an hour before, nobody came even close, all of us kids flabbergasted *Nobody'll beat that!* We didn't even bother to watch the next competitor, his throw looked so feeble, but "Don't be so mean-minded!" Henry told us. "In any other year that throw would've been good enough to win. Certainly none of *you* reprobates could do as well." Griffiths'd set a School Record with a throw of seventy-one yards, and he did it again only better a month later, a bit more than seventy-two yards at an "Inter-School Athletic Meeting" with Wolverhampton Grammar School, and we all cackled away as the visitors scattered in a hasty jumble as he threw, we had warned them and they'd not listened, old rivals so much larger, richer and posher than us, and snooty with it.

That cricket ball throw made Griffiths a star. "Just a nine days wonder," he shrugged, "Anyone can learn how to throw." And when Jim went to talk to him about Canada a year later he said "I played Baseball before I came back here, outfield. I wasn't too bad, not as good as most of the team. You have to be able to throw, accurately and fast, and we practised a lot, we all did. Learned how at school. It's not like cricket, that didn't exist where I was," and when Jim told us all this I thought how Griffiths held his bat up above his shoulder as he danced down the pitch to meet the ball mid-air, clout it. "He's not so hot at bat," Robin said, "he doesn't really direct the ball but just swings, tries to turn every ball into a yorker. He gets caught a lot. Or lbw. Lot of power though, when he connects."

Griffiths went his own way even at cricket, and he didn't seem to care what anyone thought. "He's very likeable," Jim said, "If we could see more of him we'd be friends, but he's not a boarder, goes home every day when we don't. *And* he's a Prefect." But I wasn't sure that'd make any difference.

At the beginning of Term Our Kid'd at last been made a School Prefect, not that that'd make any difference to us, he had his own stuff to do in the Upper Science Sixth, and this Term I was a House-prefect, as a result I had things to do, sometimes I'd get a bit narked when I had to be on Duty and had something else in mind, "Well, you wanted to be a Prefect" Our Kid said, "You can't complain because you've got things to do. School's not just a holiday, y'know," *Shades of Mrs Bailey!* I thought and wagging my finger chorused with him, "You're not here simply to enjoy yourself!" and laughed, in fact there wasn't any reason to get narked, I wasn't on duty all that much and had plenty of time to go off and enjoy myself, do things with Robin and Jim. We often went down Sandy Lane, perhaps we'd see Mrs Hatfield and who knows, perhaps she'd invite us in, a plump comfortable grey-haired woman quite a bit older than Mum, not a bit like her vinegary and school-teachery assistant Miss Butler, she always found a small treat for anyone on kitchen duty when she was there and she even got Miss Butler trained to reward helpers with "a little something." None of us really *knew*, and we weren't likely to if we didn't live in the village, it was none of our business anyway, but we'd been told she'd used to be Cook over at Weston Hall for the Earl of Bradford, along with her husband who we thought'd been a gardener or perhaps even a gamekeeper, but he'd died or more likely been killed in the Great War, and nobody ever talked about it. Sometimes we got glimpses of what she could do as a *real* cook. On dishes duty one Saturday I watched her squeeze elegant little peaks of coloured mayonnaise out of a paper bag she'd made into a funnel, to surround a huge salmon decorated with cucumber slices arranged like fish scales head to tail just like the pictures in Mum's copy of Mrs Beeton, and she still had time to find us a small slice of light fruit cake each. We loved the great big platters of broad beans and bacon she'd come in specially on her day off to make for Sunday supper when the beans were in season, we almost fought over that food as the Prefects carefully dished it out, everyone counted the beans on his plate, we always wanted more. I still now and again hanker for that smashing treat, chunks of thick salt bacon, the beans all glistening with bacon grease, bitter undertones from the beans, salty slight sweetness from the bacon.

None of us felt comfortable dropping in unannounced and uninvited, the second or third cottage down on the right, two-up two-down, front door straight off the pavement, a stone step straight into the parlour which opened up into the kitchen, stairs in-between on the left. On warm days she liked to keep the front door open, and the back, and you could see right through into the garden, an intense oblong of light greens and reds and yellows the other end of the dark indoors, a bit of a plum tree and an apple behind it, a low brick wall holding the raised garden back from what was immediately behind the cottage, the vague mass of a house looming up in creamish stone or plaster, the shadow of its bulk, leaves shifting and murmuring in the sun, red gingham-check curtains framing the window's beckoning delicate landscape. Lupines and daisies, picture-book tidy, the eye drawn past the brass glowing here and there in the room, a brick path outside the back door, connecting all the cottages the way ours did at Lichfield, a good place to sit. Back in the kitchen she had a favourite chair by the big iron range, and we'd walk past quickly, I'd do a little dip, bob my head down a bit and over to the right as I rubber-necked, half-hid my face behind the peak of my School cap. The three of us must have looked terribly furtive about it all, trying to see if she was there, we didn't want to intrude but we'd dawdle a bit hoping she'd see us and maybe invite us in, and of course she knew perfectly well what we were up to, and then one Sunday the bus from Wolverhampton came in just before we reached the Square and Mrs Hatfield got off, we nearly didn't recognise her in her street clothes her hat firmly on her head, she put her basket down to get at her key, I started to say something I'd no idea what, some sort of reason for being there I suppose but Jim rescued me, he said "Hullo,

Mrs Hatfield, can we help you with that?" and went a bit pink, we all did, such a pretty daft question but this glimpse of her having a life outside the School disconcerted us all a bit, Cook wearing an old comfortable-looking tweed coat just like Mum's instead of the white coverall she always wore in the kitchen, it looked like Mr Hutchings's lab coat only it was clean. "That's all right, boys, I'm used to managing" she blinked as she smiled, us bursting with curiosity picked up her basket and said "Do you want to see?" her glasses blinking in the light, "Come on in, then," and we went in and she showed us the parlour, "I like to sit just there," she said, "That's my sister's chair, we make ourselves comfortable" and as we turned to leave she said "It was nice of you to stop just now" and she smiled again. "Perhaps one of these days you'll come by and stop for a visit" and I nodded I expect the others did too as we said thank you but I felt like a great clumsy lummox, all of us galumphing in on her private life like that.

  We didn't really tell anyone what'd happened. I sort of wanted to boast, knowing Cook in a way the others didn't, but it was too private for that, knowing we could go back. It was our secret, and it was also hers. Talking about it would've been a bit like talking about life at home, personal stuff, nobody else's business. Yet what difference would it make to anybody else if we now and again went to see Cook and she'd fed us tea. I worried that we might be a nuisance and Jim and Robin said "Yes, we've got to be careful not to, but she can always just say Hullo and leave it at that, can't she," and it wasn't more than a couple of weeks before we got into the hopeful ritual of cutting our Sunday walks a bit short, loop back around the village so we could come up past her house and hope she'd notice, we could always say we'd been down to the village cricket ground across from Dolly Asprey's, we all went quite often down to Deansfield to watch anyway, lots of kids did. On our way back to School a couple of weeks later, after the game'd ended early, Mrs Hatfield's door was open and Jim knocked hard, stuck his head a bit round the jamb and leaned, "Hullo Mrs Hatfield, we're on our way back from the cricket. It's over already, and we thought we'd just say hullo as we came by. We won by seven wickets," as if we had anything to do with *that*, and I could hardly believe my ears *How'd he dare do* that? Mrs Hatfield came in from the garden and said "Oh hello boys, I thought I'd heard you. That's nice of you to drop by, would you like to come in for a bit? I haven't seen much of you lately, not even at School. I suppose we've all been busy." She looked back into the garden. "I'm just making myself a cup of tea, and I'm sure you'd like some too. Come in and make yourselves comfortable."

We looked at each other, "I don't –" I started in a low voice. Robin gave me a look and asked "Can we do anything to help?" and she said we could set the table, told us where to find things, and we Nosey Parkered our way around the room, "That's alright," she said, "but don't touch anything!", old photos on the wall, a calendar, a sampler, different kinds of embroidery stitches in all sorts of colours, a lot of them faded, the alphabet, and flowers, and a name and a date, eighteen-eighty-something-or-other, it was too far away to see clearly up on the wall above the mantelpiece and as she came in with a tray she said "I did that when I was a young girl, we all did one in those days. Careful work." I thought of the one at Alcester and told her my Aunt Dot had one on the farm done by her mother a long time ago. Jim said he'd never seen one before and Robin said in surprise "I thought everyone had one" and then nobody said anything for a while. Jim picked something up on the mantelpiece and showed it to Robin and I looked at some of the photographs on the wall as we all fell silent, I couldn't think of anything to say, Mrs Hatfield busy behind me, and suddenly "Why don't you come and sit down?" Bread and butter, little rock cakes, a bowl of watercress, celery sticks, and she looked at the whatsit Robin and Jim had got from the mantelpiece and said "The Earl of Bradford gave me that, a long time ago, when I'd been working for him for ten years, it's very old brass, it's fragile so be careful, it came from India." I sat on the edge of my chair and looked at the other two, perched on the edge of theirs, "Who are all those photographs?" I asked as Jim pointed "Are those horse brasses? I've seen some of them in shops, but mum and dad aren't interested." "Those are real ones," she said, "they're not fake. They come from the tack room at Weston Park, some from canal horses from before the First War," I thought they were smashing, probably worth a bit, but they weren't, not then, people were just beginning to collect things like that. Dad'd said that the gin palace over in Sutton Coldfield on the main road was full of them, trumpery Brummagem-ware, fake like the beams and the half-timbered outside walls, but I wondered how you could tell. "These are heavy," Robin said, "not flimsy. *Look* at 'em, they're not *machine*-made." Mrs Hatfield nodded, "the irregularities," she said, and told us the photographs were old too. "People in the village," she said, a big square man with big black muttonchop whiskers his head full of hair, wearing a leather apron, his elbow on the table at his left, his eyes looking a bit astonished over your left shoulder as you looked at him, a slightly cross and bewildered look on his face, full of contained and impatient energy. "He was the village blacksmith," she said, "he died when I was about eight or so, quite an old man by then," it must have been an old photograph then, "Oh yes it is," she said, and pointed to a sepia photo of a great big windmill, great holes in the walls and one of the vanes fallen off, *where's that? There aren't any windmills round Brewood* "There used to be lots," she said, "A big one at Wheaton Aston," and she told us about the metal works and charcoal burners in Penkridge and the maltings and forges at Brewood in the old days, we didn't even know the Spinney'd been dug out by navvies to build the canal embankments. We'd never heard of any of it. We sat there guzzling our watercress sandwiches and celery, and bread and butter and rock cakes. "Didn't anyone tell you about Ironbridge?" We all shook our heads, we'd all heard of it and Robin'd been there once, "Used to be an ironworks there," he said. "I'm surprised you don't know," she said, "It's less than twenty miles away. Where they built the very first cast-iron bridge in the world, two hundred years ago, it's famous, one of the Seven Wonders. A lot of things have happened round here, don't they tell you any of this at school?" She shook her head a bit and told us that Thomas Telford'd built the aqueduct to carry the canal over the Watling Street, we knew the Watling Street of course built by the Romans, we knew that the way we knew Julius Caesar'd invaded England in 55 B.C. "It's made of iron that aqueduct, and Telford's still a famous man," and we nodded. Nowadays a plaque on it says the aqueduct was built in 1832, but there never used to be any notice boards telling people what things were or who they belonged to or where footpaths went, at least not since they'd all been taken down in the War. Nobody'd ever said a word to us about Ironbridge. Perhaps they didn't know, like that Teacher who hadn't known how to spell Cheslyn Hay. "Were there iron works round here?" I blurted, and Jim looked at me "Well of course there were, you chump, we're right on the edge of the black country, coal and iron." "There used to be lots of ironworks, but not like Dudley or Walsall" Mrs Hatfield said, "and that's what keeps us all going isn't it, not kings and queens." She looked away. "The Earl of Bradford's a nice man. I liked working at Weston Park. I like going back to visit now and again, but not very convenient from here. You could go over on your bikes."

"I really learned a lot" I said as we three walked back to School. "She knows so much about this place," Robin said, "Who's done what and where. Not what we get in History." "Yeah," I said, "I can never sort out the two William Pitts, What difference do they make, anyway?" and Jim told me not to be so daft, "of course they matter, the way Gladstone and Disraeli matter, it's what they did then that makes us what we are now," but I couldn't see that. It wasn't like Turnip Townsend, he changed the way we grow food, changed farming practice.

We never said a word about our visit to Cook's, but something got about anyway and later that week Buddha said in class "Yes, you know nothing about local history, and you should. The best place to start would be the history of the School, it's been here a long time, four hundred years, just about," and next day he told us about famous people who'd been at the School, we'd never heard of any of them. After less than five minutes on William Pitt, he spent the whole class on Richard Hurd, son of a Penkridge farmer and "our most famous Old Boy," Bishop of Lichfield and then Bishop of Worcester until he died in 1808. "I'm going to set up a Debating Society in the School," he told us, "we'll call it the Hurd Society after him. We ought to have his works in the school library, I'll have to see what we can do about that." We knew no more about Hurd than we knew about William Huskisson, but we delighted in the fact when he told us that Huskisson was the first person in the world to've been killed by getting run over by a train. I told myself *"getting run over"* made it sound like Huskisson did it on purpose, and it was icing on the cake when Buddha said Huskisson'd got run over in 1830 by George Stephenson's *Rocket*, the most famous train of all. But Jim was scornful. "That's not *History*," he said that night, "It's just *gossip*, it doesn't say anything about why people do what they do, it doesn't tell us a thing about how they lived," and I wondered. *Why wasn't talk about the* ancien regime *or the two Pitts just Gossip?* The unbidden memory popped into my head how when I'd been taking Agriculture a couple of years ago because I thought I wanted to be a farmer Uncle Tom'd gestured at the field over the hedge. "Take a look at those oats. What d'you think?" I looked at Dad and didn't say anything, that was his and Dad's business, not mine. "No, Peter, I'm asking *you*" Tom said. "You say you want to be a farmer." *What am I supposed to say?* I hadn't even been sure they were oats until he said so, and he said "Look at the leaves, they're a touch yellowy aren't they." And I looked. "Oh," I said, "Yes!" and they were, not that lovely fresh green you get in a young plant. "Need a top-dressing of lime, don't you think?" Dad said, and Tom nodded, "A bit acid, yes." That completely flummoxed me, it wasn't the sort of thing we did at School, we didn't talk about soil conditions, we talked about crop rotation, cattle disease, different sorts of blight, and took dictated notes, but we didn't really *look* at anything. We did drawings and tables for prep, and that wasn't gossip, it was *useful* even if we couldn't actually use it.

But why had we spent so much of last Term learning about bees when there wasn't a single hive anywhere on the school grounds? At Alcester Tom'd walk down to the fields in the summer and pluck an ear of wheat oats or barley and rub it in his hands and blow off the chaff and even bite the grain left in his hand. "What do you think?" he'd ask whoever was with him, "Not quite ready yet, is it," and he'd cock an eye at the weather, so crucial as harvest-time got closer. At School we never got anything about that any more than we got told about John Bright or the Middle Passage. William

Wilberforce, yes, he was a hero, but we got nothing about the everyday, what a poet called the attractions of living recorded, just famous names and famous events, powers and agreements, wars and battles, a long way from anything local or even useful. We had to get what Buddha called a "decent grounding," that's what the School Certificate was all about, so we read about Mazarin, Metternich, and Richelieu, and I was completely lost when Buddha told us to write an essay deciding *Was Louis XIV a good king or not*. How would I know? I got an inkling of what I might say when I was complaining about it to Mike Mortimore in Mrs Roberts's tuck shop, he was nuts about history and after doing his national service a couple of years down the road he went to Oxford and got a degree in it, and a kid from the Nash waiting for a bottle of pop looked at Mike and me, "If you're askin' *me*," he laughed, "and yeah I know you're *not*, what do we 'ave kings *for*? What good are *they*?" Coming the way it did, from a Nash kid, that took me by surprise, it was the sort of question a Teacher or someone in the Sixth Form might ask, but as we walked out the door Mike nudged me "His dad probably votes Labour" he smirked, and I shrugged. I hadn't connected what we did at School with politics. It wasn't until a couple of years later and I'd left School altogether that I realised I didn't have to be a staunch Conservative like Mum and Dad but could go my own way. Not that I knew what the choices were, *Labour* and *Conservative* were just empty words.

By the time the weather got better and the days longer Jim went home for the weekend more and more, "A lot to do before we emigrate" he said, and I liked the way that word marked him off from the ordinary, "All the kerfuffle and the interruptions get in the way, take up all the time. I never get my prep done," and one Saturday with Robin and me a bit bored and Jim off at home again for the weekend Robin said, "Let's go for a bike ride?" and I gave him a look *Where?* "I don't mean *now*," he said, "but tonight, I mean *really* tonight, after everyone's gone to bed," and that was so outlandish it took me aback. "Colin James does that, quite a bit, him and a couple of others, he says it's terrific, nobody else about, it's ever so quiet, they get everywhere. 'Course, he does it at home, still has to sneak out, but we could do it here. Probably easier. Just have to be quiet." Colin lived close to Wheaton Aston. "Out to the rezzer, over to Weston under Lizard, all over the place, they cover a lot of ground." Suppressed excitement as I lay in bed that night, I didn't have a watch but Robin had his, *Have to get dressed, carry my shoes downstairs, have to be absolutely quiet* and then a quiet shuffling, Robin nudged me, hardly breathing nodding his *come on!* Scarcely a cloud on this clear night, half moon, black shadows, *Watch out! That creaks! Catch the door before it slams!* Colours all washed out, faint clatter as we got our bikes out of the bike shed but no, no sign of anybody. Climb on, a huge sigh of relief, the faint bubble of a laugh wells up, a stifled *whoop* as we pedal through the Gate *Ssssh!* and down School Road to turn past Mrs Roberts's to Church Road and another *Ssssh!* but this time with a grin as we scoot past Newport Street and turn along Bargate from the empty square, faint light behind a curtain upstairs at the Lion, faint *click, click* I can hardly hear but regular as my pedalling foot and breath, a constant register each time the rising crank arm grazed the back strut *click!* pause, and *click!* slight wobble of the pedal *I never did get that fixed!* the quiet susurrus of our tyres on the blacktop down Kiddemore Green Road, pale grass, long shadows, stir of movement in the hedge, the sudden loom of something big, heart jump as a cow shifts in the field, a pair of bright eyes and a shadow in the field as you pass by everything quiet except your breath and the tyres, magical, and *Oh!* Robin freewheels almost to a stop, stands in his saddle, points, our bikes quietly ticking as we coast neither of us pedalling *Is that a fox?* the faint hiss of our tyres scarcely a disturbance in this transformed landscape, ribbon of road pale under the moon, an owl, the sound of a distant car, flurry of wings dark shadow overhead *that owl! Hunting,* crossing the field from wood to coppice, and you stand on the pedals again to see and the edge of your shirt lifts as you crest a slope, a sudden cool breath of night air at your waist and here's a five-barred gate, soft rustles in the hedgerow *something bigger, that's no rabbit!* Way over the soft patchwork of fields and barns and houses a subdued bark, dog to fellow dog, one farm to another, *relax! it's not us it's after!* a grey and black patched hump across the field melts into a Friesian cow, and then more cows *Whose dairy farm?* A yellow glow outlines the slope ahead of us, trees on both sides, and we scramble off our bikes pull them onto the verge and lay them down *Hurry before it gets here* the doubled V stares into the sky not in a rush but not slow either down the middle of the road, a patch of nettles black behind the stark then washed-out green, yellow carlight defines a shifting patch of weirdly strange yet familiar roadside, and you crouch down to hide your face, you snatch a quick look and blink away the abrupt dazzle and the tears it brought, the light fades round a corner and the engine-sound five seconds after, silence restored. The village doctor on his way back home *who's he been to, this hour of night? Hope it's no one we know* and you resist its faint hint of inside knowledge, possible gossip, climb back on your bike the saddle cool the crossbar cold against your leg the handlebar wet with dew from the long grass you just now put it down in. "Perhaps we should go back" I breathe, "turn round" but we pedal on, down a dip and up the other side *How far is it to the rezzer?* the quiet exhilaration of this silent world as we glide between hedgerows. A light comes on as we cruise past a barnyard *Crikey! What time is it?* We zoom past Butler's farm at the head of Shutt Green Lane but no, we won't get to the rezzer not this trip, save it for the next, silhouettes of trees, the dense ribbon of the Milky Way still dusted across the sky the North Star bright, no faint light of dawn over in the east *It's long before false dawn, the birds are all dead quiet* and we stop to catch our breath and listen. Then we turn back, sneak up the stairs "Gosh, that was smashing! Do it again," get back to bed its sheets suddenly cool against my busy skin, nobody stirs, and I settle.

But "*I don't know,*" Jim said next day when we told him about it at Break, what we'd done and where we'd been, "It sounds terrific. Yes, I'd like to do that, sounds fun." He looked at me. "But I'm not so sure. We're all senior, 'n' Peter *you're* a Prefect. What'd you do if you caught someone from the first or second dorm, junior kids Third Formers doing that, sneaking off in the middle of the night to go for a bike ride, would you let them? Not *do* anything?" None of *them would*, I thought, not *them!* But then *What abut seniors?* I thought, and

"Well," I said, "Dicky Feltham went off to the rezzer a couple of weeks ago, three of 'em, for a swim in the middle of the night. Been more than once, a lot of people know about that. And they're all in the Sixth Form, they're senior to us. One of *them*'s a Prefect." I remembered what Dad'd called the perks of his job, how scrupulous he was about them. A couple of years back, he'd brought a tin of peaches from the store so we could have a treat, "We only got one case, twenty-four large tins, for the whole store, sold them all as we were putting them on the counter. Ridiculous, really," he'd said to Mum as he handed it over, "I've already paid for it, and taken the points from my ration-book." I didn't say anything about that to Jim but it's what I had in mind. You have to *earn* the privileges of rank, I thought, that's why they're called *privileges*. But Jim shook his head, "That's not honest. We all have the same *rules*. And it's not *fair*. You can't go bogging off to enjoy yourself when you've told everyone else they can't, that's hypocritical. Rules should be the same for everyone," and settling down to sleep that night I feared Jim was probably right.

As it turned out we only went off at night a couple of times after that, perhaps there was a connection. "Nothing to stop you doing it at home" Jim said, "but you'd have to tell your mum and dad what you're doing. Where you're going, too. Something could happen." As soon as I got home for the summer Mum said "*No!* It's far too dangerous, cycling all those main roads in the dark, no. Even if you've got good lights on your bike. *No.*" And "besides," Our Kid said, "who'd you go with? It's not a good idea, you can't go by yourself. And cycling in the dark even with a light, specially round here? That's completely *daft*, you'd get run over in less than'n hour!" A month or two later, almost as soon as he left school, once he'd got a job in Birmingham and was living in digs he began to bike home every weekend, Birmingham to Lichfield and back, "I'm used to traffic," he said. "You're not. And I know the back roads," I was glad it wasn't me trying that, though when I got to Nottingham three years later I cycled the three or four miles to school and back every day and it was safe enough. Everyone used bikes.

When I got back to Brewood in September I found I'd been made Head Prefect of Knightley, Our Kid gone, Jim and Robin'd gone as well, and I felt a bit lost on my first day in the Sixth Form, all the Sixth Formers so confident of themselves, so knowing, boarders not dayboys, me the only one in the Lower Arts Sixth the others a year ahead of me in the Upper, sixteen or seventeen years old, and me not quite fifteen-and-a-half. And on top of that, we didn't meet in a regular classroom but in the School Library, a room much smaller than a regular classroom, and I was the last to come in, Barton, Keale, and Mortimore already sitting at the long table, old pals who fell quiet and looked up as I came, no Teacher, nobody from when I'd been in V A the year before. Only four of us in the whole class, the other three in desultory talk. Dayboys, all of them a year ahead of me in the Upper Arts Sixth. Big window opposite the door, bookshelves all round, no desks, no blackboard, empty captain's chair at one end, nowhere I could see to keep your own stuff, and I thought of Our Kid, there'd been thirteen kids as well as him in the two Science Sixth levels and they'd all had desks and a small cupboard for their lab coats. I didn't know these three, not enough to talk to anyway.

I didn't know if I was supposed to sit in a particular place, and I didn't know where I could put my things so I just put them on the table, I'd find out what to do later but I'd better not sit in somebody else's space. I started to say hello, but I heard two voices outside the door and then an adult's laugh, and the new English Teacher came in, books and papers under his arm, talking of all people to Pete Griffiths, I knew who *he* was alright, but what was he doing *here*? I'd no idea *he*'d be in the Arts Sixth. This morning at Prayers Mr Finney'd told us Mr Illsley was "no longer here" and we had a new English Teacher, Mr Osborne. Osborne'd only teach English, nothing else, and Latin'd now be taught by Buddha Anderson, so on top of History with *him* every day I'd now have him three times a week for Latin. Barton stayed put as the rest of us shifted a bit, Griffiths across the table from me, and after we'd all settled Mr Osborne looked slightly puzzled as he said "I'd planned to spend the whole class learning all your names, but with only five of you that won't take very long at all. There's some red tape to deal with and I'll need your help with that before we can start any English. I need some of your facts," and we went through the usual boring start-of-year rigmarole, official stuff like where we lived, what our parents did, but with just the five of us we finished that in no time, and said "We've still got more than thirty minutes. Why don't we tell each other about ourselves, who we are. Just five minutes each. Be *brief! That*'s a useful exercise," and then he said, and it really *was* a surprise, "I'll start." He looked round the table, swallowed, and took a breath. "At home everyone calls me Jimmy, sometimes Jim, but not at School," and he smiled. "Here, we have to behave ourselves." I tried to hide my shock when he told us his two kids went to the Nash *that's a terrible school, just labourers' kids* and without a pause he said his wife's name was Peggy and he'd been in Coastal Command during the War. "A Catalina," he said, "cruising up and down the coast. The sea is never dull even when it's flat and grey." I leaned forward in my chair *Gosh! I think I'm going to like him* and he told us when he got demobbed he read English at Bristol University. "In the summers I'd get a job heaving big cartons of tobacco about in the warehouse, built me up. That's where I met Peggy, she worked in the factory, made cigarettes, that was wonderful, so cheap they were free, really. The sort of job you need when you're a student." He paused and said, "Now it's your turn" and looked at Griffiths. "Tell us all what *you* think we should know about you," and that surprised me no one had ever asked me for that sort of thing.

Griffiths smiled a bit, looked round the table, leaned back in his chair, "I like to be called Pete," he said, and after a sentence or two about living in Canada for the duration, he said "It's interesting when you change countries, you have to learn a lot of things all over again, the world has changed a lot from when you left." *Had it been a bit like coming home?* I wondered, *Had he felt a bit lost?* But I didn't interrupt, and when I said I liked to be called Peter, Osborne said, "Good, that'll make life easier, too confusing to have two Petes in one room" and I soon learned to call Griffiths *Pete* the way everybody else did, every morning he'd come off the bus his satchel slung over his shoulder his blazer unbuttoned deep in conversation with somebody or other, a book in his pocket. He paid no attention to how different his clothes were from ours except for his blazer, his shirts with their button-down collars – Mum and Dad frowned on such shirts and called them *"American,"* – not the sort of thing a gentleman'd wear, unlike ours they buttoned all the way down the front. *Our* shirts had three buttons to close the gap your head came through and a splendid unbroken spread of cloth down the front, we didn't have to hide that awkward and uncomfortable column of buttons behind a tie or a pullover, we could look *dressy* in them if we had to and if a soccer ball or something hit you in the chest at Break the buttons wouldn't hurt. Griffiths was so different I wasn't at all sure I could ever really like him, he knew a lot and he spoke oddly, said things like "twenty of three" and "quarter after ten," it didn't worry him at all that he was saying it all wrong. If he'd been smaller than me I'd've gone and shaken him he was so unaware of his wrongness *Why couldn't he speak properly? We're here to learn proper English, we're supposed to set a good example!* In my exasperation I'd said that to Jim one day in the Billiard Room, and Jim said he hadn't noticed. I couldn't understand that at all. *How could he not notice?* but after he said it he gave me a sidelong what's-the-matter-with-*you*-sort-of-look and frowned, his dark cowlick falling over his puzzled scowl, and a moment later I caught a *sotto voce* snatch behind me, "bit of a snob" and a laugh, "probably jealous." The blood rushed to my cheeks, I looked away, a spasm of shame, I wanted to be liked, I kept telling myself it didn't matter, and I kept telling myself I couldn't help it when now and then Pete's speech jarred in my ears. He said something was "inside of" or "outside of" a room or a window or whatever. How inefficient and wasteful. *Redundant!* is what Mr Illsley would've said if he'd seen it in an essay or even in your Rough Book, much better to save your breath; if at home I'd said something like that Mum would've pulled me up short, "You know better," she'd say. "What will people think? You're *Eng*lish."

32

Pete

That first class in the Sixth Form made me sit up a bit, Griffiths chatting like an old friend to the brand new Mr Osborne, never seen before today. *How could he just* chat *like that? To a Teacher?* But it took me less than five minutes to see that Griffiths'd talk to anyone as if he was an old friend, he had no swank or snobbery about him at all, and as I sat there in the Library that first day I remembered Jim saying what a good listener Griffiths was. When I'd seen him busy with his pals he wanted to know what they thought, he was interested in them. Later that same day, in our first History class, looking relaxed and comfortable with a fat volume of the encyclopædia resting on his waist and propped against the table, his legs stretched out in front, he looked up, he didn't raise his hand or anything he just looked at Buddha Anderson and raised his eyebrows and said "It says here that there was no real reason for Louis XIV, in 1701, to ally himself with the prince of Transylvania, but I don't understand. What's a real reason?" Buddha'd just begun to answer when Griffiths interrupted "I mean What's a *real* reason?" and Buddha looked a bit taken aback with such an interruption with no preamble, but before he could say anything Keale chimed in "What was the advantage, what was the pay-off?" and Griffiths said "No, no. You've got me wrong, I mean, What does that word *real* mean, there?" and I was a bit nonplussed, I think the others were too. I thought back to all those questions on the School Certificate history exam last year that kept asking Why did such and such happen? Always asking *Why?* And we began trying to sort it all out. "Is there such a thing as an *un*real reason?" I wondered, but no, that'd be plain ridiculous. And you couldn't have a *false* reason could you, that wouldn't be a reason at all; "That's a Self-Contradictory Term," Mortimore said, and I filed that label away for later. Whatever a "real" reason was there'd have to be more than one of it no matter what you were trying to explain, and it probably wouldn't be what you'd call a *reason*, it might be a habit or a feeling or an appetite. People do things because they want to, *like* them, we decided, or of course *not*, but none of those could be called *Reasons*, not really. "Well," Pete asked, and he laughed a bit, "d'you think *any* explanation is as good as any other, d'you think *everything*'s just a matter of *opinion*?" And we had no answer to that.

He *liked* asking questions, but *how could he show his ignorance like that? How could he just say "I don't know"?* Years ago, when I'd been at Brewood about three weeks Mum sent me a Postal Order for sixpence, that was two weeks' pocket money, I was told to take it to Mrs Roberts at the corner of School Road to cash at her tuck shop, she was busy keeping a sharp eye on all the kids, giving them change or clipping their sweet coupons, she just said "endorse it" and I didn't know what she meant, I couldn't ask when everybody except me obviously *knew*, and another kid, a bit older than me, shoved a pen at me, it'd been on the shelf by the counter, and pointed to a dotted line at the bottom with "SIGNATURE" just underneath it and I didn't know that word either, but didn't dare ask that either, certainly not of the kid who'd shoved the pen at me. But I knew what *sign* meant, *you didn't say the* G, I'd once got that wrong reading it aloud at Wheaton Aston, *sign* is what you do on letters and postcards, and then I wrote my name along the line and Mrs Roberts took the Postal Order, gave it a glance, nodded and gave me my sixpence feeling very pleased with myself for guessing what it meant and getting it right. But when Pete came back to England in 1946 he'd simply *ask* and never worry about it, after spending the whole War in Canada he didn't know what people usually did, what local customs might be, and of course nobody explains what they take for granted, they don't even notice that it's there, and you've got to fend for yourself. As soon as Pete came to Brewood we heard about him, we didn't think he knew how to behave, we heard that in Form IV A on his first day he'd simply got to his feet from his desk and crossed the room to use the pencil sharpener across the room, not even a by-your-leave and whoever was teaching the class just let him get on with it, not a word, and that disconcerted us all a bit, but by the end of the day everyone got more or less used to it, one of two kids even began to copy him. In class if he didn't understand something he just asked, he didn't even bother to put his hand up but just spoke out, right off the bat, I'd been amazed that he hadn't got into trouble for that I*sn't it rude?* but he got away with it, no trouble, and Jim'd chuckled when Robin said "Well, it'd show *someone*'d been paying attention." Before I saw the pointedness of Robin's little joke I felt a momentary rush of irritation *What if everybody did that?* and on my second day here in the Lower Arts Sixth I saw it first hand when as soon as Buddha said "and you're to hand it in on Friday" Pete looked up from his notebook his pen in his hand and asked "Do you want us just to say what the difference is, or do you want to know which we prefer and why?" and my stomach fell at his daring. "Can't you just do it?" I thought, and worried *Don't make such a fuss* as Buddha blinked and got a bit pinker. "You don't need *me* to decide that," he scowled, "*I* won't write your essay for you," and Pete shrugged. I thought Buddha sounded truly annoyed and I felt a prick of embarrassment, I didn't think there was anything wrong with Pete's question even if I'd never've asked it, Grandpa would've said let sleeping dogs lie, Buddha didn't *have* to be so short tempered but you could bet your bottom dollar he would be, he so hated interruptions.

But Pete's curiosity was irrepressible, he didn't stop thinking about English or History or whatever once a class was over, and he didn't just think about *them.* On library duty one day at Break I said to one of the Juniors how the Wolves wouldn't have had the slightest chance at winning the FA Cup against Leicester that year if it hadn't been for Bert Williams, "Best goalie in the world," I said, and started on about how I'd seen him, "lots of times" last year when a bunch of us'd cycle out to Molineux Grounds on the odd weekend, and Pete looked up and said "I'm not sure we should pay people just to watch them play a game we all play. I don't think my soccer improved just from watching," and I said you could learn a lot about goalkeeping from Bert Williams and the junior said "What about Stanley Matthews? I keep trying to do what he does, and it's impossible, except with him it's not!" The three of us enjoyed our little argy-bargy but Pete stuck to his guns, "You learn by *doing*, not by watching," he said as Break ended, "and money changes everything." As they went out two Juniors were quarrelling over whether the Gentlemen got paid in last July's Gentlemen v. Players match, "They're amateurs! They don't get *paid*, they do it because they like it! The Players won by four wickets, and that *proves* the Gentlemen weren't paid!" That was so daft I wanted to shut them up they were so annoying, but Pete chuckled and I began to laugh.

"Don't you think," Pete said, "that money turns people into spectators? Everything boils down to making money? *Doing's* better than watching, any time." But did he seriously *mean* that? *Does he really think professional sport is wrong?* And later that day in class I pricked up my ears when he asked "Who can afford to play a game that lasts for three days?" and even Barton looked up from his doodling to say, a bit testily, "Test matches last *five* days not *three*," and a moment later shrugged "they're *Aristocrats*." That really overstates it, I thought, but Pete looked towards Barton down the table and said "Does calling amateurs *gentlemen* and professionals *players* in reality have anything to do with the upper and lower classes? It's the Players who mostly win," and Jimmy Osborne looked at Pete. "You might," he said, "wonder where the middle class goes, in that picture. Look at the difference between Rugby League and Rugby Union, League pays its players, had to from the start" and Barton said "They play dirty. The League's notorious for all the injuries. Just factory hands and miners." That reminded me of those two Juniors and their quarrel about payment to amateurs. *Those two didn't have the faintest idea what they were talking about, they should've just shut up!* And then *Why can't people behave?* "Think of all the energy we all have," Jimmy said, "with nowhere to put it. Youngsters especially. What are you supposed to do with it, it's part and parcel of being alive isn't it?" "You can't *rule* it," Mike Mortimore said, "it's irrepressible. But that's what government's *for*, isn't it? Otherwise we'd be forever arguing and fighting."

On our way into the village not long after that Pete said "Filo, d'you *like* being a Prefect? I mean, *enjoy* it?" and I wasn't so sure. "Things change," I said, "you know. I was pleased and proud at first, in September, but sometimes it's a nuisance, so much I have to do. Keep my nose clean, for a start. But it's good to be trusted." "Yeah," Pete said. "I like the responsibility, and you have to live up to it. I like that, but most of the time I don't even think about it, don't need to. Life's more than that." And I wondered. In September I'd been proud and pleased to find I was a Prefect, it showed I was a success, I couldn't've borne it if I hadn't been, but I didn't say a word about the flash of sharp disappointment when I discovered I wouldn't be getting a Prefect's School cap, a sign of my importance, but once supplies ran out in the War they became relics of the past. That cap told everyone you were a Prefect and were doing well in School, I enjoyed the quiet satisfaction of Henry Houston's or Mr Finney's approval for what Finney called "meeting my responsibilities," but it wasn't all gravy, I couldn't call my time my own the way I had before, and even if I could go into the village on patrol without anybody's by-your-leave, I didn't want to do that on my own *What if I caught someone?* I dreaded having to accost a kid out in the street "Have you done your prep?" or "Who gave you permission to come into the village?" and then rebuke him in public or even give him an Imposition, put him on Rolling Duty because you had to get enough people to roll the cricket pitch tomorrow or later in the week, and do all that in front of Fatty Gwilt's dad or Gerald Wakelam's or somebody's mum in the village, her probably shaking her head a bit *tut-tut* and perhaps a touch of grin at our discomfiture, such a fuss when all this kid'd done was go into the village to meet a pal who was a dayboy free to come and go whenever he pleased. "But I must say some kids really are a pest," I said, as if Pete needed to be told *that*, "forever not doing what they should." Much later I learned to distinguish between sins of omission and sins of commission, but right now they were all just *sins*. "I get so cross sometimes," I said, that I simply want to *shake* sense into them. Don't like dishing Lines out though, you have to remember you've done that, and then you have to check up on them, make sure they've done them. And what if they haven't? What d'you do then?" "Oh that's easy," said Pete, "just don't dish them out. They don't make any difference, they never have. There are better ways to get people to behave." And I remembered Pete's question. "Sure, I like being a Prefect. It'd be a loss if I wasn't one. But what I like," I told him, "is reading the Lesson at Prayers" *To the whole School along with all the Masters*, being Somebody. "You do it well," said Pete, "you like reading aloud, don't you, and showing *that* off," and in my Lesson Reading Voice I said "Consider the lilies of the field, how they grow" and his voice joined mine, "they toil not neither do they spin." We both laughed and then polished it off together, "And yet I say unto you, That even Solomon in all his glory was not arrayed like one of these."

"Yes," I said when our delight had settled down, "and I really enjoy leading all the boarders to Church, Sunday mornings, I like being in charge of the crocodile. Wish they'd ask me to read the lesson, though." "You *do*?" Pete wondered, "That's a funny thing to want, you'd have to be there *every* week, and practise, *you* wouldn't get to choose what you read, you'd have to read what you're told to, you get ordered about. It's not like Prayers at School, and not at all the same as marching over every Sunday, the boarders in your charge with villagers gossiping on their way to church or hurrying to be on time, people watching, the sheep bell calling, the hush in church, you doing what you do now. There's a ritual in doing that, it's not just routine, it's reassuring, it keeps you comfortable." I mulled that over for a bit, and then "Remember that essay Jimmy set us," he said, "on the social function of religion?" and I remembered how that topic'd left me at a loss for the best part of a week and I felt a bit odd as I said "Well, I suppose it doesn't have much to do with believing in God. I'm not sure I know what a social function is. But it's something we do together." I wasn't at all happy with that, stumbled as I spoke. "But look at all the different kinds of rituals there are," Pete said, "like watching the Wolves on Saturdays or going to see the films at Jubilee Hall on Tuesday nights, *everyone* goes to those, the whole village goes and it doesn't matter what's on. C'mon Filo, think about it, they don't care about the film, they just like a night out with their neighbours, the whole family, all the kids playing in the back, some people hurrying over the road for a quick pint while the reel gets changed." And I was surprised, I'd never thought of ritual that way. And out of the blue Pete asked "Why do people call you Filo? There's another ritual for you. Nicknames. They tell everyone you belong." I thought of Birdie Prince. "But where did *yours* come from? It can't be after Philo Vance, nobody's heard of him except *me*." I looked a question. "He's a detective in old films, saw them in Canada." He laughed. "They're lousy. He's not a *bit* like you. He's a dandy and a fuss-pot." And I remembered my short-lived long-gone nickname *Wreck* from when we'd read "The Wreck of the Hesperus" in III A, I hadn't half been glad when John Beasley arrived and *Wreck* got transferred to him.

"Why'd you get called *Filo*?" Pete asked, and I told him I'd no idea, "I didn't know *anyone*'d ever got named Filo except *me*, not till you just told me anyway, Curly Chatham called me that about two years ago, he was a new kid in the Third Form, he simply wouldn't get his nose out of his Biggles book, he kept coming back to it over and over instead of getting on with his work, all through prep, he was driving me nuts, I was the Monitor in charge and I nagged him and nagged him and nagged him and he couldn't stop talking back to it as he read, 'Why?' he'd say, or even 'Fancy that'; once he even shouted 'No! Don't!' he was a real nuisance and I had to make sure he did his prep. So I confiscated it, just overnight, but he thought he'd never get it back, he was speechless with rage, absolutely beside himself, 'You – You – You – ' he shouted at me, red in the face, and at last, with a note of triumph, 'You – you *Filo*!' And we all began to laugh, then so did he, and now we'd all let off a bit of steam we could get back to our prep, get it done. He's a nice kid. I like him and we get on alright. His mum's a war widow, lives in a prefab out near Featherstone. I like being called Filo. His dad got shot down in his Spitfire in the Battle of Britain, and the next day after I gave him his book back he gave me a shy smile and said, 'Thank you' he hesitated, '*Filo*.' That made me feel good about him, and for a while after that he began to hang around a bit, didn't really follow me about but he kept wanting to talk, be noticed I suppose. Yeah," I told Pete, "that probably means I like being a Prefect, when that happens."

As well as being a School Prefect I was the Senior Prefect in Knightley, most of us including the Teachers called it Head Prefect, and I was proud but couldn't say anything about that, that'd just be big-headed. But sometimes I felt I was On Duty forever, aggravation always lying in wait right around the next corner, no time to myself, and when we came back from the Christmas holidays Finney'd changed things round a bit. "I need a Monitor or a Prefect in each of the dormitories," he told us, "it's a safety measure, in case of emergencies. Gives you more responsibility." "Hunh," said Steve Robinson later, "control mechanism, my dad'd call it, make sure we all behave." And Finney'd moved me miles from everybody else, to Dormitory Five up on the second floor, top of the stairs, five Juniors in my charge, thirteen or perhaps fourteen years old, one window, single washbasin with a couple of towel rails in the corner across from the door, one overhead lamp in the middle of the room, my bed just inside the door. *Lights Out* for them at nine, for me at ten, no one to talk to once I was in bed, no light to read by, forever behind in my prep. The first night there I turned the light on to get to bed and Tyler cried out "Turn that off! I'm trying to sleep!" *Tyler.* Looked like a ginger-headed tough. Impatient gaze, thin lips, lean and athletic. A year or even two younger than me, wide-awake and cross. I hardly knew him much but he reminded me of street urchins in Brummagem, and like them irrepressible in his independence, a bit scary. "I can't," I said. "Before I get into bed I've got to clean my teeth and I've got to see what I'm doing, haven't I! Get my clothes away" but as soon as the words got out of my mouth I realised I hadn't needed to say anything, and I certainly didn't have to explain why I'd turned the light on. So "Did *you* clean *yours*?" I said, everybody now wide-awake. *Prefects* don't have to justify themselves, I thought, certainly not to uppity little Juniors. "For goodness sake shut up and close your eyes. Quieten down Get to sleep! All of you!" But that was too snappish, and I remembered *Set a good example!* "Please," I said. And a voice across the room said "Use the corridor light, not this one. Leave us *be*!" "All *right*!" I said, "but I'm not going to do this every day!" I felt pretty cross, but I could calm down by reading a bit so I propped the door open with a shoe and opened my book. And it didn't work. "Do you *have* to do that?" Tyler grumbled, "Can't you turn the page *quietly*? Some of us are trying to sleep!" and I told him "It's *your fuss* that's keeping everyone awake, not *me*! Just *shut up!*" and a bed in the far corner creaked as whoever was in it muttered "Yeah, give us a break," who was he talking to, Tyler or me? I couldn't remember whose bed that was. And no matter how I tried I couldn't get back into *Eugénie Grandet* it made no sense at all, so I closed it, Balzac just too alien in all the commotion, whatever French I had *gone* for the duration.

Next night, the same thing all over again. Tyler's voice, "Shut the door! The light's keeping me awake" followed by upheaval as he got out of bed. "I'm going to the bog!" he told the whole room, me leaning into the light as I tried to read. He stumbled against my bed as he got to the door and said, "I can't see properly in all this glare!" the bed joggled my hand as I wrote in my notebook. "Oh *for God's sake*," I cried, "watch what you're doing! What if I'd been writing in *ink*?" "But you weren't, *were* you" he smirked and stomped his bare feet out the door, "You can't write in *ink* when you're in bed, that'd be really stupid!" When he came back he didn't slam the door, but he wasn't quiet either, just loud enough to keep everyone on edge and awake. "Alright, Tyler! What the hell's the matter with you? You're not even trying! Think about other people! If you can't learn to behave I'll have to give you something to worry about." "Oh yeah? You and who else?" "I could Gate you, you know, or put you on rolling duty for a whole week! Just quit it! And go to sleep. *All* of you." But ten minutes later he was at it again. "*Christ! For God's SAKE!*" I said, and clambered out of bed and over to him, "I've had enough!" I leaned over him, his eyes wide open and defiant, and my fist clenched. "Go on!" he said, "hit me while I'm down! You *daren't!*" and "Don't tempt me," I glared. He huddled under his blanket and looked up, most of his face under the covers, "Go on, then! You're *nothing*, you're just a Mouth Almighty!" and he sneered, I took a quick step back, folded my arms and legs into bony lumps and jumped against him, straight up and down, wanting to hurt him but not quite daring, hefty bounce. "Now shut *UP!*" and out of breath and still trembling with rage, the other four kids agog, back to my bed. Would *any*one on the second floor, let alone us, get a chance to sleep?

Next morning I tried to get up as if everything was okay and nothing'd happened, no hard feelings, no grudges, all friends together, I didn't say anything about last night but just said "Good Morning" to the other five, my voice and smile a bit strained, but Tyler wouldn't compromise, he wouldn't budge. He didn't quite look me in the eye and in a low voice said crystal clear to no one in particular "Mouth Almighty Muttonchops!" and shifted his gaze to the wall and my heart sank. But as I said to Pete later that day "I hate to say this, but I really like the *sound* of it, all those *em*s along with all those *tee*s in mutton and chops, too bad I can't use it" and "Uh-huh," Pete said, "it's pretty good. But you can't just let things sit there. We all live together." But how could I be friends with *Tyler*? Did I even *want* that? I started to say, "I don't want him especially to *like* me" and broke off. Was that true? Did I really not care about that? "I don't want him to *dis*like me" I thought, and then wondered what *that* meant, saying *that* even to myself. "I've got to make peace," I said, "it can't go on like this." "I suppose you could give up reading before you go to sleep," Pete said. "but you can't exactly wash and so on without a light, you've got to see where to put your clothes. If they're asleep it doesn't matter, but you could just read anyway, that won't keep anyone awake. Why don't you read to them for a bit, ten minutes, that might even take their minds off things, a book you might all enjoy?" But what book? Something they haven't already read, of course. But what if they don't like reading? I bet Tyler likes sports stories, or war stories *No, a kid like him probably doesn't read anything at all!* I laughed at my own intractability *Stop making difficulties for yourself! When they're going to bed,* ask *them, see what they have to say!* Worth trying, even if it comes to nothing. I wondered about a Biggles book, but they'd all've read whatever I found, perhaps something by Percy F. Westerman, but Tyler didn't want anything, *I just want to go to sleep!* and I got a real surprise, with just a snap of the fingers the others settled on *Just William* by Richmal

Crompton, I'd never liked those stories the way Our Kid had, but ten minutes into "William Below Stairs," that's the third story in the book but the first one I read to them a suppressed chuckle came from Tyler's bed as the others quietly chortled and I read them the whole story, that special treat made Lights Out so late I worried Finney'd come up to check, and they were all of them a bit cloth-headed in the morning, but I breathed a faint sigh of relief *perhaps we've struck a Peace Treaty*. Tyler grumped a "good morning" at me when we got up, but the others right away started laughing about what'd gone on in the story and that night at Lights Out they asked if I'd read another. I gave them a smile, "If you're awake when I come up," and I looked at Tyler. "If you *all* agree. But not a whole story, not in one go, it takes too long." And surprise, surprise, less than five minutes after I started the next story in the book, "The Fall of the Idol," Tyler said over a couple of sleepy-sounding protests "No, I don't want to hear any more, I'm tired, I want to go to sleep." Well, I had given my word. "More tomorrow," I frowned, "perhaps." And once again picked up *Eugénie Grandet*. But to see the small print on that glossy paper I had to lean into the light coming through the door, and flipping back and forth from text to vocabulary I got absolutely nowhere, just like before. I kept looking towards Tyler, breathing away loudly on the other side of the room *Is he awake? Will he behave himself in the morning?* French and Balzac would have to wait, and next day I insisted that we have a story, I'd read it at Lights Out instead of when I came up to bed, just ten minutes and I could go back downstairs again. Tyler's bedsprings jangled as he flumped heavily onto his mattress and muttered "Mouth Almighty" to his pillow just loud enough for us all to hear. But he had no choice, I was the Prefect and it was *me* in charge. The spasmodic mirth of Richmal Crompton's four ardent fans kept Tyler's everlasting grumpiness more or less in check and held our scrappy progress through "The Fall of the Idol" together in an uneasy truce, even Tyler once again reluctantly chuckling as William's adventures with Miss Drew unfolded, and when I heard Tyler telling the story to a couple of other kids at breakfast about a week later he scowled a bit as he caught my eye and his freckles suddenly stood out on as his cheek all at once flushed bright pink, a trace of unease in the *Ah! at last!* of my approving smile. Not a nice kid, he didn't like me either, we'd never be pals. But that's all right, I thought, he's one of my people now.

I no sooner thought that than I saw how daft it was. "*My* people" indeed! I thought about Pete and his endless questioning. "What does it mean," he'd ask, "to *own* somebody? That you can simply boss them about?" and I thought of Mike Mortimore and how he said you've *got* to have a party in power, that *someone* has to be in control or you get chaos. "It's complicated," I said to Pete, "I've got to think about it," and he frowned as I left it at that. Every morning at the beginning of Prayers the whole school would be chattering away like rooks and magpies, all hundred and sixty or more kids jabbering away as if they hadn't seen each other for weeks or even months, lots of news to exchange, lots of laughter, lots of argument, tremendous racket, the Prefects On Duty quietly chatting down by the door some of them ranged alongside the assembled rows of kids and Pete'd look at his watch as he climbed the steps to the stage, he'd regard the whole school assembled before him and nod agreeably, look them over, smile as he looked back at the Prefects and say a couple of things I've no idea what to whoever might be at the end of the front two rows, they were always Third Formers, really junior kids, almost everyone full of beans at the start of the day, one or two kids a bit worried because they hadn't done their prep or something, some not paying attention at all, and the noise quieted down a bit, the whole School, talkative chatterboxes, would settle. Some mornings the argy-bargy especially with a few quarrelsome kids paying attention to no one but each other, kept the noise level up, and Pete'd lift his arms up and down a bit, a shushing kind of move, and the racket'd just stop. And every morning I wondered, *How did he* do *that?* And that's when Henry Huston without fail'd stick his head round the stage-door to check then lead the Teachers in, Finney coming in last to stand at the captain's chair behind his desk, and we'd all recite the Lord's Prayer, hear a Prefect read the Lesson, and sing a hymn.

I never did understand how Pete did that. A couple of years later, him long gone and me the oldest kid in the School, what a surprise after all those years, me embarked on my third year in the Sixth Form working to get a State Scholarship to go to university and now Head Prefect, every morning I'd get up there on the stage, look out over all those assembled faces and say "All right! Let's settle down please, it's time to start" and it had no effect at all, nobody paid any attention whatsoever. I'd shake my head, make shushing motions with my arms, and shrug as the noise just went on and on with hardly a pause, I couldn't get any of the kids to take me seriously when I tried to take control. Some of them especially the Juniors down at the front'd meet my eye and give me a cheerful smile, stop talking and even shrug back at me, look round as the noise went on its unabated way and start talking again *yammer yammer yammer* until Gordon Hughes with his fierce blue eyes and his strong hook nose climbed the bottom two steps to the stage and looked over the whole school, his long black hair undisturbed as it swept back from his brow, and the noise cut off like a knife. He'd not needed to say a word to get that sudden quiet, and he looked round again as he stepped down and returned to his place by the door, unsmiling and watchful. We knew hardly anything at all about his life at home, we knew he was Welsh he was proud of that, but we didn't know where he came from, at least I didn't, except that his dad was a sheep farmer out in Merioneth or Montgomery somewhere, steep hill country up near Snowdon, a hard life in that country's hard winters and uncertain summers. It took a while to learn that his parents were very strict, chapel people of some sort. Gordon didn't play cards or board games much though he might watch for a bit, and he seemed indifferent to music, at least I never heard him singing or whistling away the way most of us did, but he played hard and worked hard, everything a duty. When he came into the Billiard Room, everybody laughing or squabbling or just gossiping away there'd be a brief hush, a sudden lull as everybody looked up, his presence inescapable and uncompromising, hard to be friends with, just as hard to dislike. He was simply who he was.

When Gordon was off sick one morning Henry Houston stuck his head round the stage door for a quick look, he glanced back into the corridor and nodded, the hubbub instantly settled and he led the

Teachers in, me still vainly trying to get everyone quiet, I hadn't even begun to leave my post at the side of the stage yet. I saw yet again how utterly useless I was as Head Prefect, *every*body knew it, all the Teachers and everyone *It's Gordon who's in charge, not me. I don't have their respect at all*, and I was glad it wasn't me reading the Lesson that morning, I knew I'd only stumble through it instead of doing it well the way I usually did. With everyone on the way out at the end it was hard to answer at all when Chatwynd smiled at me from the Third Form row and said, "Where's Hughes this morning?" he was just as friendly as ever. My cheek went hot and I mumbled "he's not very well this morning, he'll be here later" and smiled feebly back. But Hughes's power was a problem it kept me awake that night and the night after, I tossed and turned, ran the cold tap and cupped my hands for a drink, threw the covers off, pulled them back on *Hughes! Hughes! What can I do? This is hopeless* got up for another drink, went to pee, wondered what time it was, heard an owl, listened to the creak of bedsprings down the hall as somebody turned over, heard someone down on the second floor stumble sleepily to the bog, sighed, heard a car somewhere. *Hughes. Hughes.* I sighed again *I'm not a Prefect at all* My heart pumped away *not even the Third Form pays attention to me* and I turned over yet again *This is plain daft! I've* got *to do something* and after a deep breath *But what?* stifling a yawn I clenched my jaw and then yawned anyway, couldn't stop it, but sleep a long way off.

I turned over for the umpteenth time, thought about Prayers in the morning and *Oh! Ask Henry! He'll know what I can do, I can talk to him alright* and *wham!* I fell asleep to wake early, the sound of doors opening and closing down near the Billiard Room. I felt tired out and untidy *I must look a wreck* and I scurried through my wash, combed my fingers through my hair. I didn't *dare* look in the mirror, but nobody said a word, and first thing after breakfast, yawning my head off, jittery and apprehensive *I hope he can help. But what* will *he think of me?* I got to the Staff Common Room, straightened my tie, not everybody there yet, and asked Henry if I could come and see him "I have to talk about something" I said. His sandy eyebrows lifted a little. "After supper," he said. "I'll be down at the Rodney, in the snug. Jasper'll show you, Not before seven-thirty."

It was a bit later than that when I took my School cap off as I came through the bar door and Jasper nodded in approval, "Yes. Better not wear that in here" and he nodded towards the door. "Back through there," he said, "duck through under the stairs" and turned away to serve someone. A couple of tables in the snug, maybe more but I didn't count, a scrap of worn hearth-rug, a coal fire set but not yet lit, a few wooden captain's chairs, Henry's with a cushion, and a bench against a wall. Stale cigarette smell, beer mats, ashtrays, pictures on the wall, a pint in front of Henry. He gestured towards the other chair at his table and he reached over to press a bell-push. "I've ordered you a half-pint of shandy," he said, "I hope that'll be alright," and I said "Oh, yes. Thank you, Sir. He looked at me. "Not in here," he said, "I'm not *Sir* here. *Henry*. Now let's wait for your shandy, relax a little." And Jasper came in, my lemon shandy on a tin tray. "Before you tell me what's on your mind," Henry said as he put his glass down, "I want to tell you how *wise* I think you are, letting Hughes manage things for you at Prayers. Not many people have the maturity to do that. Hughes enjoys it, and he does it well and you don't interfere. You preserve the unity of Prefects' authority, and you don't lose any respect." He took a sip from his tankard and nodded at my glass "Why don't you try that shandy, Jasper keeps a good cellar, and he balances the lemon and the malt very nicely." And I was completely flabbergasted, the sheer relief completely knocked the wind out of my sails. "Now, tell me what you want to talk to me about." And I was speechless *What could I say?* And I floundered about in silence, Henry gazed into his beer, and at last I stammered something about worrying about how lousy I am at Sports and it didn't take him long to ask how Our Kid was doing now he'd left school. As I got up to leave after I'd got through my shandy Henry looked me in the eye and shook my hand as I thanked him, that must've been the first time he'd ever done so. "Don't worry," he said, "You're doing a fine job, I know it's not an easy one" and I felt exhilarated and relieved as I went back up Dean Street to the School.

When I'd come back in September for my third and final year in the Sixth Form, to sit the State Scholarship exams, Pete'd already been gone for a year, off at a teacher-training college in North Wales, well over a hundred miles from Wolverhampton to Bangor, you'd have to change trains at Crewe and even change again at Chester on top of that, it might take all day to get there from Codsall or Brewood, so I didn't see Pete at all once he'd left, him swotting away at Teacher Training, and anyway Old Boys never came back to School *What grown-up'd want to spend his time with a bunch of kids if he wasn't their teacher?* and, what with Tyler and Hughes and everything I had to do as Head Prefect of Knightley and the whole school, I didn't have much time to myself anyway. It struck me that the only other kids in the Arts Sixth, both of them in first year Arts, both of them two years younger than me, were Wilfrid Parker and Harold Alcock, they'd hardly got out of the Fourth Form when I'd started in the Sixth, and as I struggled in French through Alfred De Vigny's *Moïse*, "*puissant et solitaire*," my mind strayed off onto what responsibility entails and how De Vigny was right, "that's what power does" I said to myself and I suddenly wondered what Jim and Robin and Pete were up to, how they were all doing now their lives had changed away from Brewood. Now, as I look back after all these years, I see that Pete and I had one of those intense friendships teenagers get into, we shared everything, we jabbered hammer and tongs endlessly at one another, each a talking post for the other, and it truly astonished me one mild Saturday afternoon early in the Term to see Pete right out of the blue. He'd dropped in for the afternoon, and for once I had no duties, no Games to patrol, nothing on my plate besides prep. "*Filo!*" he said, "You're who I came to see." He took my arm. "Come for a walk" he said. "Let's get into the village," that familiar loping stride driving me alongside him. "Hold on a minute," I said, "my cap! Boarders *have* to wear their caps, out in the village!" and he gestured impatiently "No," he said, "That doesn't matter! Nobody'll care! And I'm only here for the afternoon. Got to get the bus back at four." At the corner of Church Road he said, "Hang on!" and darted into Mrs Roberts's shop. "Here," he said, and thrust a bar of Cadbury's into my hand as he came out. "Have some chocolate." He broke his own open, "go on. Now we can both have some," and I discovered how much I'd missed him. He took a bite of his chocolate bar, looked at me, said something as we turned into Bargate Street and he dropped a pace behind me, a sudden short spate of low-voiced words. I didn't understand his quick gabble. "What?" I said. "What did you say, Pete? I didn't hear" and he said nothing. I looked at him, the faint pink of his cheek, as he looked across the street at Speedwell Castle.. In my head I listened again to what I'd heard. Ah yes. *peterlikesfilo* said so fast it had to be sorted. *Oh!* I was a bit nonplussed "I like you too." I took his arm. As we ate our chocolate and walked he told me he'd been in hospital a long time with meningitis, *months!*, and then been at home convalescing, "I'm not as strong as I was," he said. "But I'm better. I've got to get back to Bangor, though, on Sunday" and I remembered someone from Codsall saying that he'd heard Pete wasn't very happy out in Bangor. He shrugged. "I've a lot of catching up to do."

And as we walked we fell into the old familiar talk, he told me one of his courses was about how to cope with adolescents, it was the only thing he told me about his life in Bangor, not a word otherwise. I scarcely knew where Bangor was let alone what it looked like, I'd never even seen a photograph, and I said, "What's an adolescent?" When he told me I said "I'm not sure I like that idea, people aren't all the same, and you can't just say that when you're fifteen you're going to do what everyone else does when they're fifteen! People aren't *like* that!" And he told me "Filo, we've got to be able to analyse people's behaviour, if you're a Teacher you have to know what people are like, be able to sort them all out, know what to expect" and as he talked I began to feel quite cross, it sounded like some scientist or other busybody telling me what I was supposed to be, someone telling me who I really am when he hadn't the faintest idea about me, hadn't even met me or talked to me. Dad would've been enraged by that. "Officials!" he would've scornfully said, "politicians!" I asked Pete "D'you actually believe all that?" and he said "I don't know. I'm not sure. I'm curious, though, need to know more" and as we walked and talked it was exactly like old times. I reflected as we waited for his bus that until Pete'd turned up earlier today I hadn't quite known I felt a bit lonely. I hadn't talked so freely to anyone that way since Pete'd left, and I began to wonder why. None of them's truthfully interested in what I think or might have to say, Buddha Anderson just wants to make sure I understand history the way he does, all he wants to do is correct me, and Frank Evans'll only pay attention to how good my French is, not to what I might think, look at how he'd smiled over a "famous" French pun on *Leviathan* and *Levy attends* but he hadn't bothered to explain the politics that made it so famously successful. With a small shock I remembered the great revelation in Henry's "how wise you are," but I knew I could never have a proper conversation with him, he was always enjoying his own wisdom while being so wise.

Pete's visit left me wonderfully refreshed and invigorated, and I felt a bit restless and even rootless on the Monday after. At Break told Jimmy about seeing Pete. "Oh yes," he said, "I know he was here, but only saw him for a few minutes I had too much to do. Wish he could have been here longer." Then he said "Filo, I want your advice. Seeing Pete reminded me I've been wanting to talk to you about a lot of things, where you'll go to University for instance, and what you'd like to do, but more than just that. Peggy and I wonder whether you'd like to come to us for the weekend, come on Saturday, we can have a good talk, you can meet all of us, stay till Monday." And that weekend became the first of many, the three of us long talking after the two children had gone to bed. Jimmy and me sometimes went for long walks or mucked about in his garden, the children off somewhere on their own. We'd spend some time with them. On that first weekend when I said something about working with the farm hands at Alcester Jimmy smiled at Peggy and said "Peg, you were just a hand, weren't you" and she laughed. "Fingers more like." and she waggled them for a long second before at last the penny dropped. "Working in that cigarette factory in Bristol. That's how we met, isn't it Jimmy" she said, and that night in bed I wondered what sort of difference it made, thinking of factory workers as Hands and not as people, Mum and Dad might've said "that's not worth bothering about, *of course* they're people, we never forget that" but it'd never occurred to me that calling people *hands* might make you think that's *all* they are, "a part for the whole," Jimmy said next morning, "there's a name for that, it changes people's attitudes," and the three of us drank tea and talked about how words got to *hide* things, "persuade and control" Jimmy said, "make them want what they don't want" until at last Peggy said "Well, this is all very interesting, but some of us have got work to do" and as Jimmy and I went to the garden "I've got some pruning to catch up on" Jimmy said, and I thought how much Pete would've enjoyed that talk, such a long way from anything in a classroom.

Then one day in November word ran like wildfire through the whole School, I heard it from a Junior asking one of his pals "Did you hear about Pete Griffiths?" and the hushed "Yeah. Terrible. He stuck his head in the gas oven!" I couldn't believe it at all, I hadn't even known he wasn't away in Wales, and I can't be sure any more when I heard, what month it was, it was utterly as if I'd been hit, and all I can remember is the whole room in a hush, lots of younger kids but no talk except in whispers, me standing motionless in the Billiard Room looking out of the window past the monkey puzzle tree, my hands resting on the hot radiator all I could feel, my mind a complete blank, not a thought, just the hot metal under my hands, and after a while someone came up to my elbow and shyly said "He was your friend wasn't he" and I stood there, not even a question in my mind, not a thought but I must've nodded or said something, and slowly the other kids came up to me and said something I have no idea what and I just stood there, my hands hurting, red and hot from resting on the metal, and I didn't know what I felt at all, didn't know I felt anything, couldn't even think when I'd last seen him, and a small voice in my head said "Is this what grief is? Is this what it feels like?" and I didn't have an answer to that, I just stood there, empty, and the bell rang from the belfry the way it always did, Young Nunc doing his job, a tractor strained away in a field, and they all went back to their classes as I stood there.

Next day Mr Finney called me to his study and said that as Senior Prefect I should write to Pete's father on behalf of the School and I said "Yes, of course" and I wanted to but when I tried I could not, there was nothing I could say, just a blank, wooden words trying to fill the gap but dying in their turn. As I tried I realised I knew absolutely nothing about Pete except that he lived in Codsall with his dad, I'd never even laid eyes on his dad and had no idea at all what he did for a living, I didn't even know his initials, and I was a bit flabbergasted when somebody told me Pete didn't live in Codsall but in the big housing estate down the road at Bilbrook, how could I know so little, when he was supposed to be a friend of mine, how could I ask Mr Finney all these things, what would people think, me not knowing, and what could I possibly say?

Finney looked weary on Monday morning, we all looked a bit grey and somber, and as we dispersed to our various classrooms after Prayers Jimmy got hold of me and said "Me and Peg, we want you to stay with us this weekend, no ifs or buts." My smile must've looked a bit feeble as I said "Yes, I'd like that, very much" and as I said it I realised how true that was, a glow of anticipation right away *Yes!* a stir of excitement and relief. A week later, right after Prayers, I knocked on the door to the school secretary's small office, Angus's old sitting room, to deliver a report for Matron, and Nancy gestured me away from the door, "Hello, Filo" she smiled. "Come in for a moment," and she paused. "I know you've met Bob a couple of times, my husband, though you might not remember, and we wondered," and she hesitated, she fiddled with a paperclip as she looked up from her desk and I blinked in mild puzzlement from my post at the doorjamb. "No," she said, and shook her head. "Come away from that door, Filo, please," and she hesitated again, swivelled her chair to face me. "This is a bit difficult," she hesitated, then smiled. "Anyway we were talking about what's happened, him and me, how terrible it is, Pete Griffiths. We know he was your friend…" Her voice trailed off. She started again. "We've been thinking, and Bob said we should try and get you away from school a bit, and…" she grimaced and then just blurted "Could you come to tea this weekend, Filo? Saturday or Sunday? I'm doing some baking on Saturday, Bob says I always do too much, but we always eat it up and it never goes stale. And if the weather's nice we can go for a drive, get out of the place. That'll do us all good" and I said "Oh yes, please," I didn't have to think about it for a second, "I'd like that, thank you very much." And, like Jimmy and Peg. Nancy and Bob gave me ground, as my centres shifted.

Afterword

My English Teacher Jimmy and his wife Peggy, the school secretary Nancy and her husband Bob, along with Pete, never tested me, but allowed me to follow my enthusiasms and passions. In fact, they shared them and taught me to enjoy thinking and arguing without worrying about how it looked to others. It didn't matter what other people thought, and it was wonderful to be free of the social roles school had imposed. We felt like a family.

For a while, I was really astonished that Pete and I became friends, he was so much the school hero, good at sports and academics, and I was so much the opposite. I wasn't a star in anything. I was convinced I came to be a Senior Prefect by default, not through any virtue of mine, after the boys in the form ahead of me got disqualified. But Pete was an exotic, he'd lived overseas, and his whole approach to life felt so casual and informal that some kids and some Teachers couldn't quite take him seriously.

He was actually a maverick, but hardly anyone saw him that way because he never offered a boast, a see-here, or a threat to anybody. He didn't do the expected, and he refused to be defined by others. He valued the personal, the individual, not conformity with expected values and class mannerisms. He was interested in other people, talked to them, argued. He and Jimmy got on like houses on fire. Pete knew how to enjoy life, and he loved new ideas and challenges, and so was perhaps the most gregarious person I knew.

It took me years after Brewood to form the kinds of relationships I'd had with Jimmy and Pete. They created a space for me where I could finally be myself. I think this undemanding approach to other people, taking them seriously and listening to their ideas, shaped the things I later tried to do in my teaching career. Pete taught me never to hide my ignorance, and like Jimmy I tried to share my enthusiasms and get students to argue passionately for what mattered to them.

It also took me a long time as a teacher to be able say to students that I simply didn't know the answer to any given question. I'd learned that the teacher was always the final authority on rightness and wrongness, and that therefore I must know the correct answer. Pete would have laughed at the idea that the teacher always knew, and Jimmy often laughed at his own ignorance. They got me to see that it was alright in the classroom to change my mind about things. And if I didn't know something, I could always go and find out, or ask a student to look into it.

Still, I could not imagine that graduate students did not know everything I expected they should know. I'd get hot under the collar about that, and like many colleagues I'd come to swift judgement. It was so easy to condemn the student for his own ignorance. I had to learn that, after all, students are students because they don't know. They're here to learn. At the same time, I had to discover that linguistic habits vary widely from one culture to another, that there are many Englishes and that apparently neutral diction could be deeply offensive in a different cultural context. That was a hard lesson to learn because it threatened to undermine my authority as a teacher, an authority based on assumptions which came from a colonizing British Empire.

That empire was in decline, it was losing its grip, former colonies were asserting their own identities and languages. My own study of American literature, and especially of American poetry, eventually showed me what a mistake it was simply to impose a British and especially English literary canon on my students. I was reading in non-British writing an extraordinary diversity of experience and form that was nowhere found in the English canon I'd been trained in, which didn't even include Scottish and Welsh writing. I began to abandon inherited notions of correctness, and through my delight in the poetry of William Carlos Williams connected to poets and writers outside the academy and outside the canon, like Basil Bunting, Robert Creeley, and Robert Duncan. I developed a taste for experimental writing and for the unconventional. Some of my colleagues came to see me as a bit of a rebel, and that has turned out to be a great blessing.

Appendices

Appendix 1

People and Places

Some names have been changed to protect the guilty.

The Davises, Wheaton Aston shopkeepers, family we were evacuated to
Mr Davis, Mrs Davis, Peggy, Timmy

The Farm, Alcester
Uncle Tom [Thompson], managed The Farm
Aunt Dot, Uncle Tom's wife
Brenda, Dot and Tom's daughter
Daphne, the Land Girl, part of the Women's Land Army during the War
Fred, farm labourer

Quartermain Family Relationships and Households
Grandfather and Grandmother Quartermain (Dad's parents), who lived in Little Marlow
Uncle Allan, Uncle Gilbert and Uncle Geoffrey, Dad's brothers
Grannie and Grandpa [Wilson] (Mum's parents) who lived at Spalding
Aunt Kath, Aunt John, Mum's sisters
Mum, Ada Bessie [Wilson] Quartermain
Dad, Clifford Philip Quartermain
Phil, a.k.a Our Kid, Philip Geoffrey Quartermain, my brother
Alice, Mum and Dad's maid
Mary, one of the maids at Spalding
Uncle Edward: married to Aunt Kath, he was a Mess Officer in the Air Force, a school teacher in civilian life who enjoyed his authority

Wheaton Aston School
Mr Button
Pearl, Mr Button's daughter
Miss Chapman, school teacher

Woodroughs School, Rushbury (Shropshire), the school evacuated from Birmingham
Mr Stephen J Belben, Headmaster

Brewood Grammar School, Brewood, Staffordshire
Headmasters
Mr Bailey (Percy W) [Pussy Bailey] (1932-1943)
Mr Brogden (Harry S) [Broggie] (1944-48)
Mr Finney (Jack) (1948 – 196?)

Teachers
Angus Beaton, Art master
"Belsen Bill" Barnes, Chemistry master
Broggie [Mr Brogden]
Dolly Asprey
Henry Houston, Assistant Headmaster
Hutch Hutchings, Chemistry master
Jimmy Osborne, English master, and Peggy, his wife
Mr Godfray, French master
Bill Illsley, English master
Mrs Bailey, prep school teacher
Mr Page
Frank "King" Evans, French master
Nosey Parker, Religious Instruction master
Ticker Ranson, Gym master
Tubby "Buddha" Anderson, History master

Staff
Mrs Grant, Matron
Mrs Hatfield, Cook
Nunc, a.k.a. Nunc Whitehouse, or Mr Whitehouse, school caretaker and gardener
Young Nunc, a.k.a. Alf Whitehouse, Nunc's son, janitor and groundskeeper at Brewood

Boys
Arthur Wardle
Birdie Prince
Brian Harley, bullied kid
Bud Flanagan, senior kid
Fatty Bullimore, senior kid
Gavin "Olive" Frost
Graham Harvey
Gravette
Jeremy Ascough, prankster
Jim Costley, close friend
Ken Hatton
Morris West
Paunch Chatterton
Pete Griffiths, close friend
Ray Shaftsbury
Rex Farran
Robin Salmon, close friend
Shag Callahan, Prefect
Taffy Evans
Taffy Hughes, Prefect
Tyler, unruly kid in fourth dormitory
Willy Pratt, boarder

Dormitory 1 Boys at one time or another
Peter Quartermain [Filo]
Ron Malpas
Smithe
Jones
Blondie Hart
Morris West
Martin Franks
Tom Fearnley
Gravette
Birdie Prince

Incidental People

Mrs Roe and her son Sammy. She ran the kindergarten next door in Shirley.

Mrs Spencer, ran the sweet shop at Spalding

Nash boys, boys who attend the National school, the state funded village school

Squire Giffard, Chairman of the Brewood School Board of Governors, lived at Chillington Hall

Places

Alcester, Warwickshire, where The Farm was

Ayscoughfee Gardens, public park in Spalding, Lincolnshire

Favre & Picard, where Grandfather used to work

Hanbury Crater, left by underground munitions explosion

Lower Hillmorton, small village outside Rugby, Warwickshire

Moseley, Birmingham suburb

Rugby, where Dad managed a Woolworth's during part of the war

Shirley, Birmingham suburb

Spark Hill, Birmingham suburb, where Dad managed a Woolworth's

Stanway Manor Farm, where Woodroughs school was at Rushbury, Shropshire

The Quad 1936

Appendix 2
Sketch of Brewood Village

Sketch of School Grounds

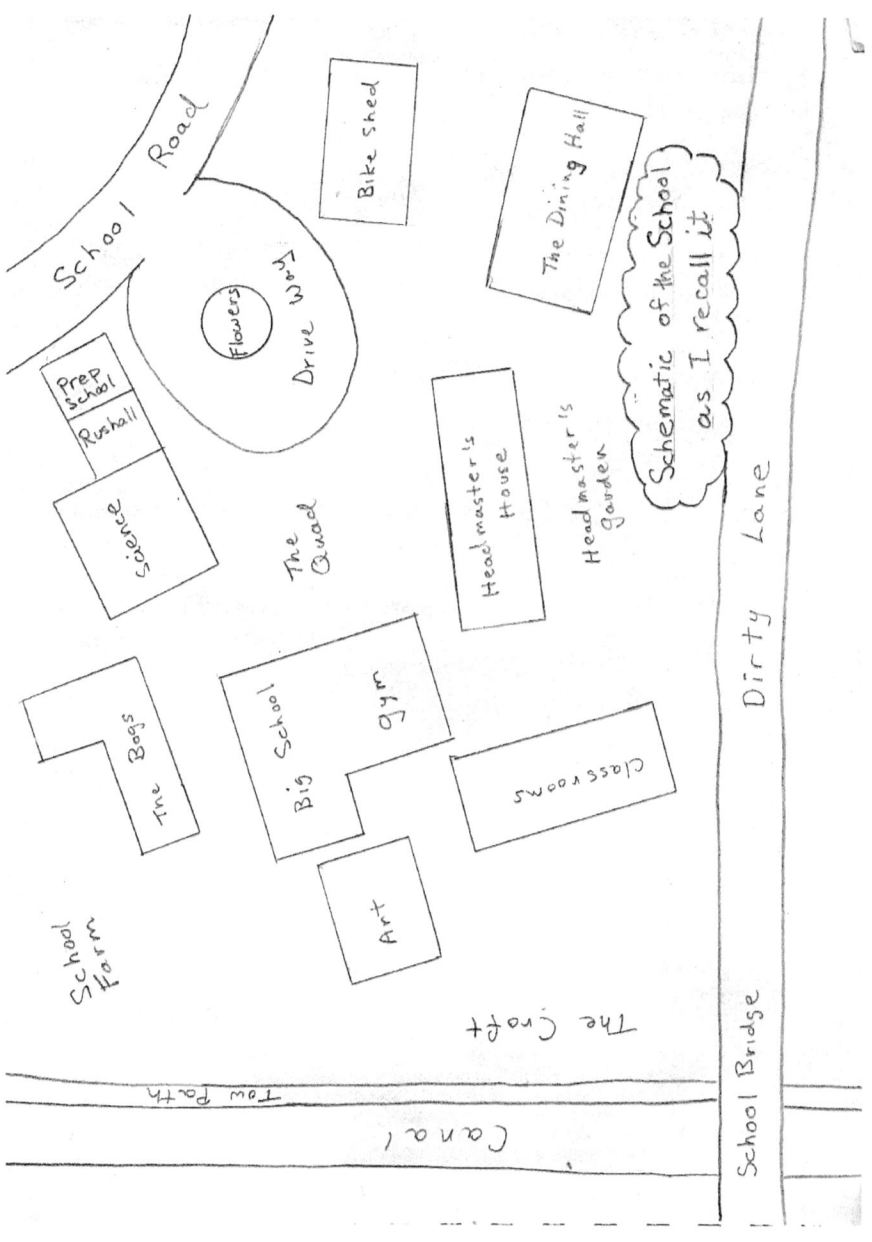

Glossary

billy-oh, run like billy-oh: *very energetic*

civvy street: *civilian street, and therefore civilian life*

facer, a bit of a facer: *something that takes you aback*

Great Aputh: *aputh means half penny worth; Great Aputh is slang for being an idiot*

Headmaster: *the principal of the whole school*

House: *in school, the kids were divided into "houses" and the houses competed for prizes in everything from sports to academics. At Brewood, the Houses were Knightley (the boarders' House), Kempson, and Parke*

Housemaster: *the teacher who was in charge of a particular House*

gym knicks and pumps: *gym shorts and plimsolls, i.e. rubber-soled shoes*

Land Girls: *women who lived and worked on farms, replacing male hired hands during the war, from the Women's Land Army*

lbw: *leg before wicket, a cricket term*

Lord Haw Haw: *German propaganda broadcaster, born British*

lp: *long-playing record, i.e. vinyl*

pink 'un: *every local newspaper had a coloured sheet or edition dedicated to sports results, especially soccer; the Saturday evening Express & Star printed on pink*

primus: *one-burner camp stove*

rezzer: *slang for reservoir*

rissoles: *meat patties made with minced leftover meat*

scarpered: *ran off*

sweet jars: *jars for storing candies in sweet shops, which sell mainly a great range of candies and chocolate bars, etc.*

swot: *a kid who loves schoolwork*

swozz: *music with an obvious energetic beat*

worriting: *worrying*

Acknowledgements

Thanks to:

Lou Rowan for publishing several chapters in *GHR*

David and Jill Evans (for their extensive file of the Brewood Grammar School magazine)

David Horowitz (his wonderful history of *Brewood*, and *Memories of Brewood*)

UK Public Record Office

Phil Quartermain (phone calls, reminders, corrections, accommodations, tours, &c &c; gift of *Brewood and Penkridge in Old Photographs*)

The Capilano Review and The Capilano Review Society for granting me a Koerner writer-in-residency in 2003, and publishing part of it

Jimmy Osborne who made his part of it tolerable and indeed a delight.

Many thanks to Rachel Blau DuPlessis and Marjorie Perloff, who read the whole manuscript and cheered me on. I'm also extremely grateful to my editor Marguerite Pigeon who thoroughly edited the complete manuscript and thereby enabled me to make the final amendments. My debt to Erín Moure is immense for designing the book, copy-editing, and liaising with Lulu.com to get the book into the world. Thank you both for all you've done to support this project.

Above all, deepest thanks to Meredith for unflagging encouragement and practical assistance, and for preparing the sketch maps.

I've been blessed with many other appreciative and helpful readers including: Robin Blaser, George Bowering, David Bromige, Colin Browne, Guy Davenport, Ulla Dydo, David Farwell, Paolo Javier, Bridget Mackenzie, Daphne Marlatt, Jimmy Osborne, Aaron Peck, Jenny Penberthy, Kyle Schlesinger, Geoff and Brigid Smedley, Harry and Pat Wrennall, Karen Yearsley, and my brother Phil.

Much gratitude to the following publications for including selections (since revised) from this project:

"Delivering the Bread" *The Capilano Review* 2.38 (Fall 2002)

"Feeding the Chickens" *THE NEWS* (Fall 2003)

"When It Snowed" *Kiosk* 3 (2004)

"Marbles" *Terminal City* (18 Nov 2004)

"Getting The Milk" *Terminal City* (25 Nov 2004)

"Nickname" *Terminal City* (2 Dec 2004)

"Blitz. 1942" *Terminal City* (9 Dec 2004)

Winter Mostly Keefer Street Press (Dec 2004)

"Getting Caned" *2nd Ave* (2006)

Home and Away Keefer Street Press (Dec 2006)

"Proper Talk" *Origin* 6th Series (2007)

Learning Keefer Street Press (Dec 2007)

"Growing Dumb: Chapter One" *Golden Handcuffs Review* 1.10 (2008)

"Fun And Games" *Golden Handcuffs Review* 1.13 (2010)

"The Farm" *Golden Handcuffs Review* 1.17 (2013-4)

"The Village" *Golden Handcuffs Review* 1.20 (2015)

"Boarding School" *Golden Handcuffs Review* 1.22 (2016)

"Teachers and Pupils" *Golden Handcuffs Review* 1.24 (2017)

"Queuing for Food" *Sustenance* Ed. Rachel Rose (2017)

"Robin and Jim" *Golden Handcuffs Review* 2.30 (2021)

The irrepressible **Peter Quartermain** taught modernist poetry and poetics at the University of British Columbia in Vancouver, Canada for over thirty years, retiring in 1999. He has had a major impact on poetic scholarship in English; his work brings together late 20th century English-language avant-garde poetry from both sides of the Atlantic. He is the author of *Basil Bunting, Poet of the North* (1990), *Disjunctive Poetics: From Gertrude Stein and Louis Zukofsky to Susan Howe* (Cambridge U Press, 1992) and *Stubborn Poetries: Poetic Facticity and the Avant-Garde* (U Alabama Press, 2013). He edited, with Richard Caddel, *Other: British and Irish Poetry since 1970* (Wesleyan U Press, 1999) and, with Rachel Blau DuPlessis, *The Objectivist Nexus: Essays in Cultural Poetics* (U Alabama Press, 1999). Recently, he edited two volumes of the collected works of Robert Duncan—*Robert Duncan: The Collected Early Poems and Plays* (U California Press, 2012) and *Robert Duncan: The Collected Later Poems and Plays* (U California Press, 2013). Sections of his memoir *Growing Dumb* have appeared in such magazines as *Golden Handcuffs Review* and *The Capilano Review*.

bio prepared by Elisa Sampedrín

Praise for *Growing Dumb*

Beautifully written and consistently interesting and fascinating.
Marjorie Perloff

The depiction of stuff (corporal punishment, loneliness, fear and its repression) in the child's point of view is uncanny. So you get this individual tiny beam of light at the same time that whole bunches of people seem to be present/presented in the sentences. It is a remarkable effect and it floods into and from the past like waves, so that there is a tidal suck back, and then one of these sentences comes forth and emerges with a whole bunch of sea wrack, shells and old plastic on our shore. It is really a remarkable prose rhythm.
Rachel Blau DuPlessis

www.ingramcontent.com/pod-product-compliance
Lightning Source LLC
Chambersburg PA
CBHW021757220426
43662CB00006B/85